Die Reihe „Weltwirtschaft und internationale Zusammenarbeit“ wird herausgegeben von

Prof. Dr. Hartmut Sangmeister, Universität Heidelberg
Prof. Dr. Oskar Gans, Universität Heidelberg
Prof. Dr. Detlef Nolte, GIGA Institut für Lateinamerika-Studien Hamburg

Band 9

Leslie Wehner

Explaining Failed Free Trade Agreement Negotiations

Cases from Latin America

Nomos

Gedruckt mit Unterstützung des Deutschen Akademischen Austauschdienstes.

Die Deutsche Nationalbibliothek verzeichnet diese Publikation in der Deutschen Nationalbibliografie; detaillierte bibliografische Daten sind im Internet über http://dnb.d-nb.de abrufbar.

Die Deutsche Nationalbibliothek lists this publication in the Deutsche Nationalbibliografie; detailed bibliographic data is available in the Internet at http://dnb.d-nb.de.

Zugl.: Hamburg, Univ., Fakultät Wirtschafts- und Sozialwissenschaften, FB Sozialwissenschaften, Diss., 2010

ISBN 978-3-8329-5806-0

1. Auflage 2010

Foreword from the Editor

Bilateral free trade agreements have come into fashion since the mid-1990s, not only in Latin America, but also in other parts of world. Most free trade agreement negotiations have come to successful conclusions. This is not surprising, given negotiations of this kind are generally introduced by governments with the intention of arriving at an agreeable outcome. Nevertheless, there has been a small number of free trade agreement negotiations, which, despite the participating governments' efforts, could (at first) not come to a successful conclusion—for instance, between New Zealand and Hong Kong, South Korea and Japan, South Korea and Mexico, and Canada and Central America. This book analyses two stalled free trade agreements from the period between 1996 and 2002: the negotiations between Chile and Panama (1996-1998), and those between Costa Rica and Panama (2000-2002). Both sets of negotiations resumed a few years later (2005-2007) and were successfully concluded.

The study clearly defines the external and internal constraints and dynamics of bilateral free trade agreements. The author is aware of the limited explanatory power of a comparison of two cases, which conditionally allows for only generalised conclusions. Nevertheless, he assumes that his heuristic framework can also be used to analyse other cases of stalled free trade agreement negotiations. The extent to which this framework is also valid for multilateral free trade agreements, such as between the EU and the MERCOSUR, remains to be verified, as in this case the dimension of regional coordination must be incorporated into the analysis.

The author takes an original approach to explaining the reasons for the failure of free trade agreements. While he takes into consideration the domestic political factors that influence foreign policy preference formation (especially foreign trade policy), he still acknowledges the importance of the negotiation strategies of the governments in question. In the jargon of international relations, the author looks both into the black box of foreign-political preference formation and likewise into the black box of international negotiations, which usually take place behind closed doors and which he attempts to reconstruct by analysing relevant documents and interviews.

This theoretically interesting and empirically demanding study provides an important contribution to the academic debate about the reasons for the failure of bilateral free trade agreements and, in doing so, also indirectly conveys the necessary conditions for the successful completion of free trade agreements.

Hamburg, May 2010 *Detlef Nolte*

Acknowledgement

I would like to express my deepest gratitude to all those who gave me support without which I might not have been able to complete this work that was originally presented as a doctoral dissertation at the University of Hamburg. The German Academic Exchange Service (DAAD) granted me a three year doctoral scholarship. The German Institute of Global and Area Studies (GIGA) provided additional support to conduct my field research. I am also grateful to Prof. Dr. Klaus Bodemer who provided additional feedback on different chapters of this study. I also thank my second supervisor Prof. Dr. Cord Jakobeit who gave me additional feedback to improve this final manuscript. My deepest gratitude is reserved for Detlef Nolte whose supervision and criticisms made my original dissertation a better work.

During my field trips to Chile, Costa Rica, and Panama, I had the privilege of interviewing trade negotiators and representatives of the different business associations and labour unions. They shared with me their experiences in both successful and failed negotiations. They also taught me unknown aspects of the dynamics of negotiations. These real experts deserve a special thank you for sharing their knowledge and giving their testimonies without which this research and other studies on FTAs would not have been possible. This is also extended to the staff at the information centres of the Ministries in charge of conducting the FTA negotiations in these three countries. They gave me access to the draft texts of the negotiation as well as minutes and different documents related to these processes. In Panama, I received strong support from the Garisto Family who provided friendship and guidance to establish contacts with different actors of these negotiations. I also thank Roberto Echandi from Costa Rica who helped me to contact different trade negotiators. Despite the fact that I received intellectual support, advice and essential information from the above mentioned people, any errors in this book are entirely my own.

On the personal side, I want to thank my wife Anne-Mette Ribov for her emotional and intellectual support over the years and for giving me feedback and criticisms on the entire manuscript. I also want to thank the unconditional support of my parents Peter Wehner and Marcia Venegas. I also thank my brother Oliver Wehner for arranging some of the interviews I conducted in Chile. The final and biggest "thank you" is for my two "Große Jungen" Loui and Oliver for giving me their unconditional love and keeping me connected to the basics of life, and making me laugh and play during the "ups and downs" of writing this doctoral work which now becomes a book.

This book is dedicated to Anne-Mette, Loui, and Oliver.

Contents

Figures and Tables

Acronyms and Abbreviations

ABC	Asociación Bancaria Costarricense/ Costa Rica's Bank Association
ABC-COMEX	Asociación Bancaria Costarricense–Ministerio de Comercio Exterior/ Costa Rica's Bank Association-Ministry of International Trade
ABIF	Asociación de Bancos e Instituciones Financieras-Chile/ Association of Banks and Financial Institutions-Chile
ACE	Acuerdo de Complementación Económica /Complementary Trade Agreeement
AFP	Asociación Fondo de Pensiones-Chile/ Pension Fund Association-Chile
ALCA	Área de Libre Comercio de las Américas (see FTAA)
ANAFEREC	Asociación Nacional de Fabricantes de Embutidos de Res y Cerdo-Panamá/ National Association of Cattle and Pork Sausages, and Cold Meat Producers-Panama
ANAGAN	Asociación Nacional de Ganaderos-Panamá/ National Association of Cattle Growers-Panama
ANALMO	Asociación Nacional de Molineros-Panamá/ National Association of Rice Producers-Panama
ANAPOR	Asociaciación Nacional de Porcinicultores/ National Association of Pork Meat Producers
ANAPROLE	Asociación Nacional de Procesadores de Leche-Panamá/ National Association of Milk Processors
ANAVIP	Asociación Nacional de Avicultores de Panamá/ National Association of Poultry Farmers-Panama
ANBER	Asociación Nacional de Bebidas Refrescantes-Chile/ National Association of Beverages and Refreshments –Chile
APA	Asociación de Productores Avícolas-Chile/ Association of Chicken Producers-Chile
APADEA	Asociación Panameña de Aseguradoras/ Panamanian Insurance Association
APEC	Asian Pacific Economic Cooperation
APEDE	Asociación Panameña de Ejecutivos de Empresa-Panamá/ Association of Executives-Panama.
APEX	Asociación Panameña de Exportadores/ Panamanian Export Association
APEXMAR	Asociación Panameña de Exportadores del Mar/ Panamanian Association of Exporters of Sea Products
ASEAN	Association of Southeast Asian Nations
ASEXMA	Asociación de Exportadores de Manofacturas-Chile/ Association of Exporters of Manufactures–Chile
ASOEX	Asociación de Exportadores- Chile/ Export Association-Chile (fruits)
AUZLC	Asociación de Usuarios de la Zona Libre de Colón-Panamá/ Association of Bussiness Owners within the Duty Free Area of Colon–Panama
AZUCALPA	Asociación Azucarera y Alcohol de Panama/ Panamanian Association of Sugar and Alcohol

BATNA	Best Alternative To a Negotiated Agreement
BCN	Biblioteca del Congreso Nacional-Chile/ Congress National Library-Chile
BIT	Bilateral Investment Treaty
BONLAC	It is a name and not an acronym as such. It is the name of a Panamanian dairy company
CACIA	Cámara Costarricense de la Industria Alimentaria/ Costa Rica's Chamber of the Food Industry
CADEXCO	Cámara de Exportadores de Costa Rica/ Chamber of Exporters-Costa Rica
CANAVI	Cámara Nacional de Avicultores-Costa Rica/ Costa Rica's Chamber of Poultry Farming
CARICOM	Caribbean Community
CB	Caribbean Basin Initiative
CCIA	Chamber of Commerce, Industries and Agriculture-Panama
CENA	Consejo Económico Nacional-Panamá/ National Economic Council-Panama
CEPAL	Comisión Económica para América Latina y el Caribe
CICR	Cámara de Industriales de Costa Rica / Chamber of Industries of Costa Rica
CMP	Cámara Marítima de Panamá/ Maritime Chamber of Panama
CNAA	Cámara Nacional de Agricultura y Agroindustria-Costa Rica/ Nacional Chamber of Agriculture and Agro-industry-Costa Rica
CNPL	Cámara Nacional de Productores de Leche-Costa Rica/ National Chamber of Dairy Producers-Costa Rica
CNTP	Central Nacional de Trabajadores de Panamá/ National Union of Panamanian Workers
COMEX	Ministerio de Comercio Exterior- Costa Rica / Ministry of International Trade-Costa Rica
CONAPYME	Corporación Nacional de Pequenas y Medianas Empresas-Chile/ National Corporation of Small and Medium Enterprises-Chile
CORFOGA	Corporación de Fomento Ganadero- Costa Rica / Corporation of Cattle Growers- Costa Rica
CORMA	Corporación de la Madera / National Wood Corporation-Chile
CPC	Confederación de Producción y Comercio-Chile / Confederation for Production and Commerce- Chile
CTU	New Zealand Council of Trade Unions
DINECI	See MICI
DIRECON	Dirección de Relaciones Económicas Internacionales-Chile / General Directorate for International Economic Affaire-Chile
DR-CAFTA	Dominican Republic – Central America Free Trade Agreement
DTO	Decreto / Decree
ECLAC	Economic Commission for Latin America and the Caribbean
EFTA	European Free Trade Association
EU	European Union
EUI	Economist Intelligence Unit
FATF	Financial Action Task Force
FDI	Foreign direct investment

FEDAP	Federación de Asociaciones Profesionales-Panamá/ Federation of Professional Associations-Panama
FENASEP	Federación Nacional de Servidores Públicos/ National Federation of Public Servants
FEPACH	Federación de Procesadores de Alimentos y Agroindustriales-Chile/ Federation of Food and Agroindustrial Processors-Chile
FSLN	Frente Sandinista de Liberación Nacional/ Sandinista National Liberation Front
FTA	Free Trade Agreement
FTAA	Free Trade Association of the Americas
GATT	General Agreement on Tariffs and Trade
GDP	Gross Domestic Product
GTEICA	General Treaty for the Economic Integration of Central America (see also SIECA)
IANSA	Industria Azucarera Nacional-Chile / National Sugar Industry-Chile
ICE	Instituto Costarricence de Electricidad/ Costa Rica's Institute of Electricity
IMF	International Monetary Fund
INTECH	Instituto Textil de Chile / Textile Institute of Chile
IR/IPE	International Relations / International Political Economy
ISI	Import substitution industrialisation
KJFTA	Korea-Japan Free Trade Agreement
KOPA	Korean People's Action against FTA & WTO
LAILA/ALADI	Asociación Latinoamericana de Integración/ Latin American Integration Association
MERCOSUR	Mercado Común del Sur/ Common Market of the South
MFN	Most Favoured Nation
MICI	Ministerio de Comercio e Industrias-Panamá / Ministry of Commerce and Industries-Panama
MIDA	Ministerio de Desarrollo Agropecuario-Panamá / Ministry of Agricultural Development-Panama
MIDEPLAN	Ministerio de Planificación/ Ministry of Planification
NAFTA	North American Free Trade Agreement
NTB	Non-Trade Barriers
OECD	Organisation for Economic Cooperation and Development
PAC	Partido Acción Ciudadana-Costa Rica/ Citizen's Action Party-Costa Rica
PDF	Panamanian Defence Force
PIN	Partido Integración Nacional-Costa Rica/ National Integration Party-Costa Rica
PLN	Partido de Liberación Nacional- Costa Rica / National Liberation Party- Costa Rica
PRD	Partido Revolucionario Democrático-Panamá/ Democratic Revolutionary Party-Panama
PUSC	Partido de Unidad Socialcristiana-Costa Rica/ Social Christian Unity Party-Costa Rica

PYME	Pequeñas y Medianas Empresas / Small and Medium Enterprises
SICA	Sistema de Integración Centroamericana/ Central American Integration System
SIECA	Secretaría de Integración Económica Centro Americana/ General Agreement - (Permanent Secretariat)- on Central American Economic Integration
SIP	Sindicato de Industriales de Panamá / Union of Industrials of Panama
SME	Small and Medium Enterprises (see also PYMES)
SNA	Sociedad Nacional de Agricultura-Chile/ National Agriculture Association-Chile
SOFOFA	Sociedad de Fomento Fabril- Chile / Federation of Chilean Industries
SUGEF	Superintendencia General de Entidades Financieras- Costa Rica/ General Superintendence of Financial Institutions- Costa Rica
SUGEF-COMEX	Superintendencia General de Entidades Financieras-Ministerio de Comercio Exterior / General Superintendence of Financial Institutions-Ministry of International Trade
SUGEVAL	Superintendencia General de Valores- Costa Rica/ General Superintendence of Securities Markets- Costa Rica
TB	Tariff barriers
UNPAP	Unión Nacional Productores Agropecuarios de Panamá/ National Union of Agricultural and Livestock Producers-Panama
UPANACIONAL	Unión Nacional de Pequeños y Medianos Productores Agropecuarios-Costa Rica/ National Union of Small and Middle Sized Agricultural Producers-Costa Rica
US or USA	United States / United States of America
WB	World Bank
WTO	World Trade Organisation

Concepts and Definitions

Access points: are defined here as the entrance points provided by agents and agencies, where domestic constituencies and/or interest groups in FTA negotiations can lobby for a policy option of its preference.

BATNA: Best Alternative To a Negotiated Agreement is the alternative action a negotiating party can pursue if the negotiation between two or more parties fails to reach an outcome of agreement. BATNA can also be the status quo ex ante, if the gains of the negotiation are below the status quo. In this dissertation, BATNA may be the status quo ex ante, and/or it may serve to launch FTA negotiations with other countries.

Comparative Advantages: (see inter-trade).

Distributive Strategy: (see value-claiming strategy).

Encaje: is an unremunerated reserve requirement. It is a mechanism to control the inflow of capital by depositing part of the incoming investment in a non interest bearing account in the Central Bank. The rate of the total investment to be deposited in Chile was 30 percent, and it should be kept in the Central Bank for a year. The main purpose of the *encaje* system in Chile was to influence the composition of its capital inflows by increasing the costs of speculative and/or short term capital (see Williamson 2000).

Escalatory Effect: (see spiral effect).

Integrative Strategy: (see value-creating strategy).

Inter-Trade: The principle of inter-trade in international trade says a nation should specialise in producing and exporting that which it can produce at relatively lower costs vis-à-vis another country. Thus, a country should also import those goods whose costs of production are relatively high vis-à-vis the costs of production of another country (Samuelson and Nordhaus 2005: 734).

Intra-Trade: refers to possibilities of developing -or boosting the extant- trade between the parties of a negotiation in similar products with differentiated "subjective" varieties such as cars, different types of apples, or rice, and services. The definition for this dissertation is based on the process of Intra-industry trade developed by scholars of New Trade Theory.

Mixed strategy: is the combination of value claiming and value creating strategies in a negotiation process. A negotiation as a whole presents a mixed strategy.

Non-tariff barriers: are all barriers to trade that do not take the form of tariffs. Thus, they are also protectionist measures to discourage or prevent imports in the form of regulatory proceedings, domestic laws, voluntary exports restraints, technical barriers to trade, as well as obstacles to the establishments and delivery of services, etc.

Rapport: It can be defined as the achievement of an agreement through the building of trust. Developing trust facilitates the negotiation process as parties develop a sense of mutual understanding for the reasons of conceding or not conceding in issue-areas and the different items of a negotiation.

Resistant points: are the bottom line of what it is acceptable in a negotiation for the parties involved in such process. In other words, it is the least favourable point in the negotiation in which one party will still accept an agreement. Resistant points are also known as reservation price, or simply the bottom line.

Spiral Effect: For the purpose of this work, this concept is defined as the pattern in which the use or overuse of an offensive distributive strategy increases the severity of a conflictive negotiation relationship between the parties. In other words, a threat brings to another threat, or intended omission of relevant information for the negotiation is counteracted by the same or another form of distributive tactic creating a spiral effect of distributive strategy.

Stalemate: means the impossibility of continuing negotiations, making the parties of a negotiation leave the process with an outcome of non-agreement. Stalemate is also associated to the concept of failure to reach agreement.

Tariff barriers: is a number of protectionist measures by which a country discourages or prevents the imports of goods. Tariff and Quotas are the most common forms of trade barriers in international trade.

Tariff: "A levy or tax imposed upon each unit of a commodity imported into a country" (Samuelson and Nordhaus 2005: 752).

Trade creation: means the creation of trade between the parties of an FTA that would not have existed otherwise (taken from Viner 1950; Baldwin 2006)

Trade deviation: means that a free trade area diverts trade away from a more efficient supplier outside the FTA toward a less efficient supplier within the FTA. Thus the trade deviation effect will act as an incentive for the country outside such trade area to materialise an FTA with the members of the trade area, and/or establish its own web of FTAs (taken from Viner 1950; Baldwin 2006).

Trade-off: is commonly known as concessions in a negotiation. Trade off is conceding on something valuable in exchange of something which is equally or more desirable of what was given up in a negotiation to trigger such concession. The concessions in a negotiation may be triggered by using either distributive or integrative strategies.

Value Claiming Strategy: is "…a set of actions that promote the attainment of one party's goals when they are in conflict with those of the other party" (Odell 2000: 31). A value claiming strategy is also called distributive strategy and zero sum bargaining.

Value Creating Strategy: "…involves actions that promote the attainment of goals that are not in fundamental conflict -actions designed to expand rather than split the pie" (Odell 2000: 34).

Win-set: is "the set of potential agreements that would be ratified by domestic constituencies in a straight up-or-down vote against the status quo of "no agreement"" (Moravcsik 1993b: 23).

Zone of Agreement: is the area in which both parties may find an agreement satisfactory for both parties. This zone is delimited on its two extremes by the resistant points or the bottom line of what it is acceptable for the negotiating parties. This zone is also the overlap between the minimum and maximum of acceptable agreements between two parties, that is, the minimum for one party is the maximum for the other. Outside the zone of agreement there is no agreement or there is failure and BATNA.

1. Introduction

1.1 Empirical Puzzle, Aims and Questions

The consolidation of economic globalisation in the economically interdependent world is expressed in the extant and growing number of bilateral and multilateral Free Trade Agreements (FTA) that countries from different continents have signed or are negotiating. While some countries have opted to negotiate FTAs as part of a regional group such as the European Union (EU), European Free Trade Association (EFTA) and the Common Market of the South (MERCOSUR), others have chosen a bilateral path without totally excluding a multilateral one. Amongst the latter, it is possible to find countries with different levels of development e.g. less developed, developing and developed such as Chile, Singapore, South Korea, Japan, the United States (USA), Canada, Australia, New Zealand, Panama, Mexico, Costa Rica, Guatemala, Egypt, and Thailand. Whichever path countries decide to follow and whatever their level of development, they share a common goal: to maximise their economic welfare and that of their domestic constituencies by achieving FTAs. For these pragmatic reasons, countries seek to negotiate FTAs with their neighbouring countries (intraregional) as well as with countries from other continents (cross-regional).

However, the economic integration achieved through FTA negotiations is by definition not an easy task, since the parties involved in this process have to integrate the government positions, as well as the policy preferences of the different domestic constituencies that have stakes in an eventual FTA. These domestic constituencies are not homogenous and usually have diverging interests, positions and policy preferences with regard to specific FTAs. These interests are dependant on whether they have more or less comparative advantage (inter-trade) than the counterpart, whether there is potential or not for intra-trade between the parties, and whether the FTA threatens to reduce or remove the tariff and non-tariff barriers (TB & NTB) that protect some economic groups from external competition. In other words, a negotiation of an FTA always carries benefits and losses for domestic actors. Despite the fact that the negotiation process of an FTA is constrained by the interests of these domestic groups, the majority of these negotiations end with an outcome of agreement.

Yet, there are a few numbers of FTA talks that halted for months and even years vis-à-vis FTA negotiations which were successfully concluded.[1] The results of agreed and stalled FTAs suggest a priori that global conditions have not substantially changed in the economically interdependent world. If this is so, then *why do some FTA negotiations fail in reaching an outcome of agreement? Under what conditions do these FTA negotiations fail?* These two simple questions guide the present research.

This study thus deals with a particular aspect of bilateral (state to state) FTA negotiations: *outcome of non-agreement.* This study has both theoretical and empirical aims. The theoretical aim is to make a contribution to the study of international economic negotiations. I present a framework that allows us to set conditions and delineate the cause or causes of halted FTA negotiations, as well as to determine how, and by what channels protectionist domestic groups influence this process more than those groups that support the FTA. Therefore, I intend to develop an inside-out theoretical framework to explain the domestic constitution of policy preferences for FTA negotiations, especially those preferences against a particular FTA; the responsiveness of the government to these pressures either *pro* or *contra* a specific FTA; and the government's own agenda towards the sensitive issue-areas that makes a negotiation comes to a standstill. I rely on existing theoretical approaches in an eclectic way i.e. I take elements from theories of economics, IR/IPE, and negotiations to elaborate a framework that can help to explain the cases at stake here.[2]

The empirical aim of this study is to present a plausible explanation for the non-agreement outcome of two FTA negotiations. The case studies are taken from Latin America i.e. Panama-Chile's (1996-98), and Costa Rica-Panama's (2002) FTA negotiations. These negotiations were stalled for years before their resumption and conclusion. Resuming the negotiations in 2005 (Chile-Panama) and 2006 (Costa Rica-Panama) meant starting all over again as the items in the first FTA negotiation had become anachronistic.[3] Therefore, the exclusive focus of this research is on the reasons for stalling these two FTA negotiations in 1998 and 2002 respectively and not on the relaunching process in 2005 and 2006.

1 Examples of stalled FTA negotiations are those between Chile-Panama (retaken after years and concluded), South Korea-Japan (stalled), US-Egypt (stalled), Singapore-Mexico (stalled), South Korea-Mexico (stalled), US-Thailand (stalled), EU-MERCOSUR (stalled), Free Trade Area of the Americas (FTAA: stalled), ASEAN-India (stalled), and Panama-Costa Rica (retaken and concluded), New Zealand-Hong Kong (stalled), Canada-Singapore (stalled), and Canada-Central America –El Salvador, Honduras, Nicaragua, and Guatemala (stalled).

2 On the benefits of using analytical eclecticism see the various publications of Peter Katzenstein who was one of the first scholars to highlight the convenience of an eclectic approach when attempting to explain/understand empirical puzzles. See especially, Katzenstein, Peter J and Sil, Rudra (2004) Rethinking Asian Security. A Case for Analytical Eclecticism, in Suh, J.J.; Katzenstein, Peter; and Carlson, Allen (eds) Rethinking Security in East Asia. Identity, Power, and Efficiency. Stanford: Standford University Press; pp. 1-33.

3 Interviews with Rodrigo Contreras, DIRECON, 28/03/2008; Laura Rodríguez, COMEX, 08/07/2008; Amparo Pacheco, COMEX, 02/07/2008; Melissa Davis, DINECI, 17/07/2008).

Though the cases selected are connected through Panama, the reasons that brought both negotiations to break down are varied. The failures in these negotiations are not Panama's exclusive responsibility. Therefore, Panama should not be labelled as the main stalemate creator of these two negotiations as the following pages of this work will show. In this regard, the case selection of Panama as the centre for this research is purposive rather than random. Each FTA negotiation has its own dynamic that makes it different from the other, despite the presence of the same country and certain common aspects. These common aspects and differences i.e. each FTA negotiation's own independent dynamics are brought up, contrasted and compared.

1.2. The Argument

In a nutshell, I argue that the outcome of non-agreement in FTA negotiations is not only the product of negotiating sensitive issues, such as interests and strategies, but also the product of factors external to the bargaining at both the domestic and international levels. Therefore, *external factors*[4] to the negotiation as well as the responsiveness of the government to these because of social, economic and political costs (job insecurity, politicisation, and electoral costs: closeness to elections) should be seen as complementary forces to the "internal" negotiation process. These together provide a better understanding of the reasons that lead to reach a stalemate.

The constitution of domestic pressures favouring or opposing an FTA negotiation begins even before the formal negotiation starts, which to some extent determines the strategy the government is likely to use in a particular issue-area at the intergovernmental level. However, the intensity of pressures from domestic groups increases during the FTA negotiation as a way to assure a satisfactory outcome. Government actions in the international sphere - in this case in the negotiation of an FTA - are seen as a reaction to domestic influences or as instruments that can concede or resist the policy preference options that interests groups try to put forward in the decision-making at intergovernmental level (Moravcsik 1993a, 1993b and 1997; Schirm

4 External factors will be understood as the background conditions in which domestic actors constitute their policy preference options i.e. the government is constrained by organisations and important domestic constituencies that it must represent and whose interests they must include in the negotiation. Other important external factors to the negotiation process have a domestic and an international dimension. The former includes legal, technical and socio-economic constraints at the domestic level, and the latter the importance of other FTA negotiations. The global market conditions are not considered an external constrain i.e. economic crises do not stop FTA negotiations as such. During the economic crises of 1998-2000 (Asian crises), and 2008 (sub-prime crisis) countries like Chile, Costa Rica and Panama continued negotiating FTAs and in most of these negotiation processes they reached an outcome of agreement. This is also the case for countries in Asia and Latin America such as New Zealand, Australia, Japan, China and Singapore as well as Mexico, Peru and Colombia.

2002:7). The negotiation of an FTA is thus a two level game. With regards to why in certain occasions one or both governments of an FTA decide to stall the negotiation and consequently favour protectionist oriented domestic groups, I rely mainly on the ideas of collective action i.e. small protectionist groups tend to organise better vis-à-vis the bigger and diffused pro-FTA groups (exporters and consumers). In this latter group, agents tend to free ride (Olson 1965).

1.3 Reasons to Study Stalled Negotiations

FTA negotiations are about trade, strategies, and external relations and diplomacy between states. In these negotiations there is thus a convergence of the fields of economics, negotiations and international relations. If one wants to capture or re-build part of the negotiation process, a scholar should be able to integrate these different theoretical lenses. In the literature on theory of negotiation there are often references to negotiations that face impasses, or reach a stalemate, but these are usually treated as reference points to impede the breakdown of a negotiation. In this regard, part of the literature on negotiation has a prescriptive connotation i.e. how to do better in a negotiation and overcome impasses (see Lebow 1996; Plantey: 2007). Especially important is the work of Fischer and Ury (1981): *Getting to Yes*, which has contributed to the field of international negotiation because of its prescriptive nature, and its contribution to the development of the concept, and category of negotiation, known as joint-problem solving.[5]

In addition, the literature that focuses on the process of negotiation, i.e. strategies and their tactics, shows that a stalemate is reached because parties tend to use aggressive-distributive rather than integrative strategies (Odell 2000); or because one of the parties has a best alternative to a negotiated agreement (BATNA) (Odell 2006: 15; Hopmann: 1996). On the other hand, game theory approaches have also refereed to non-agreement as a reference point for the negotiation process i.e. the interest of one or both parties over an issue at stake is either beyond the possibility frontier, or underneath the threat point, or resistance point (Holzinger 2001:75; Raiffa 1982: 45).

Whereas there are clear references to the problem of stalemates, the extant works do not provide a clear and detailed account of the process that leads both parties to reach a stalemate in a negotiation, either in theoretical or in descriptive terms. In other words, we do not know much about the steps -in qualitative terms- that domes-

5 Anatol Rappaport (Fights, games and debates (1960)) set up initial conditions for the development of the category of joint problem solving in the field of negotiation. Another seminal contribution on joint-problem-solving is the work of William Zartman and Maureen Berman (The practical negotiator (1982)). A good account of the development of the two predominant schools of negotiation is given by Terrence Hopmann (Two Paradigms of Negotiation: Bargaining and Problem Solving (1995)).

tic actors take before and during the negotiation in order to impede an agreement. Neither do we know much about the conscious process a government follows to respond and satisfy these groups over the sensitive issues at stake in the negotiation. The lack of studies on these aspects also applies to bilateral FTA negotiations. One reason for the lack of studies is precisely the normative or prescriptive nature of negotiation theory, which focuses on how to do better in negotiations and on how to achieve a satisfactory outcome of agreement for the parties involved in the bargaining.

A common answer to explain stalled FTA negotiations is to highlight the deadlocks created by lobby groups that benefit from TB e.g. agriculture, and manufacture. However, the process by which FTA negotiations reach deadlock has not been comprehensively assessed. In this regard, more attention has been paid to the successful cases of FTAs, because in economics -and partly in political science- scholars advocate free trade as the optimal policy. If free trade is the optimal policy in economics, and agreement the main goal in the theory of negotiation, why not explain the process that impedes final agreement in FTA negotiations as a way to obtain insights that could help overcome such deadlocks in the future?

The governments involved in FTA negotiations hold free trade as their optimal policy; if the case were otherwise, these governments would not risk their reputation entering into an FTA negotiation that would not end in a final agreement. When governments decide to pursue an FTA policy, it is because they believe that the overall economic welfare produced by an FTA is higher than the associated costs for some sectors of their national economies. Moreover, they believe that the domestic bargaining with these groups can be solved by offering side payments, by using issue-linkages approaches, or directly by overcoming these groups in the intergovernmental bargaining process. However, there are still FTA negotiations that stall, but the explanations of why and of the conditions under which they stall lack.

Stalled FTA negotiations are not only originated in the oft-blamed agricultural-manufacturing issue-areas, but also in the difficulties to reach agreements over other areas such as services, investment, banking, telecommunications, phytosanitary measures, property rights, and rules of origin. Economic negotiations are no longer circumscribed by TB (tariffs and quotas), as was the case from the 1960s to the 1980s, but are moving more and more from TB to NTB encompassed in domestic laws (Landau 2000: 6; Milner 2006: 449). Neither are there accounts of the difficulties involved in reaching agreement on these issues, nor studies that elucidate the whole processes of these areas, be these with an outcome of agreement or non-agreement.

The academic focus on multilateral and bilateral economic negotiations has mainly been limited to the so-called Triad (Europe-US-Asia), with a lack of theoretical and empirical studies concerning the developing world.[6] Yet the focus of some of the extant works, bilateral and multilateral accords, is on their contribution to the institutional building, and the growing issue of global governance (see Woolcock 2006; Dür 2007: 185-188). Latin America has not been excluded from this wave of FTA negotiations with the developed world. However, it is novel that countries like Chile, Colombia, Panama, Costa Rica, Peru and Mexico have also sought to conduct FTA negotiations with each other in a South-South context.[7] In fact Chile, Mexico, and Costa Rica are amongst the leading Latin American countries in the numbers of FTAs.

Theoretically there is also the need of offering more consistent analytical frames to explain FTA negotiations processes, when hard economic issues are at stake. Most of the theoretical frames to analyse free trade policy are within the field of economics, particularly new trade theory. Although they do not directly assess FTA negotiation processes or the states' positions within the negotiations as such, they offer some insights on the role of protectionism for free trade in an imperfect market i.e. TB and NTB.

Regarding explanations within the field of international relations and international political economy, these accounts focus on how institutions and their regulations affect the outcome of a negotiation, or on how the contextual background shapes the form of an institutional setting, neglecting the role of the negotiation process in that outcome. Therefore, negotiations are seen as a procedural step, which are secondary to explaining an outcome in regime theory. Theory of negotiation focuses on how a negotiation process works and the characteristics that such processes present, such as domestic actors, intergovernmental actors (Moravcsik 1993b) or both integrated (Putnam 1988). However, they do not refer to how actors (domestic and government) move to assure a non-outcome in FTA negotiations. Theories of negotiation and international relations/international political economy should be able to explain why some FTA negotiations stall and the conditions in which they reach a stalemate.

1.4 Delimitation of the Study

It is important to further clarify the scope of this study. First, this is a study of reasons for failure in FTA negotiations, so the analysis will be limited to the issue-areas in which agreement was not reached i.e. an ex-post analysis. The problematic topics of the negotiation usually range from one to four issue-areas. Sometimes these issues are linked with each other, and sometimes they are linked with other areas that are less sensitive or conflict-absent.

6 John Odell and the contributors to his edited volume (2006) take this task of analysing developing countries' economic negotiations. However, the focus is on their participation in multilateral settings such as regional arrangements and the WTO.

7 Here it also possible to find cases of non-agreement.

Second, the study at stake here will partially reconstruct the negotiation process. Even though an overview of the whole negotiation will be given, the focus is on the issues that blocked the agreement. Therefore, the full reconstruction of the negotiation will be on these issue-areas. Moreover, it seems impossible to reconstruct "the whole" in a highly-detailed way. Nonetheless, some references to other issues will be used when they exert a certain level of influence on the sensitive issue-areas and the final outcome of the negotiation.

Third, this study deals with the background conditions as well as the pre- and the negotiation processes that lead to a stalemate. Therefore, this work does not go into the legal ratification process as such.[8] The process of ratification opens a venue of new negotiations, in which the possible outcomes are either ratification or non-ratification. These types of negotiations are mainly limited to the domestic level i.e. it is between the government, domestic constituencies and the congress.

Finally, when one decides not to use a contrasting comparison between two cases e.g. agreed and stalled negotiations, there is always the risk of over-dimensioning a case when the focus is one-sided or selected according to the dependent variable i.e. failed cases. It is thus important to clarify that the cases of stalled FTA negotiations are a minority vis-à-vis the agreed ones. Yet, it is precisely this anomaly in bilateral FTA negotiations that make these few cases worth studying on their own merit. In other words, this study does not directly seek to compare the cases of agreed and stalled FTA negotiations.

1.5 Conceptual Clarifications

Having a final agreement or not in an FTA negotiation will be associated with the concepts of *success* and *failure* in this work. Failure may be understood here as the process in which both parties of an FTA negotiation could not reach a final agreement, deciding one or both actors to postpone or leave the negotiation for an unlimited period of time. Failure here is also used synonymously with outcome of non-agreement, breakdown of the negotiations, and negotiations at a standstill as well as stalled, halted, and frozen negotiations. Yet the stalemate of a negotiation for this research has the characteristics of a certain level of durability in a time-setting of years i.e. ex-post observation. In addition, failure is constituted as such when parties leave the negotiation table without concrete intentions of going back.

8 This ratification is usually carried by the legislative power. Putnam refers to the latter ratification as well as that carried informally by domestic actors during the negotiation. Despite the problems in identifying what type of ratification Putnam is referring to, it is possible to assume a sequential order in the ratification i.e. domestic actors decide whether to accept the agreement over their issue-areas (informal). The preliminary approval of domestic actors allows the overall agreement to be legally ratified by the legislative branch (Putnam 1988). Yet this legal ratification should not be taken for granted as the losers of the negotiation will try to lobby Legislators to amend the agreement or to impede its ratification.

In this work a bilateral FTA is defined as an arrangement that establishes a preferential treatment of trade between two governments. An FTA has the purpose of securing a commercial preferential treatment between signatory countries vis-à-vis a third country that is excluded from such agreement (Corning 2007: 45). The negotiation process of an FTA is thus the means to realise the goal of achieving such a preferential treatment.

The negotiation of a bilateral FTA is composed of strategies and tactics. A strategy is conceived as a gamma of behaviours observed, and used by the negotiators, in the negotiations to achieve a particular outcome during the process. Tactics are then specific actions embedded within a strategy. In other words, a strategy will not always apply the same tactic in every situation (Odell 2000: 31). For example, a government can use a distributive strategy in the negotiation, but within this strategy a government can use different tactics such as using a threat like imposing sanctions against the counterpart, or using the manipulation of information during the process.

A strategy can be classified as distributive (value-claiming) or integrative (value-creating). Distributive, value-claiming, and hard-bargaining are used as synonyms as well as integrative, value-creating, and win-win bargaining. On the one hand, a distributive strategy is "...a set of actions that promote the attainment of one party's goals when they are in conflict with those of the other party". On the other hand, an integrative strategy "...involves actions that promote the attainment of goals that are not in fundamental conflict -actions designed to expand rather than split the pie" (Odell 2000: 31-34). In real terms a negotiation as a whole presents a mixed strategy which is a combination of value-claiming and value-creating strategies. However, in some issue-areas of FTA negotiations it is possible to observe the predominance of one of the two strategies.

Power is also present in this type of negotiations since an FTA policy is one of the multiples aspects that constitute a country's foreign policy. In this work power is conceived as means to achieve an end rather than as the primary end of the negotiation. If power is conceived as means then power is an instrument embedded in the strategies and tactics used by the negotiators and the representatives of domestic actors in such process as well as in the external factors to the negotiation that may affect such a process in its domestic or international dimensions. Therefore, power is also present and embedded in the conditions outlined in the following chapters; power will not be given its own label and will not be presented as a primary condition that determines the result of agreement or non-agreement in a negotiation.

1.6 Case Studies

The theoretical framework in chapter 3 will be applied to the bilateral state to state negotiations between Chile-Panama, and Costa Rica-Panama in 1996-98 and 2002 respectively:

1.6.1 The Negotiation between Chile and Panama

The FTA negotiation was first launched in 1996 under the initial request of the government of Panama. Between 1996 and 1998, 15 rounds of negotiations were held between the parties (Ferrer 2001). In August 1998 the negotiations reached a stalemate. They were only resumed in 2005 and concluded with an agreement in 2006 (DIRECON: July 2006).[9] From the beginning Panama and Chile were involved in highly complex negotiations to reach agreements on investment, as well as on professional and financial services and some agricultural products such as rice, oils, beef, chicken and pork meat, milk products and mainly sugar and sugar based food products (DINECI 26/06/2006). Both parties included the services, commerce, and agricultural associations in the previous consultation process to analyse the possibility of having an FTA with the counterpart. The inclusion of domestic groups was expanded in the intergovernmental negotiation to specific issue-areas groups such as banking, trade unions from the financial sector, aquaculture industries and fishermen workers, the forestry sector and meat as well as rice producers. In this regard, domestic lobby groups from both parties not only channelled their demands through their confederations or associations, but also by pressuring the government directly either individually or by forming a coalition with other alike domestic groups.

Even though the amount of trade between both countries as well as the number of domestic groups participating in the negotiation was low[10], the outcome of the negotiation suggests that the amount of resources, time, and energy to lobby the government was intense. The toughness of the negotiation was presumably due to the eventual consequences that a rule binding FTA agreement could create for the less competitive domestic groups. The domestic groups' mobilisation pro or contra particular economic negotiations between parties with middle or low trade should present similar characteristics as those in which the trade between the parties is high.

1.6.2 The Negotiation between Panama and Costa Rica

Both countries are part of the same region and are trade partners. In fact both countries signed a preferential trade agreement in 1973. However, the scope of this agreement is very limited. Therefore, Costa Rica and Panama as well as the other Central American countries sought to establish FTA negotiations.[11] In 1997 the

9 This agreement was implemented in March 2008.

10 The economic exchange in each year from 1998 to 2002 did not surpass 45 million US dollars. In 2003, the economic exchange between both countries was 106,63 million dollars; in 2004 it was 172, 62 millions and in 2005 122,21 million dollars. The trade balance throughout these years was always favourable to Chile (DIRECON 2006: 1).

11 These countries are Costa Rica, El Salvador, Guatemala, Honduras, Nicaragua and Panama. This FTA is only binding in bilateral terms i.e. the trade relation between each Central American Country vis-à-vis Panama.

Central American countries signed a memorandum of understanding to explore and assess the possibilities of launching negotiations to build a normative frame between Central America and Panama as well as conducting bilateral negotiations on market access, rules of origin and financial services between each Central American country and Panama (Ferrer 2001). Yet the formal negotiating rounds only started in 2000 and it ended with a common frame to negotiate the respective bilateral FTAs in May 2001. In 2002 the bilateral negotiation between Costa Rica and Panama started. However, this negotiation stalled after two rounds during the same year, due to lack of agreement over issue-areas such as financial services, rules of origin, phytosanitary measures as well as over agricultural products such as tomato products, onions, beef, chicken and pork meat, and dairy products (COMEX 14/03/2006: CP 597 and CP 646). These negotiations resumed in August 2006 and after seven rounds of negotiations the negotiations concluded -the FTA was signed on 7 August 2007. Domestic groups took an important role in shaping the legal common frame for the negotiations between the Central American countries plus Panama. In fact, more than 800 companies from Costa Rica participated in the negotiations as well as 45 Trade Associations (COMEX 2000: CP 077).

1.6.3 Justification of the Case Studies Selection

On the one hand, Panama and Chile were not and are not significant trade and political partners for each other. Despite the fact that the trade relation has grown in the last years (1998-2005), it is not considered significant.[12] On the other hand, Costa Rica and Panama are important trade and political partners. This is reflected in their trade indicators, in the extant limited FTA implemented in 1973, and in the idea of establishing bilateral FTAs among the Central American countries plus Panama. Therefore, I have chosen one case in which the countries are highly dependent on each other due to their geographic proximity i.e. Costa Rica and Panama, which are border countries; and another case in which no previous significant economic ties existed i.e. Chile and Panama. Most of the FTA negotiations underway at present show such relevant trade and political partners (e.g. South Korea- Japan) and low political and economic contact (e.g. Mexico-Singapore) as the cases chosen for this research. Thus, stalemates in FTA negotiations happen in cases where low and high economic ties exist between the states.

One could argue that the causes for both stalemates lie in Panama's interests and strategies to negotiate. This interpretation is misleading for the following reasons: first, Panama's trade policy presents cases of agreement and non-agreement in trade accords of lower scope and multilateral negotiations. In addition, when it negotiated with Costa Rica already signed its first FTAs with Central America (normative frame) and with El Salvador. Therefore, Panama could successfully conclude FTAs.

12 See footnote number eleven for data on the trade relationship Chile-Panama.

However, the negotiation with Chile was its first FTA negotiation experience. Yet, the actor that pursued the hardest negotiation strategy in the case of Chile-Panama was the former and not the latter. Chile was the first to defect in the FTA negotiation before Panama, following a "tit for tat" strategy (see Axelrod 1984). Of course, Panama also has some degree of responsibility for the outcome of non-agreement because none of the parties were capable of fulfilling each other's expectations in the negotiation. Finally, in the case of Costa Rica and Panama, both sides have shared responsibilities for the stalemate, because they pursued aggressive tactics to include both Costa Rica's dairy products and Panama's financial and insurance sector as part of the deal as well as other agricultural products.

Second, the phenomena of FTAs and the negotiation processes of these types of accords between Latin American countries, or involving one party from this continent, have been understudied. One exception is the case of MERCOSUR and its negotiations with the EU and the US (FTAA) (see Genna 2007). Most of the extant literature on FTAs focuses on the potential benefits that these types of agreements bring to a national economy as a whole i.e. the field of economics. However there are to date no studies on the political process of state to state FTA negotiations in Latin America. An exception again is the case of MERCOSUR (see Bouzas 2006)

Using cases of stalled negotiations from Latin America should not undermine the attempt and aspiration of creating a theoretical framework, since the only requirement to pursue an FTA negotiation between countries is to share the *ideology* of economic liberalisation, although this ideology is adapted to a country's own national institutional context, called varieties of capitalism (Hall and Soskice 2001). Putting aside the differences countries have in terms of development, the sharing of a common road map (that being economic liberalisation) through negotiating FTAs is not intended to solve the extant North-South division, but rather to give tools to the countries to manage their insertion into the global economy (Landau 2000:2). This common goal indicates that countries with different levels of development also share similarities in terms of domestic constraints when they pursue FTA negotiations.

Third, if one wants to study failed experiences of FTAs, then one should go for the case that had the most cases of failed negotiations in proportion to its own successfully concluded experiences: this is Panama. This country did not have successful FTA experiences until 2001, except the normative FTA frame with Central America and the bilateral FTA with El Salvador. However, after this problematic start, Panama's performance in FTA improved substantially as it has already signed ten FTAs (see www.dineci.go.pa).[13] Some of these successful negotiations were achieved in a short time after the failed negotiation with Costa Rica, such as Taiwan. In addition, studying these FTA negotiations with Chile and Costa Rica are interesting as these two countries, along with Mexico, are the most proactive in terms of

13 The current impact of previous failed experiences has diminished for Panama's record, as it currently has more FTAs than stalled cases.

promoting the benefits of achieving FTAs. In fact, Chile is currently one of the countries with most FTAs in the world, and it was already the most proactive country in the race of FTAs on the Latin American continent when it negotiated with Panama. Costa Rica is the leading country in the Central American region in terms of economic liberalisation. Therefore, due to the experience of Chile and Costa Rica, officials of the three countries perceived the respective FTA negotiations Chile-Panama, and Costa Rica-Panama as realisable, i.e. with high chance of concluding with an outcome of agreement.

Fourth, language and strong cultural differences are ruled out as an explanatory variable in these two FTA negotiations. Despite the fact that there is abundant relevant literature on how language and culture affects "bargaining", in these cases these factors lack explanatory power. This fact helps us to focus more on finding common general material patterns on the process of negotiating an FTA as well as on the role of domestic actors in the making of the FTA policy of a country.

Fifth, the relatively small size of the countries chosen allows us to identify in a clear way the relevant domestic actors and their channels of influence on the negotiation process as well as the eventual coalitions they build to lobby and exert pressure more efficiently over the negotiators. Moreover, relevant actors and interests as well as the process that leads to a stalemate may be traced back in a more complete way.

Finally, and as a clarification, both negotiations were re-launched after many years as mentioned before. The resumption of both negotiations does not erase or minimise the fact that these FTA negotiations failed in the first attempt in 1998 (Chile-Panama) and 2002 (Costa Rica-Panama). On the contrary, the resumption of these negotiations after many years enhances the case study selection criteria as the respective re-launching processes took the dynamics of new negotiation processes. Both negotiations had to start from zero in the market access area, because the failed negotiation was seven years back in the case of Chile-Panama, and four years back in the case of Costa Rica-Panama. Thus what was negotiated in 1998 and 2002 became anachronistic in 2005 and 2006 when both negotiations were resumed.

1.7 Methodological Considerations

Following the categories of studies on negotiation i.e. descriptive, prescriptive and normative (Raiffa 2002b), this study fits the first category. First, it uses descriptive analysis to recreate how actors performed in two real negotiations, although the empirical cases are used to test the theory and the hypotheses derived from it. Moreover, this work is also theory grounded as it intends to develop a theoretical framework to explain the process that makes an FTA negotiation stall.

Recreating a negotiation is rather complex, since a researcher can only aspire to analyse negotiation processes as an outsider and thus only in a limited way. On the other hand, insiders of the process have occasionally used years of first hand experience to publish in highly detailed ways their experiences of particular negotiations. A good amount of literature is available on negotiations, especially on episodes of the cold war. In contradistinction to the abundance of such publications, there is no such material available on state to state FTA negotiations. A plausible reason for this is that the phenomenon of bilateral FTA negotiations is rather new and the task of writing a book on these issues is time consuming for negotiators. Another reason might be that the nature of FTA negotiations impedes a first hand observer who wishes to give a detailed account of the whole process, since these types of negotiations are highly technical. Therefore, governments use different negotiators for a broad range of issue-areas, based on their topics of expertise e.g. a specialist over public procurement does not necessarily know how the issue-area of agriculture is negotiated, because he or she has not been able to participate in the negotiation of that issue due to his or her lack of expertise.

Despite the limitations for an outsider, there are alternative ways to recreate the process of stalled FTA negotiations. In order to gather empirical information on the case studies, and test the plausibility of the hypotheses of this study, I use qualitative techniques i.e. process-tracing. Process-tracing provides a series of possibilities to reconstruct, and trace the causes of stalemate in FTA negotiations (see George and Bennett 2005: ch. 9-10). I mapped out the respective FTA negotiations based on the evidence provided by internal documents of the negotiations such as minutes of the rounds of negotiations, draft text of the FTA, documents elaborated by the domestic interest groups on the FTA policy of their country, and the texts with these groups' specific demands on the FTA negotiations. I also used national newspapers and the magazines published by the different business associations with declarations or analyses of the different domestic actors' and government representatives' interests over the FTA policy in general, and the negotiations of this study in particular. Moreover, I interviewed the teams of negotiators and the representatives of the different interest groups of each party of the period in which these negotiations were conducted in order to reconstruct the parts missing in the written sources, and to supplement and confirm what the official documents and the media sources say.[14]

Using qualitative means for a study usually limits the number of cases to which one can choose to apply a theoretical frame. Beyond the understandable reasons of limited time and reduced funding to carry interviews during field trips, there is the limiting factor of non-existence of statistical data over the processes of FTA negotiations e.g. background conditions such as legal constraints as well as the strategies and tactics used by actors before and during the negotiation. This is something that limits the possibility of choosing *many cases and few variables* and the aspiration of making far reaching generalisations (see Hague et al. 1992; Landman 2002).

14 On the importance of interviews as an essential component of the process tracing method (see Tansey 2007: 765-772). I also interviewed members of the negotiation teams of these three countries that were inderectly related to these processes.

This is thus a comparative study with few cases. Having a comparative study of this type can still contribute to refining extant theories that fall short in scope to explain the case of stalled FTA negotiations. Moreover, a focused comparison may help to shed light over other cases of stalled FTA negotiations or future ones, when similar antecedents and contextual factors are present (see Landman 2000: 4). However, shedding light over other cases of stalled FTA negotiations or future ones does not imply that far reaching generalisations can be made in a research with as *'few cases and many variables`* as this one. The scope of the book is thus rather modest, since this study as a whole has to be taken as a heuristic attempt in its additive sense to test whether the conditions outlined here are applicable to other cases that were omitted in this work, and to the ones that for sure will emerge in the future.

Because this research has *few cases and many variables* in an already small universe of possible choices i.e. anomalies are fewer than agreed FTAs, this work becomes heuristic. It is an invitation to add new cases of stalled FTA negotiations, and by that I mean challenge, confirm, or refine the theoretical framework and the conditions presented in this work (on heuristics see Pólya 1957; Abbot 2004). As part of this heuristic invitation, I keep the research questions open and not closed in order to pinpoint the need of assessing other failed FTA negotiation experiences. Keeping the research question open should not invalidate the conclusions of this work. In other words, using the research question *why do some FTA negotiations fail in reaching an outcome of agreement*; instead of asking: *why did the FTA negotiations Chile-Panama and Costa Rica-Panama fail in reaching an outcome of agreement in 1998 and 2002 respectively* does not mean generalisations. It just means there are other empirical cases that deserve research attention, and that this work may be taken as a starting point for such enterprise.

1.8 Material: The Constraints of Qualitative Sources

This theory-guided research relies on a broad range of material. In the development of the theoretical frame, I mainly use secondary sources i.e. books, articles published in peer review journals, and edited books from the fields of international political economy, international relations, economics, and theory of negotiation.

I use primary sources to carry out the analysis of the two case studies. A great deal of these sources are public documents of various kinds, such as government declarations, and internal analysis reports, minutes, and a draft text of the FTA negotiations written by trade diplomats. Economic negotiations to achieve FTAs are certainly part of a country's foreign policy. The goals of a country's foreign policy are often shaped by government representatives through public statements before and after the meetings with the counterpart/s of the negotiation, either in bilateral or multilateral forums. In the latter, governments usually conduct bilateral meetings. Therefore, I rely on public speeches, and interviews for newspapers.

Domestic actors usually go public about their policy preferences when they are not heard by their governments. This is the case when a specific FTA negotiation might jeopardise the benefits that some groups have in the forms of TB and NTB. Therefore, evidence of domestic interests groups' participation and policy preferences are likely to be found in statements through newspapers and media as well as through the think-tanks that are economically supported by some of these economic groups. Moreover, these domestic groups tend to channel their demands through sector associations. These sector-economic associations usually distribute internal papers, magazines, and memoirs to their affiliates about the steps they are following with regards to the government economic negotiations. Yet, sometimes these associations represent economic sectors that have divergent interests in an FTA negotiation. I also rely on interviews with representatives of these economic associations and the key representative of sub-sectors that blocked the FTA talks.

The use of the aforementioned material is compared with the evidence gathered in face to face interviews with key government officials as well as the representatives of interest groups that participated in these negotiations.[15] One goal of these interviews is to be able to corroborate and contrast the information obtained in the government documents, articles in newspapers, documents from think-tanks, as well as public speeches and official reports.

A methodological problem of using interviews is that participants of negotiations usually tend to recall events with certain biases i.e. sometimes they magnify a specific event or recall some facts erroneously. A researcher using this method should be aware of these biases in negotiations. It can also be the case that these biases are intended rather than "pure lack of memory". When negotiators and interest groups' representatives refer to some events giving excessive importance to some aspects over others, one should ask himself whether the policy-makers or the representatives of interest groups have a hidden agenda. Therefore, the evidence obtained in these interviews has to be cross-checked and corroborated by other written sources as well as by other members of these negotiations.

However, I confront another problem with regards to the interviews. There are internal aspects of the negotiation that are relevant which do not have written material to use to corroborate the evidence gathered in interviews. This is an inherent feature of negotiations. Therefore, I use the material obtained in the interviews, but I make sure this evidence is confirmed by a number of persons that have divergent interests in the issue-area at stake. Another dilemma is that some of the people want to remain anonymous. These interviews are included in this study since I was able to contrast and corroborate important parts of their testimonies with those who have authorised the use of their names in this study.

15 These interviews were conducted in Spanish during the year 2008. All translations of these interviews are my own.

1.9 Organisation of the Study

This work is divided into two parts. *Part I* consists of two chapters. *Chapter 2* gives an overview of the state of the art on the issue of failed FTA negotiations, and on the study cases. *Chapter 3* presents the theoretical frame, the hypotheses, and the conditions to explain the stalemate of some bilateral FTA negotiations.

Part II has five chapters that deal with the empirical cases of this study. *Chapter 4* consists of a brief historical account of the external trade policy of each country as well as an overview of these countries' respective FTA negotiation processes as a whole. In addition, I identify the key economic agents of the FTA negotiations i.e. interest groups, agencies, and negotiators. *Chapter 5* focuses on the internal and external domestic factors of the negotiation between Chile and Panama, and on the role played by domestic groups regarding the sensitive issue-areas that explain the failure of this negotiation. *Chapter 6* pays special attention to the intergovernmental negotiation and the internal and external factors at this level that explain the failed process between Chile and Panama. *Chapter* 7 has the same purpose as *chapter 5*, but with regards to the FTA negotiation between Costa Rica and Panama. *Chapter 8* analyses the state to state negotiation between Panama and Costa Rica in a similar way to *chapter 6*. *Chapter 9* compares the similarities and differences of the empirical cases of this study. It also puts the issue of failed FTA negotiations in a broader perspective by giving an overview of failed FTA negotiations that have occurred in Asia and the Americas.

The conclusion, *chapter 10,* has four parts. The first section answers the key questions of this research. The second section answers the questions by giving an overview of the process of failure in the two negotiations, as well as it evaluates whether the conditions and hypotheses are confirmed accordingly with the empirical results. The third section of the conclusion deals with the possible theoretical implications of the theoretical frame and conditions I have presented for studying these two cases of stalled FTA negotiations for the fields of international relations, international political economy and negotiation. The last section sets a road map for future research.

Finally, I have also added an epilogue, in which I briefly present the re-launching process of these FTA negotiations as a way to complete the two sides of the story in the bilateral economic relationships of Chile-Panama and Costa Rica-Panama. I only describe in a general way how the re-launching of these FTA negotiations was produced in 2005 and 2006.

Part I: The State of the Art and Theoretical Framework

2. The State of the Art

2.1 Introduction

There are theories from different fields of study that can provide some tools to explain the phenomenon of stalled FTA negotiations. The theoretical approaches presented below span the field of economics; the field of international relations and international political economy; and the field of negotiation. Nevertheless, none of the extant works tackle the issue of stalled negotiations in a direct way. Therefore, I highlight the key issues of these fields, their theoretical shortcomings, and the aspects that can be useful to analyse failed FTA negotiations. I also explain why I have chosen to exclude some theoretical approaches of particular schools of thought such as constructivism in the field of IR/IPE and negotiation. Even though the theory of negotiation is a middle range theory embedded in the grand theories of IR/IPE, I present it in a separate section. Finally, I give an overview of the extant empirical literature on the external trade policy of Chile, Costa Rica and Panama.

2.2 The Field of Economics

2.2.1 New Trade Theory

New trade theory assumes that the market is imperfect, because firms interact strategically with each other to change prices in order to maximise their profits. In the real world, perfect competition does not exist since most of the prices are set up by companies that hold a monopoly or are part of an oligopoly (van Marrewijk 2002). New trade theorists also seek to supplement the idea of comparative advantage, by introducing the notion of increasing returns to scale as a cause of trade. Observing increasing returns to scale helps explain the occurrence of specialisation and intra-trade, understood as possibilities of importing and exporting products and services within the same industry (Krugman 1992a, and Helpman and Krugman 1999).

The first generation of new trade theorists focused on the relative importance of simultaneous exports and imports of similar manufacturing products in a given country (Gandolfo 1998: 228). Another group of scholars has focused more on the issue of protectionism, arguing that temporary import protection can lead to a better specialisation and export promotion (Krugman 1992b, Brander and Spencer 1984, Balassa 1971). Protection gives domestic firms the chance to reduce their learning curves, lower production costs and increase their market shares in both national and international markets (Krugman 1989, Venables and Smith 1986). New trade theorists expect that short-term protection and the efficient allocation of these measures will limit rent-seeking behaviour, and will create good conditions for specialisation and efficient production of goods (Kibritçioglu 2002: 2). There are types of protection that are ruled out in new trade theory, because they are more damaging for free trade i.e. quotas are worse than tariffs (Bhagwati 1965). Moreover, new trade theorists point out that inter-trade needs more protectionism than intra-trade firms (Schirm 2004: 37-38). Even though protectionism is in theory an option, most economists do not recommend translating its premises into concrete policies, because policy makers usually go beyond what the theory recommends when they have to implement such measures (Krugman 1992a).

A weakness of new trade theory is its ambiguity regarding the exact length of "short-term" temporary protection should run i.e. development of an infant industry that without protection would otherwise not have existed. Authors (Helpman 1999, Krugman and Obstfeld 2006, and Tornell 1991) acknowledge the fact that once protectionist measures are implemented, their removal becomes extremely difficult in the future. Moreover, new trade theory neglects how difficult it is for a government to separate strategic interventions from non-strategic ones (Hart and Prakash 2000: 253). New trade theory thus indirectly attributes explanatory power to the role of domestic actors (rent-seeking); the cleavages that allocation of protectionist measures create or enhance within a country through time; and the institutional setting that constrains the intergovernmental bargaining process.

The stalemate of some FTA negotiations is thus possibly related to the fact that protectionism in the forms of TB and NTB becomes difficult to remove, especially when inter-trade economic issue-areas are at stake, because it empowers domestic lobby groups in the economic and political spheres (rent-seeking, and government as office-seeking) as well as amongst the public opinion. Yet not all is about pure domestic interests in FTA negotiations; there are also conditions for governments to respond or not to these pressures. Otherwise, if governments were always more responsive to protectionist groups because of its better organisation, then there would not be successful stories to tell about FTAs. Due to its different goals, new trade theory does not consider why governments are, in some cases able to and in others not able to overcome protectionist lobby groups at the national or at the intergovernmental negotiation levels. This theory does not explain the process by which a government changes its initial preference from an FTA to stall these negotiations, nor does it consider the role of the counter-part in such negotiations. However, these aspects are important to explain why FTA negotiations stall.

2.3 *Theories of International Relations/International Political Economy*

2.3.1 Liberalism

The preference of domestic actors for freer trade and their impact on governments' decisions have often been used to explain trade policy in the field of international political economy (Milner 1998; Keohane and Milner 1996; Ladewig 2006; Krueger 1997; Moravcsik 1993b). Others have studied the consequences of changes in international trade for domestic groups that advocate more or less free trade (Rogowski 1989; Frieden and Rogowski 1996; Rodrik 1997).

The focus on domestic actors has widely been used in negotiation theory in general (Putnam 1988; Evans, et.al. 1993; Mayer 1992), and in economic negotiations in particular (Friman 1993; Odell 2000; Milner and Rosendorff 1996). Most of this literature focuses on how governments have to simultaneously negotiate both the domestic and the international level to assure success in inter-state negotiations. This literature has been path-breaking, when it comes to paying attention to how preferences of domestic actors are formed around an issue-area at stake, and how domestic preferences become essential to explaining outcomes in negotiation analysis. Although this double-edged diplomacy has been used for issues dealing with economic negotiations, the topic of stalled FTA negotiations has not been considered.

At a general level, liberal theory establishes the preponderance of domestic preferences to explain state behaviour in international politics (Moravcsik 1997). Liberal theory provides some arguments to analyse why some FTAs have stalled, especially if two forms of liberalism are used i.e. commercial and republican. Here, reasons for stalled FTAs can be due to the fact that protectionist-oriented actors pressure the government to include their policy goals, which encourage a disaggregated policy option with regards to free trade. This implies that a possible agreement over an FTA is a difficult process, because a government has to represent the preferences of both export and protectionist oriented domestic groups, both being powerful groups. Moreover, the government will tend to include the policy preference of both groups because of its office-seeking goals. While these arguments can lead to explain FTA negotiations in part, they do not capture the conditions in which an FTA stall, or the conditions in which the eventual losers of an FTA overcome the winners. A way to understand the formation of domestic actors' and governments' preferences in an FTA policy, as causes for domestic policy preferences for having or not having an FTA with another country, is to complement them with aspects of new trade theory, such as whether these actors belong to an inter-trade and intra-trade sector as well as whether they enjoy high, medium, low or nothing of TB and NTB. However, the final attribute to stall a negotiation between states are the governments. Thus, can intergovernmentalism explain the process that leads to a stalemate?

2.3.2 Intergovernmentalism

Intergovernmentalism or interstate negotiations are synonymous words taken from the neorealist tradition. A difference with most traditional versions of neorealism is that intergovernmentalism seeks to integrate the domestic and the interstate dimensions. In this regard, intergovernmentalism is a theory synthesis attempt of elements of neorealism and neoliberalism to explain international phenomena.[16] Nevertheless, it seems appropriate to make a brief account of what "traditional" neorealism is and has given to this intergovernmental approach.

The neorealist theory highlights the anarchic nature of the international system. Nation-states are the primary actors and their survival and power position are the most important goals for each state in the international system (Waltz 1979). For neorealism, economic issues are at a secondary level. However, survival and power can also be achieved by enhancing economic means (Gilpin 1987). Yet, when states cooperate they do it for instrumental reasons i.e. alliances are short term to overcome security threats posed by a common enemy (Lamy 2001: 186). Even though most of the neorealist literature is concerned with security and power positions in the international system, cooperation has been taken into account by the theory, also in economic issues (see Grieco 1993). Whether a state decides to cooperate or not is a matter of relative gains i.e. how much power and influence one state will get if another one decides to cooperate with the former (Grieco 1988, 1990). Joseph Grieco (1990) neglects the role of domestic interests as causes for the formation of relative gains. As with most neorealists, he does not open the *black box* of the state, to analyse the domestic actors' preferences formation. According to the neorealists, state interest is superior to domestic ones in security as well as in trade issues. The argument of an extant unitary interest of the state leads neorealists to rule out the power of initiative that resides within the units of analyses (Linklater 1995: 251-259).

The usage of the concept of relative gains has also been applied to negotiation theory, which is often named *distributive strategy* (Hopmann 1996: 48). However, an economic negotiation is not only based on distributive strategies but also on integrative ones (absolute gains: liberal theory) (Friman 1993: 396). Even though the concept of relative gains may help to explain why FTA negotiations sometimes stall, it does not establish circumstances that make some economic issue-areas part of a distributive (or value-claiming) or an integrative strategy (or value-creating). In other words, the concept can be useful to describe how the process develops to reach a stage where zero-sum bargaining predominates, but it does not delineate clear causalities of why non-cooperation sometimes happens.

Since Waltz's rigid systemic theory and the subsequent discussion over relative and absolute gains in the 1990s, new insights into the role of neorealism have been

16 As liberalism was already presented in the previous sub-section, I will only focus on what neorealism has given to this approach.

developed. One middle range theory is the liberal intergovernmental approach. This theory is inspired by both the liberal and neorealist tradition, and it seeks to complement the domestic and international level. This approach opens the *black box* of the state by integrating the dimension of domestic politics to explain foreign policy behaviour (Moravcsik 1993, 1997). However, this theory was thought to explain regional cooperation, and it became one of the main explanatory models for the study of the European Union (Tonra 2001: 27). Despite the fact that this theoretical approach is Eurocentric, it is possible to extract general aspects to explain the stalemate of some FTA negotiations. If regional cooperation is extrapolated to FTA negotiations, it can be said that FTAs are another form of cooperation. What matters is that intergovernmentalism seeks to establish endogenous causalities for state behaviour vis-à-vis other states. Those interests that the government negotiates at the international level by using either value-claiming or value-creating strategies are constituted at the domestic level. Governments' external policies are thus reactive to the policy preference options of domestic actors and each step governments take in the intergovernmental level is conceived either to accede or resist these domestic forces (Schirm 2002)

Nonetheless intergovernmentalism presents some shortcomings that make its sole applicability to the case of stalled FTA negotiations difficult. One of the main shortcomings of the theory is that the formation of governmental interests at the domestic level is developed in an analytical vacuum (Ibid.). The theory shows how interests are formed and shaped, but it does not determine why interests in or opposing FTA negotiations emerge. Neither does it establish which conditions predominate to make groups advocating for keeping "protection" successful vis-à-vis freer trade groups. Whereas Moravcsik (1993: 474) mentions the term *interdependence* as a driving force for cooperation, the term is a static label that does not help to establish clear causalities for non-cooperation (stall) or cooperation (agreement), if the term is applied to FTA negotiations. In other words, if governments' preferences either for agreement or non-agreement in an FTA negotiation are constituted by domestic actors, what drives these domestic actors to advocate for one of these two options? If the stalemate of an FTA negotiation sometimes predominates, then what conditions make the governments protect these interests to the extent that no final agreement is reached during the intergovernmental bargaining process? As intergovernmentalism cannot answer these questions, it seems promising to take elements from new trade theory (inter-trade and intra trade as well as the strategic use of TB and NTB), liberal theory (commercial and republican liberalism), and intergovernmentalism (state to state and responsiveness or not to own domestic actors) to explain the context and the negotiation process that lead to a stalemate. Yet, constructivism has also developed a solid case to understand negotiations, but: can constructivism as a school of IR and with its new developments in negotiation provide a frame to understand the cases of this study?

2.3.3 Constructivism in IR/IPE and in Theory of Negotiation

Constructivism highlights the role of ideas, norms and values as key elements for the constitution of governmental interests as well as those of domestic actors in international politics (Kratochwill 1989; Onuf 1989). Agents do not interact in a vacuum, since structure, which is socially constructed, constrains the acts and behaviour of the different actors that participate in the international sphere. In other words, agent and structure mutually constitute each other (Wendt 1999).

For constructivism there is no such a thing as an objective reality "out there", but a social constructed one "in here" (Pettman 2000: 19). The construction of this social reality is produced by intersubjective exchanges between actors. Thus for the constructivist, reality is a socially constructed phenomenon, in which agents act depending on what is *appropriate* in a particular situation i.e. agents will tend to act according to the values, ideas and rules that are associated to their particular identities (Risse 2000; March and Olsen 1998; Adler 2006; Checkel 1997). Constructivism thus rejects the idea that actors make their policy preferences based on a cost-benefit analysis as rational choice presupposes.

Using a broad constructivist lens to analyse FTA negotiations in general and the process that makes some bilateral FTAs stall in particular seems inappropriate. The broad range of issue-areas negotiated in these trade negotiations can always be expressed in material or quantifiable terms. The eventual losses or benefits for one or more domestic groups as well as for the government in different issue-areas of an FTA negotiation have always a tangible monetary value or they are interest loaded. This is the case when actors negotiate the removal or not of tariffs; when they negotiate a certain number of quotas over specific products; and when the negotiators have to deal with issue-areas in which NTB play a major role, or in which workers can be benefited from (more jobs or better wages), or affected by, an eventual deal (job insecurity or wage reductions).

2.3.3.1 The Logic of Arguing in the Field of Negotiation

The logic of arguing has mainly been developed by the German academic community. One of its founding fathers is Jürgen Habermas (1984), who distinguishes between strategic and communicative action. The former mode of action is based on the rational choice paradigm, which takes actors as utility maximisers, whereas communicative action presupposes an ideal speech situation, in which actors try to realise societal goals by negotiating a common definition of reality. Negotiation is thus about mutual understanding. This mutual understanding presupposes the exclusion of "egocentric calculations of success" (Habermas 1984: 286). To achieve such mutual understanding for a social-normative setting, it is necessary that the parts involved in communicative action achieve a reasoned consensus over the presented arguments. A reasoned consensus can be achieved if none of the parties involved try to manipulate the communication process, and if their arguments are open to mutual deliberation about their validity (Habermas 1984). Therefore, the parties involved in communicative action should be open to change their preferences if a better argument is presented by the counterpart.

Even though Habermas' work is thought in terms of truth-seeking through deliberation and argumentation in the public sphere, his ideas have been applied to the "closed" process of negotiations. A negotiation, no matter what it is about, is all about presenting the better argument. For Thomas Risse (2000: 20-21), however, arguing matters in the different stages of a negotiation, although to different degrees. The one in which arguing matters the most is the pre-negotiation in which actors set the agenda, and establish a common knowledge on the topic to be negotiated, by defining collectively the situation and the rules to negotiate a given issue. The next step at which arguing plays a key role to achieve a reasoned consensus is to try to find an optimal solution to a common problem i.e. actors should pursue a problem-solving attitude through the negotiation process.

A Habermasian-based approach has also been used to analyse why, in some negotiations, actors pursue their goals in bargaining (cost-benefit analysis), or in an arguing mode (Kotzian 2007; Esser 2004; Payne 2001). Such analyses have claimed that actors are able to *frame* a negotiation and apply these frames, depending on the aims and the topics at stake in the negotiation. Frames are not automatically activated. Actors are able to activate either a frame of bargaining or arguing. In this regard, actors choose their frame, depending on their calculations on what the situation is about (Kotzian 2007: 83-84). Therefore, the frame selection is a rational decision. For example, in a negotiation over human right issues it is very likely that actors will activate an arguing frame rather than a bargaining one, but in trade negotiations such as bilateral FTAs, it is more likely that both domestic actors and the government from both parties of the negotiation will activate a bargaining frame. In this example, we can see why the logic (or frame) of arguing as well as the logic of appropriateness are not suitable to analyse and explain FTA negotiations.

"Bargaining is the baseline model and only if certain conditions are met will actors engage in arguing" (Kotzian 2007: 95). One important condition is that the actors are involved in a long-term socialisation process, and that the relation between the parties is highly institutionalised. However, in negotiations between eventual trade partners in which the negotiation is limited to trade and where the parties are not necessarily part of a long socialisation process, the rational election of actors will tend to be the frame of bargaining. Otherwise, the actors' bad choice over the most suitable frame for a negotiation will create a power asymmetry that will be used by the counterpart for its own benefit.

Therefore, as the aim of this book is to analyse stalled FTA negotiations, in which the issue-areas at stake can be expressed in monetary terms or are interest-loaded; where actors' interests predominate over presenting or not a better argument; in which actors will get more of their "wishing list" by analysing the situation in cost-benefit terms, then it is better to take the frame of bargaining as a starting point for this work.

2.4 *Theory of Negotiation*

I have already mentioned some aspects of the theory of negotiation throughout this review and the introduction because of the difficulties involved in separating it from the theories of IR/IPE. Nonetheless, this review allows me to highlight the analytical and conceptual tools that I am using in this study.

One of the most systematic works on negotiation within the field of IR is that of Terrence Hopmann (*The Negotiation Process and the Resolution of International Conflicts*, 1996).[17] Hopmann's book presents the basic concepts and types of negotiation within the discipline of IR applied to security issues. Hopmann distinguishes between the concepts of bargaining and negotiating. Whereas bargaining belongs to win-lose situations, negotiating is used to describe win-win situations. In addition, the book presents a clear and systematic definition of BATNA, which here is the prior status quo. The book analyses competitive and joint problem solving negotiations in both bilateral and multilateral settings. It also considers the impact of power and the influence of extant symmetries or asymmetries between the parties as well as the influence of bureaucracies and the human dimension.

The focus on security issues of this study problematises its applicability, beyond the conceptual contribution, to economic negotiations. Whereas there are many references to situations in which real negotiation stalled, there are not systematic explanations of why this is so. Moreover, the costs of having a stalemate in security issues is rather different than that of a stalemate in economic ones i.e. the outcome of an enduring stalemate in security issues between two countries can in the worst case scenario escalate to an armed conflict. Thus these high costs for both parties will tend to create special conditions for third party mediation in security conflicts (Hopmann 1996: 242-243). Mediation through a third party is also rarely present to redirect or relaunch bilateral FTA negotiations. Rather than mediation in bilateral FTA negotiations, new waves of lobbying from domestic groups can better explain the relaunch of this type of negotiations. Using the theoretical approach developed by Hopmann is inappropriate for this study. Therefore, the use of this text is limited to conceptual aspects of negotiation such as BATNA, win-win, and win-lose situations.

Other general works on negotiation are Howard Raiffa's (1982) *The Art and Science of Negotiation,* and (2002) *Negotiation Analysis* (with John Richarson and David Metcalfe). In the first work, Raiffa analyses different topics, from business negotiations to the negotiation of the Panama Canal. He uses game theory to explain the different phases of a negotiation process. In this scheme, non-agreement is a

17 A vast amount of literature on negotiation is available on business and other issues, having a prescriptive view. In fact some of this literature has had a strong influence in the development of the theory of negotiation within the fields of IR and IPE. Some classical cases are the works of Walton and Mckersie (A Behavioural Theory of Labor Negotiations, 1965); and Fisher and Ury (Getting to Yes, 2007).

static depiction of a two-tale continuum of a zone of agreement for bilateral negotiations. Raiffa names the limits of the zone of agreement as reservation price (Raiffa 1982: 42). This reservation price is also named prior status quo, resistance points or simply BATNA.

Whereas the issue of stalled negotiations is not analysed directly, Raiffa distinguishes between two types of stalemate. The first originates in inefficiencies of the parties when attempting to find the zone of agreement. The narrower the zone of agreement, the more difficult the negotiation is. However, for Raiffa, the number of stalled negotiations is very low, because negotiating parties will always commit to find an agreement if there is a zone of agreement, even if it is a reduced one. The second possibility is that negotiations stall because such a zone does not exist (Raiffa 1982: 57). Following this line of arguing, whether it is possible to find or detect a zone of agreement is part of the pre-negotiation stage. In the negotiation process, this zone of agreement can be expanded or reduced depending on the tactics used by the actors and the possible realignments of domestic coalitions triggered by the process as such or by external factors to the negotiation such as elections, politicisation, and uncertainty.

In the case of stalled FTA negotiations, a stalemate is caused by the inefficiency to detect the zone of agreement and/or to expand it. Yet, if a zone of agreement does not exist, then negotiations will not start and will not go beyond the mutual consultations and studies on whether an FTA with another country is plausible. Despite this distinction between these two types of stalemate, this work does not explain in detail how actors lead a negotiation to a stalemate. This aspect is also present in Raiffa's book *Negotiation Analysis,* in which he seeks to integrate the individual dimension of negotiation with game theory as well as decision-making theory. Even though he analyses the possibility of deadlocks, even when a zone of agreement exists, he only mentions the aggressive value-claiming strategies used by the parties or the inexistence of a zone of agreement as possible causes (Raiffa 2002: 295-298). Moreover, he switches the focus to prescriptive mechanisms of negotiating when one has to negotiate with a difficult counterpart, because he presents to his readers how to prevent a deadlock (Raiffa 2002: 298-306).

A seminal contribution to the field of negotiation in International Relations is Robert Putnam's article (1988) "Diplomacy and Domestic Politics: the Logic of Two Level-Games". Putnam argues that government's negotiations at the international level (or level I) are constrained by endogenous actors at the domestic level (level II). The government has thus to be aware that what is negotiated internationally needs to be ratified domestically. Following this need of ratification, the negotiator has to find along with its counterpart an outcome that is satisfactory enough for the divergent interested groups. In addition, some negotiators will take some steps at level I to trigger realignments at level II to facilitate goals that seemed unachievable for the domestic politics and for the approval of the negotiation (Putnam 1988: 427-435).

In order to get ratification at level II of the game, having a larger win-set makes a final agreement more likely.[18] Putnam argues that the win-sets for domestic actors should overlap so that domestic actors with stakes in the negotiation may ratify the agreement. The larger a win-set is, the more likely an agreement is; and the smaller a win-set is the higher the chance that a negotiation will breakdown or stall. In Putnam's work reaching a stalemate is a real possibility. In fact he distinguishes between voluntary and involuntary defection. The former concept "… refers to reneging by a rational egoist in the absence of enforceable contracts". The latter concept "… reflects the behavior of an agent who is unable to deliver on a promised because of failed ratification" (Putnam 1988: 438). Whereas Putnam refers to stalemate in negotiations, he does not go into the details of how one of these two types of defection occurs. In fact, he recognises that sometimes it is difficult to find out whether a defection is voluntary or involuntary, because negotiators who defect voluntarily will try to blame the costs of non-agreement on the domestic actors i.e. to make a voluntary defection look as an involuntary one (Putnam 1988: 439).

A problem in Putnam's work is that voluntary and involuntary defections are presented as two different processes. While this differentiation is useful to keep a methodological order, he does not mention the possibility that a negotiation may stall because of an overlapping of both types of defection. It is plausible that a negotiation stalls because of a convergence between the forces of domestic actors opposing the deal and the lack of political will of the government to ratify the agreement due to previously unseen costs at the beginning of the negotiation. In other words, the deal is both blocked by endogenous forces and by a tacit agreement of the government because of socio-economic and political costs.

Another problem of Putnam's work with regards to this study is the ambiguity in the delimitations of the meaning *ratification*. Whereas he distinguishes between a ratification of domestic actors and that of formal institutions like the Congress, it is not clear to which type of ratification he refers when he analyses both cases i.e. ratification and lack of ratification –or involuntary defection. Despite these shortcomings, the two-level game approach provides two useful concepts –voluntary and involuntary defection– to explain stalemate in FTA negotiation. Putnam's work has been extensively analysed through these years. In fact, some special literature dedicated to the two level game has been published such as the work edited by Peter Evans et.al. (1993) *Double Edged Diplomacy: International Bargaining and Domestic Politics*. This work as well as others has sought to refine and substantiate the metaphor of two level games. Nevertheless the effect has been more cumulative than theory building. Works using Putnam's two-level game range from rational choice

18 A win set for a given Level II (domestic level) is defined by Putnam as "…the set of all possible Level I agreements that would "win"-that is, gain the necessary majority among the constituents –when simply voted up or down" (Putnam 1988: 437).

models to descriptive ones as well as from issues of security to issues of economic negotiations.[19]

Economic negotiations have grown as consequence of the end of the Cold War and the consolidation of economic globalisation. John Odell (2000 & 2006) has tried to capture this phenomenon of economic negotiations.[20] However, his focus has been on the US bilateral economic negotiations as well as on multilateral economic negotiations such as those of NAFTA and the WTO. Odell (2000: 1-6) argues that economic negotiations have special features that make them different from other type of negotiations. The scope as well as the outcome of an economic negotiation are not only determined by the process as such, but also by the variations, either positives or negatives, of the markets in the short run.

Odell (2000: 31-34) develops a conceptual frame for economic negotiations in a continuum of value-creating and value-claiming strategies, although in practice negotiations present a mixed pattern of both strategies. The author presents a simple model to understand negotiations based on dependent variable *outcomes* and the independent variable *strategy* which is operationalised according to the changes of the market, the beliefs of negotiators and domestic politics. To put this matrix forward, Odell argues that cost-benefit analysis on the vein of rational choice is not possible, so he uses the concept of bounded rationality i.e. actors are constrained by their beliefs on what they think is the best option for them. In other words, negotiators are satisfiers rather than utility maximisers (Odell 2000:18; 2006: 11).

Regarding the issue of stalemate, Odell does not provide any account of the issue of non-outcome in economic negotiations. Non-agreement is only used as a referential point that increases the leverage of one party during the negotiation, in case the non-agreement option makes one party worse-off than the other (Odell 2000: 27). Yet, BATNA's characterisation shows that non-agreement is not only status-quo ante, but it can also make the parties lose a share of expected utility in case an FTA

19 Mon, Jongryn seeks to expand Putnam's work in (1995). "Domestic Institutions and International Bargaining: The role of agent veto in two-level games". The American Political Science Review. Vol. 89: 4, pp. 914-924. A critique on the win-set issue is presented by Mayer, Frederick (1992). "Managing domestic differences in international negotiations: the strategic use of internal side payments". International Organization, 46:4, pp. 793-818. Some good applications of the two level game to empirical cases are: Boyer, Marc (2000) "Issue Definition and Two-Level Negotiations: An Application to the American Foreign Policy Process". Diplomacy and Statecraft, Vol. 11: 2, pp. 185-212. Al-Ghamdi, Salem (1999) "Success and Failure in Saudi-American Negotiations: American Views". International Negotiation 4, pp. 23-36. It seems impossible to give a full detailed account of works published that use a two-level game approach since this focus is what predominates in contemporary negotiation analysis.

20 It is necessary to distinguish between authors that focus on the process of negotiation as such and those that use an IPE lens, which usually put aside the fact that the bargaining process shapes and alters outcomes. For the latter group, the goal is to analyse how institutions play a major role in the outcome or how the outcomes coincide or try to set a new institutional setting.

agreement is not signed. The reason is that FTAs will tend to create trade between the parties of the agreement (Baldwin 2006). While this aspect helps to justify why to study stalled FTA negotiations, it does not provide a systematic approach to the process that leads to reach a stalemate.[21]

Finally, economic problems often emerge in the global economic markets. However, one actor can decide to start negotiations with another party to solve them, or take unilateral action. Another option is to wait until new markets condition emerge in order to make a negotiated solution feasible (Odell 2000: 206-207). Odell's argument is more likely to occur during the rounds of consultation i.e. whether to negotiate or not rather than when the negotiation has been launched. In this regard, I follow a different path than John Odell. I argue that adverse global market conditions do not affect the process of the FTA negotiation to the extent that they cause negotiation failure. Global market conditions for sure play a strong role in multilateral negotiations but in bilateral state to state these conditions are limited to the national market conditions for specific products or sectors. Countries of Latin America, North America, and Asia have continued their respective FTA negotiations even during the Asian (1997) and Sub-prime economic crises (2007-10). What may play a factor in leading to a stalemate in FTA negotiations are changes in the conditions for domestic actors rather than the market conditions at the global level. Therefore, I prioritise an inside-out lens in this study, and exclude "fluctuations in the global market" as an explanatory factor for failure in FTA negotiations.

The issue of bilateral and multilateral economic negotiations is also assessed in Victor Kremenyuk and Gunnar Sjöstedt's (eds., 2000) *International Economic Negotiation: Model versus Reality*. This text provides an overview of economic negotiations conducted by different types of actors beyond the nation-state and its domestic constituencies. It includes cases of negotiation between governments and multinational corporations; multilateral negotiations, and financial and monetary issues; macroeconomic aspects; trade and trade related issues. However, the treatment of this broad range of cases is instrumental to the assessment of the functionality of economic theory and theory of negotiation to explain the negotiation process in different settings. The conclusion is that neither economic theory nor a pure focus on theory of negotiation can provide a full account of the different patterns of economic negotiations. Therefore, an integration of both theories seems promising to explain economic negotiations. However, there are divergent opinions within this text on which theory of economics should prevail i.e. neoclassical or new trade theory (see Chapters 1, 13, 14 & 15).[22]

This text does not provide a clear account of the case of stalled economic negotiations. Nevertheless it shows in which phase an economic negotiation is likely to stall

21 On page 24 I have referred to another possible explanation for stalemate that Odell mentions i.e. the use of aggressive value-claiming strategies. However, he only mentions this as a possibility without giving a further explanation.

22 The reasons not to use neoclassical theory in this study have been presented above.

if it does. "The formula phase is cooperative and integrative by nature, the detail phase conflictual and distributive" (Kremenyuk and Sjöstedt 2000: 25). The authors refer to the detail phase as the quantifiable issues, such as the discussion on how many pears or apples (quotas), how many years of transition to remove TB, how to delimit the use of NTB in the eventual FTA. In this regard, a stalemate is produced because of the incapacity of parties to worsen the outside alternatives (i.e. BATNA) of the counterpart during the negotiation in order to make it commit to reach a final agreement (Ibid: 20).

Other seminal contributions in the field of negotiation and conflict resolution are those of I. William Zartmann (1989, *The ripe for resolution: Conflict resolution in Africa*; 2000, *Ripeness: The hurting stalemate and beyond*). Zartmann develops the concept of mutually hurting stalemate. His argument is that both parties perceive that they cannot make further progress in a conflict and that the winning option through the use of escalatory means in conflict is not succeeding. Therefore, the author suggests that a mutually hurting stalemate in a conflict is the initial step for de-escalating and negotiating a peaceful settlement of the conflict (i.e. ripeness theory). In this regard, stalemate means the impossibility of escalating more in the conflict, which opens the venue for starting the negotiation. Yet in trade negotiations the costs of a mutually hurting stalemate are rather different than the cost involved in a conflict that may involve deploying troops or triggering an armed conflict between the parties if they do not negotiate. In a trade negotiation even if it is conflictual in nature the parties will have more room to continue escalating with the hopes that the counterpart will weaken its position due to the time constraint in the long run, although this may create a spiral effect of value-claiming behaviour that brings the parties to leave the negotiating table.

However, FTA negotiations do not start due to a perceived conflict between the parties i.e. mutually hurting stalemate. Countries start such negotiations because they perceive mutual gains and complementarity between their economies. Thus an FTA negotiation is always started because it was perceived, in the previous analysis of the parties, as a cooperative game, in which the framing of the overall negotiation was in a win-win way. Zartman's work is not largely used in this work, since he focuses on the conditions to start a negotiation when conflict has reached its peak, and not in analysing the conditions once the negotiation has started. In this regard, the concept of stalemate in this study is rather different to the one of Zartman as I focus on the process that develops inside the negotiation. Here stalemate seeks to capture the dynamics and conditions in which both parties cannot continue negotiating, and one or both sides left the negotiating table without having the intention of going back unless the other party gives the necessary concessions to resume such process.

A similar use of the concept stalemate to that of Zartmann is used by Dean Pruitt and Sung Hee Kim in (2004) *Social Conflict: Escalation, Stalemate, and Settlement.* However, Pruitt and Hee Kim avoid using the concept of mutually hurting stalemate and instead use 'perceived stalemate' of one party and the optimism of the other to reach an agreement to describe how a conflict de-escalation begins, and how the conditions for a negotiated settlement develop. For Pruitt and Hee Kim (2004: 172) a stalemate is a "situation in which one (or better, both) of the parties perceives that it cannot make further progress in the conflict at an acceptable cost or risk that further efforts to win through escalation are unworkable and/or unwise".

Zartmann and Rubin (2000) have contributed to the study of power in international negotiations. One of the main contributions of these authors is that they demystify the common assumption that a structural power will impose its conditions and interest over a small or weaker party in a negotiation. They show how the weaker party can still get a satisfactory outcome in a negotiation in which the power is distributed asymmetrically between or amongst the parties (Zartmann and Rubin 2000: 289). Although this study considers the breakdown of negotiations as a reference point to impede the fall of the negotiation and to create the conditions for finding a satisfactory outcome, it poses in a coherent way the importance of power in the negotiation process. However, as it was explained in a previous section,[23] power is conceived as a means or an instrument embedded in the strategies and tactics displayed by negotiators, leaders, and representatives of domestic actors in the current negotiation, or in another setting that may influence the negotiation process i.e. external domestic and international factors to the negotiation.

An enduring deadlock may be considered a breakdown, or the halt of a negotiation. Guy Olivier Faure (2005: 25) differentiates deadlock and stalemate. "A deadlock is an impasse in terms of position, a situation in which no concession or constructive actions takes place. A stalemate is an impasse in terms of movement and offers no more possibilities for escalation". I shall add to specify that a stalemate is an enduring impasse that impedes progression during the negotiation which make parties stall the negotiation for an undetermined time-period. Yet I use the two concepts as synonymous because both refer to the impossibility of moving forward in a negotiation.

Faure (2005: 36) also presents the incentives to break a deadlock following Zartman's statement that "Only time resolves conflicts, but time needs help" (Zartman 1989: 273). To escape a deadlock and in that way move the negotiation towards an outcome of agreement, the costs of the deadlock for the parties have to be important. Yet Faure suggests that if the costs of the deadlock are not perceptible and the advantages of breaking such a deadlock are not palpable or evident, then there is no incentive to escape such a status in a negotiation. Faure uses an interesting example that may shed light on the issue of stalled FTA negotiations. He uses the case of business negotiations in which, he argues, there is no such incentive to escape a deadlock because the parties negotiate in a parallel way with other counterparts in a form of multi-track negotiations, which provide certain leverage in the deadlocked negotiation to keep it in such status. Therefore, parties in business negotiations do not feel the time constraint which would usually result from the cost incurred by not moving in such negotiation as well as by the lost opportunities for the parties. More-

23 see section 1.5, Conceptual Clarifications

over, a standstill status is also difficult to quantify in business negotiations. These may be reasons to keep the deadlock as each party may think that its counterpart position will weaken in the long-run, which gives the powerful party the chance to impose its position if the negotiation is eventually resumed.

Although Faure's counterintuitive argument is persuasive and provides some aspects that can be used in FTAs (for example the time constraint in a negotiation) he tends to minimise the costs involved in trade and business negotiations. FTA negotiations that end in non-agreement have certain costs for the parties some of which can be quantified and others not, even if this negotiation was part of multiple negotiations conducted within the same time-setting. It is difficult to quantify the reputation or loss of status caused by the parties' failure to agree.[24] However, there are quantifiable costs such as the time of preparation for the negotiation, the elaboration of studies previous to the formal negotiation to analyse the viability of having an FTA, the pre-negotiation, the human resources involved that could have been used on dedicating more time and preparation for other FTA negotiations, the elaboration of studies and reports by domestic business associations with the proposal for that FTA negotiation, and the costs involved in each round of negotiation before the negotiation came to a standstill. All these aspects have a monetary cost. Finally, trade deviation can also count as an associated cost if an FTA negotiation does not conclude in agreement.

Nevertheless, Faure (2005) highlights the importance of time in a negotiation. Yet it is not clear whether time is an intervening variable, or whether time is conceived as a tactic in the negotiation by one of the parties to trigger concession on the counterpart. In this book I include time as a tactic which can become part of a value-claiming or value-creating strategy. Parties use time constraint with the intention to push the negotiation towards an outcome of agreement. For example parties may use the tactic of time as part of a distributive strategy in the following way: one party with more room to bargain says: "there are elections or a change of presidencies soon in *my country* or *in yours* so we need the agreement now or never". Or the party with the best BATNA can also state that "a new negotiation with a bigger player is forthcoming which will need all our human resources available so we cannot postpone a decision once again i.e. take it or leave it". Negotiators can also use time as inaction, which means that the stronger party may have a tactic that was developed during the difficult negotiation: "I will wait all the necessary time because I know my counterpart leaders cannot afford ending his presidential term without a final agreement. This will weaken its position and I win the big price". Time is important, it is there and it constrains, but the time constraint can also be manipulated and used instrumentally by negotiators as a tactic to trigger concessions from the counterpart.

24 A possibility to analyse whether a party has reduced its reputation because of its failed FTA negotiations, is to analyse whether these previous failed experiences prevented this country from launching new FTA negotiations with other countries.

Though it is impossible to provide a complete account of the literature on negotiation, I have provided an overview of the main contributors to the field, the main issues and approaches. None of the extant works and views presented here provides a systematic account of the process that leads to stall an FTA negotiation. Parties' resistance points are not only theoretical and abstract depictions to delimit the zone of agreement, but they are also there to be manipulated by the negotiators either to expand or reduce this zone. The increasing number of bilateral FTA negotiations either intra or interregional make the *status quo ante* appear to be far from the best scenario, because the parties excluded will reduce their gains due to the trade deviation effect that other bilateral FTAs produce. However, it can also be the case that the costs of stalling are not high for the parties involved as most likely there will always be another state with whom it will possible to negotiate an FTA despite the previous history of failed attempts. The reason may be associated to the fact that FTA and regional economic integration in the 1990s and 2000s were phenomena in vogue in the global economic world.

Considering all these circumstances, negotiators usually face the dilemma of whether to choose to stall a negotiation, or to continue and negotiate an FTA that does not necessarily satisfy all their expectations i.e. protect their less competitive sectors and include all their competitive sectors in the deal. Yet, what steps do actors take to cause such problems that a negotiation will stall? Is this only explained by the actions of the domestic actors' lobby? Why is the government more responsive to these domestic groups that oppose a specific FTA? These questions are not answered in the literature on negotiation and thus it is one of the tasks of this work to address such questions. However, I will firstly turn to assess the extant state of the art on the empirical cases of this study.

2.5 The Literature on the Case Studies

2.5.1 Chile

The literature on Chile's FTA policy is not broad, despite the fact that Chile is one of the most active countries in the world in pursuing FTAs and economic negotiations. In fact, Chile has relied heavily on its external trade policy to promote and achieve its strategic goals in the Latin American continent and throughout the world. Most of the extant works cover the benefits and losses that certain FTAs will carry for the Chilean economy (see Mesa and Pinto-Agüero 2004; Mesquita Moreira and Blyde 2006). Other economic works focus on the impact of Chile's FTAs with major powers such as the US, which analyse the potential benefits and costs for the economy (Cabezas 2003). The economic benefits and costs of the FTA between Chile and the EU are also studied, specifically the impact for the Chilean export sectors (Nowak-Lehmann, Herzer, and Vollmer 2007). There are also some legal and economic studies that seek to analyse some issue-areas of the FTAs such as rules of origin. One study presents how these rules of origin have to be interpreted (Vergara Hernández 2008), and another concentrates on how these rules of origin should be used to boost the national economic production (Witker 2004). Another academic work puts a stronger emphasis on the outward oriented economic reforms Chile conducted, and on the mechanism to control the flows of capital investment in Chile (Urriola 2000).

Studies on Chile's external relations are varied, though they touch upon the issue of FTAs in a general way. Alberto van Klaveren (1998) analyses the international insertion of Chile into the global system after democracy was re-established. However, he argues that the historical roots of the authoritarian legacy and the international context made Chile not only recuperate a place in the international scene, but also reformulate the principles and aims of its external policy (p. 122). In a new international context (i.e. open regionalism), the integration into the world through economic means became one of the pillars of this new insertion to the international system. Van Klaveren (1998) mentions how the US from the beginning became the main aspiration for Chile's FTA policy. Moreover, he also observes how Chile included the issue of trade promotion in the traditional agenda of border issues and security aspects with its neighbours. However, van Klaveren does not detail the FTA negotiations processes as such, since it is not the aim of his article. Nevertheless this work offers a good overview of Chile's key issues on its foreign policy in the 1990s, in which the FTA negotiation between Chile and Panama was conducted.

José Morandé (2003) highlights along with the state level, the importance of the domestic and the individual level (leadership) as key drivers of Chile's Foreign Policy. Morande also goes back to the periods of Eduardo Frei Montalva, Salvador Allende and Augusto Pinochet to contrast and find out the patterns of continuity and change in Chile's foreign policy priorities, and strategies vis-à-vis the new democratic governments. Chile has rebuilt its status and image in the international system partly because of its goals of achieving economic integration in a world of open regionalism (p. 263). Claudio Fuentes (2006) also analyses Chile's foreign policy, yet is limited to the period of President Ricardo Lagos (2000-2006). The author highlights the progress of the external trade agenda during this period in contrast to the previous presidencies of Patricio Aylwin and Eduardo Frei. Yet the base for such pro-active FTA agenda was cemented under the previous periods. Despite the fact that Fuentes (2006) pays particular attention to the achievement of FTAs with South Korea, the US, the EU and Japan, these particulars are presented as part of broader picture of a multidimensional and multi-track foreign policy. Yet he does not refer to specific dynamics of FTA negotiations.

Verónica Silva (2004) shows the interplay between private and public institutions in the making of the trade policy of Chile in general and that of FTAs in particular. The author goes trough a diverse set of topics such as the composition of Chile's trade and the issue of FDI; the three dimensions of Chile's external trade policy i.e. unilateral, bilateral and multilateral economic liberalisation; and the interplay between private and public agents in economic negotiations. The latter aspect provides a departure point for this study in the sense that Silva's work identifies the key interests and policy preference of domestic and public agents as well as the relevant actors in the process of FTA negotiations. Nevertheless this work as well as the others presented above do not refer directly to specific negotiations, or to the one of Chile and Panama.

Sáez and Valdéz (1999) give an interesting account of Chile's 'lateral' trade policy in the 1990s. They combine different variables of economics and politics to analyse Chile's goals in conducting an FTA policy. In other words, they go beyond the economic justification of trade creation and diversion for negotiating FTAs. They also incorporate security reasons for negotiating trade accords with neighbouring countries. However, the prescriptive nature of this work and overall picture of the trade policy of this country, limits the possibility of detailing the different set of negotiations Chile has conducted. The works above presented will be used to set the context in which the FTA negotiation of Chile and Panama was developed, as part of this strategy of becoming part of the global world and of improving the possibilities of competitiveness for the Chilean economy.

Regarding the experience of Chile in its FTA policy there are some works that analyse the structure of FTA negotiations i.e. actors such as business associations and negotiators and institutions such as the Ministry of Foreign Affairs and of Finance, the congress and political parties as well as how these interact in such economic processes (Bull 2008). Moreover, there are overviews of the early negotiation processes such as those with the USA, the different complementary agreements in Latin America, and the shift to the Asia-Pacific region (see Porras 2003). Verónica Silva (2001) also focuses on the specific interests of domestic actors and government agents on the FTA negotiation process. She describes how the negotiation agenda is articulated by the private and public sector in an overall way without going into specific negotiations. She also analyses the specific interests on the trade agenda of the different sectors of the Chilean economy with regards to FTA negotiations. Here the author presents the economic sectors that may gain and lose with such negotiations. Whereas there is certain prescriptive ambition in Silva's work i.e. how to do better, this is a valuable analysis as she identifies the different interests of domestic sectors of the national economy, and how they interact with the agents that conduct the intergovernmental process of negotiating.

A work that analyses the FTA policy and aspects of Chile's FTA negotiation is that of Sáez and Sáez (2006), who describe and analyse Chile's negotiation processes over financial services with the US and the EU. The authors identify the key issues of both negotiation processes and also outline the strength of Chile's financial regulation system as well as the well-functioning banking sector, which helped to sustain a good bargaining position vis-à-vis the two actors with the largest and most powerful banking and insurance sectors in the world. This work is rather useful for this research as it identifies the key interests of the financial sector in FTA negotiations, though Sáez and Sáez restrict themselves to two specific cases. Nevertheless much of these interests and positions of the financial sector were the same in previous, and have remained in subsequent FTA negotiations.

Although the above literature and other works will be widely used in this book, no extant titles refer to failed negotiation processes as such. Whereas there are references to some negotiation processes, the extant works do not analyse positions and the negotiation dynamics of Chile's FTA in a detailed way. Therefore, there is a gap in the literature of political science on the analysis of Chile's FTA negotiations in both cases: FTAs with outcome of agreement and non-agreement.

2.5.2 Costa Rica

The academic work on Costa Rica's FTA policy has similar shortcomings to those that analyse Chile's case. Moreover, the literature on the most part does not address FTA negotiations in particular, with the exception of that of DR-CAFTA, and the issue of the referendum (Castillo Araya 2005; Quinteros, Ochoa and Salcedo 2005: 9-49; Mansfield, Milner, and Pevehouse 2007: 403-432). Part of this literature is anachronistic with regards to this research as the bilateral negotiation between Costa Rica and Panama was conducted before those with the US (2002). However, it is interesting to know and understand the dynamics of the DR-CAFTA in a general way since it apparently played a role in the stalemate of the FTA negotiations between Costa Rica and Panama.

Most of the literature on the trade liberalisation experience implemented from the mid 1980s onwards has been elaborated by economists. The extant analyses put a special emphasis on the definitive erosion of the model of import substitution industrialisation (ISI) in the early 80s, and in advocating for the economic liberalisation of Costa Rica. In this regard, there are a series of publications coming from 'La Academia' which is a think tank located in San José. This vast area of the literature assesses the causes, implications and consequences of the definitive shift to a market oriented economy (see Monge and González Vega 1995; Lizano 2003; López and Herrera (eds) 2005).

Other studies by 'La Academia' justify the need for such a switch in the economic pattern of development, and they also assess the economic sectors in which the reforms have had a positive impact on Costa Rica's economic growth (see Messalles and Céspedes (eds) 2007; Monge and González Vega 1995; López and Herrera (eds) 2004). In addition the same literature also poses the challenges for the future but always advocating the path of economic liberalisation. In this regard, following a path of economic integration through FTAs becomes a natural step for a national economy whose essence is the promotion of exports.

The works published by 'La Academia' are of great value for this research, since most of the authors of these studies were also or are still part of the political establishment that led and implemented such economic reforms, including the FTA policy. In this regard, the extant literature of this think tank reflects what the leading people of the financial, labour and external trade reforms think about the model. They also present clear positions with regards to the economic integration and on whether certain economic sectors should be liberalised or kept with certain protectionism. This debate on liberalising or keeping restricted protection for specific issue-areas of Costa Rica's economy may also help to detect the positions in specific economic sectors for the FTA negotiations.

One of the core texts for the case of the negotiation between Panama and Costa Rica is the text published by Eduardo Lizano (2001) *La Política de Comercio Exterior de Costa Rica*, in which the author presents the unilateral, bilateral, and multilateral dimensions of Costa Rica's external trade policy. He also pays special attention to the integration process in Central America. Even though he advocates for further liberalisation, Lizano is also able to detect and present in a succinct way the interests and future challenges of Costa Rica's FTA policy. Within this setting he briefly presents the ongoing FTA negotiations at that time (2001), in which that of Panama and Canada have a special importance. This article also offers some comments as appendixes in which trade diplomats present their opinions with regards to Lizano's arguments. Two important comments are those of Anabel González and José Manuel Salazar who were vice-minister and minister of commerce respectively. These comments, although personal, reflect the overall orientation, priorities and positions of the government in the FTA policy.

More critical works on the economic transformation of Costa Rica and on the external trade policy are presented by Luis Vargas Solís (2002, 2007). Vargas Solís assesses in his work *La estrategia de liberalización económica* the economic changes between 1980 and 2000. He covers the changes in the economic structure of the country and the negative side of such changes such as the un-protection for still weak SME. He also criticises the failure of economic reforms to improve living conditions and create more jobs for the national economy.

An aspect of particular interest for this research is the liberalisation and privatisation of the banking system. Vargas Solís (2002, 2007) highlights the fact that the privatisation of banking created a new powerful elite, which prevented competition from abroad. Yet due to global pressures, Costa Rica's banking system started to open with certain restrictions to keep the exposure to the global financial markets to a minimum level. Thus, Costa Rica only allows the location of bank branches and not the establishments of bank subsidiaries. This issue is of special importance for this work as it seems to be one of the sensitive issues, along with rules of origin and agriculture that provoked the breakdown of the negotiation with Panama. The latter sought to locate subsidiaries and facilitate the opening of branches in the FTA with Costa Rica. Therefore, the identification of elites groups within the financial sector helps to understand the dynamics and the interests in keeping certain restrictions within the financial sector in FTA negotiations. The reasons are not only because of the stability of such a system, but also because of specific domestic interests to which the government pays special attention due to its office seeking goals.

Interpretations and analyses from the field of political science on Costa Rica's trade policy are limited. Bruce Wilson (1999) presents an interesting study on Costa Rica, in which he argues that the National Liberation Party adopted neoliberal policies abandoning its traditional programs that involve more state intervention, and the party still got re-elected. What is relevant for this study is Wilson's general assessment of the trade policy priorities of each government since the early 1990s onwards, as well as the presentation of the economic reforms in a process oriented way. This work will be used to set the context in which Costa Rica's FTA policy has been conducted.

None of these extant works assesses the reasons for failure in FTA negotiation between Costa Rica and Panama in 2002. Despite the fact that there are no accounts on this negotiation, the literature that focuses on Costa Rica is useful to create the context for this negotiation. It also helps to detect the government's and interest groups' positions with regards to external trade agenda.

2.5.3 Panama

The literature on Panama's external trade policy is not abundant. Most of the literature on trade policy has a legal orientation and assesses the legal frame of the banking and insurance sector (Ley Bancaria Panameña 1998; Urbina 2001; Ley de Lavado de Dinero 2001; Legislación sobre Seguros 1999). A good study on the issue of banking regulation and competition policy in Panama is that of Paredes and Morales (2007). Despite its legal orientation, it provides a useful overview on how the banking system is structured in this country. Moreover, the article of these two authors also puts the issue of banking and its problems within the frame of international law. The above mentioned text gives an overview of the banking economic sector, and it gives blue-prints to understand why Panama's counterparts in FTA negotiations are averse to include this issue in the FTA negotiation.

There is also another legal oriented study that highlights the general conditions of competence under the neoliberal model implemented in Panama (Fernández 2005). The main focus of this study is on Competence Law that was introduced in 1996, and the functions of the Commission of Free Trade and Consumer Affairs. This commission deals with issues of competence, consumer protection, and dumping. This study is important because it provides an overview of how certain matters were covered in this law to fulfil the criteria for the accession to the WTO and interests for FTA negotiations. Competence, consumer protection, and dumping issues are important aspects in the making of an FTA. Therefore, understanding the dynamics of these matters provide clues on how these issues are tackled and negotiated in FTAs.

Economic studies on Panama's trade policy concentrate on the aspects that articulate the systemic competitiveness of this country (see Saied and Estribí 2004: 319-391). They present the interaction of the four levels of systemic competition: Meta, Macro, Micro, and the Meso Level, in which the three previous levels interact in the making of infrastructure and non-physical infrastructure for the country. Yet such study concentrates on the Meso level and calls for effective interaction between the civil society and the public organisations that constitute each level of competition. In addition, the study recommends focusing on controversial institutional design such as the judiciary system, and tackling corruption in the state as well as pushing for a general societal consensus at the Meta Level on the best economic model for Panama. This study also presents the internal dimensions of the national economy, and pinpoints the different flaws of Panama's economic model. Saied and Estribí (2004) indirectly bring up the issue of winners and losers in a trade policy as they are more focused on improving systemic competitiveness. Nevertheless, identifying losers and winners in internal trade policy also helps to detect the sub-groups of losers and winners of an external trade policy.

Political studies that both describe and suggest the best policy for the country are more abundant for the case of Panama. The study 'Strategy and Nation' (Cordero and Jované 1990) assesses the plan for the 1990s launched by Panama's Government in a document "National Strategy for the Development and Modernisation of the National Economy". In this regard, both authors present a critical view on such strategy but also recommend steps to make Panama achieve a permanent path of economic growth in the near future. These critics refer not only to economic issues as such, but also include the need of achieving a more inclusive democracy, in which civil society directly participates in the decisions on which economic path is more convenient for Panama to follow. The national strategy of the government advocates adopting a neoliberal model, whereas Cordero and Jované emphasise the costs of such policies. Nevertheless, these two authors presents an important analysis of the process in which Panama was starting to implement a neoliberal pattern. This work is useful for providing a context in which the new model was adopted as well as its benefits and costs for the different groups of civil society. Within this economic shift, Panama sought to tie up its domestic reforms at the international level through joining the WTO and achieving FTAs.

Other critical views on the neoliberal policies implemented in Panama are focused on specific national economic policies proposed by then president Mireya Moscoso (1999-2004). José Torres Abrego's work (2000) analyses the financial strategy of Moscoso's government proposals and prescribes alternative strategies. Such strategies include: better allocation of resources for industrialisation; better tax collection system; and land redistribution. Although Torres Abrego critises the economic policies of Moscoso's government, he also gives a description of issues that dominated the debate in the previous governments. Therefore, the current study uses this work to describe the external setting in which the FTA negotiations of Panama-Chile and Panama-Costa Rica were conducted.

Horacio Rivera's article (2005: 63-81) "The FTAs of Panama, its consequences and impacts and the forthcoming negotiations with other countries" analyses in detail the FTA policy of this country. In this regard, Rivera identifies the main actors of this external trade policy on both the state and domestic levels. Moreover, it describes the content of these FTAs and the priority areas for Panama. Whereas the issue of failure is not present in the article either for the case of Chile or for the case of Costa Rica, this article presents an overview of the origins of such trade policy as well as its process of implementation in which actors, interests and outcomes are constitutive parts. Therefore, Rivera's work becomes one of the main background sources to understand the overall FTA policy of this country.

2.6 Concluding Remarks

To sum up, the empirical literature does not explain the failed FTA negotiations of Chile-Panama and Costa Rica-Panama. The extant theoretical works cannot provide a full account of failed negotiations. Whereas the reviewed literature on theory of negotiation provides some fuzzy blue-prints to follow and develop the issue of failed FTA negotiations, it misses the exogenous factors to the negotiation in both the domestic and international levels. Moreover, approaches on international relations and international political economy suffer the reverse problem i.e. they cannot give an account of the internal aspects of the negotiation, in which most conditions that lead to the breakdown of negotiations originate. However, these approaches provide a good overview of the external factors to the negotiation in both levels. Therefore, presenting a theoretical frame that includes the internal and external aspects of negotiation in both the domestic and international levels, as well as the conditions for the breakdown of bilateral FTA negotiations, is the immediate task to which I will now turn.

3. Theoretical Framework

3.1 Introduction

The theoretical approach that I will use to explain the process of non-agreement in an FTA negotiation relies on an inside-out framework of analysis that takes elements from new trade theory, liberalism, intergovernmentalism and theory of negotiation. The theoretical framework highlights the material capabilities of domestic interests groups and governmental ones as well as the conditions in which they interact. These aspects will determine a material outcome with regards to the issue-areas negotiated. However, this material outcome does not occur in an isolated matrix box. The rationality of actors is usually constrained and shaped by exogenous factors and the context in which such interaction occurs (Pollack 2006: 3-6). The rationality of actors is bounded i.e. it acts as satisfiers rather than utility-maximisers. As actors lack complete information and frame the information they have in a subjective way in a negotiation, they have to pay a cost, which is to choose an option that is satisfactory rather than optimum (Simon 1957; Odell 2006). Therefore, actors will tend to choose an option which is available to them, given the context as well as the internal and external constraints to the negotiation process. This option is not necessarily the optimal for actors' purposes but it is a realisable one.

There is a growing number of works that use rational models that aggregate interests in international relations, such as those of domestic and government units. Such works thereby make use of models that utilise variations on preferences. However, the predominate approach in the literature is to use fixed and stable preferences (Snidal 2006: 84-85). Contrary to the assumptions of the more popular approach, observing FTA negotiations reveals that preferences are not always constant i.e. they can change based on other rational calculations and parallel games, such as nested games (Tsebelis 1991). In fact, governments can shape and manipulate FTA negotiations before and during the formal negotiation process by using side payments. The negotiation can also be shaped by interest groups, who at times will exert pressure over, or offer compensation to, other interest groups, in order to create a coalition against or favouring a government policy. In the case of interest groups, that receive protection from the state, its purpose in FTA negotiations is to create a strong coalition opposing to such accord. This opposition of domestic actors could make the government change their preference on the topic(s) at stake.

3.2 *The Process: Internal and External Dimensions*

3.2.1 Formation of Endogenous Policy Preferences in FTA Negotiations

Introducing the notions of intra and inter-trade as well as protectionism in the forms of TB and NTB can help to explain why domestic groups opt either for freer trade or for protectionism. Despite the fact that the initial goal of TB and NTB in new trade theory was to protect infant industries until they became competitive enough, some industries do not reach this stage in the imperfect economic market (Kjeldsen-Kragh 2001). Therefore, these economic sectors become highly dependent on government protectionism, which creates the incentives for these domestic groups to spend energy, resources and time on lobbying the government in order to increase, maintain or minimise the eventual losses caused by these TB and NTB. The differentiation between intra and inter-trade as well as the government allocation of TB and NTB thus allows us to establish why certain domestic actors favour, while others oppose, an FTA with another country (see figure 1: 65). The causal process inferred from these aspects of new trade theory can explain not only why some economic groups prefer or oppose an FTA negotiation, but also why groups like labour unions from specific economic sectors would tend to oppose an FTA agenda.[25] In the services areas domestic groups also tend to protect or seek liberalisation of their own or their counterpart's national market. However, services tend to use more NTB as mechanisms of protection from international competition.

To limit the analysis to the direct beneficiaries of TB and NTB would leave us with too narrow a view of the process of configuration of domestic interests that favour or oppose an FTA. The costs of a stalemate mostly fall to domestic actors that are protected by the government. In fact the core groups, which benefit directly from TB and NTB, can usually mobilise a network of supporters. These supporters are not only labour unions from the economic sectors jeopardised by the FTA negotiation, but are also from other economic groups that depend on a well-functioning core group, even if what is understood by "well-functioning" is based on extant protective measures. In other words, the losses produced by an economic agreement go beyond these core groups, because the production of goods and services depend on production chains or value chains. Almost all companies are involved or are part of a value chain, including state-owned, or semi-private companies, and even companies without a global orientation. No company can produce or provide all the needed inputs by itself to produce a final service or good for the consumers (Kaplinski and Morris 2001). Therefore, the larger the national production chain, the

25 Following Ricardo-Viner's theory, the mobility of production factors is low in this time-setting since specific FTA negotiations are conducted in the short and mid-term. This means that in FTA negotiations there are more sectoral constituents coalitions rather than factoral coalitions, as the Stolper-Samuelson theory predicts (see Ladewig 2006: 71; see Hiscox 2002).

more potential to create a broader coalition against the removal or reduction of TB and NTB vis-à-vis a specific FTA negotiation, because members of these chains are not only economic but also potential political agents.

Nevertheless, the eventual opposition or support to an FTA is neither *per se* nor automatic, because the domestic groups can realign themselves depending on: a) whether they have more or less TB and NTB than the negotiating counterpart in an eventual FTA; b) whether they have similarity in the products and the production process with the counterpart's domestic actors; and c) whether they enjoy more or less comparative advantages (inter-trade). In some cases an economic sector loses as a result of liberalisation through bilateral FTA negotiations, whereas on other occasions the same sector may also gain if they decide to liberalise vis-à-vis another country. The latter could occur, for example, in cases where the sector enjoys better comparative advantages. Comparative advantages are not static; on the contrary, they are relative to the country with which an FTA is negotiated. Therefore, the winners in some FTAs can also become potential losers in other bilateral economic negotiations.

Regarding the reasons for stalled FTA negotiations, the government allocations of TB and NTB to protect key inter-trade issue-areas become constitutive parts of the process that leads to stall an FTA negotiation (see figure 2: 66). The maintenance through time of TB and NTB generates high flows of power for domestic groups that oppose an FTA. These high power flows will help to create the conditions in which these groups (along with supporters located within the production chain and other potential losers from other sectors) can overcome other pro-FTA groups.

Therefore, these protected groups will tend to refuse to be part of a package deal, and object to their issue-areas being part of a government strategy of issue-linkages. In other words, these groups will seek to lobby the government to pursue a value-claiming strategy over their issue-areas rather than a value-creating one (Odell 2000: 109-135). Yet the ideal for these groups is that the government signals to the counterpart the non-negotiability of these issues. This fact suggest that governments also pursue an "own" strategy in the negotiation.[26]

26 This argument is developed below.

Figure 1: Domestic preference formation in a specific FTA negotiation

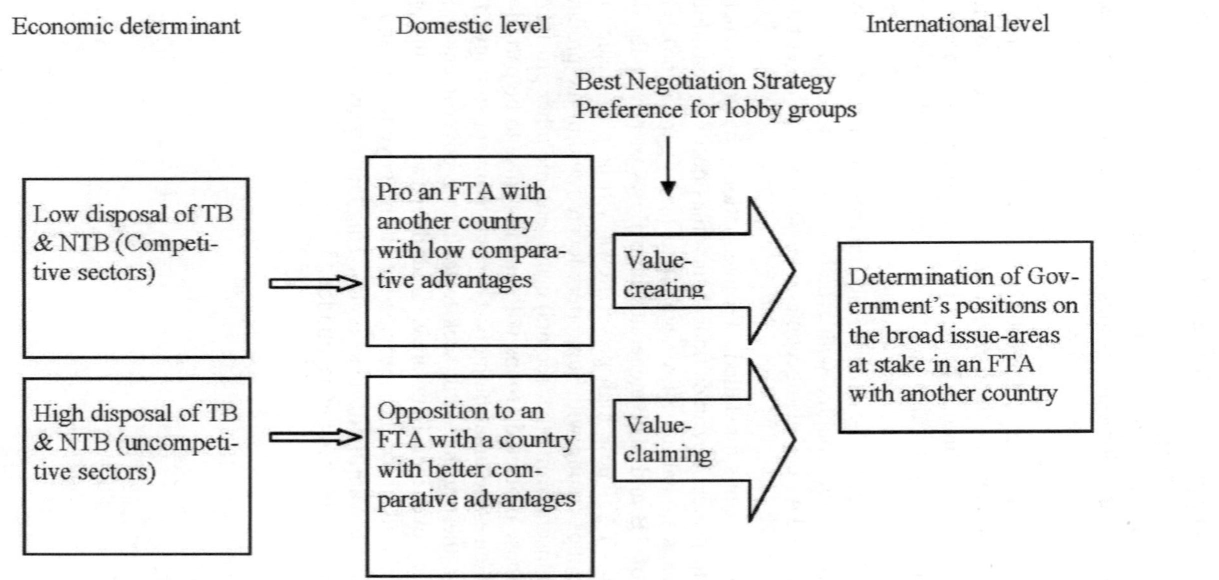

Figure 2: Model to explain failed FTAs

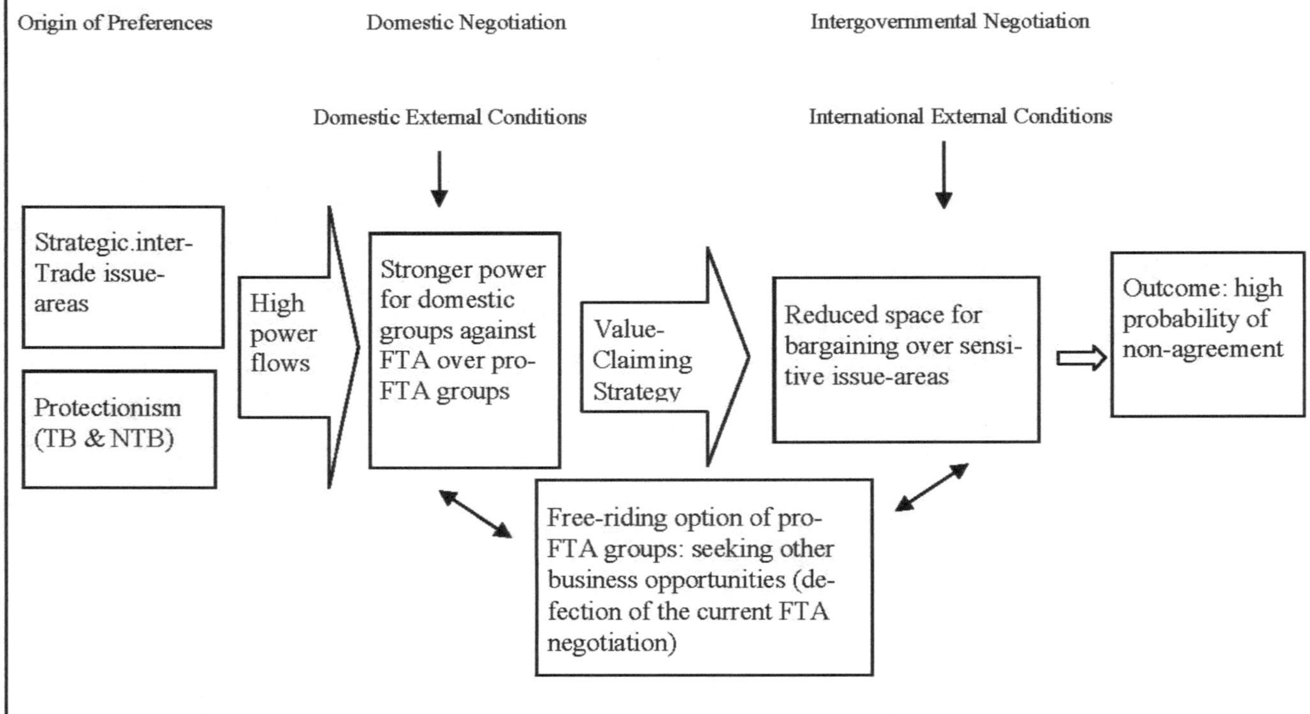

Moreover, pro-FTA groups will presumably develop parallel options to the eventual FTA, when they realise that an FTA is unlikely to happen in the short term. These groups will establish or enhance extant trade relations on the sidelines of the eventual agreement with domestic actors from the counterpart nation. In addition, they may lobby the government to start other FTA negotiations in which a less conflictive negotiation can be conducted. This exit option (free-rider problem) within pro-FTA groups weakens their representative members vis-à-vis protectionist members at the negotiation table. Consequently, the initial interest in an FTA will tend to diminish among the members of the former group. Therefore, protected inter-trade areas are plausible causes for non-agreement in FTAs.

Despite the fact that pro-FTA groups also lobby for their best outcome in the negotiation, they are surmounted by lobby groups either protected by tariffs, subsidies and quota systems or by NTB. The reason that anti-FTA groups are able to overcome pro-FTA groups in the negotiation process is that they can articulate a more coherent group. It is thus more likely that a member will free-ride in pro-FTA group than in an anti-FTA group. In an FTA negotiation, the benefits of lobbying for keeping protectionist measures are concentrated, whereas the benefits of getting freer trade through a bilateral FTA are dispersed because of the collective action problem (see Olson 1965 & 1982).

There is a majority of successful FTAs vis-à-vis failed cases. This means that freer trade groups can also get the outcome they want when they lobby a government to do so. Therefore, in most cases pro-free trade groups can overcome the collective action problem, allowing them to transfer products or inputs more easily from one location to another (Milner 1988: 290-297). The overcoming of the collective action problem of the groups favouring an FTA in successful cases is facilitated by the state. A government's willingness to support this liberalisation and assume the political and socio-economic costs is an important aspect that makes these groups more successful vis-à-vis protectionist groups Thus, in the successful FTA it is possible to observe a common interest between the government, national companies and their multinationals partners to lower tariffs.[27]

Whereas free trade groups lobby and organise themselves to get a desired outcome, there is no clear evidence of whether they ease the collective action problem as well as, or better than those groups that advocate keeping or implementing protectionist measures. It can be presupposed then that the costs of lobbying for these groups are lower than for those favouring a specific FTA. Thus the protectionist groups dominate the lobby system even when there are high chances that their goals will not be fulfilled (Ehrlich 2007: 581-582). Not only has a negotiation many veto-players capable of vetoing ratification (Tsebelis 2002); but there are also different access points to lobby for a specific outcome over the issue-areas of their interests (Ehrlich 2007: 578). An FTA negotiation provides access points in different stages

27 This convergence of the state and domestic groups in favour of economic liberalisation is also present when the states decides to pursue an unilateral liberalisation policy.

of a negotiation. Groups that advocate keeping tariffs, subsidies or quotas and technical barriers to trade will use the access points provided by institutions and the negotiation system to make, if possible, decision-makers veto a possible negotiated outcome with the other state. These domestic groups will primarily advocate a veto on the issue-areas that jeopardise their market privileges.

Access points for those who lobby for a particular outcome in these negotiations are provided by the same executive power that usually conducts these negotiations. Negotiators need an input from the domestic constituencies regarding what is acceptable or not in the negotiation on the issues that concern them.[28] The executive usually implements rounds of consultation before the negotiation, and also implements a "next room" during the negotiations to consult directly with the interest groups with stakes on the plausibility of accepting certain offers and counteroffers from the counterpart.[29] The domestic actors included in the consultations have a direct effect on the outcome of the negotiation in both specific issue-areas which are segmented agreements, and as a whole i.e. final agreement or non-agreement. This system of constant consultation with domestic actors acts as an accurate indicator of what is plausible to achieve or not during the negotiation (Landau 2000: 4-14). In this way, a government is able to anticipate what the final agreement should be in order to assure a final ratification by the Congress.

Congress plays an indirect role in creating the outcome of the FTA negotiation, yet an important one. The Congress role constrains the steps a government can pursue in the negotiation since the legislative power may act as a veto player and therefore it offers an additional access point for lobby groups which seek to block, in this case, an agreed FTA (Mansfield, Milner and Pevehouse 2007: 405-406). When the government anticipates high costs to assure ratification or it sees no ratification in the Congress, then it is likely that the negotiation will stall, unless the sensitive issues that anticipate a veto are completely excluded from, or modified in, the agreement. A government would prefer to burn the costs of non-agreement on the lobby-groups rather than on the Congress in order to prevent a deterioration of the executive-legislative relation that can have spill-over effects on the internal legislative agenda.[30]

28 Ehrlich argues that lobby groups use access points to lobby for protectionism in institutional settings from a comparative perspective i.e. executive and legislative power. The more access points a group has to the policymaking, the more likely they are to encourage protectionism (Ehrlich 2007: 583). Here I argue that international economic actions of states such as FTA negotiations also provide access points to the lobby groups in order to shape the FTA agenda-setting and the agreement-making.

29 This process is sometimes used by governments to offer side-payments and to manipulate the situation to break resistant coalitions that oppose a specific deal on their issues in the FTA negotiation.

30 The Congress is considered an intervening variable. Both actors, government negotiators and domestic groups, know they have a congress to convince in order to assure ratification or advocate its veto role. Yet this is an indirect influence in the negotiation, since the congress or its members are not included in the negotiation process. However, the existence of this further

I have presented so far how preferences are formed around an FTA negotiation in both cases pro-FTA or contra-FTA. I also introduced how and why groups that advocate keeping or minimising eventual losses in an specific FTA negotiation will tend to lobby more than pro-FTA groups. Yet this does not explain the stalemate of FTA negotiations in itself. In the previous argument I have mentioned the fact that a government has to be responsive enough to these pressures. There are cases in which the government has a similar agenda to pro-FTA groups, and sometimes the government seems more constrained by groups advocating for the maintenance of the status quo ante, at least in their issue-areas. Therefore, the government faces a dilemma during the negotiation which is to respond to the pressures of protectionist oriented groups, jeopardising the negotiation and the commitment to the counterpart, as well as respond to its own pro-FTA domestic actors and the counterpart with the purpose of making an agreement that creates trade between the parties.

3.2.2 Domestic Actors' and Government's Policy Preferences

A government allows domestic groups to shape its position within the interstate bargaining process because of political and socio-economic reasons. In the case of stalemate, the government's national economic interest converges with the commercial interests of the protectionist groups with regards to a specific FTA, which is already at a negotiation stage.

When a government defends the eventual losers of an FTA, it uses a *distributive logic*. However, it is primarily domestic level interests that turn the negotiation strategy of a government from value-creating to value-claiming with regards to the removal of TB and NTB. The government makes the interests of domestic groups fit, when they match its own internal agenda in an issue-area. Governments become responsive to these groups, because the allocation of protectionism among domestic groups is not only based on an economic, but also on a political rationale (rent-seeking and office-seeking). In other words, governments either cannot distinguish between strategic and non strategic interventions (Hart and Prakash 2000), or they can only do so once protectionism is introduced. The short-term socio-political costs of removing such measures become higher than the overall long-term welfare that a liberalising path creates for the national economy as a whole.

step to a FTA agenda constrains actors and makes the government anticipate what is ratificable or not. The domestic actors influence is still the provider of direct feedback on how the formal ratification process is likely to be.

One specific negative effect of liberalising or pursuing a free trade agenda is a sense of job insecurity among some domestic constituencies, which has a consequent impact on the popularity of the government e.g. losing electoral support among the citizen-voters (Kapstein and Landa 2000: 133-148; Mughan and Lacy 2002: 531-533). This process of *clientelistic* relations enhances extant political cleavages that favour protectionist groups, because losses of freer trade are usually concentrated (supply side of the economy) and the benefits are dispersed (consumers, importers and export oriented groups). A government needs to prevent an eventual creation of job-insecurity which implies a loss of electoral support when carrying a freer trade policy or when negotiating a specific FTA. Therefore, a rational government decision would be to allow the eventual losers of the agreement to lobby before and during the negotiation, in order to prevent conceding so much as to damage not only specific economic sectors, but also its own popularity.

Eventual preferences for protectionist domestic groups in an FTA negotiation that involve protected inter-trade areas are: First, to exclude the protected issue-areas from the final agreement; second, to stall the negotiations; third, to restrict the entrance of products by quotas; and finally, to liberalise these issue-areas after a long transition period. The latter two options usually go together. However, governments in cases like the Mexico-Singapore, Costa Rica-Panama, and South Korea-Japan have preferred to stall the trade negotiations rather than to exclude their sensitive protected issue-areas from the deal. The status quo prior to the negotiation is also a policy option when the deal makes protectionist domestic groups worse-off (Odell 2000: 38-39). Yet, why not exclude these issues and continue with the negotiations so that parties can find solutions and lock-in agreements over the rest of the topics of the negotiation? Whereas it can be argued that the solution I am suggesting is below any optimal equilibrium point, the reality of bilateral FTA negotiations shows that this is usually the path that countries choose in some FTAs (see Chile's FTAs, Japan's FTAs, Mexico's FTAs). Moreover, negotiators and decision-makers can barely or never achieve an agreement that is pareto-optimal due to their bounded rationality, in which they choose an option that according to their ideas and external constraints satisfy both negotiators and domestic constituencies yet is below any optimal equilibrium.

When countries face deadlocks that seem endurable, threatening to stall the entire negotiation and keep it in that condition for a long time, they opt to exclude certain issue-areas from the final agreement. For example, Chile-Japan chose to do so; they included a clause in the final accord to review the exclusion of some items like milk and some fruits like oranges in 5 years time (*Business Latin America* 2007: 1-2). If this solution was also chosen in the FTA between the US and South Korea with the purpose of preventing a stalemate, then why did Chile and Panama, and Costa-Rica and Panama not choose a similar path to continue with their negotiations?

Counter-intuitively I can presume that these issue-areas were also the ones in which one of the governments expected maximal economic benefits for their own national markets, making all the other areas, in which benefits could also be realised, complementary to those that caused the stalemate. Therefore, this factor could have encourage the winners of the negotiation to free-ride, and find alternative options to continue with their bilateral FTA policy. In other words, the threat of stalling and the free-riding option of pro-FTA groups indirectly tend to empower the eventual "own" losers as well as those of the counterpart in the negotiation of that FTA. However, the exact time at which the negotiation is stalled is the prerogative of the government, although this option as well as that of excluding the sensitive issue-areas is presented through all the phases of the negotiation by the economic sectors that lose with the agreement.

3.2.3 Intergovernmental Negotiation

Another plausible reason to stall, other than excluding the controversial issues at stake from the negotiation, is governmental pursuit of a parallel agenda in the intergovernmental process. Governments use inter-trade issue-areas as a strategic bargaining tool to extract concessions from the counterpart in its respective inter-trade issues. Here the government will use an offensive value-claiming strategy.

The government does not exclude the sensitive issue-areas from the beginning by signalling their non-negotiability to its counterpart. It rather waits to see whether it is possible to make a good package-deal, and whether it is good enough to seduce its opposing domestic actors to change their preferences, and in that way expands the zone of agreement. This does not mean that domestic actors give up on their initial intentions, but the government intends to use small concessions that do not excessively affect these groups, in order to trigger concessions in areas that are difficult and sensitive for the counterpart. The government uses this tactic to prevent losses and at the same time realise high gains in sectors in which some of its domestic groups are highly competitive. However, this option will develop during the intergovernmental negotiations, because through this intergovernmental interaction, government A and B will mutually realise what the counterpart's real expectations and negotiation strategies are. Though using protected inter-trade issue-areas is a marginally risky means to a value-claiming predominant negotiation, governments will take this risk in light of the likelihood of obtaining satisfactory compensations from their counterpart's inter-trade areas:

> Value-creating approaches should never be used, however, in a situation of heavy losses. In such cases, negotiators generally opt for extremely risky approaches –unlike in value creation- to resolve conflicts. Only highly risky approaches hold the potential for recapturing the status quo or moving into a position of gains (Elms 2006a: 406).

15Failing to highlight the non-negotiable issues is a risky option for the parties, because it shows to the counterpart that there is a window of opportunity to negotiate over those issues (Ortiz Mena 2006: 193). This gives the incentive to the other government to push strongly for concessions. Yet these concessions are dependant on the counterpart's concessions on its highly protected areas. Whereas the initial steps of the negotiation over these issues can be pursued in a value-creating mode, the context of the issue makes the parties switch to value-claiming strategies. Consequently the overuse of this strategy pushes the counterpart or both parties towards their resistant points. In this way parties reduce their zone of agreement (see figure 3: 72).[31] The value claiming strategy, especially its offensive variant, is likely to have a "spiral effect" which makes it difficult to reverse and find other plausible alternatives to solve the negotiation of the issue-areas at stake (Olekalns, Smith and Walsh 1996:70; Pruitt 1983; Elms 2006a: 414).

As a whole an FTA negotiation presents a mixed strategy used either sequentially or simultaneously. However parties isolate sensitive issue-areas from other issues (de-linking). The use of a pure offensive distributive strategy on these de-linked issues reduces the chances of getting a final agreement. Yet this reduction of chances to get an agreement is not deterministic, and it depends on a case by case basis. Nevertheless, governments are likely to use defensive value-claiming strategies to protect their sensitive issue-areas, which are triggered by an offensive value-claiming strategy from the counterpart. Pursuing an offensive value claiming strategy aims at removing the resistance of the other government on reducing TB and NTB on the FTA negotiation. This use of offensive value-claiming strategy as a strategy for one government, and the use of defensive value-claiming for the other, are likely to reduce the zone of agreement. When governments pursue these strategies, rather than a mutual defensive value-claiming the counterpart (exclusion counteracted by exclusion), the option of excluding the issue-area or part of the issue-area from the negotiation no longer seems a plausible option. The reason is that one government is compelled to offset the exclusion of its issues against its own offensive demands on other issue-areas (see Ortiz Mena 2006: 197). This latter option reduces a government's leverage in the negotiation, because one has to retract its demands in other products or issue-areas that were anticipated as sectors in which high benefits were possible.

31 This figure gives only an example in a rather abstract way of what a zone of agreement is and how parties can reduce the possibility of having an agreement by pursuing value-claiming strategies, or how parties can expand the zone of agreement by pursuing value-creating strategies. Here A use an aggressive value-claiming strategy which moves its position from A to A1. Even after this movement there is still a zone of agreement in which to set up an accord; this has narrowed extremely, which makes it difficult for both parties to negotiate in such a zone to reach a final agreement, because they are rationally bounded.

Figure 3: Zone of agreement

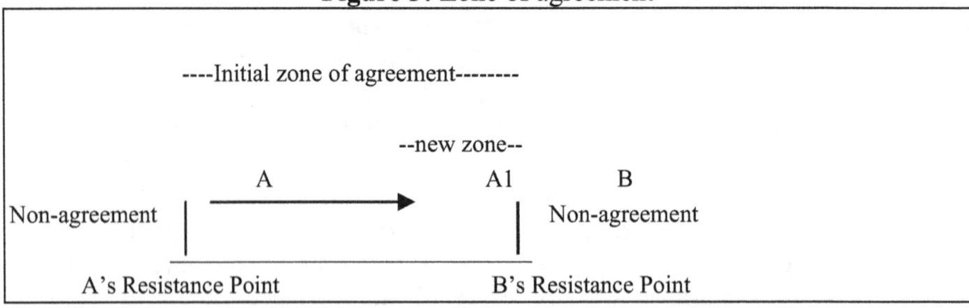

Excluding a sensitive issue in exchange for reducing one's own demands on other profitable issue-areas will tend to reduce one's own interest in the possible benefits of a final FTA. The strategy chosen to counterbalance offensive aims has thus to be carefully chosen because it can constrain a government's demands in other issues of the negotiation. The problem is that if both parties choose an offensive value-claiming strategy the entire negotiation can be at stake since parties go into a zero-sum bargaining which can escalate to a negotiation stall (Elms 2006a). To follow this latter path could only be possible if the BATNA for both countries is worse than the current negotiation. Therefore, a final agreement is more likely by using defensive against defensive value-claiming (excluding one sensitive issue counteracted by another sensitive issue exclusion from the counterpart). On the contrary, it is more difficult, when using a defensive against an offensive value-claiming strategy; or an offensive value-claiming against another offensive value-claiming strategy (see table 1: 74).

Yet the final agreement or the lack of one in many negotiations is only possible due to the exertion of leadership (Young 1991).[32] The presence or lack of leadership acts as a causal variable and explains a great deal of the results of economic negotiations (Deese 2008). Leadership exerted by members of the team negotiators as well as external ones such as ministers or even the involvement of the head of the government can save impasses at critical junctures of the negotiation, and give certainty to the losers of the FTA that satisfactory compensations will be provided. Moreover, leadership is about finding creative and expert solutions to redirect the process, whenever it is jeopardised, towards a path of agreement, as well as to bring the negotiation mode from hard bargaining towards integrative bargaining. The display of these leadership skills serves the purpose of showing commitment to finding a satisfactory agreement to the counterpart. The lack of leadership to breakthrough impasses serves as an extra indicator for pro-FTA groups that the negotiation will be time consuming, and the impasses time-enduring for their purposes. Therefore, this apparent lack of leadership enhances the free-riding option for pro-FTA groups, and

32 Young (1991) also presents two other types of leaderships: structural and intellectual leadership.

also encourages protectionist lobby groups to be noisier about their demands for keeping protection. Leaders can act as facilitators to find negotiable solutions for a final agreement, which could work to reduce the domestic demands in two ways: first, by backing up compensatory measures or by providing new ones, and second, by showing to the counterpart the real interest in achieving a final agreement. In other words, a failed negotiation could be explained by absence of leadership skills to redirect the negotiation process to find creative solutions for the governments and domestic groups, to help deescalating conflicts, and thus to save sensitive impasses.

Whereas some conditions for stalling a bilateral FTA negotiation have been mentioned in the previous pages, in which I presented the dimensions involved in an FTA negotiation, this has not been presented in a systematic and operationalisable way. First I present the hypothesis of this work and then the underlining conditions that plausibly leads to a failed FTA negotiation.

Table 1: Possible outcomes of using variants of a value-claiming strategy

	Country B	
Country A	Defensive	Offensive
Defensive	• Exclusion by exclusion • Likely agreement if exclusions are reduced. • Low conflict-bargaining over sensitive issues.	• The initiative is on country B: • Country B takes advantage by pursing an aggressive value claiming strategy and A adopts a defensive position of containment. • B agrees on A excluding some sensitive issues only if A offsets its demands on B's most sensible sectors and if A grant access to B to the rest of B's competitive products. • Outcome of agreement is still possible despite the fact that the win-set is reduced if the alternative options are worse than the current process. • If the outside alternatives are better the negotiation may stall.

	Country B	
Country A	Defensive	Offensive
Offensive	• The initiative is on country A: • Country A takes advantage of country B's defensive position as country A agrees on B excluding some sensitive issues if B off-sets its demands on A's most sensible sectors and if B grants access to A to the rest of B's competitive products. • Outcome of agreement is still possible despite the fact that the win-set is reduced if the alternative options are worse than the current process. • If the alternatives outside are better than the negotiation, this may stall.	• Aggressive bargaining on both sides • Both demand concessions without reciprocity on their most competitive products without compensating by giving certain access to the counterpart on their most sensitive areas. • Using an offensive variant counteracted by offensive variant produces an escalatory spiral effect of tough bargaining that spills over to other issue-areas which are less sensitive. • The outcomes are a reduced space to bargain and a reduced win-set and finally the stalemate.

3.3 Hypotheses

3.3.1 Hypothesis I: On Domestic Actors and State Responsiveness

A stalled FTA negotiation is caused by some powerful domestic actors who intend to preserve the extant economic rules of the game at the national level, which assures them a constrained or no external competition in their issue-areas. The allocation of TB and NTB fulfils the criteria to impede the advantageous position that external goods and services have in the national (and regional) markets. Moreover, a government's embedded autonomy (Evans 1995), and thus its constant concerns on short-term electoral and social costs, will impede high concessions to its negotiation counterpart over a wide range of protected inter-trade areas. These aspects lead to the first hypothesis:

> H1: If the defence of protected inter-trade areas of the national economy in the different spheres of the political process determines the course and the momentum of the negotiation by empowering protectionist interest groups which politicise the negotiation; by reducing the incentive for export-oriented groups to participate actively in the negotiation; and by increasing the socio-political costs for the government, then the initial governmental position of aspiring to an FTA is expected to change to a position of non-agreement.

3.3.2 Hypothesis II: On Intergovernmental Bargaining

The intergovernmental negotiation over protected inter-trade will presumably create a reduced space to bargain and pursue a win-win solution on specific but important issues. Hence, the concern over *distributive logic* in the intergovernmental negotiation will dominate sensitive issue-areas at stake as well as spill over to lesser sensitive-issue on the FTA negotiation. The early pursuit of value-claiming strategies will tend to limit *the political will* between the parties to advance towards an agreement, even if this could still make sense economically. These considerations lead to a second hypothesis:

> H2: If governments have limited room to manoeuvre in the interstate negotiations as a result of their mutual distributive concerns over previous and current removal of TB and NTB; of not manifesting the non-negotiable issues of the negotiation at the outset of the process; of the lack of exerting entrepreneurial leadership skills; of prioritising other negotiations; and of predominantly using an offensive value-claiming strategy to get high concessions from the counterpart strategic inter-trade areas, then the negotiation is likely to stall.

3.4 Conditions to Stall a Negotiation

The conditions outlined in this section are contained in a general way in the above hypotheses. However, I make the conditions explicit here, and present their main characteristics and rationales. The conditions to stall a negotiation are presented in two parts for analytical clarity: First, I will discuss the domestic level of the negotiation; I will also present the external factors to the negotiation that have an impact on it, which originate in the domestic sphere. Second, I introduce the intergovernmental level of the negotiation -or state to state negotiation- and I also outline the external factors to the negotiation that have an international dimension or that originate at this level and directly affect the result of the FTA negotiation process. These conditions unfold in a similar timing and they together constitute the setting for failing to reach an outcome of agreement in the FTA negotiations analysed in this work. Moreover, these conditions are part of a whole and should not be taken as a mere aggregation of them. It is the interrelation of these factors that explain the failed cases of Chile-Panama and Costa Rica-Panama in 1998 and 2002 respectively.

3.4.1 Domestic Factors

a) Divergent Interests: The policy preference of domestic groups usually diverges in an FTA negotiation. This divergence is based on whether they enjoy a better comparative advantage than the counterpart or not. The divergent interests constituted at the domestic level are represented by states at the international level. In this regard, the divergence is given by the fact that the counterpart sees the country and domestic sectors as more competitive in some categories and as less competitive in other items. This makes the country seek liberalisation in the counterpart market when domestic sectors perceive economic gains, and protection when they perceived economic losses. However, the stalemate is usually triggered by a constant lobby of powerful domestic actors that can outweigh the costs of organising of other groups as well as the FTA policy-making of the government. Even if a powerful domestic group is threatened by an FTA, this does not mean that it will always block an agreement. Context in this sense matters. The loser groups in a specific FTA are powerful groups that have access points to influence and lobby both the executive and the legislative power (Ehrlich 2007). This influence over veto players increases the extent to which the group threatens the realisation of the FTA, if: they are able to politicise the negotiation; if there are any sort of electoral process ongoing or coming soon; and if they are able to co-opt or displace other domestic groups that have favourable stakes in the negotiation.

b) Job Insecurity: One specific negative effect of liberalising or pursuing a free trade agenda is a sense of job insecurity among some domestic constituencies, which has a consequent impact on the popularity of the government e.g. losing electoral support among the citizen-voters (Kapstein and Landa 2000: 133-148; Mughan and Lacy 2002: 531-533). A government needs to prevent an eventual creation of job-insecurity when carrying a freer trade policy or when negotiating a specific FTA. This can be done in two ways: first, by conducting negotiations way before elections, though there is a time extension factor in the process which to some extent is unknown: *one knows when the negotiation starts but not when it will be concluded.* Second, government's can prevent job insecurity by allowing the eventual losers of the agreement to lobby during the negotiation in order to prevent making too many concessions that will damage not only specific economic sectors, but also the government's own popularity. The first option for these loser groups is that the government excludes the issue from the negotiation, and the second is to have a long-term phase-out along with restricted quotas for goods. In the case of services, the less competitive sector in the country goes for exclusion. But governments sometimes cannot agree on excluding these issues. As I have argued above, I presume that these issue-areas were also those in which one of the governments expected maximal economic benefits for own national markets, making all the other areas, in which benefits could also be realised, complementary to these. Therefore, this factor could have encouraged the winners of the negotiation to free-ride, and find alternative options to make gains.

c) Politicisation: Here there is a convergence of the government's office-seeking goals (close elections), in the sense that a government must address the possibility that an FTA will create losses for workers (job-insecurity), and the fact that the negotiation is a closed process but not completely secret. Protectionist groups have different access points available to influence the negotiation process, and have access to information on the likely consequences if a government takes specific steps that threaten their level of protection. Politicisation also involves fragmentation or polarisation of positions with regards to the FTA negotiation as well as the entire trade agenda of a government.

Domestic groups usually use multiple channels to politicise the negotiation. They encourage media coverage to publicly complain about their losses in order to present a focalised negative consequence as evidence of how the government's actions in its external trade policy would damage the whole civil society.[33] Other concrete ways to politicise a negotiation are to threaten the government with demonstrations on the streets, and to leave the negotiation at the domestic level as an act of discontent with the process. The level of politicisation has not only a direct effect on the negotiations, but it also makes Congress plays an indirect role by sending signals of non-ratification, which constrains what the negotiators could offer and counter-offer to its counterpart.

By politicising the negotiation, protectionist domestic lobby groups seek to tie the hands of negotiators on what they can offer to the counterpart. This tie of hands will limit the negotiators capability to use *side-payments and package deals* as compensations for eventual losses. When the government does not use attractive side payments or package deals, the negotiators do not have enough tools to breakthrough resistant domestic groups. In other words, the higher the level of politicisation, the lower the chances for the government to overcome hard-core protectionist interest groups during the pre and formal FTA negotiation.

c.1) Elections: Elections are considered as a sub-condition within the politicisation factor. The reason to include election as sub-condition of politicisation and not as a condition of its own is that the likely effect of an upcoming election over a launched

33 I assume that the government has the conviction that its trade policy will benefit a majority. Therefore, such policy will increase the welfare of civil society as a whole. However, domestic groups losing with such trade policy will use a rhetoric, in order to protect its particular interests, that government's actions in FTAs will not only damage their interests, but also those of other groups of civil society.

FTA negotiation process is its politicisation, or the augment of the already existing politicisation level of this FTA negotiation. Candidates for Presidency, Congress and City Council will seek to obtain political dividends by attempting to protect the losers of such FTAs who are part of their electoral base to get into office.

Electoral years affect the relative autonomy governments have to conduct and execute their internal and external trade policy. Governments are exposed to criticisms from the opposition and domestic groups that feel threatened by its policies, because they want to get their candidates elected in the forthcoming elections. Therefore, in an electoral year, the opposition will frame the movements of the government in FTA negotiations as a negative step that threatens key and big sectors of the national economy. Under high divergence over interests and positions, along with the upcoming elections, the government will tend to move towards a more defensive position in the negotiation over the most sensitive issues as a way to prevent losing electoral support (Milner and Rosendorff 1997: 140-141). Both governmental and opposing parties threaten the government with exerting its veto role in congress if the FTA includes uncompetitive sectors that constitute an important part of their electoral base. As a government wants to be re-elected in presidential elections, to keep a majority in congress and get many majors in municipal elections, bringing the negotiation to a standstill is one rational option, amongst others, to regain electoral support from the resistant coalitions of the FTA.

However, the parties of the negotiation may be caught in the middle of such an economic negotiation in parallel electoral processes or referendums. These electoral processes may not seem connected to the FTA negotiation as such, but they may also affect the way the international trade negotiation develops. In addition, a previous electoral process may also limit the level to which a government pursues a trade agenda, depending on the results of such elections. Whereas these aspects may seem irrational at a first glance, it has the rationality of nested games (Tsebelis 1991). Any electoral process or referendum, in which the civil society has to vote, can be used by domestic groups or political opponents of the government to obtain concessions or to block other ongoing processes e.g. in the case at stake here an FTA negotiation. Depending on the electoral result i.e. if the government's support decreases, then this loss may act as a mechanism of self-constrain on the actions the government can pursue in the nested or parallel games, since the mandate of the leader will weaken.[34] Yet this connection between parallel games or nested games does not develop on its own; it is articulated by the groups opposing the government and its policies, in this case, including the economic ones.

34 As this work is assessing causes and conditions for stalemate, I focus on this side of the story. However, the reversed argument applies for conditions of successful policy making in parallel or nested games i.e. it could be also be the case that the government in such electoral processes or referendums may obtain a high support. Therefore, the government may be empowered in parallel games.

d) Pro-FTA Groups' Free-riding and Finding Other Economic Alternatives: When the government opens to many access points to get feedback on the different issue-areas of the negotiation, these tend to be overused by groups that lose with the eventual FTA negotiation. In addition, the level of politicisation will create conditions to slow down the speed of the FTA talks. This perceivable potential time extension of the process will affect the pro-FTA group's cohesiveness in the negotiation vis-à-vis the protected groups. Pro-FTA groups will try to find other alternatives to realise economic gains on the sidelines of the eventual agreement with the counterpart domestic trade partners, or with other external trade partners. Potentially the pro-FTA groups will lobby the government to start other FTA negotiations with countries, in which the level of politicisation and uncertainty for protected FTA groups are low. These pro-FTA groups will lobby to pursue FTAs, in which the eventual losers are domestic groups that are not strong enough to block an agreement, or are willing to accept economic compensations for their eventual losses. When the pro-FTA groups seek to get other alternatives to assure economic gains, these moves debilitate their representatives in the FTA negotiation, because the protected oriented groups remain strong to assure a satisfactory outcome. Therefore, the higher the probability of a time-enduring negotiation, the more incentives pro-FTA groups have to find alternative ways outside the FTA negotiation to maximise economic gains.

3.4.2 Intergovernmental Factors

e) Non-negotiability: The most difficult parts of a negotiation are the issues, areas or products governments do not negotiate or are unwilling to negotiate (Mladinic 2000: 69). Yet some governments do not make clear the non-negotiable to its counterpart. The government does not announce at the outset of the negotiations the non-negotiability of its most sensitive issues, because it wants to use them as a bargaining chip to extract concessions in the sensitive areas of the counterpart. A government rather waits and sees how the negotiation develops and then, on the late stages of the negotiation, presents the claim of the non-negotiable. This tactic confuses the counterpart, since it increases the expectations of getting a bigger benefit by claiming value over those issue-areas. Waiting and seeing and then deciding the non-negotiability because of unsatisfactory offers from the counterpart sensitive issues reduces the zone of agreement. The fewer signals one sends on eventual non-negotiable issues at the outset of the negotiation, the lower the final chance to exclude them from the negotiation, because the temptation for the counterpart to pursue an offensive-value-claiming strategy to get concessions in those issues increases. This choice, when the negotiation is difficult and the win set is small because of high divergences, reduces the options to continue the negotiation under such unfavourable conditions for one of the parties.

f) Lack of Leadership Skills in the Negotiation: The negotiations are usually conducted by technical experts as a way to facilitate the dialogue in the diverse array of issue-areas that are part of such negotiation, and not to give advantages to the counterpart in the making of the agreement. However leadership matters. It may facilitate a final agreement and the lack of it may hamper the reach of such agreement. In other words, effective leaders try to create some legacy by getting things done or moving the negotiating agenda forward; by detecting and recognising the constraints in their political environment -(and also in the interstate agenda)- and working to overcome or mitigate such constraints (Blondel 1987). Leadership skills are attributes that negotiators, government officials and elected members should display in a negotiation. Leadership skills are also constituted by intellectual leadership. This type of leadership is based on expert solutions and ideas to shape the way of thinking of principals in a negotiation. However, leadership skills in a negotiation is also about displaying entrepreneurial leadership. This form of leadership skills are based on the person skilful negotiating techniques, creative ideas and expert knowledge to put together win-win deals that were previously impossible to reach (Deese 2008: 24-5; 35-6).

Negotiators, top officials, and political leaders displaying leadership skills in trade talks can act as honest-brokers, can prevent negotiation parties from overusing value-claiming strategies beyond the most sensitive issues, and can make the spiral effect de-escalate (On leadership theory see Deese 2008; Young 1991; Blondel 1987; Hermann 1995). Therefore, the less the display of leadership skills, the higher the chance the parties will not be able to overcome a stalemate.

g) Predominance of Value-claiming Strategies on Key Sectors: When a government does not signal to the counterpart the non-negotiability of the sensitive issue-areas at the very outset of the negotiation, the government is likely to use offensive value-claiming strategies to get high concessions on the counterpart inter-trade issue-areas in exchange for minor concessions on its own issue-areas that do not threaten its own domestic coalitions. If the counterpart resists the offensive strategy and no substantial concessions are given then it will be likely that the counterpart will seek to adopt a similar strategy, which will create a spiral effect of using offensive value-claiming strategies.

On the other hand, it is also possible that one party will use a defensive value-claiming strategy to try counterbalancing an offensive value-claiming strategy from the counterpart. If this is the case then a government's defensive strategy (e.g. exclusion of the issue or a highly restricted quota system along with a long transition period) has to be offset by reducing its own demands on other attractive issue-areas rather than by both parties reducing their demands. This defensive strategy to counterbalance offensive claims is likely to reduce the interests of a country's pro-FTA groups on the negotiation, because these groups will see their government reducing its demands on issues that were taken for granted as to get maximal utility. Therefore, the more value-claiming strategy that is used, especially its offensive variant, without being mixed with integrative approaches, the higher the chance that the negotiation will stall.

h) The Weight of Other FTA Processes: Alternatives to the current negotiation could emerge before, during and after the negotiation (Singh 2008: 42). If countries are having their first FTA negotiation experience, these countries usually would like to make a precedent of an FTA text to follow in the next negotiations. Therefore, negotiators refuse to exclude key issue-areas in which they are competitive because these may give the country more bargaining power in subsequent negotiations. At the same time, negotiators will seek to exclude the most sensitive products and services in which openness may trigger negative effects for their national groups. The logic is to claim in other negotiations that concessions on these issues have not been given to any counterpart.

In addition, if the parties of the current negotiation have had certain experiences in negotiating these accords, then the consequences of extant FTAs may be used by domestic actors as an example of the negative effects produced in its sector by pursuing FTA negotiations with direct competitors. Finally, negotiators take care of making precedents when the country is having parallel negotiations, because what is given to one country will have to be given to the other; or at least this is an argument that the counterpart in the other negotiation is likely to use.

Future negotiations also have an impact on current negotiations especially if a higher trade relation exists with the future counterpart and when this future counterpart nation has a strong bargaining power. The current defensive government can thus anticipate that the future counterpart will hardly push on specific sensitive issue-areas that have not been liberalised at all in previous negotiations. Not giving concessions today is used as a way to prevent giving unnecessary concessions in a future negotiation (Crump 2006; Watkins and Passow 1996).

It may be the case that one of the countries in the current negotiation wants to save such sensitive issues for another occasion in which it will have to face countries or regions which dominate the economic system such as the US or the EU. Therefore, one or both countries of the present negotiation will reject the idea of negotiating such issues as they know a structural power will put this issue on the negotiation table. The country in the ongoing negotiation may be better off waiting and liberalising this issue in a negotiation with a structural power in order to use this issue-area as a bargaining chip to get a better deal in market access or services sectors of the largest economic powers of the world. In this argument, there is a certain inevitability of negotiating these sensitive issues for the small or middle sized country vis-à-vis the structural economic powers. To some extent the latter wants to be the first in liberalising a closed sector, and this may also be the immediate economic reason to negotiate with small or middle sized countries, putting aside the eventual commitment to a free trade ideology that the structural powers might have. Therefore, the possibility of having parallel or future negotiations with other states, especially global economic powers, reduces the interest of the parties in the current negotiation.

3.5 Operationalisation

Hypothesis 1: To asses the plausibility of the first hypothesis the explanatory factor "defence of protected inter-trade issue-areas" is defined here as: a process where domestic groups advocate vis-à-vis their national governments to keep protective measures without which these sectors would not be competitive enough to face external competition. This definition partly leads to the operationalisation of interests. To complete this picture, the interest formation for an FTA negotiation comes from domestic groups that are able to perform in the global economy and have the need to increase their market share by increasing factor mobility and reducing the transaction costs (Schirm 2002: 15). In this regard, it has to be clarified that most of the pro-FTA groups are already part of the global markets. However, in an FTA they seek to increase the benefits by assuring a ruled-binding agreement (governance) that reduces the cost of uncertainty about possible market fluctuations that can lead to diminishing the future transactions of goods, capital and services. The aggregation and interaction of divergent lobby groups will create the formation of endogenous preferences (or interests) for either freer trade or non-liberalisation.

Interests are based on a cost-benefit analysis that guide domestic actors either to increase, to keep or not to lose material capabilities as tools for economic performance and for exerting pressure to shape and constrain certain government positions in the national and international arena. Therefore, the economic foreign policy of a nation-state is to a large extent influenced and determined by powerful interests groups that either act alone or through coalition-building. In this research it is assumed that domestic actors are exposed to the market, even those that advocate keeping protection when an FTA is negotiated, because their increasing exposure to external competition can trigger negative effects in their economic sectors i.e. unemployment and severe reduction of profits. On the other hand, export oriented groups in the service and goods areas will have a positive attitude toward an FTA, because such agreements will potentially increase their market shares. Finally, endogenous forces coming from dominant groups either from protectionist or from market oriented groups are not only sources of an initial position with regards to an FTA, but also a source of change through the process of negotiating such agreement (change for non-agreement: dependent variable).[35] Some preliminary indicators of interests of domestic groups can be found in statements, documents and speeches from the representatives of confederations and business associations as well as labour unions.

Government Position is not a static label; it can change through the process of the domestic and intergovernmental negotiation, because of the domestic pressures exerted by lobby groups as well as by the counterpart position over the issue-areas at

35 I presented a more detailed argument in the Methodology section in chapter 1, on how I have got empirical evidence (sources) to show how material interests shape and determine government's positions within an FTA negotiation.

stake in the FTA negotiation. A national position is an "official" statement coming from expert government representatives of first line i.e. presidents, prime ministers, and ministers of foreign affairs, minister of finances, official trade negotiators, and ambassadors. In this regard, an initial position with regards to FTAs will be found in official documents, public statements, as well as in speeches in international summits and bilateral meetings (where government representatives seek to establish conditions for FTA negotiations). However, as a government position in the process of an economic negotiation may change, it is necessary to follow the process through different issue-areas i.e. a disaggregated position through sectors. It could be that a position in one issue-area, such as services, is to liberalise, but in another like agriculture or rules of origin the position is to keep protection. Therefore, a unitary government position is present in the overall idea of having an FTA and the benefits that this may create for the welfare of the national economy and consumers on a whole, but once specific issue-areas are discussed the government position tends to be segmented. Evidence of segmented positions within the government is likely to be found in public speeches, draft-texts and minutes of the FTAs, and white and green papers from the economic sections of the respective Foreign Affairs Ministries.[36]

Job-insecurity is an issue that trade liberalisation produces. Domestic groups losing in the negotiation may try to get sympathy from citizens by claiming, and by creating discourses on eventual job losses with this FTA. An indicator to assess the job-insecurity is to analyse the press and documents of trade unions and economic sectors that are subject to economic liberalisation in an FTA. In these texts one is likely to find indicators of how an FTA negotiation represents a threat for workers in some economic areas. I contrast and compare data from interviews with the representatives of trade unions and economic sectors against a specific FTA with the data obtained from press, magazines, and documents outlining the positions of such groups. I show that job-insecurity of domestic groups causes negotiators not to concede too much on sensitive issue-areas of the negotiation. In other words, I will ascertain whether lobby groups use their arguments, on potential job-losses produced by an FTA, publicly, in meetings with trade unions or when lobbying government through an access point.

It is appropriate to differentiate between job-insecurity and job-losses. The former is the threat of losing a job because of the trade policy of the government, and the latter is the real fact of losing jobs because of such trade policy. The job-insecurity is to some extent articulated by leaders of trade unions and political parties representing the interests of workers. However, the job-insecurity is based on previous mate-

36 Now I operationalise the specific conditions to measure the plausibility of the first hypothesis. Interest was already operationalised. The conditions job insecurity, politicisation, elections, and free riding option of pro-FTA groups are embedded in a general way in the first hypothesis.

rial experiences i.e. previous economic liberalisation that created job-losses. Job losses may be the material consequence of a particular orientation of trade-policy in general. As workers and leaders do not know for sure the real effects that a particular FTA will have on the economy or on specific issue-areas, though they may estimate them (by using proxies), it is better to refer to the job-insecurity effect that an FTA negotiation produces rather than job-losses, since the real effect produced by a specific FTA is likely to be seen when the FTA is implemented, i.e. when the outcome of the FTA is agreement.

Politicisation is measured by analysing the phrasing and articulation of public complains of domestic lobby groups. These groups publicly pinpoint the negative consequences of the negotiation through media and newspapers as well as through assemblies and meetings with members of domestic groups that feel jeopardised by an FTA negotiation. Moreover, they also seek to spread their concerns on the specific eventual losses with an inclusive discourse of politicisation in order to attract other groups. Evidence of politicisation is likely to be found in the press of the period of the respective negotiations, in which the domestic groups complained and made economic-sectors losses look as if they were for the economy and the society as a whole (this also acts as an indicator of politicisation).

Other indicators of politicisation are the recurrent threats to the government from domestic groups to mobilise and demonstrate on the streets. A way to obtain empirical evidence of politicisation is to conduct text analysis of newspapers and magazines. Moreover, the existence of local referendums, congress and national elections may be another indicator of the level of politicisation during the negotiation. However, politicisation implies a certain level of mobilising forces against the current policy-making as a whole or in this case against trade issues, or against the project of the government proposed by the current incumbents. Therefore, careful attention should be paid to the strategies and messages of the political parties and domestic groups which oppose the government i.e. the messages to the voters from the opposition that criticise the government's trade policy in general and the FTA negotiations in particular. Moreover, I also analyse the way in which the debate between political parties from both government and opposition articulate their strategies against each other.

In addition, politicisation manifests in the level of polarisation within the domestic groups' positions with regards to an FTA negotiation as well as against the government trade agenda. Polarisation within an issue-area can be measured by the number of domestic positions with regards to the negotiation of that issue and whether they diverge or converge. I also analyse the texts of the negotiations, and I contrast the data with interviews conducted with the negotiators on whether they have internal problems with presenting a unified position in overlapping issue-areas or within one issue-area.

Therefore, politicisation as such is not a homogenous force in the different FTA processes a country conducts. Politicisation shows different degrees of intensity (high, medium and low) due to the interests as well as due to tactical reasons. A group or a coalition losing with an FTA can politicise a negotiation from within the process (by articulating blocking positions from inside), as well as from outside (by leaving the negotiation table at the domestic level and going to the streets).

Elections are the number of electoral processes the countries holding FTA negotiations have. These electoral processes are diverse and include city council elections, elections for congress, presidential elections and referendums. Creating indicators on elections is redundant and self-explanatory. Yet the level in which elections have an impact on the FTA negotiation is analysed using the results of the electoral processes i.e. whether the government loses power in the electoral processes, which may be an indicator of reducing the importance of FTA negotiations in general. Another important aspect is to assess whether the electoral campaign for the electoral process was also taken as an opportunity to assess the trade policy of the government, beyond a specific FTA negotiation, but which may have an impact on it. When the government loses support in the electoral process, it is expected to redirect its policies in order to regain electoral support in the near future, including policies on trade issues. When the election is forthcoming in the near future, the level of compromise of the government in the negotiation on sensitive issues is relatively low, or it will not tend to compromise at all with its negotiating counterpart, since the opposition and domestic groups opposing the trade policy will use the electoral campaign to obtain political dividends. Indicators of the impact of elections are likely to be found in the press and also in the information provided by the people interviewed, for example, how the actors postponed an agreement, as well as how the electoral process increased the politicisation level or hampered the negotiation of the FTA.

Pro-FTA Groups' Free-riding and the Finding of Other Economic Alternatives. Trade negotiators were asked, in the interviews I conducted, whether they perceived a diminishing interest of pro-FTA groups in the negotiation when the process got more difficult to manage and the costs of agreeing started to increase. These opinions from interviews are contrasted with the ones provided by the representatives of pro-FTA groups. In addition, free-riding can also be measured by the lobby efforts of these groups to open new FTA negotiations with other countries in which a less conflictive negotiation is expected. I pay special attention as to whether during the period of the negotiation, new FTA negotiations with other countries where launched or were advocated. Moreover, I assess whether more priority was given to FTA negotiations that were conducted in a parallel way, or to the preparation of the negotiations that were forthcoming, than to that which finally stalled.

Hypothesis II: It is plausible that the factor "limited room for manoeuvre" in an intergovernmental negotiation is not only produced by domestic actors, but also by the negotiation process as such (e.g. the predominance of value-claiming negotiating strategies over sensitive issues-areas) and by seeking to burden the costs of eventual non-agreement on the counterpart. In this regard, limited room to bargain (manoeuvre) is defined as the process in which governments are unable to go further in the negotiation by giving new offers to the counterpart, by re-reframing the issue-area at stake and the conditions to pursue a win-win solution. In other words, limited room for manoeuvre will tend to constrain and shape government positions in the FTA negotiation to the extent that no-agreement is possible i.e. stall (dependent variable). Indicators of non-agreement are likely to be found in green papers, minutes of the negotiation, draft texts of the negotiation and memos of governments as well as by interviewing officials from governments. The operationalisation of *interests* and *government positions* that lead to a stalemate in FTA negotiation has already been presented above.

Non-negotiability refers to the specific set of products or services that the parties are unwilling to negotiate or include in the FTA negotiation due to its high sensitivity or its strategic character for the national economy. These non-negotiable issues are sometimes tacitly included or at least the counterpart assume so due to the "confusing" or "unclear" signalling coming from the other government. Indicators of non-negotiable issues are whether both counterparts stated to each other at the very outset of the negotiation the status of non-negotiable over certain sensitive issues. On the contrary, if they indirectly or tacitly include these issues, then it augments the hopes that the issue will be negotiated, which also increases the expectation of the counterpart. I expect that the possible non-negotiables were used strategically to trigger concessions on the counterpart's sensitive issues. This work studies evidence of signalling the non-negotiables at the outset of the negotiation, which is likely to be found in draft texts of the negotiation, and in the interviews conducted with the teams of negotiators of Chile, Panama, and Costa Rica.

Lack of Leadership Skills is defined as the non display of skills related to political, intellectual and entrepreneurial leadership types in the negotiation. The mere presence -or absence- of high profile political leaders such as Presidents in episodes of the negotiation should not be taken as an indicator of leadership exertion as such. In other words, it also involves certain qualities of leadership techniques in a negotiation process. What I mean by leadership are the skills and the ability of presidents, ministers, negotiators, diplomats and government officials to display and create innovative solutions, to attract and convince the counterpart through putting together win-win deals on sensitive issues, and in their capacity to redirect the process whenever it is jeopardised by the high divergence over interests.

Examples of these leadership skills are the role of negotiators, ministers or leaders of acting as honest brokers with the purpose of redirecting the negotiation process at difficult junctures, and the creation of knowledge-based arguments to persuade the counterpart or the domestic groups to follow and accept a certain course of action. Acting as honest-brokers is a role of leaders in the negotiations. This honest-broker role or its absence can be measured by analysing the declarations when the head of negotiators, the leaders of the government, and ministers involved in a negotiation meet either in multilateral and bilateral settings. For example, it may be the case that leaders meet but they do not make direct statements about the negotiation or possible solutions to overcome problematic issues. Here I also rely on internal documents of governments and interviews with the actors of the negotiation and also on the testimonies of advisors to presidents, ministers and negotiators.

Indicators of lack of leadership can also be the absence of mutual support for the process from the leaders of both parties, or that only one party publicly supports and the other publicly omits such willingness to redirect the process to achieve a final agreement. In addition, whether leaders, ministers and negotiators respond to questions about the FTA in press conferences about the meeting with its counterpart in a direct or indirect way, or not at all, can also be considered as indicators of leadership failure to redirect the negotiation process. Other indicators are the inability to reduce the tensions and the hard rhetoric between negotiators of the two countries as well as the inability to focus on a win-win negotiation. The inability to control the use of value-claiming strategies in issues that were not conceived as sensitive as such may be another indicator of lack of leadership skills. Empirical evidence of lack of leadership skills is likely to be found in the press of the period, internal documents of the ministries involved in the negotiations and in the face to face interviews with the team of negotiators.

Predominance of a Value-claiming Strategy on Key Sectors is the use of a set of actions that seek to realise one's own goals when they are in conflict with those of the counterpart. This is restricted to the interstate negotiation in which governments may use this strategy to prevent loses and obtain gains at the expense of the counterpart, following the indication of its domestic constituencies or its own priorities. A value-claiming strategy is compounded by an offensive and a defensive variant that can be used sequentially or simultaneously. The use of the offensive variant is to get value from the other important issue-areas, along with marginal concessions or no concessions at all. This variant can spill over on other issues that were not considered sensitive at a first glance. On the contrary, the defensive variant is used to prevent the counterpart taking value from one's own sensitive issue-areas. The indicators of such strategy are considered a set of tactics that form a strategy. Therefore, indicators of this strategy and its offensive variant are: when a government uses threats such as non-agreement to get concessions; when the government seeks to worsen the counterpart BATNA by establishing new FTA negotiations; when it claims exclusion of issues-areas without giving concessions in other areas of the negotiation; when it uses the time-setting in a manipulative way e.g. 'there is no more time so take it or leave it'; and when it manipulates information on the issue-area at stake. A defensive variant will qualify as such when a government seeks to defend itself from the offensive strategy used by the other government; and when a government defends the issue-area by reciprocating the exclusion of issues from the offensive party with the intention of excluding areas that are attractive to the counterpart. When both governments display offensive strategies to negotiate, then a threat is counteracted by threat; and the manipulation of the other or own BATNA is counteracted by a manipulation of BATNA, and/or of the extant information over the issues of the negotiation.

The Weight of Other FTA Processes is what it is usually called BATNA in negotiation theory. Whenever countries decide to open their economies by pursuing bilateral FTA negotiations, they are usually looking for more trade partners for future negotiations. The weight of other FTA processes is thus the relative attention that a negotiating country will give to a third country with which it already has a trade accord, with which it is currently negotiating, or with which it expects to negotiate in the near future. Indicators of the weight of other FTA processes are the debate and the direct references regarding the previous FTA experiences, and regarding the importance of launching negotiations with other countries rather than the current one. These indicators are likely to be found in reports of domestic groups with stakes in FTA negotiations, and documents and public declarations of government officials and negotiators. A great deal of attention will be paid to potential or parallel negotiations with structural powers and the references to other negotiations, especially when those arguing for waiting for other trade partners are government officials and the most important business associations of the country.

3.6 Concluding Remarks

In this chapter I outlined the elements that make domestic actors favour or oppose an FTA. I also presented the circumstances in which a government is more likely to coincide with the demands of domestic groups favouring an FTA, and in other contexts to the demands of groups opposing a negotiation. I relied on elements of collective action and liberalism to see why protectionist groups lobby more, and exert a more efficient pressure than domestic groups favouring an FTA and attempting to influence the negotiation through the access-points provided by the same governments. Liberalism in its republican form (office-seeking goals) and commercial form (domestic groups influence) helped to explain the external goals of a government that may change its initial perception of having an FTA for one in which a final agreement is no longer possible to be approved. In addition, I presented the specific conditions external or internal to the negotiation in both its domestic and international dimension that plausibly act as forces that bring a negotiation to a standstill. The application of such conditions to two different failed negotiations and the assessment of these conditions' explanatory value for the empirical cases here presented is the task to which I turn in the following chapters.

Part II: Empirical Cases: Chile – Panama & Costa Rica – Panama

4. The Road to the FTA Policies of Chile, Costa Rica and Panama

4.1 Introduction

This chapter assesses the context in which the FTA policies in each case study were generated and conducted. Therefore, this section has to be taken as a contextual description of the origin, development and implementation of the neoliberal trade policy of each country. I also describe the initial steps of Chile, Costa Rica, and Panama towards an FTA policy, and present their respective trade negotiating experiences conducted before the negotiations Chile-Panama, and Costa Rica-Panama. Finally, I present the main actors, and groups of the FTA negotiations as well as how they interact in these negotiations, conceiving this processes as having a domestic and international dimension i.e. double-track diplomacy.

4.2 Chile

4.2.1 Chile's Economic Model

Chile's neoliberal model was implemented in 1975 under an authoritarian rule, which facilitated the introduction of radical reforms. The first period of economic transformation, between 1973 and 1981, has been called *pure neoliberalism* due to its strict economic measures. These measures included a strong shock therapy and the liberalisation of the different economic sectors to promote exports (Ffrench-Davis 2005). A second period of reforms was introduced between 1982 and 1986 to boost economic growth and leave behind the economic crisis of the early 80s. As part of these reforms, the government privatised the pension schemes and electricity companies. In addition, it continued reducing the fiscal spending in education and health as the privatisation of these sectors increased (Huneeus 2000: 437-485).

The new democratic governments did not change the economic model of the previous regime. As Patricio Navia (2006) has persuasively argued, the first three governments of the centre-left coalition -and I include that of the socialist Michelle Bachelet (2006-2010)- have learnt to live with the economic model and they have also legitimised it.[37] However, the democratic governments have put a special em-

37 These governments were that of Patricio Aylwin (1990-94), Eduardo Frei (1994-2000), and Ricardo Lagos (2000-2006).

phasis on levelling the playing field for every one (Engel and Navia 2006; Muñoz Gomá 2007: 96-104). One of the main goals has been the reduction of the poverty level, which was around 40 percent under the last years of Pinochet, and it went down to 18.7 percent in 2003, and to 13.7 percent in 2006 (MIDEPLAN 2007: 3).

Nevertheless, the success of the Chilean model, when measured only in terms of economic growth, has been based on the promotion of exports which are mainly commodities. The external trade policy of Chile has been based on a unilateral, bilateral and multilateral liberalisation. The unilateral liberalisation was started under the authoritarian government, in which tariffs were dismantled to create competition for the local economic sectors by facilitating the imports of products at a cheaper price. The rationale was that only the efficient companies would survive. From a simple average tariff of 94 percent in 1973 the average tariff went down to 10.1 percent in 1979. Along with this tariff reduction, the government also eliminated non-tariff measures that restricted the level of imports, measures such as deposits and the payment of rights to people, companies and regions (Ffrench-Davis 2005: 119-120). During the crisis in 1981-82, the flat tariff was raised to 35 percent, although this was transitory. This unilateral liberalisation also deepened by the first democratic government, in which the average tariff was brought from 15 percent to 11 percent in 1991. Thereafter the flat tariff was reduced one percent per year from 11 percent to 6 percent between 1999 and 2003 (Silva 2004: 28-29).

Whereas unilateral liberalisation reduces the costs of imports, it does not imply reciprocity from the other countries as Chilean exports still have to deal with high tariffs. In this regard, a bilateral track of liberalisation makes sense for the Chilean economy. Moreover, the bilateral path also has a political connotation as it was conceived as a strategic tool to achieve Chile's foreign policy goals, which were to gain the acceptance from the other countries of the region after its authoritarian period, to change the focus on security and border issues with neighbouring countries, and to achieve international recognition (Wehner 2009a).

The unilateral and bilateral path of Chile's external trade policy was also embedded in a multilateral track, such as Chile's participation in the World Trade Organisation (WTO) (Mladinic 2000). Chile's trade policy has been created following the extant rules of the GATT/WTO regime. Chile joined the GATT/WTO in 1947. On this multilateral level, Chile has advocated for enhancing the regulation of free trade from 1975 to the present. Yet Chile's impact on the creation of global economic governance at this level is minimal as Chile's status in this context is that of a small power. Therefore, Chile's bilateral path gives the country more negotiating leverage vis-à-vis its role on the multilateral level. Moreover, the bilateral path also gives Chile the possibility of making trade agreements in which its own interests are better reflected in the wording of such accords, even in the FTAs with global economic powers such as the US and the EU.

Chile's bilateral path was thus conceived as a way to respond to the endogenous pressures of domestic actors as well as to realise strategic goals of the government's foreign policy. Yet these endogenous interests and power issues in pursuing trade accords are also facilitated by an overall societal acceptance of the economic model

(Wehner 2009b). Nevertheless, in the immediate time-setting Chile's external trade policy and specifically the FTA talks "...can be used as a tool to improve countries' status and image by allowing them, on the one hand, to display 'benign leadership' through collaborative economic projects" (Solis and Katada 2008: 249).

4.2.2 Chile's Trade Accords

Chile's first step on its bilateral path was to negotiate low scope trade agreements or trade complementary agreements within the regulatory frame of the *Asociación Latinoamericana de Integración* (ALADI). These accords are of low scope, because they give preferential treatment to a reduced list of products. The so called ACEs were negotiated with Latin American countries. In terms of negotiating experience, these accords gave Chile the chance to develop expertise not only on how to negotiate these accords, but they were also seen as a stepping stone to negotiate more complex trade agreements such as the FTAs. In fact, for some Chilean negotiators of FTAs, the latter are simpler to negotiate vis-à-vis the ACEs.

Every time that a zone of free trade is created, the former low scope accords are over passed and absorbed totally by these FTAs. In addition, the negotiation of broad scope agreements *–FTAs–* is much simpler than the old 'product by product' negotiations, and they are also less costly than the FTAs in terms of economic efficiency. Therefore, the new agreements have a lesser distortion effect than the other type of agreements in the allocation of resources (Rebolledo 1996: 15).[38]

Nevertheless, the low scope agreements provided the first negotiating experience on the making of trade accords. At the time of the negotiation with Panama, Chile had already eight ACEs and an FTA with Canada signed in 1996. Moreover, it became a member of Asian Pacific Economic Cooperation (APEC) in 1995 and was attempting to negotiate a NAFTA membership, which failed. Chile then tried to negotiate a bilateral FTA with the US, which also failed due to the internal political dynamics in the US. In a analogous way, Chile became an active negotiating member of the Free Trade Association of the Americas (FTAA), which started in 1994 and stalled in 2005. Moreover, Chile was also negotiating an FTA with Mexico, which was signed in April 1998. In other words, Chile had already a wide variety of negotiating trade accords in both multilateral and bilateral settings. Moreover, Chile had other chances to negotiate trade accords beyond the negotiation with Panama.

Chile-Argentina (ACE 16): These two countries signed a low scope trade agreement in 1991 with the purpose of facilitating and creating new niches of economic exchange. In addition, this accord also aimed at promoting and stimulating investment, and cooperation in areas such as infrastructure, mining, energy and tourism (ACE 16 Chile-Argentina 1991). This accord was absorbed by ACE 35 between Chile and MERCOSUR in 1996.

38 Author's translation.

Chile-Mexico (ACE 41 and FTA): This accord was signed in 1991 and established a free trade zone. This accord also removed the non-tariff restrictions, and established the liberalisation of maritime and air transport, the national treatment of investments and a system to solve controversies. This low scope trade accord was later replaced by an FTA, signed in 1998 (ACE 41 Chile-Mexico 1991; FTA Chile-Mexico 1998). The negotiation of this FTA was conducted in a parallel way to that of Chile and Panama.

Chile-Venezuela (ACE 23): This accord was signed in April 1993 and included the new trade issues negotiated with Mexico such as commercial promotion, investment, technical norms, services and transport (ACE 23 Chile-Venezuela 1993, summary).

Chile-Bolivia (ACE 22): This accord was signed in April 1993. The accord has both a trade and a political purpose, which were to boost economic exchange and broaden the bilateral agenda, beyond the focus on security and border issues (ACE 22 Chile-Bolivia 1993, summary).

Chile-Colombia (ACE 24): This agreement was signed in December 1993, ensuring that each country was given free access to the vast majority of the other's markets within a period of three years. This ACE excluded 300 products, which were mainly textile products (200 out of 300 exclusions). Colombia is highly competitive in textiles and Chile was experiencing a severe crisis in this area (ACE 24 Chile-Colombia 1993, summary).

Chile-Ecuador (ACE 32): This accord was signed in December 1994. This accord was easy to reach as both countries have complementary economies and enjoy a long-term bilateral partnership in political issues. The accord has parallel protocols such as a bilateral investment treaty and a treaty on sanitary and phytosanitary measures (ACE 32 Chile-Ecuador 1994, summary).

Chile and Cuba (ACE 42): The accord was signed in 1998. The negotiations were conducted in a parallel way to that of Chile and Panama. This negotiation was highly criticised not only because of the sensitivity of the industries (e.g. sugar cane production), but also because of the political connotation and the ideological division created in Chile by Cuba's political stance. In fact, the Congress of Chile only approved this accord in March 2008 and it was not implemented till August 2008 (Boletín BCN Legislativa 11-24 March 2008; www.direcon.cl).

Chile-MERCOSUR (ACE 35): This accord was signed in June 1996. This ACE has currently developed into an economic partnership agreement as there have been many side agreements, in which new issue-areas have been included such as services in 2008 or physical integration agreements as well as scientific and technological cooperation. Moreover, Chile became an associate member of this regional block in 1997. Nevertheless, the original scheme of this ACE 35 negotiated in the mid-1990s includes areas such as controversy resolution, competition policy, safeguard measures, the use of technical rules, sanitary and phytosanitary measures, export promotion measures and intellectual property (see ACE 35 1996, summary).

The most sensitive products of this agreement were to be completely liberalised in 10, 15, 16 and 18 years. These are mainly agricultural products such as beef, dairy products, pork meat, sugar and wheat products. Sugar products will start a linear and progressive liberalisation from year eleven onwards and wheat products were negotiated in 2003 with the liberalisation process due to begin in 2014 (see ACE 35 1996, summary). The negotiation with MERCOSUR was highly politicised as there were several concerns from Chilean endogenous groups with regards to their lack of competitiveness vis-à-vis the Brazilian industrial sector and the Argentinean agricultural sector. The mobilisation of agricultural sub-sectors implied high polarisation, and mobilisation against this accord. Yet the accord was approved in Congress because of the allocation of generous compensation packages to break the resistant coalitions and their representatives in Congress. In addition, such liberalisation was also facilitated by the lack of elections in that term, which did not constrain the office-seeking goals of the centre-left coalition *La Concertación*.

Chile-Canada (FTA). This is Chile's first FTA, signed in 1996. Chile's rationale was to negotiate with Canada a NAFTA-like agreement with the purpose of preparing a negotiation with the US. Therefore, negotiating with Canada and then with Mexico were seen as logical steps on the way to approaching the US (Morande 2003; Silva 2004: 31-32). However, Chile was careful not to negotiate its most sensitive issue-areas, such as financial services and certain agricultural products such as dairy products. This was a way to protect these sensitive issue-areas, which were to be used as a bargaining chip in an eventual negotiation with the US. In this agreement, there are products that have a phase out of 17 years such as pork-meat, vegetable oils, beef, potatoes, wheat flour, sugar and sugar based products, and corn flour. The accord covers areas such as services, investment, dispute settlement, competition policy, government procurement and customs procedures, and side agreements on labour and environment cooperation (FTA Chile-Canada 1996).

Future planned negotiations: As already mentioned, Chile's priority was to achieve an FTA with the US either bilaterally or regionally i.e. joining NAFTA. Therefore, the negotiations with Mexico and Canada were taken as preparatory negotiations for an agreement with the US (Porras 2003: 36-39). Nevertheless due to the deterioration of the Clinton government's approval of NAFTA and the American rescue of Mexico from the Tequila crisis, the US had to postpone other NAFTA memberships (Palmer 2006). In addition, the US launched the FTAA, in which Chile also put resources and hopes in getting a free trade zone for the Americas.

The negotiation between Chile and Panama was articulated in this setting. This negotiation was constrained by the conduction of other negotiations and by giving priority to other FTA process. These previous accords allow us to detect the sensitive products and issue-areas such as services, and Chile's non-compromise stance on financial services in FTAs. These previous negotiations also show that Chile was expert in negotiating trade accords. Therefore, these different experiences suggest that the negotiation with Panama did not fail because of amateurish behaviour in negotiating FTAs.

4.2.3 Chile's Domestic and Governmental Actors

Domestic economic groups: these domestic groups first channel their demands and expectation for a particular FTA through the business associations, but also participate in the so-called next room during the negotiations, either individually or represented by their respective business associations.[39] For example, producers of wood and wood-related products channel their policy preferences on an FTA through the National Wood Corporation (CORMA). The food producers do the same but through the Chilean Food Association; and the agricultural producers and the Milk Producers Association channel their demands through the National Agriculture Association (SNA). The small and medium enterprises present their demands to the National Council for Small and Medium sized enterprises or through the National Association for Small and Medium-Sized Industries.

Fruit exporters channel their demands through their own association, which is the Export Association (ASOEX). Chilean textile producers articulate common positions on FTA negotiations through the National Institute of Textiles (INTECH). Beverage and Refreshment producers present common positions on FTAs through the National Association of Refreshments (ANBER). The *Federación de Procesadores de Alimentos y Agroindustriales* (FEPACH) have a strong position on the liberalisation of other countries' markets with the purpose of exporting their products. In addition, they also lobbied for eliminating the price band system on sugar, wheat and wheat flour, and corn in order to be able to import at a cheaper price for the production of food.[40] Salmon producers present their position on FTA negotiations through *Salmon Chile*; the chicken producers through Association of Chicken Producers (APA), and the manufactures exporters through the National Exporter Association of Manufactures (ASEXMA). Wine producers express their interest on specific FTAs through Wines of Chile or the Chilean Corporation of Wine. Those within the financial sector express their positions on the negotiation of financial services through the Chilean Bank and Financial Institutions Association (ABIF) (see Bull 2008; www.sofofa.cl; www.cpc.cl).

The role of business associations in negotiations: The SNA, National Chamber of Commerce, the Federation of Chilean Industries (SOFOFA) and ABIF are horizontal institutions that have the same weight in representing the diverse array of

39 The individual companies that participate in the 'next room' during the negotiation are usually the big companies. These companies only participate when the counterpart is a big market and the winning and losing options are high, such as with the negotiations with MERCOSUR, the US and the EU. Otherwise, they are represented in the next room by their sector associations. Here, I will only include the most relevant endogenous groups by sector rather than identifying the companies. I focus on the sectors with most weight on the FTA negotiations rather than naming all the different associations that exist in Chile. The purpose of this is to grasp the way in which interests and policy preferences are articulated and processed in FTA negotiation in an inside-out way.

40 This was finally eliminated in the negotiation with the US.

economic sectors in FTA negotiations.[41] However, for strategic reasons of efficiency these associations chose SOFOFA as the institution to channel all their demands about each FTA process with the government. This was also because of the technical expertise on FTAs SOFOFA developed before the other associations, as well the fact that it addresses less sensitive issues in FTA negotiations, which facilitates a strong partnership between the government negotiators and the private sector (Bull 2008: 214). In other words, associations like the ASEXMA, SNA, CORMA, ABIF, ASOEX and AMBER, etc. do channel their demands through SOFOFA in the negotiations as a way to present common positions and exert more power during the negotiation at the domestic level. Nevertheless, these powerful associations still have the option of lobbying on their own, whenever they feel that their demands for liberalisation or protection are not being met in the process. A special case is ABIF, which represents the Banking sector positions on financial services to the Ministry of Finances. This ministry articulates a national position for the FTA negotiations that involve financial services. SOFOFA brings and presents the policy preferences of each sector, which still gives enough room for each association to lobby on their own. Yet SOFOFA also acts as a lobby group for each association and defends its own interests. All these associations named above are part of an umbrella institution which is the Confederation for Production and Commerce (CPC), which also leaves the role of FTAs coordinator to SOFOFA (see Porras 2003, Silva 2001: 33-60, Bull 2008).

The role of governmental institutions and agents in the FTA negotiations.[42] Under the presidency of Eduardo Frei, under which the negotiation with Panama was conducted, the elaboration and control of the trade policy was in DIRECON's hands. This meant that all the inputs for the negotiations coming from the private sector and the elaboration of a 'sector by sector' negotiating strategy was centralised in this institution, which belongs to the Ministry of Foreign Affairs. Yet there were still some exceptions, specifically regarding those who negotiated the accord in sectors like financial services (Interview with Marcela Klein, Ministry of Finances, 24/03/2008). Even though DIRECON won more capabilities to control the trade agenda, the Ministry of Finances had the prerogative to negotiate financial services. Yet the Ministry of Finances also coordinates negotiating positions with the experts of DIRECON.

41 A detailed analysis on the role and functions of the different business associations in Chile see Scapini 2006.

42 Congress is not considered a direct player here as it has the role of approving or disapproving the FTAs once they have being signed by the executive power. Nevertheless, the representatives of Congress may also lobby on behalf of associations. Yet Congress is considered as an intervening variable as the same business associations also lobby the negotiators directly, and they also participate in the negotiations in the next room. Therefore, their interest and positions on a specific FTA are always given directly to the DIRECON negotiators.

In 1995 an Inter-ministerial committee on International Economic Negotiations was created in order to have a better coordination of the elaboration and execution of the trade agenda between the different governmental actors involved in such processes. This committee replaced the former inter-ministerial committee on International Economic Relations formed in 1992. The role of the new committee was to coordinate common positions for a negotiation on the different issue-areas that an FTA involves; to propose setting teams of technical experts for the preparations of the negotiations; and to inform the private sector on the developing of such negotiations. In addition, a committee on negotiation was also created with the purpose of assessing the different negotiation processes as well as setting an agenda for the Interministerial Committee. Both new committees were lead by the head of DIRECON (see Gobierno de Chile 1995, DTO-419; Porras 2003: 20-22; Sáez 2002: 35-43).

Even though the Chilean government initiated the trade policy by showing interest in negotiating FTAs with other countries, the articulation of common interests and positions for the negotiation was conducted in a bottom up way. The overall assessment of the benefits or losses of having an FTA with another country starts with the companies sending their individual assessments to their respective associations, and then the associations send the positions to the government negotiators i.e. bottom-up.[43] However, when it comes to lobbying, the economic groups can go directly to the government or indirectly through their associations, if they think their losses are too high or their winnings too low.

4.3 Costa Rica

4.3.1 Costa Rica's Economic Model

Costa Rica's economic neoliberal model started to be implemented in the early 1980s, specifically under the presidency of Luis Alberto Monge (1982-1986). As with most countries in Latin America, Costa Rica was also affected by the economic crisis of 1981-1982. During this crisis, the national economy experienced a deterioration, in which the external debt and inflation increased. The GDP was –2.3 percent in 1981 and –7.3 percent in 1982. Inflation jumped from 17.8 percent in 1980 to 65.1 percent in 1981 and 81.8 percent in 1982, and the public external debt reached 3.117 million dollars. These three factors partially explain the change from an import substitution industrialisation pattern to a neoliberal one.

In addition, the lack of access to external credits and the level of internal debts facilitated the change and acceptance of a new economic model. This process of economic change was also possible due to the external pressure exerted by the IMF and

43 This is also the case for Costa Rica and Panama and most countries involved in this type of agreements which enjoy democracy.

the World Bank, with which Costa Rica had to renegotiate its external debt and its access to credits (Rojas Bolaños 1997: 39-53; Charpentier Brennes 2004). However, the economic transformation implemented in Costa Rica was gradual, because it was implemented in a democratic context.

The internal dynamics of politics kept certain room for economic compensations for the social sectors that were affected the most, not only for the economic crisis of the 80s, but also for the adjustment programs implemented by the Monge's government and continued by the governments of Oscar Arias (1986-1990), Rafael Calderón (1990-1994), José Maria Figueres (1994-1998), and Miguel Angél Rodriguez (1998-2002). Costa Rica thus followed a unilateral trade policy at the beginning of its economic transformation. Consistent with this unilateral policy, the government reduced the tariff levels. The average tariff levels went down from 53 percent to 16.7 percent between 1985 and 1987 and to 6.1 percent in 2000. The tariff ceiling for all products, with the exception of some agricultural goods, went down from 80 percent to 40 percent at the end of the 80s. The tariff ceiling is currently 15 percent. Another measure was to attract FDI through tax benefits, which allowed the location of multinational technological companies such as INTEL, and the Laboratories Abott, Baxter, and Procter and Gamble were located in Costa Rica (Rodriguez-Clare, Sáenz and Trejos 2004: 123-124).

In addition, the financial system was reformed (1984-1990) and the role of the Central Bank of Costa Rica changed as it adopted a less politicised role, it became an autonomous body, and it implemented, supervised and controlled the monetary policy. Yet the financial reform also involved the privatisation of some banks, creating a mixture of public and private national institutions. Moreover, the government created a General Superintendence of Financial Institutions (SUGEF) in 1996, whose role was the prudential supervision of the banking system as well the monitoring of each financial institution to ensure that they have enough assets and capital to operate (Villasuso 2007: 269-270).

This unilateral liberalisation was also based on the purpose of facilitating the exports of the most competitive products such as commodities and the products of INTEL. Yet the unilateral liberalisation did not assure the reciprocity of the markets from the counterparts. In this regard, Costa Rica started to pursue a bilateral liberalisation process with the purpose of achieving preferential treatment for its exportable goods. The external trade agenda was firstly focused on achieving an FTA with the US or joining NAFTA. The lack of support for this idea on the American side pushed Costa Rica's external trade agenda towards negotiating accords with other NAFTA members such as Mexico and Canada, and possible candidates such as Chile, in a way to prepare a NAFTA membership for the future.

As part of the strategy of export promotion, Costa Rica also sought to re-launch the Central American Integration schemes, though in a rather pragmatic way as Costa Rica intended to give more emphasis to the economic dimension of integration rather than to the political aspects.[44] The integration of Central America is and was not seen as an impediment for Costa Rica to follow trade negotiations with other countries (Lizano 2001). Costa Rica had negotiated trade accords with countries as a regional group. This was the case with the negotiations with Chile and the Dominican Republic in the normative part of the negotiation, as well as the DR-CAFTA and the negotiations with the EU. In other cases, Costa Rica had negotiated on its own, as it was with its negotiations with Mexico and Canada. Yet Costa Rica had, at the same time, been one of the leading countries in pushing the Central American regional scheme to focus on economic integration, since a neoliberal region served the purpose of opening both regional and global markets for its products:

This setting is obviously very different to the existing one of the decade in which the Common Central American Market was formed. Now there is the common interest in reactivating the process of economic integration amongst the countries of the Central American region, but now with two essential goals: to improve the working of the free trade zone and to use these Common Market to achieve a re-insertion into the global economy. In other words, this is about integrating the national markets of the five countries to look for other markets abroad (Quinteros de Aguilera 2000: 460).[45]

Moreover, Costa Rica's external trade policy is also embedded in the multilateral level. Costa Rica is a small country that follows the rules of the game rather than creating them. What matters is that Costa Rica has sought to put its trade accords within the frame of the WTO trade regime. Overall the tariffs of the different sectors have gone down in the accords negotiated by Costa Rica (Lizano 2001). However, some FTA regulations go well beyond the extant rules of the WTO. These new rules were adopted by Costa Rica after negotiating with Canada and with the US within the DR-CAFTA's frame. This is an indirect way for the US to set the rules for a system of global economic governance and to push for its interests at the WTO negotiation rounds (Woolcock 2006: 22; Reiter 2006; Okamoto 2003). Nevertheless, Costa Rica has adopted an economic path in which external trade is the core driver for its economic development. As shown in this section, the paths to FTAs were preceded by economic transformations in which the unilateral, bilateral, regional 'economic' integration and multilateral tracks complement and facilitate the achievement of its external trade and foreign policy goals.

44 The other member countries are: Salvador, Guatemala, Honduras and Nicaragua.
45 Author's translation.

4.3.2 Costa Rica's Trade Accords

General Treaty for the Economic Integration of Central America (GTEICA): This integration scheme was created in the early 1960s. Because of different internal conflicts in some Central American countries, the economic integration process halted until the end of the 1980s. In 1992, the five member countries of this accord signed a reformation of the treaty with the purpose of adapting the GTEICA to the new conditions of the global market. In 1991, El Salvador and Guatemala also signed an accord to deepen economic integration by creating a Customs Union, which Costa Rica joined in June 2002 (COMEX 2006: 5). The GTEICA is embedded in the Central America Economic Integration System (SICA) formed in 1991. SICA includes four core areas of integration, which are economic, social, environmental and political integration (see www.sica.int).

The GTEICA covers the economic dimension which Costa Rica has paid more attention to. The economic liberalisation covers 99 percent of the products. It includes areas such as rules of origin; safeguard measures; unfair trade practices regulations; sanitary and phytosanitary measures; normalisation measures, standardisation, metrology and authorisation procedures; and a dispute settlement body. The economic integration of Central America has thus been a continuous ongoing process of integration as shown by the creation of a Customs Union and the conduction of group FTA negotiations with external countries.

Costa Rica's and Panama's FTA and Preferential Agreement: This accord was signed in 1973. Even though both countries named this accord an FTA, the scope is rather limited. It fits the criteria of a partial trade agreement. This low scope is evidenced by that fact that the FTA negotiation was launched between Central America and Panama in 2000. In fact, the accord of 1973 excluded around 75 percent of the tariff headings (COMEX 2001a: 12). This accord show the limitations but also the sensitivities on both sides to negotiate a new FTA. These sensitivities caused by the high numbers of exclusions in 1973 re-emerged during the bilateral FTA negotiation between these two countries in 2002. The accord of 1973 includes the following sections that show its limited scope: the system of market access for a reduced list of tariff headings; the rule of origin for such products; problems of trade competence; a short scope dispute settlement mechanisms for the issues included in the agreement; the Customs regulations; and transport conditions for goods in transit (Costa Rica-Panama preferential trade agreement 1973).

Costa Rica-Colombia: These two countries signed a partial trade agreement in 1984, which has been valid since 1985. The accord is extremely limited in terms of market access as it only includes 30 products (see Acuerdo Alcance Parcial Costa Rica-Colombia 1984).

Costa Rica-Venezuela (ACE 26): Both countries signed a partial trade agreement in March 1986. This ACE only covers 27 products. It also covers rules of origin for the products liberalised, safeguard measures, differential treatment, commercial promotion and mechanisms to solve trade conflicts (ACE 26 Costa Rica-Venezuela 1986).

Costa Rica-Mexico (FTA): This FTA was signed in April 1994. This is Costa Rica's first FTA. The negotiations to reach an FTA were conducted from April 1993 onwards. The main purpose for Costa Rica, beyond the direct trade creation effect, was to prepare itself for a NAFTA membership (COMEX: 1994: 10). It was expected that around 98.5 percent of all products will be liberalised in both countries in 2009. The issue-areas of this FTA include market access, rule of origin, sanitary and phytosanitary measures, Customs procedures, safeguard measures, services such as national and MFN treatment, normalisation measures, government procurement, investment, temporary entrance of business people, intellectual property, and dispute settlement mechanisms (COMEX 1994: 13-16).

Costa Rica and the Dominican Republic (FTA): This accord was signed in April 1998 and was negotiated between the Dominican Republic and the Central American countries. However, the market access section of the agreement was negotiated bilaterally between the Dominican Republic and each country of this regional grouping. In the case of Costa Rica this accord came into force in 2002 (COMEX 1998).

Costa Rica-Chile (FTA): In August 1998 Chile and the countries of Central America agreed on launching FTA negotiations. The normative frame of this accord was signed in 1999. However, the bilateral FTA between Chile and Costa Rica became valid in 2002. First the Central American countries and Chile agreed on achieving a common normative frame, and as a second step they would negotiate bilaterally with Chile the issues-areas of market access and the specific rules of origin for each country. The negotiation of the normative frame for the FTA between Central America and Costa Rica had six rounds and the bilateral discussion between Costa Rica and Chile was finished after 4 rounds. It is expected that in 2013, 95 percent of Costa Rica's and 95.1 percent of Chile's tariff headings will be totally liberalised. The exclusions represented 3.8 percent of products in each country. Chile excluded the products which are part of its band system price, such as wheat, wheat flour, comestible oils and sugar, whereas Costa Rica excluded meat, chicken sausages and chicken cold meat, dairy products, horticulture products, forestry products and wood furniture (COMEX 2003).

Costa Rica-Canada (FTA): These two countries signed an FTA in 2001 after seven rounds of negotiations. The agreement came into force in 2002 (COMEX 2001b). The approval of the Congress in Costa Rica was difficult and time consuming for the team of negotiators as they had to prepare the approval by justifying the concessions over sensitive agricultural issues like potatoes. In order to approve such accord in the Congress, the executive had to present some compensation packages for the potato producers since the FTA granted preferential access to Canadian processed potatoes (washed, cut and fried potatoes) with a quota without paying tariffs on 2.273 tons.[46] This quota increases by five percent each year until year nine of the

46 Canada has one of the world leading industries in processed potatoes, which is McCain Foods Limited (Ulett: 2001).

FTA, in which these products will not have any restriction for importers (*La Nación* 19/07/2002). Canada automatically granted free access to its market to 86 percent of Costa Rica's products, and the latter liberalised 65 percent of its tariffs headings for Canada (COMEX 2001b).

Other negotiations: In a parallel way to the negotiations with Panama, Costa Rica was in a process of conducting technical studies to negotiate an FTA between the Central American countries and the US (2002). Yet the process of preparing the launching of such negotiations started in 2001. The formal negotiations between the US and Central America began in January 2003. Costa Rica was also participating in the FTAA negotiations, in which trade diplomats had to prepare negotiating positions. Moreover, Costa Rica was negotiating an FTA with Trinidad and Tobago. This accord was signed in 2001. This agreement was later absorbed by the FTA between Costa Rica and CARICOM, which was launched in October 2002. Therefore, Costa Rica also had a vast trajectory in negotiating FTAs as part of its strategy of economic development. In other words, the possible claim of inexperience of Costa Rica's trade diplomats as a cause for failure in the negotiation with Panama should be dismissed.

4.3.3 Costa Rica's Domestic and Governmental Actors

Domestic Actors: Unlike Chile, Costa Rica does not have one single institution that channels the demands of all economic sectors for an FTA negotiation. Whenever a negotiation is launched the Ministry of Commerce (COMEX) informs the different economic sectors and companies on the possibility of starting FTA negotiations with another country. Once the information reaches the different sectors of the economy, the process reverses in a bottom-up way as the different companies send their letters stating their positions to COMEX.[47] An average of around 800 companies sent their policy preferences to COMEX during the consultation process for the negotiations with Panama (see Comex 2000a).

Business Associations in the Negotiations: Even though COMEX asks the different companies for their positions on specific FTA negotiations, the different sector economic associations still have a strong representation and a voice in the different stages of an FTA negotiation i.e. pre-negotiation (preparation), negotiation (next room) and ratification (lobbying Congress). COMEX asks these associations for their positions on specific negotiations. In this regard, COMEX trade negotiators want to have all the actors in its proposals to negotiate with another country. These positions do not diverge from those submitted by individual companies to COMEX as they also submit a copy of their preferences to their respective associations (interviews with Luis Obando and Jack Liberman, CICR, 30/06/2008; Carlos Céspedes,

47 It will be meaningless to name all the different companies that operate in Costa Rica in this section.

CADEXCO, 25/06/2008; Ronulfo Jimenez, Banking Association, 27/06/2008; Erik Montero, CNLP, 27/06/2008; Mario Montero, CACIA, 07/07/2008; William Cardoza, CANAVI, 01/07/2008).

COMEX also asked 45 sub-economic sectors for their policy preferences with regards to the negotiations with Panama (COMEX 2000a: 2). Amongst the most important ones in the process of preparing a negotiation and the formal process as such in the area of market access were the Chamber of Milk Producers, National Chamber of Pork Producers, National Horticulture Corporation, National Rice Corporation, National Federation of Coffee Producers, the Agricultural-Industrial League for Sugar Producers, Chamber of Textile and Confections, National Chamber of Agriculture and Agro-industrial Products, Chamber of Bananas Producers, Costa Rica's Industrial Association of Plastic, National Chamber of Poultry Farming, and National Chamber of Exporters of Sea products.

In addition, certain chambers of economic sectors participate in the Advisory Council for the Ministry of Commerce, which was set to give advice to the executive power on external trade policy and foreign direct investment matters as well as to promote public-private coordination in trade negotiations. The private actors of this initiative are the Costa Rica's Union of Chambers and Associations of the Private Companies, Chamber of Industries, Chamber of Commerce, Chamber of Exporters, and the Chamber of Agriculture. There are other sub-sector chambers which participate sporadically depending on the issue address by the meeting of this advisory panel. These different chambers also submit their policy preferences to COMEX before a FTA negotiation starts and participate in the "next room" during the process. The public side of this panel is constituted by the ministers of COMEX, Agriculture, and Foreign Affairs (COMEX: 2000a: 1).

On matters of Services in the negotiation with Panama as well as in the previous and subsequent FTA negotiations, the most common and important actors from the private and public sector are: National Bank of Costa Rica, Central Bank, Superintendence of Pensions, Superintendence of Values and Stock Market, General Superintendence of Financial Institutions, Chamber of Private Banks and Financial Institutions of Costa Rica, University of Costa Rica, Costa Rica's Institute of Tourism, Costa Rica's Institute of Electricity, Federation of Workers with University-Professionals Degrees, National Chamber of Tourism, Costa Rica's Chamber of Commerce, and Costa Rica's Social Security Fund. These institutions submit their own policy preferences on a negotiation to the COMEX representatives (Interviews with COMEX's trade diplomats 24/06/2008 to 14/07/2008).

The role of Governmental Institutions and Agents in FTA negotiations: the Ministry of International Trade (COMEX) controls and has all the prerogatives to initiate talks on trade accords and conduct such processes. However, there are other governmental institutions that provide feedback depending on the issue-area involved in the negotiation. The governmental institutions that provide these inputs to COMEX's negotiators are the Ministry of Agriculture (market access), the Ministry of Foreign Affairs (strategic choices on Foreign Policy), the Ministry of Finances (Services), and the Ministry of Environment and Energy (Services). COMEX has a minister and vice-minister who delineate the executive overall policy for an FTA negotiation. The overall policy choices for a negotiation are expressed by the head of the negotiation and his/her respective teams for each section i.e. market access, rules of origin, investment, services, financial services, dispute settlement, etc. Usually the minister and vice-minister of COMEX act as the main voices, and the negotiators of last resort in the FTA talks whenever the negotiation becomes complicated or deadlocked in one of the issue-areas (see ww.comex.go.cr; interviews with Laura Rodriguez, COMEX, 08/07/2008; Amparo Pacheco, COMEX, 02/07/2008; Esteban Agüero, COMEX, 02/07/2008).

4.4 Panama

4.4.1 Panama's Trade Policy

Panama experienced its economic transformation from an inward to an outward economic pattern of development much later than Costa Rica and Chile. Panama was ruled *de facto* by General Manuel Antonio Noriega from 1983 to 1989. Noriega was never president of Panama. However, he controlled the military (Panamanian Defence Force: PDF), and was able to appoint his favourite candidates for presidency and manipulate the results of the elections. His power was partly based on the support of the US under the context of the Cold War as Noriega gave the US the rights to set listening posts to control and monitor Soviet and Cuban activities as well as the general movement and guerrillas operations of the *Frente Sandinista de Liberación Nacional* (FSLN) in Nicaragua (Harding 2006: 89-95). Therefore, Panama was used by the US as a strategic site to conduct military and security operations in Central America. These acts not only violated Panama's sovereignty but also that of the rest of the Central American countries (Sánchez 2007: 162-163).

In 1989 the Cold War was coming to an end and also the internal conflicts in Central America. Therefore, the cost of keeping Noriega increased as he was also participating in, or allowing, illegal activities in Panama such as drug-trafficking, human rights violations and money laundering. There were many military attempts to remove Noriega from his de facto power. The last attempts of *a golpe* against Noriega backed by the US were conducted in March 1988 and in October 1989. Yet both failed in removing General Noriega. The definitive end of Noriega's *de facto* regime was due to the manipulation of the electoral results in the presidential election of 1989. Noriega's candidate was Carlos Duque, who led the National Liberation Coalition. The opposition, Civic Opposition Democratic Alliance, was led by Guillermo Endara (Harding 2006).

The results of the election broadly favoured Guillermo Endara. As there were international observers including former American President Jimmy Carter, Noriega claimed external interference in Panama's 'democratic process' in a way to alter the course of elections and to justify appointing his favourite Carlos Duque.[48] The US did not recognise Duque as the President. This rejection from the US was not only based on the defence of the pillars of democracy, but also on the need to protect its strategic goals in the Canal. The Canal was to be passed to Panama on the 31st of December 1999. The US were concerned about giving control of the Canal to Noriega's de facto dictatorship. However, two episodes precipitated and justified the invasion. One was the assassination of a US soldier, Roberto Paz, at the checkpoint of the PDF, and the other was the arrest of an US Navy officer and his wife, who were beaten and tortured (Sánchez 2007)

On December 20 1989, the US deployed 24000 troops to remove Noriega. This triggered a transition to democracy in Panama. Guillermo Endara (1990-1994) took power under the tutelage of the US. In February 1990 the US pulled out most of its military, though some remained in the US bases at the Canal's Zone. Endara had to deal not only with restoring democracy, but also with a severe economic crisis. The estimates of the damage to Panama as a consequence of the occupation and errant economic policies under Noriega's years were about USD 1.5 billion. Yet the US granted 450 million in aid and more than 500 million in credits and guarantees for rebuilding the economy (Harding 2001: 182).

The poor economic conditions were reflected in the capital flight from the banking system, which is estimated at 18.7 billion from 1987-1989. The country's GDP dropped 15.6 percent in 1988. The unemployment rate grew significantly between 1987 and 1989, from 11.8 percent to 16.3 percent. The external debt was USD 5.99 billion in 1992 (Ferrer 2001: 26-29). The unstable political setting and the need to bring back FDI in the national economy, led the Endara's government to adopt a severe adjustment package following the advice of the World Bank and the IMF. The orthodox fiscal policies and the privatisation measures were kept under the following presidencies of Ernesto Peréz Balladares (1994-1999) and Mireya Moscoso (1999-2004). However, Endara's government rapidly brought the national economy onto a healthy track and created a stable democratic system.

Under the mandate of President Peréz Balladares, key public companies were privatised such as the sugar, cement, rail, electricity and telecommunication companies (Ministerio de Economía y Finanzas-Panamá: 2000: 5). Moreover, the state passed laws to give more transparency to the economic system such as an anti-monopoly law and a money laundering agreement to regulate and control money transactions in the financial sector. In 1998, a banking law to comply with the Basel Accords was also approved to fulfil the transparency criteria of multilateral accords.

Panama's GDP grew 5.5 percent in 1993, 2.9 percent in 1994, 7.6 percent in 1995, 0.5 percent in 1996, and 4.4 percent in 1997. Inflation averaged 1.1 percent from 1993 to 1997 (*Economist Intelligence Unit* 1996 & 1998). Despite these good

48 The exit polls at voting centres showed that 73 percent voted for Endara and only 26 percent for Noriega's candidate Carlos Duque (Harding 2006: 112).

macroeconomic results the unemployment rate reduction was modest as a consequence of the diminution of state employment, which had been one of the main employers in the national economy. From 16.3 percent of unemployment in 1989, the numbers only dropped to 13.6 percent in 1992 and 13.2 percent in 1997 (*Economist Intelligence Unit* 1998a: 12).

The then President Mireya Moscoso from the Arnulfista Party did not change the course of the economic pattern. Moscoso's government achieved a growth average of 3.4 percent between 1999 and 2004. Yet in 2004 the economy grew 7.6 percent. The inflation rate averaged 0.8 percent between 2001 and 2004. The unemployment rate went down to 11.8 percent during her last year as president. During the previous years the unemployment had remained around 13 percent (*Economist Intelligence Unit*, 2005: 5 & 23).

One of the key parts of Panama's strategy of market liberalisation was to promote economic growth through exports (Ministerio de Economía y Finanzas-Panama 2000: 4). In this regard, the main trade partner of Panama was and still is the US. The latter received 46.2 percent of Panama's total exports in 1997. Panama was and is also trade dependent on its imports from the US, which came to 36.9 percent of total imports in 1997. In 2005, the US was still the main market for Panamanian exports and imports, accounting for 44.5 percent of its total exports and 27.4 percent of its total imports (*Economist Intelligence Unit*, 1998b: 5; 2006: 5).

As part of its external trade policy agenda, Panama sought from the beginning to achieve preferential treatment from the US for its exportable products. In order to open the possibility of a trade accord with the US, Panama was asked to join the WTO. The WTO membership negotiations were taken by Endara in 1990, and continued by Peréz Balladares. In fact the formal negotiations at the WTO started as such in 1993 (Ferrer 2001).

The accession to the WTO was a hard process because of the challenge to negotiate the accession both multilaterally and bilaterally whenever any of the WTO members requested to do so in order to negotiate market access item by item within the GATT/WTO regime. In addition, the most difficult part of the accession was to convince the endogenous economic actors of Panama's need to be part of the multilateral trade regime. Negotiators also had to break the domestic resistance of the industrial and agricultural sectors, which were used to having high levels of protection in the form of tariff and non-tariff barriers. However, the accession to the WTO was also used as a way to 'lock-in' the domestic economic reforms, and prevent an eventual reversion of them. Panama's definitive accession to the WTO was in 1997. The WTO accession became a focal point in the elaboration of an external trade policy for Panama, in which one of its core issues was to achieve an FTA with the US (interviews with Carlos González, APEDE and ex-MICI 21/07/2008; Alejandro Ferrer, MICI, 29/07/2008).

Panama felt that it was falling behind the web of FTAs that were proliferating in the Western Hemisphere. Moreover, it also saw how direct economic competitors were lobbying to launch FTA negotiations with the US such as Costa Rica and the rest of the Central American countries. Therefore, Panama implemented a multi-track foreign economic policy, following the Chilean example, employing unilateral, bilateral and multilateral economic liberalisation. Chile's insertion into the global economy was taken as a role model. Once the accession to the WTO was granted, it became imperative to negotiate an FTA with the US either bilaterally or through a NAFTA-membership. Nevertheless, the US focus on the FTAA and the deterioration of the US economy due to the Asian crisis as well as the difficult approval of the NAFTA accord in the US Congress postponed such enterprise for the future. Meanwhile Panama sought to get expertise on negotiating this type of accords with its role model of economic integration: Chile.

4.4.2 Panama's Trade Accords

Accession to the WTO: Panama's most recent experience of negotiating a trade accord before negotiating with Chile, albeit a multilateral one, was its accession to the WTO. Here Panama had to articulate, create and coordinate common positions at the national level to be presented at the multilateral level in issue-areas such as market access, services, investment, and property rights. The team of negotiators that participated in the WTO accession process remained after the accession to negotiate the failed FTAs with Chile and Costa Rica. Most of the team-members, such as Leroy Sheffer and Diana Salazar, are still part of the negotiations as heads of negotiating teams.

The negotiation in the WTO was intense as Panama had to introduce new systems of tariffs, reduce its tariffs and commit to a tariff ceiling.[49] Moreover, it also had to negotiate non-tariff barriers, intellectual property, sanitary and health measures, commercial services, professional services, telecommunications, banking and other financial services. Not only were the staff from the Ministry of Trade to negotiate the WTO accession, but they were also responsible for the implementation of the WTO rules in the national economy. Nevertheless, the accession to the WTO implied a broad adaptation of national legislation in order to fulfil the WTO criteria.

One episode of the accession to the WTO that played a significant role in the FTA negotiation between Panama and Costa Rica was the bilateral negotiation over market access conducted by both countries at the WTO. Although conducting bilateral market access negotiations as a part of the process of accession to the WTO is consistent with the extant multilateral trade regime, it was seen as an obstacle for Panama in its process of joining the WTO. This was only the second time in the history

49 Panama negotiated a total of 8394 tariff headings: The agreement at the WTO was that only 0.99 percent of the headings were to be above a 40 percent tariff; 68.24 percent of products should have progressive reduction from 40 percent to 30 percent in five years time of the tariff ceiling; from 40 percent tariff to less than 30 percent tariffs there would be 2.36 percent of products; below 40 percent tariff there would be 31.51 percent of products; And in services Panama would keep the status quo with the exception of tourism which was to be further liberalised (Abrego 2000: 120).

of access either to GATT or the WTO that a developing neighbouring nation asked another developing country to conduct such negotiations (Ferrer 2001).

The previous experience was between El Salvador and Honduras, yet the former had to withdraw its request. In this regard, common practices sometimes matter more than legal rights, even with well established multilateral institutions. Moreover, Costa Rica presented the second largest request for negotiating market access after the EU. The negotiation was conducted in a very confrontational way according to the testimonies of Panama's negotiators Carlos González (21/07/2008) and Diana Salazar (30/07/2008). The difficult process of negotiating between these two countries was also confirmed by Costa Rica's trade diplomats Roberto Echandi (26/06/2008) and Irene Arguedas (03/07/2008), and by former Vice-minister of International Trade between 1994 and 1997, Mr. Francisco Chacón (14/07/2008).

In a strategic move Panama negotiated first with the US, Japan, and the EU and kept the negotiations with Costa Rica at a low pace. Panama sought to make Costa Rica give up on its difficult demands by negotiating at a slow pace in order to create a more levelled playing field to negotiate at a later date. In addition, the delay and the noise claiming the unfairness of Costa Rica's demands also constituted a strategic move to prevent other developing countries from being tempted to request bilateral market access negotiations with Panama (see Ferrer 2001: 93-95). Nevertheless, this episode re-emerged during the negotiations of the FTA from the beginning, as Panama depicted Costa Rican negotiators as untrustworthy and ready to push hard unexpectedly, whilst Costa Rica's negotiators perceived those form Panama as hard and immovable without hard bargaining.[50]

Before the accession process to the WTO, Panama also conducted other trade negotiations that helped to build 'learning by doing' expertise on trade issues. However, these negotiations involved a restricted set of products. In addition, other trade agreements with the goal to facilitate trade were not used in practice as the real trade exchange did not increase in the same manner as 1981's exchange with China. The non-use of the agreements as such is not an aspect relevant in this section. What matters for this research is the negotiating experience gained and the development of negotiation skills as well as the fact that Panama was able to reach final agreements in its trade negotiations. The main aspect is that Panama was neither inexperienced nor non-agreement oriented in its history of trade negotiations.[51]

Panama-El Salvador: These two countries signed an FTA and Preferential Trade Agreement on October 1968, which has been valid since 1970. The scope of this accord is limited as it only includes 316 products. It also includes a section over rules of origin for the products included in the accord, dispute settlement mecha-

50 This shows that past experiences, although in different settings, matter and affect current ones. It also shows the bounded rationality of actors to conduct such negotiations, as any attempt of pushing hard was automatically associated to past experiences.

51 In the following short description of other trade agreements I skipped the low scope preferential trade agreement with Costa Rica as this accord was presented in the section that deals with the case of Costa Rica.

nism, custom issues, and transport facilitation measures for the products of the two countries (Preferential Trade Agreement Panama-El Salvador 1970).

Panama-Nicaragua: Both countries signed an FTA and Preferential Trade Agreement on July 1973, which came into force in January 1974. The agreement included 246 products of which 213 were to be traded without restrictions, 4 were subject to quotas and 29 to import/export restrictions. This agreement also includes rules of origin for the products included in the agreement, dispute settlement mechanisms, custom issues, and transport facilitation measures (Preferential Trade Agreement Panama-Nicaragua 1974).

Panama-Honduras: This Preferential Trade Agreement was signed in November 1973 and was implemented in February 1974. The accord includes preferential treatment for 190 products of which 130 are traded freely, 40 have a tariff reduction, two have quotas, and 18 have import/export restrictions. As with the rest of the agreements with the other Central American countries, this includes rules of origin for the products included in the accord, dispute settlement mechanisms, custom issues, and transport facilitation measures for the products of the two countries (Preferential Trade Agreement Panama-Honduras 1974).

Panama-Guatemala: Both countries signed an FTA and Preferential Trade Agreement in June 1974 that has been valid since April 1975. This accord covers 261 products of which 138 are to be traded tariff free, 116 with tariff roll-back, 2 have quotas and 5 import/export restrictions. It also includes rules of origin for the products included in the accord, dispute settlement mechanisms, custom issues, and transport facilitation measures for the products of the two countries (Preferential Trade Agreement Panama-Guatemala 1975).

Panama-Mexico: Both countries signed a partial scope agreement within the framework of the Latin American Integration Association (LAILA/ALADI) in May 1985. The ALADI allows partial scope trade agreement with non-member countries such as Panama.[52] The accord covers 120 products (Preferential Trade Agreement Panama-Mexico 1985).

Panama-the Dominican Republic: These countries signed an FTA and Preferential Trade Agreement in July 1985. The treaty came into force in June 1987. It has similar characteristics to those agreements Panama signed with the Central American countries as it covers rules of origin for the products included in the accord, dispute settlement mechanisms, and transport facilitation measures for the products of the two countries. The liberalisation of goods includes 120 products that have reciprocal free trade: 26 extra products have zero tariffs to access the Dominican market for Panama; 24 extra products of the Dominican Republic have free access to Panama's market; and there is free reciprocal access for 29 products produced within the Duty Free Zones of each country (Preferential Trade Agreement Panama-Dominican Republic 1985).

52 Mexico is an ALADI member from 1980, and Panama only became member in 2009 (see www.aladi.org)

Panama-Colombia: Both countries negotiated a low scope partial trade agreement within the frame of ALADI. This accord was signed in July 1993 and came into force in January 1995. Panama reduced the tariffs for only 12 products for Colombia and the latter liberalised the same number of products for Panama. However, none of the countries granted free access for any product; instead they gave preferential treatment to each other by reducing the tariff levels. The accord also covers matters such as rules of origin, safeguard clauses, unfair practices to trade, trade cooperation, normalisation measures, transport facilitation, cooperation over banking and financial services, government procurement, and dispute settlement measures. Even though the thematic is broader than other low scope preferential trade agreements that Panama negotiated, the scope of this accord is smaller than those of the proper FTAs or last generation trade accords negotiated in the end of the 1990s and during the 2000s (Preferential Trade Agreement Panama-Colombia 1993).

Panama-Central America: Panama and the Central American countries signed an FTA common normative framework. The normative framework with Central America was achieved in 2001 (www.mici.gob.pa).

Panama and El Salvador: They signed their bilateral protocol in March 2002. This is the first proper FTA that Panama achieved in terms of scope and depth. It replaces the partial trade agreement valid since 1970. This FTA was achieved before Panama and Costa Rica launched their bilateral negotiations (FTA Panama-El Salvador, bilateral protocols 2002).

Other trade accords: Panama also signed trade accords which are no longer valid, such as the agreement with the Soviet Union signed in 1989. This agreement granted a most favoured nation treatment and promotes the growth of trade relations. Similar agreements were also signed with Bulgaria (1979), Hungary (1979), Poland (1979), and Romania (1980). These agreements gave a most favoured nation treatment in all trade related matters (Ferrer 2001: 65-67).

When Panama launched negotiations with Chile, it did not have other ongoing negotiations, as Panama saw an FTA with Chile as an easy negotiation which will give Panama not only the experience but also an FTA text-model to follow and be used as a precedent in subsequent negotiations.[53] When Panama launched the negotiations with Costa Rica in 2002, Panama was preparing the negotiations with Taiwan, had FTA talks with Mexico, and also had the hope of launching negotiations with the US. Panama was also participating in the FTAA negotiations into which both countries had to put time and human resources. This is also the case for the negotiation with Chile as the preparatory process of FTAA negotiations was conducted between 1994 and 1998.

53 When started to negotiate with Chile, Panama also initiated preliminary talks with Mexico for an FTA in December 1996 (Ferrer 2001: 227).

4.4.3 Panama's Domestic and Governmental Actors

Domestic Actors: During the process of formation of interests for a negotiation, it is the government which first calls for an FTA negotiation in order to receive feedback from the different domestic economic groups regarding their interests for the upcoming negotiation. However, after the government calls for the presentation of policy preferences on an FTA, the process becomes bottom-up. Panama integrated its different domestic actors, either losers or winners, within the liberalisation discussion in the WTO accession negotiation. This participation of domestic actors was maintained during the pursuit of FTA negotiations.

The different economic sub-sectors and companies presented their policy preference over negotiations directly to the ministry of trade and industries, which conducts the international trade negotiations. However, these domestic actors also submitted their policy preferences to their respective associations and the Chamber of Commerce, Industries and Agriculture which acts as a sort of umbrella association for Panama's different economic sectors (interviews with Carlos González, ex-DINECI 21/07/2008; Diana Salazar, DINECI, 30/07/2008; Victor Cruz, SIP, 16/07/2008; Manuel Ferreira, Chamber of Commerce, Industries and Agriculture 25/07/2008).[54]

Business Associations: As previously mentioned, the different domestic actors also send their policy preferences to the different associations in order to coordinate group positions. This empowers the positions of an economic sector vis-à-vis the negotiators. However, the different domestic groups, depending on their size and importance for the economy, may have the multi-track choice of lobbying. Most groups in Panama lobby on their own and also as part of the business associations in order to exert extra-pressure on the government's negotiators. The business associations use the Chamber of Commerce, Industries and Agriculture as an umbrella association, which also presents its policy preferences based on the feedback provided by the different sub-economic sector associations (interviews with Panama's trade negotiators and representatives of business associations 16/07/2008 to 05/08/2008).

54 The most relevant agricultural and food producers in negotiations include rice, sugar cane, pork, chicken, bovine, milk, fruit, tobacco, and fish producers. In services, broadly defined, the most relevant players are: banks, saving institutions, stock market investment companies, money transfer companies, insurance companies, factoring companies, and credit card institutions as well as hotels, restaurant, tourist offices, casinos, professional services (lawyers, doctors, accountants, engineers, etc.), universities, shipping companies, air and sea transport, and editorials. Amongst the industrialist sector (vis-à-vis either export or internal consumption) the most relevant players in a trade negotiation are: food producers, beverage and liquor producers, retailing companies, plastic producer, metallurgic companies, paper producers, and clothing and shoe producers. Within the technological sector the relevant parties include telecommunication companies, software importers and producers, and call centres.

Amongst the most important associations that play a major role in the negotiation process of an FTA, there are: the Union of Industrials of Panama (SIP); Panamanian Insurance Association (APADEA); Panamanian Professional Association (FEDAP); Panamanian Export Association (APEX); National Union of Agricultural and Livestock Producers (UNPAP); National Association of Milk Producers (ANAPROLE); National Association of Business People Executives (APEDE); National Association of Cattle Growers (ANAGAN); and Banking Association (interviews with Alejandro Ferrer, DINECI, 29/07/2008; Joaquin Jácome, DINECI, 17/07/2008; Estif Aparicio, DINECI, 18/07/2008).[55]

The role of governmental institutions and agents: The role of conducting the negotiations as well as processing the inputs from domestic economic groups is part one the prerogatives of the Ministry of Trade and Industry. Within this ministry and below the minister there is the Vice-minister of International Trade, who is directly involved in all stages of the negotiations. The Vice-minister of International Trade serves as a chief negotiator, who sets the directives for the negotiation and coordinates the negotiation positions in the different issue-areas. There is also a director of economic negotiation below the chief negotiator. Under the direction of this director of economic negotiations there are different departments that prepare a negotiation and conduct this process by issue-areas organised in three pillars: market access; rules of origin and Customs procedures; and investment, services and other juridical issues.

The Ministry of Trade and Industry also coordinates the negotiation of positions with other ministries such as the Ministry of Agricultural Development (market access, rules of origin, and sanitary and phytosanitary measures), Ministry of Economics and Finances (industrial goods, financial services, services and investment), Ministry of Health (sanitary and phytosanitary measures), National Customs Agency (Customs issues and rules of origin), Superintendence of Banks of Panama (financial services), Superintendence of Insurance and Reinsurance of Panama (financial services), and the National Commission of Values (investment and financial matters); (see www.mici.gob.pa; interviews with Leda Arrue, DINECI, 17/07/2008, Diana Salazar, DINECI, 30/07/2008, Gabriela Diaz de Morales, Ministry of Agriculture, 28/07/2008).

55 Other relevant associations in the FTA negotiations are the National Association of Milk Processors, National Commission of Values, "Asociación Azucarera y Alcohol Panama" (AZUCALPA), National Association of Chicken Meat Producers (ANAVIP), National Association of Pork Meat Producers (ANAPOR), National Association of Rice Producers (ANALMO), Association of Producers, Processing and Exporters of Sea Products (APEXMAR), National Association of Cattle and Pork Sausages and Cold Meat (ANAFEREC), National Association of Milk Producers (ANAPROLE), Maritime Chamber of Panama (CMP), Panamanian Chamber of Commerce and Investment, Association of Business Owners within the Duty Free Area of Colon (AUZLC), and the Association of Producers of Tropical Exotic Fruits of Panama.

4.5 *Concluding Remarks*

The purpose of this chapter was to give a complete overview of the trade policy of each country, the previous trade negotiations each country conducted, and how the different actors articulate common positions to negotiate an FTA. To sum up, the three actors of this study had different levels of expertise in negotiating FTAs when they launched the negotiations between Panama and Chile, and Costa Rica and Panama. Even though Panama was the most inexpert, it was not amateur in negotiating trade accords. This suggests that neither amateur behaviour nor lack of experts were causes for the breakdown of these FTA negotiations. Moreover, it was highlighted in this chapter that the staff of negotiators from the three countries found their negotiating experience of low scope trade agreements more complex. For Panama, the accession to the WTO was also perceived more difficult and complicated than negotiating an FTA. Then: why did the FTA negotiations Chile-Panama and Costa Rica-Panama fail to achieve agreement? Answering this question by conducting an empirical analysis of each FTA negotiation process is the task I turn to in the following chapters.

5. The FTA Negotiation between Chile and Panama: Domestic Dimension

5.1 Introduction

The aim of this chapter is to explain the process of the negotiation between Chile and Panama and assess the conditions that brought this FTA negotiation to a stalemate. Here I analyse the domestic dimension of the negotiation (internal and external factors) that play a direct role in such a stalemate. Before focusing on the conditions that explain the breakdown of the negotiation, I give an overview of the process and I present the most sensitive issue-areas of the negotiation. I will show that problems in these sensitive areas caused the end of the talks between these two countries.

5.2 The Negotiation Process

The FTA negotiations between Chile and Panama were held from November 1996 to August 1998. The negotiation had 15 rounds (see Table 2: 116).[56] Chile opted to negotiate an FTA with Panama for political reasons rather than economic ones. Some of the leaders of the government coalition, "La Concertación", criticised Chile's excessive focus on a possible NAFTA accession, leaving aside a further economic integration in Latin America beyond the extant low scope trade agreements (Fermandois 2005). This tension was in part due to the overlapping of competencies between the Ministries of Finances and Foreign Affairs with regards to trade issues. The Ministry of Finances wanted to concentrate on an accession to NAFTA, and the Ministry of Foreign Affairs prioritised Latin America. "The program of the second government of the Coalition sought to clear up the alternative Latin America/NAFTA, by setting a priority on Latin America. Commercially, this priority

56 See Ferrer 2001: 226. There were two rounds in 1996, nine in 1997, and four in 1998. However, the last round was rather brief as the negotiation was already dead and the presidential power in Panama was weakened due to the referendum loss days before this presidential meeting. It seems that Chile, in their capacity as guest country, tried to give a symbolic gesture to Panama's president by manifesting its wish to conclude this accord in the future. Only authorities met during the presidential meeting and not the technical groups of negotiators in September 1998. The round that became the definitive stalemate of the negotiation was held the 13-14th of August 1998.

meant the signature of an accord with Ecuador (1995), and the launching of FTA talks with Peru and Panama" (van Klaveren 1998: 125).

The FTA negotiation with Panama was seen as easy to manage, and represented a good chance to start another round of integration on the continent after the highly politicised negotiation with MERCOSUR. Hence the political logic predominated, and displaced the economic rationale, which constrained the capacity to detect all the sensitive issues for the negotiation. A trade diplomat, describing the failure of this negotiation, explained that "We miscalculated the minimums and maximums in the negotiation with Panama" (Interview with Mario Matus, DIRECON, 28/02/2008).

Table 2: Formal Negotiation Rounds between Chile and Panama.

Rounds	**Date**
First	20-21 November 1996
Second	December 1996
Third	30-31 January 1997
Fourth	03-05 March 1997
Fifth	24-26 March 1997
Sixth	21-22 April 1997
Seventh	19-22 May 1997
Eight	06-08 June 1997
Ninth	15-16 June 1997
Tenth	10-12 October 1997
Eleventh*	20-22 October 1997
Twelfth	first weeks of March 1998
Thirteenth	(12) 13-15 June 1998**
Fourteenth	13-14 August 1998
Fifteenth	04 September 1998
Meeting of ministers, Insulza and Heras	10 September 1997
Meeting of Chile's undersecretary of ForeignAffairs with DINECI staff	13 February 1998
* Also presidential meeting	
** Not clear whether the round started the 12th or the 13th.	

Sources: Ferrer 2001: 226; FTA Chile-Panama's draft Text 24-26 March 1997; Minutes of the 4th and 5th rounds of negotiation; March 1997; *La Nación* 1996-1998, *El Mercurio* 1996-1998; *El Diario* 1996-1998, *La Prensa* 1996-1998, *El Panamá América* 1996-1998; interviews with negotiators from DIRECON-Chile, and DINECI-Panama.

Conversely, for Panama the FTA negotiation with Chile was its first experience in negotiating an FTA. Yet this does not mean that Panamanian trade diplomats were inexperienced in negotiating trade accords, as shown in the previous chapter of this work. Moreover, Panama was implementing its WTO membership. In its accession to the WTO, Panama's tariff ceiling was limited to 40 percent for goods (Ferrer 2001; Abrego 2000: 114-120). However, the then President Pérez Balladares passed a law in 1997 to speed up the reduction of the tariff ceiling to 15 percent (*Martes Financiero* 25/11/1997: 10-11; Ferrer 2001: 208). This law came into force in 1998, which meant an extra challenge for the negotiation with Chile, since the market access issue was already well advanced. Negotiators thus had to harmonise the goods already negotiated under the old tariff system with the new one (*El Panamá América* 22/11/97: E-3).

Panama chose to negotiate its first FTA with Chile because the latter was seen as a role model in terms of economic reforms. Panama also aimed for integration with the global economy, as well as an opportunity to learn how to negotiate these types of accords (interviews with Samuel Moreno, MICI, 22/07/2008; Melissa Davis, MICI, 17/07/2008; Estif Aparicio, MICI, 18/07/2008). Moreover, a former trade diplomat and then vice-minister of trade proposed that Panama should follow the Chilean path: "As I have said before, I recommend that negotiations be concentrated on free trade agreements with countries or existing FTA's, as Chile has done, rather than trying to go into deeper levels of integration" (Ferrer 2001: 228). This is confirmed by the then ambassador of Panama in Chile Mr. Bruno Garisto: "In my own opinion […] the experience of this accord with Chile is the underpinning for following FTA negotiations with other countries or regions, because no one can deny the leadership of the southern country" (*El Panamá América* 13/09/97: 5-C).[57] A further two factors that influenced the negotiation with Chile was the countries' low economic ties, and the fact that their economies were seen as complementary.[58]

An agreement with Chile was perceived, before the negotiation rounds were launched, as relatively easy to reach because of the low costs of adjustment for the different sectors of the economy (Interview with Manuel Ferreira, Chamber of Commerce-Panama, 25/07/2008). This misperception was based on the assessments of agricultural products as both countries saw potential complementarity between them. The misperception of possible complementarity on market access was based on the fact that Panama produces tropical agricultural products to export and Chile produces Mediterranean agricultural products. Nevertheless, this misperception has a certain logic as the most difficult issue to agree on in most FTA negotiations is agricultural products, especially the reduction of respective tariffs, despite the growing importance of NTB and of services in this kind of negotiation.

57 Author's translation.

58 In 1995 Chile exported to Panama 14.1 million US dollars and it only imported from Panama for 9.4 million US dollars (La Prensa 21/11/1996: 33a).

The formal negotiation process started in November 1996, although assessments and studies were conducted prior to this to ascertain the possibility of realising this FTA. Despite the fact that these studies are technically written, they are politically used to justify the need of opening trade negotiations with a specific country. These studies focus more on the overall gains for a country. Whereas these studies detect eventual losses they do not go in depth to assess the economic impact of such losses for specific economic sectors (interview with Roberto Pizarro, DIRECON, 25/03/2008).

The negotiation between Panama and Chile followed an easy development during the first rounds. The first round addressed the mode of negotiating i.e. in what order the issue-areas will be negotiated. Both countries decided to use the text of the negotiation between Canada and Chile as the core text for the FTA, although it was modified in order to adapt it to their respective economic contexts and trade relation (interview with Oscar Quina, DIRECON, 08/04/2008).

Despite the easy development of the negotiations during the first rounds, Panama asked from the beginning to include the issue-area of financial services as a topic to negotiate. Chile gave rather ambiguous signs of its willingness to negotiate such an issue-area. Whereas Panama wanted a parallel negotiation over market access and services, Chile convinced Panama to move these sensitive issue-areas to the last rounds by stating that financial services would not be left off the negotiation table (interviews with Diana Salazar, MICI, 30/07/2008; Melissa Davis, MICI, 17/07/2008; Samuel Moreno, MICI, 22/07/2008).[59] Moreover, Chile asked Panama to include the issue of professional services which was seen as one of the most sensitive sectors for Panama as there is a nationality requirement for foreigners to work in this country (Interviews with Carmen Paz Cortes, DIRECON, 25/03/2008; Catalina Bau, Ministry of Finances, 11/04/2008). By stating the need to negotiate professional services Chile was able to convince Panama to move the issue of financial and professional services as well as investment matters to the last rounds.

5.3 Domestic Factors

5.3.1 Divergent Interests

The conflictive issue-areas of the negotiation were concentrated in services, investment, and some agricultural products. Within the services area, those that jeopardised the negotiation were financial and professional services. Panama had an interest in including a chapter on financial services with clear rules to allow the free move-

59 This does not mean that the issue emerged in the last rounds. The sensitive issues were always there. The negotiators talked about the issues, discussed possibilities, and conducted analysis over these issues. However, both parties agreed to devoting exclusive attention to these issues at the end of the process.

ment of capital, its competitive off-shoring bank, and insurance sector (Interviews with Bosco Quintero and Carlos Berguido, APADEA, 18/07/2008). Conversely, Chile has a protected and regulated banking system that does not allow the operation of off-shoring societies. Moreover, Chile had a system that makes investors keep part of their investments in the Central Bank as a way to prevent capital flight and speculation i.e. *encaje system*. The main goal was to assure a liquid economy in times of economic turbulences or crises (Ffrench-Davis 2005: 347-366). Thus Chile had a strong defensive position on this issue.[60]

Chile's position on the financial system is based on past experiences. Chile had a severe economic crisis in 1981-1982, in which the banking sector collapsed, despite the government's bailouts to overcome the eventual bankruptcy and the lack of liquidity. The state took over five banks and closed another three. Chile fell into default with its external creditors and had to renegotiate its external debt (Teichman 2001: 77-84). In order not to create similar conditions that brought the financial institutions to bankruptcy in the 80s, Chile developed a regulatory framework in order to prevent speculative investments (Phillips 2004: 76-77).

Chile saw Panama's legislation on the banking sector and the investment regime as too liberal, especially because of its tolerance of investment that could come into the country without the state knowing the owner of such investment. Moreover, the public limited company regime in Panama also protects the identity of the holders of a company which makes it difficult to trace the origin of the money. According to Chilean legislation, every investment has to be backed up by the name of the institution making an investment as well as its owners. The specifics of the 'encaje' system (unremunerated reserve requirement) to prevent short term speculation operate in the following way: First, in order to assure a liquid economic system, part of the foreign direct investments should be in Chile for a minimum period of a year; such investment would not be subject to restrictions to move the capital out after this period.

60 This position has been made more flexible in recent years, after Chile negotiated with the US and agreed to change the 'encaje' from an anticipatory to a reactive measure in case of crisis (Fazio 2004). According to Hornbeck (2004: 55), Chile still has the right to re-impose its capital control laws, especially the Encaje law. Yet, US' investors can use the dispute settlement mechanism of the FTA to protect their investments in case Chile uses such laws under adverse economic circumstances. The encaje can be used for a year as stipulated in the FTA with the US (FTA Chile-US 2003). In practice, the encaje was not operating since 1998 as it was set to a 0 percent. The encaje was then eliminated in 2001 (Le Fort and Lehamann 2003: 35). Conversely, many analysts maintain that the 'encaje' was severely reformed due to US pressure to the extent that it was eliminated within the frame of the US-Chile FTA negotiations. Before, the encaje was active even when the economy was growing in order to prevent the attraction of speculative investment. Some analysts believe that this change from a preventive to a reactive nature of the encaje was intended to give US investors, the necessary time to move their capital out when there is symptoms of a crisis (see Fazio 2004: 138-144). Paradoxically enough, and despite its elimination, the encaje mechanism is still present in some FTAs, which were negotiated after 2001 such as that of Japan (FTA Chile-Japan 2007, Annex 8)

Second, commercial loans, deposits in foreign currency, loans associated with FDI and the emission of bonds have an 'encaje' of 30 percent of the total financial operations according to the regulations which were valid in 1998. This 30 percent is deposited in the Central Bank (Ffrench Davis 2005: 360).

So far the positions or interests of Chilean domestic actors such as the banking sector (ABIF, Superintendency of Banks, and insurances, Chilean Pension Fund Administrators' Association AFPs, and the Superintendency of AFPs) favoured keeping the status quo after an eventual negotiation with Panama. The reasons were those described above which in the most part can be summarised as the threat of offshoring societies and the threat of reduced restrictions on capital movements within Panama's legislation. The key ideas of this argument were also shared by the Chilean Central Bank and the Ministry of Finances. The latter also participated in the negotiation at the international level.

However, these were not the only concerns for these domestic actors. They also sought to postpone any negotiation on financial services with medium and small sized countries. These domestic groups as part of a national strategy were only thinking on an eventual negotiation on financial services with structural powers, which have the largest share of world trade i.e. the US and the EU. One of the main goals of Chile's FTA strategy was to achieve an FTA with the US which was the main trade partner in this period (1995-1998) (Silva 2001). Chile knew that the US or the EU would exert pressure to put the issue of financial services on the negotiation table. In this regard, Chile's logic was not to liberalise this sector until an agreement with the US was reached (Sáez and Sáez 2006). Chile was more concerned with the US than the EU in a negotiation over financial services as they saw the US as having a more liberal banking system than its European counterpart. Therefore, Chile adopted the position of waiting to negotiate first with the US over financial services in order to include this issue in other FTAs.[61]

Therefore, the interests of protecting the status quo on financial services was not only based on Chile's assumption that Panama has liberal and lax regulations, but also on the eventual loss of bargaining power on a subsequent negotiation especially with the US if the issue was to be included in the agreement with Panama. Moreover, Panama's domestic actors rejected the exclusive option of stating the mutual recognition of financial sectors and stating national treatment in each country. They also refused to comply with the domestic regulations for operating in one another's countries, as WTO regulations demand (see Ibid.:10, 17-18).[62] Panama also wanted the free movement of its capital investment in Chile in a similar way to the US approach on investment and financial services.

61 I return to this issue in the next chapter.

62 The WTO approach on financial services is to assure national treatment, to protect the investment, and to confirm one another's legislation, which produces a double charge of regulations that financial institutions should comply with (Sáez and Sáez 2006).

Another criticism from Chile's domestic actors, both public and private, concerned the speculative nature of the investments originated from Panama's financial sector, as the latter allowed free transfers of capital in the short term. However, adopting the Chilean regulatory system would require applying it to all external investment in Chile, so if any of the members of Panama's financial sector wanted to invest in Chile they would have to adopt the law of the Southern American country (interview with Cristina Farah, ABIF, 26/03/2008).

Panama's domestic actors' specific interests in services were already mentioned in the previous paragraphs, though in tacit way. At the risk of repeating the argument, I will briefly present the interests of Panama's domestic actors over the issue of services. Panama advocated including financial services in order to legitimise its banking system. Moreover, it also wanted to set a precedent for subsequent negotiations i.e. Panama negotiates FTAs if the issue of financial services and other services are constitutive part of such agreements.

Domestic actors related to this issue area included the Banking association, Panamanian Insurance Association (APADEA), National Association of Business People Executives (APEDE), National Commission of Values, Maritime Chamber of Panama (CMP), and the Panamanian Chamber of Commerce and Investment. All these groups converge on the idea of including a chapter of financial services and another one that frames the relationship over services and investment in general. However, there were differences amongst these domestic groups on the scope of these two chapters. On one hand, the Banking Association and Panamanian Insurance Association wanted a highly detailed and large scope chapter over financial services including matters over the provision of cross-border financial services. They primarily wanted their government to push Chile to liberalise its 'encaje system' in order to facilitate the movement and transference of capital in the short run, similar to the way that Panama off-shoring institutions operate. The Chamber of Commerce and Investment wanted a less ambitious chapter over financial services as it also wanted a good chapter on investment matters due to the diverse economic interests in its constituency. This is also the case for the National Association of Business People Executives (APEDE) which also has members working on services that are not part of the financial sector as such and members working on insurance and banking sectors (interviews with John and Irving Bennett, APEDE, 25/07/2008; Manuel Ferreira, Chamber of Commerce-Panama, 25/07/2008).

On the other hand, the Maritime Chamber of Panama (CMP) paid particular attention to getting a strong chapter on services, especially with regards to the issue of maritime services, as the shipping industry in this country was the second most important after banking (interview with CMP representative 04/08/2008). However, Chile's maritime sector was rather defensive on this negotiation as its interests may have been affected if Panama's shipping companies were allowed to locate in Chile under a favourable treatment (interview with Rene Muga, CPC, 07/04/2008).

Even though Panama's financial services sector wanted a chapter with a far reaching scope on the FTA with Chile, the lobbying to push through for its interests was not particularly intense, according to Panama's representatives of both the insurance and banking systems. They argued that they do not need FTAs as such, as their total revenues come from the benefits international and national banks have in Panama, and by attracting investors to Panama. Nevertheless they supported the FTA negotiation with Chile as it could have given them the opportunity to obtain more economic gains, although as Chile did not represent an attractive market as such for financial companies, such gains would be marginal. Moreover, they also supported the liberalisation process for ideological reasons and because banks would indirectly benefit if Panama producers were to export to Chile, as they would need access to credit (Interviews with Bosco Quintero and Carlos Berguido, APADEA, 18/07/2008; representative of the Banking association, 23/07/2008). In this regard, the Chilean banking and insurance lobby groups had an advantage as they were extremely defensive and they saw a real threat in Panama.

The then Chilean President Eduardo Frei (1998: 2) argued that an FTA negotiation should reflect the extant realities and sensitivities of each country. He also gives the example of the negotiation of Chile and MERCOSUR, which did not include services, in order to justify the Chilean lack of interest over this issue in the FTA with Panama. However, president Frei highlighted the diverse economic benefits that MERCOSUR has created for Chile, despite the lack of a chapter on services. At the same time Frei recognises the competitiveness of Panama's financial sector vis-à-vis Chile:

What happens is that, in these negotiations, we need to comprehend the extant realities of each country. There are countries that have progressed in some issues and other countries have progressed in other issues *–liberalisation.* For example, the MERCOSUR accord, which we signed last year, includes a rapid liberalisation in a diverse array of products, but at the same time, there are phase outs of 15 years for some agricultural products. In the concrete case of services, in order not to skip the question and we talked about it with the President of Panama, the issue, which impedes a final agreement such as services in general and financial services, is not only a problem in this negotiation it was also a sensitive issue with MERCOSUR. Yet this is also a sensitive issue in most FTA negotiations. Usually the most sensitive issues of a negotiation are services and agricultural products. With regards to services, Panama has progressed much more in a liberal system than Chile. However, Chile is also interested in following this path (ibid.).[63]

Panama's Labour code guarantees a nationality requirement that must be fulfilled in order for someone to work in Panama's professional services (Républica de Panamá-Código de Trabajo 2008). However, foreign professionals can work in Panama if they deliver temporary services in the form of consultancy and advice. Panama had a strong opposition to including the issue of professional services in the FTA, an opposition that came particularly from the Professionals Associations. These associations were even suspicious of their own government as they thought the latter wanted to liberalise this sector through FTA negotiations.

63 Author's translation.

Chile had an offensive position, since it sought to abolish the nationality requirement that Panama has in order to deliver professional services. The then Minister of Trade Alejandro Ferrer (2004-2008) stated that one of the causes of the stalemate in the negotiation in 1998 was the professional services issue-area, "in which there was a deep demand from Chile to accede to our market" (*Terra/EFE* 31/01/2006).[64] Panama's professional services association (FEDAP) had defended the status quo, which rejected the idea of eliminating the nationality requirement. FEDAP, which congregates around 25 sub-groups of professionals, argued that Panamanian professionals had a better level of wages than the Chilean ones. Moreover, this association also highlighted in its speeches to the media that Panama pays for professional services in dollars, which may be an attraction for possible Chilean professionals to relocate to Panama with the goal of working.

The then president of the Union of Lawyers stated that:

> This negotiation may jeopardise the level of wages in Panama, since Chile has a devaluated currency vis-à-vis the dollar. Therefore, when Chilean professionals come they will bring the wages down as they will offer to work for less money than Panamanian professionals due to the favourable conversion they have (*El Panamá América* 23/04/1997: C1).[65]

This argument was also posed by the representatives of FEDAP such as Hatuey Castro (21/07/2008) and Luis Cheng (21/07/2008) in interviews with them. Yet, Castro and Cheng also stated that they knew in advance that "the probability of Chilean professionals coming to Panama was relatively low". However, in the press they also argued that "Chile was a real threat for the professionals of Panama". This comparison between what they thought at the time of the negotiations and what they thought in 2008 when I conducted these interviews suggest that the main concern over liberalising the professional sector was not only and exclusively about Chile, but also about what was coming after the FTA with this South American country. The main concern was a subsequent possible negotiation with the Central America countries, which were considered Panama's natural trade partners due to the geographic proximity.Yet the level of wages of professionals in these countries were comparatively lower to those of Panama, which may trigger a growing migration of professionals to Panama (Interview with Hatuey Castro, FEDAP, 21/07/2008). Moreover, the Panamanian government did not have a fluid relation with FEDAP in the negotiation process as FEDAP predicted it would be used as a bargaining chip for the government in order to trigger more concessions in the Chilean financial service and market access sectors (*El Panamá América* 09/04/1997: C4).

In agricultural issues, the interests were less divergent than in services. Nevertheless, Panama sought to have more market access in beef and chicken meat, milk products, rice, coconut oil, melon, water melon and sugar. These were the open issues to close during the last rounds of the negotiation (*El Diario* 15/01/1998: 29). Moreover, national producers complained about Chile's price-band system on sugar

64 Author's translation.
65 Author's translation.

and wheat, and over the elaboration of food products for exportation in which the main inputs are sugar and wheat (Interview with Manuel Ferreira, Chamber of Commerce-Panama, 25/07/2008).

Chile's position on agricultural products, represented by the National Society of Agriculture (SNA), had a defensive position on products like beef, pork, chicken, turkey, dairy products, coconut oil and other types of oils, barley, oats, corn and unprocessed and processed sugar. These products were almost those same products that jeopardised the ratification of the agreement with MERCOSUR. The government had to implement generous programs of compensations and agricultural reconversion for traditional producers in order to assure ratification in Congress of the agreement with MERCOSUR (*La Epoca* 12/09/1996: 3B; interview with Luis Schmidt, SNA, 01/04/2008).

The initial position of the SNA in the negotiation with Panama was not to include the sensitive issues, and as a second best strategy the SNA was against liberalising these products on top of those that were already liberalised with MERCOSUR. The SNA thought that broadening market access for other countries may even put the reconversion process at stake. Yet the acceptance of the second best option in Chile's early FTAs, according to Luis Schmidt (SNA, 01/04/2008), Raúl Opitz (DIRECON,10/04/2008), and Carlos Furche (DIRECON,18/03/2008), had to be encouraged by speeding up the transfers of money promised as compensation in the MERCOSUR agreement.

Two interest groups, which are for pro-liberalisation of sugar and the price band system in general, were FEPACH[66] and AMBER. The members of these two associations had historically complained about the excessive costs they face when producing food products and beverages, as the government protects national producers of sugar and wheat through a band price system. According to ANBER, sugar consumers overpaid US$ 523 million between 1986 and 2003. 44 percent of this went to the national sugar industry (IANSA), which is the only national company that produces sugar and it is the only buyer of sugar beet. The sugar beet producers received 29 percent of the overpayment and the government 24 percent (ANBER 2005: 9, in Bolivar Ruiz et.al. 2005).

Panama is a sugar producer, although a small one in the world market. Therefore, the negotiating parties have divergent views. On the one hand, the Chilean government wanted to keep restrictions on the sugar importation regime and did not give concessions to its negotiating counterparts. On the other hand, ANBER and FEPACH wanted not only the liberalisation of sugar as input for their production, but also a better market access for their products in the counterpart's market. Then FEPACH president stated with regards to the FTA negotiation with Panama that "[...] we want to get to this country, to stay in this market and not become a stock

66 FEPACH does no longer exist. FEPACH associates and other food producers became members of Chile Alimentos.

business as we are now" (Callario 27/02/1997).[67] Food producers maintained that every time Chile negotiates with a sugar producer country, the government will have to restrict its position on market access for sugar based food products as the government will not accede to grant preferential treatment to the other country on the products which belong to the band price system (Interviews with Jaime Gatica, ANBER, 01/04/2008; Rene Muga, CPC, 07/04/2008).

Panama's sugar producers were unhappy with Chile's demand to exclude sugar from the negotiation (interviews with representative of AZUCALPA, 28/07/2008; Gabriela Diaz de Morales, Ministry of Agriculture, 30/07/2008). Moreover, Panama's government wanted to at least include quotas for its sugar producers (interview with Diana Salazar, MICI, 30/07/2008; Melissa Davis, MICI, 17/07/2008). Chile's position was to exclude sugar from the agreement, but its demand for better treatment for its sugar-based food producers created a source of conflict within the negotiation. Panama asked Chile for immediate liberalisation, whereas Chile put sugar on the exclusion list. In addition, on the items of food products such as cookies, biscuits, juices, powder juices and sweets, Chile asked for immediate liberalisation and Panama asked to exclude them (FTA Chile-Panama's draft text, 24-26 March 1997). Panama asked for exclusion on these food products in order to counterbalance Chile's position of excluding sugar. If Chile was willing to give certain concessions, Panama was willing to give a better treatment on Chile's food products which use sugar in their production process (interviews with Diana Salazar, MICI, 30/07/2008; Samuel Moreno, MICI, 22/07/2008; Leda Arrué, MICI, 17/07/2008; Melissa Davis, MICI, 17/07/2008; Alejandro Ferrer, MICI, 29/07/2008).Whereas divergence on this issue alone does not stall a negotiation, it reduces the win-set of a negotiation if this issue is taken along with other highly divergent issues such as services and financial services.

To sum up, the interests at the domestic level in each country were highly divergent in issue-areas that are conceived as strategic for the respective national economies, such as services, and those traditional areas such as the aforementioned agricultural products. The liberalisation of these sectors is a costly decision to assume for any government. The difficulties with reconciling one another's interests to satisfy domestic actors were seen as contributing significantly to the negotiation stalemate.

In addition, there is also the contributing factor of divergence over interests between the government and their own domestic actors in the case of professional services. The divergence of interests was due to the fact that Panama was willing to satisfy Chilean demands with some changes on its professional sector in exchange for more market access and a better deal on financial services. In the case of agriculture, Chilean government was not willing to give concessions to Panama in sugar against the opposition of ANBER and FEPACH. Yet this position of excluding the products that are part of the band price system was highly supported by the SNA. As

67 Author's translation.

it has been argued "Free trade policies create winners and losers", and in an FTA negotiation there are certain issues that may be liberalised against the will of domestic actors to make possible a final agreement that creates overall gains for the national economy.

However, these evident high divergences do not entirely explain the stalemate of the negotiation as most negotiations have them, which are solved by package deals and side payments. Although these divergences over interests help us to understand the difficulties of reaching agreement, the reduction of the zone of agreement, and the time extension of the negotiation, it does not provide a complete picture for the reasons for such a failure in this FTA negotiation. Therefore, interests are not alone in causing stalemate; they have to be put on a multi-factor perspective to comprehend what brought both countries to the end the FTA talks.

5.3.2 Job Insecurity

The fear of losing jobs was especially salient for the union of professionals FEDAP, which saw a threat in the FTA with Chile. They saw the negotiation over professional services as a way to bring competition into the system that was protected by law. The union of professionals framed the issue as an attempt of the government to deepen its neoliberal model and trigger an internal reform by pursuing an FTA negotiation. Therefore, FEDAP presented the idea of including this issue in the FTA negotiation with Chile as a threat to Panama's sovereignty and the economic well being of its people (*La Prensa* 15/11/1997: 5 A).

If the data on unemployment is analysed in the period between 1995 and 1999, it is possible to appreciate a certain stability in the level of unemployed people despite the decreasing numbers (see table 3).

Table 3: Unemployment index in Panama (1988-1999) (%)*

1988	1989	1991	1992	1993	1994	1995	1996	1997	1998	1999
16.3	16.3	16.0	14.7	13.3	14.0	14.0	14.3	13.4	13.6	11.8

* There is no official data available for 1990.
Source: Dirección de Estadística y Censo-Panama (2001: 266)

These numbers suggest that the neoliberal package introduced by the governments in Panama did not increase the unemployment and the effectiveness of such reforms to create jobs was rather marginal. The marginal reduction of the unemployment also suggests that the Panamanian economy had a structural problem that impedes the entrance of people of the working age into the labour market. Moreover, the level of unemployment has to be linked to the fact that workers in Panama felt the threat of liberalisation and the possible incoming wave of foreign workers. They also observed that if their sectors were to be exposed to external competition the chances of getting new possibilities to re-enter the labour market was restricted as the economy was not able to absorb incoming professionals and blue-collar workers, despite the economic growth of the country.

However, this overall view of the labour sector does not necessarily represent the reality of the FTA negotiation. In this regard, FTA negotiation threatened the professionals in Panama. Yet this sector framed the situation as a national problem and it linked the issue of liberalising its sector through an FTA to the rather marginal benefits of the neoliberal reforms and the costs of the adjustment measures.[68] The constitutional referendum in Panama in 1998 and the subsequent presidential elections campaigns were articulated around the issue of economic reforms as well as the benefits and costs the model was bringing to the Panamanian median voter. In fact, the defeat of President Pérez Balladares in the referendum in 1998, and the triumph of Mireya Moscoso in the presidential race in 1999 were partly based on the continuous references to the socio-economic costs of the model (Adames Mayorga 2001; Harding 2006; Sánchez 2007; Jované 2003).

On the Chilean side, the fear of losing jobs with this FTA was lower. The impact of the job insecurity was lower than in Panama as the actors that felt possibly jeopardised in the negotiation were the sugar beet producers and the state company IANSA.[69] However, IANSA and the sugar beet growers felt relatively calm about this FTA negotiation as the government was willing to keep the status quo for its sectors as well as for the rest of the agricultural products that were protected through the band price system (Jana 2005: 177-178). More than feeling a threat from Panama's competitiveness, the traditional agricultural producers felt the threat from FTAs in general. The difficult experience for this group in the negotiation with MERCOSUR, made them less keen on supporting this type of accord, unless their most sensitive products were protected through exclusions, quotas and long term phase out schemes. In fact they asked the government to protect the products mentioned above; otherwise, ratification would have been an issue (Interview with Luis Schmidt, SNA, 01/04/2008).

Even though Chile agreed to open its sugar industry through a phase out period of 16 years with MERCOSUR, it protected this industry in subsequent trade accords, as well as the rest of the products in the price band system by refusing to negotiate these issues, and/or to put them in similar schemes as those of the negotiation with MERCOSUR as a second best option. The idea was to use the products in the band price system along with financial services as bargaining chips in the negotiation to join NAFTA. In the case of MERCOSUR, the sugar issue was beginning to be liber-

68 I come back to this issue in the following sections.

69 Workers in financial services did not feel a real threat from a liberalising option. On the contrary, the overall position, beyond a particular negotiation, was that incoming banks located in Chile tend to create job places (Interview with Cristina Farah, ABIF, 26/03/2008).

alised after 11 years. In other words, MERCOSUR countries had an initial access in 2007 with a reduction of 17 percent in the tariffs, 33 percent in 2008, 50 percent in 2009; these countries would also have access through a reduction of 67 percent in 2010, 83 percent in 2011, and 100 percent in 2012 in order to complete the 16 years of transition (Jana 2005: 178).

In conclusion, the job insecurity issue was strong on Panama's side and low in Chile. Although job insecurity, and the economic transformations taking place in Panama did not stall the negotiation, understanding the increasing level of politicisation of the negotiation as well as the role this issue played in the electoral process is a 'sine qua non'. As neither job-insecurity nor divergent interests explain the stalemate alone, despite their partial explanatory power, they have to be understood along with the politicisation level (electoral process), and the free riding options of domestic pro-market actors. I analyse these elements in the following sub-sections.

5.3.3 Politicisation

The politicisation of the negotiation was triggered by FEDAP, and by a parallel game, in which the FTA negotiation was caught due to the extension of the talks with Chile, produced by the divergent positions over the issue-areas previously presented. On the Chilean side the politicisation level was not an issue at all and to some extent the controversies between the government and domestic groups were associated with the agreement with MERCOSUR that made the SNA reluctant to accept new FTAs that include conditions beyond those agreed in that accord.[70]

The parallel game that increased the politicisation level in Panama concerned the aspiration of President Pérez Balladares to amend the constitution through a referendum in order to be re-elected for a second consecutive term. FEDAP created in part the conditions to polarise the FTA negotiation with Chile at the domestic level. However, the presidential call for a referendum at the beginning of 1998 to be formally conducted at the last day of August of that year became an important source of politicisation. The referendum campaign affected the course of the negotiations and empowered FEDAP as a lobby group during the development of the talks between Panama and Chile, especially during 1998.[71]

The referendum in Panama concerning a re-election amendment vote also became an opportunity for the opposition to mobilise different groups of civil society to vote against the government's trade policy. This referendum process was also used by

70 I only mentioned the low level of politicisation in Chile as it seems to be the case that politicisation in this country did not play a major role in the outcome of the agreement. Therefore, the focus of this section is mainly on Panama's internal process.

71 The role of elections or in this case a referendum will be developed in detail in the next sub-section, 5..3.3.1 Elections, so here I only mentioned that the referendum played a role and how it played a role in a brief way.

FEDAP to increase the pressure on the government negotiators with regards to the FTA with Chile. Even though the overlapping of the FTA negotiation and the referendum was not planned as such in Panama, it was used for domestic groups and political parties to realise their economic and electoral aspirations.

The governments of Panama and Chile expected to complete the FTA negotiation by mid-1997, which would not have posed any problem for the referendum or for the FTA negotiation.[72] However, the extension of the negotiation due to the politicisation level and the high divergences on key issues during the talks between both countries made possible this undesired overlapping. This overlapping constrained not only the capacity to move the negotiation forward, but also hampered the overall agenda-setting capacity of the government of Panama.

Although FEDAP's representatives participated in the initial consultation of the FTA negotiation, they left the table in order to not back up the negotiation process. Tactically it was more convenient for them to be outside the negotiation between the government and the interest groups. Outside the negotiation table they were able to mobilise and refuse to recognise a final agreement that might include their area of interest. The politicisation was increased through lobbying congressmen to impede a ratification of the FTA if the issue of professional services was included, and by going to the streets to show FEDAP's discontent.

> We stepped back from the negotiation because our name was being used to say we were participating and supporting the negotiation, but to be sincere we were the 'unwanted guests' in the process (Carrizo in *El Panamá América* 23/05/1997: C2).[73]

The professional associations had the conviction that Chile was pursuing a rather offensive strategy to liberalise this sector in Panama (interview with Luis Cheng, FEDAP, 21/07/2008). Although in many occasions the Chilean Ambassador stated that professional services will not be included as such, the professional associations did not take these statements as valid (*La Prensa* 05/05/1997: 2 A; *El Panamá América* 23/05/1997: C 1). The reason is that some of Panama's negotiators used a confusing rhetoric over the issue: "[...] No Chilean professionals can come here tomorrow to work because, they will first have to fulfil the national criteria to get residence permissions" (*El Panamá América* 05/05/1997: C5). "Professionals will have to fulfil the migratory and labour laws" (*Martes Financiero* 08/07/1997: 2).[74] Although what the negotiator or government representative intended to say in this quote was that professionals will be protected by other national law, the government also kept the option open for the negotiators to remove the nationality clause to work in Panama. Nevertheless, both countries wanted to facilitate the delivery of professional services in form of consultancy. Yet negotiators in principle agreed in includ-

72 After the self-imposed deadlines to conclude the negotiations in May and June, the negotiators established November as a new deadline which was also moved to 1998 due to the difficulties with closing a deal.

73 Author's translation.

74 Author's translation.

ing an annex to set minimum standards for the recognition of university diplomas (*El Panamá América* 01/07/1997: C1). According to FEDAP the idea of working on minimum standards were also problematic as the University of Panama homologates diplomas without mayor assessments for Panamanians who studied abroad. If this principle is applied to foreigners with universities studies from abroad it could create competition problems and the displace of national professionals. Therefore, the nationality requirement was essential to prevent incoming workers from Chile and elsewhere (interview with Hatuey Castro, FEDAP, 21/07/2008; Luis Cheng, FEDAP, 21/07/2008).

Moreover, the lack of trust that FEDAP had towards the government negotiators also played a role in politicising the negotiation. This lack of trust was not only based on the ambiguous rhetoric negotiators used over this sector. This lack of trust is also based on the past experience and the ideological commitment that Pérez Balladares' Presidency had over a market economic model. Although Panama excluded professional services from the WTO liberalisation package (Ferrer 2001), the professional services actors knew that their sector was to be included in a liberalisation process sooner or later.

As a former negotiator of Panama (anonymous interview 25/07/2008), and a representative of FEDAP both suggested (Luis Cheng, FEDAP, 21/07/2008), one of the only possibilities to liberalise professional services would be through an international agreement rather than a pure unilateral decision that will have to be negotiated between domestic actors with the considerable erosion and possible stalemate of the government legislative agenda. What they intended to create was the need of ratifying an accord that included professional services, but that also included major benefits for the economic sectors of the national economy. Government officials agreed that negotiating professional services to trigger the willingness of Chile to put financial services on the table will be a major win for Panama, which might have allowed a swing of support in Congress from the professional services interests to those of the government FTA agenda (Interviews with Melissa Davis, MICI, 17/07/2008; Diana Salazar, MICI, 30/07/2008).

The major win was based on the fact that Panama has other legislation to control eventual flows of foreign professionals such as immigration laws and the application process to assess the equivalence of the education of foreigners with that of Panama. In other words, the negotiators of Panama thought that the removal of the nationality requirement would be cosmetic rather than real as FEDAP will still have other legal mechanisms to be protected from external competition. As the then Ministry of Finances Miguel Heras stated:

> In order to be in Panama, first a Chilean worker needs to fulfil the legal migratory regime. In other words, a Chilean worker will need to apply for permanent residency and working permission at the Immigration Office, which is not easy at all (*La Prensa* 05/05/1997: 2A).[75]

75 Author's translation.

FEDAP perceived the problem in a different way from the government, as it had the conviction that other laws may be easy to change in the future if the nationality requirement would be removed in an FTA negotiation. They also knew that it was only necessary for one FTA to liberalise its sector as Panama was planning to negotiate more FTAs. Here it is important to show the level of knowledge FEDAP had over the issue of FTAs as they knew that future FTAs may include professional services only if the negotiators granted an MFN treatment clause on this issue to advance the liberalisation on this sector.

Therefore, FEDAP could anticipate the direction of the negotiation a great deal and also knew through informal channels that putting the issue on the negotiation table due to the Chilean insistence was also inevitable (Interviews with Hatuey Castro, FEDAP, 21/07/2008; Luis Cheng, FEDAP, 21/07/2008). As they were informed on what was coming FEDAP was able to take preventive measures to block the eventual liberalisation of their economic sector. These actors were able to articulate a strong strategy to oppose the government FTA negotiation with Chile by creating simple messages for the population with regards to the government economic policy as a whole and how this rush to adopt a neoliberal model was eroding the social bases of Panamanian population. In other words, the professional services actors which include rather powerful sectors such as medical doctors, lawyers, engineers, economists, veterinarians, and school teachers, were capable of linking one FTA negotiation with the trade policy of the country, and in that way achieve a certain level of support for their cause of resisting their status as a bargaining chip for the FTA negotiation.

> For FEDAP, as it has been proved to the public opinion, the behaviour of our government with regards to the inclusion of the liberal professions in the FTA negotiation with the Republic of Chile is against the national interest. Therefore, this Federation as it has already expressed to the pertinent governmental officials, DENOUNCE to the country that signing such agreement under such adverse conditions for the national interest will severely affect the highest interest of our nation (FEDAP in *El Panamá América* 25/08/1997: C2).[76]

This kind of publication was part of the strategy to politicise the negotiation as the formal talks with Chile were undergoing. This strategy also included demonstrations on the streets and in front of the Chilean embassy (*La Tercera* 28/08/1997: 24), lobbying Legislators to send signals of non-ratification, lobbying political parties from the opposition, and the use of newspapers and TV to state their positions on FTA processes both in general and with regards to Chile in particular. The mobilisation of FEDAP against the FTA negotiation with Chile also made the Chilean diplomats jump into the debate in Panama. They attempted to calm down the situation, but used rather unfortunate phrasings with regards to FEDAP members. For example, the then Chilean Ambassador in Panama, Mr. Eduardo Ormeño, referred to the complaints of FEDAP about the possibility of Chileans coming to work in Panama in the following way:

76 Author's translation.

> If we analyse realities and not fantasies *–in clear reference to FEDAP-* we can see that in 1996 five thousand foreign workers came to Chile to work; and this is because the economic development of the country needs it….In consequence if we are here to talk about immigration of professionals it is more logical to think that Panamanians may migrate to Chile rather than the other way around (*La Prensa* 09/06/1997: 35A).[77]

The words of this Chilean representative were taken by FEDAP representatives and also by government representatives as arrogant and unfortunate for diplomats as they contributed to the increased perception in Panama's public opinion that professional services were being negotiated between both countries (interviews with Luis Cheng, FEDAP, 21/07/2008; Hatuey Castro, FEDAP, 21/07/2008; anonymous, 26/07/2008; Manuel Ferreira, Chamber of Commerce-Panama, 25/07/2008). Moreover, Chilean diplomats participated indirectly in internal political affairs with their own declarations, which only frustrated the Panamanian government. Such words also helped to increase the public's and the opposition political parties' sympathy for FEDAP's goal, as it looked to the rest of civil society as though the government was not fulfilling its role of defending the interest of Panamas' workers.

> If the government is not defending the interests of professionals with degrees from University, what else could we expect for blue collar workers and other sectors of the economy which are displaced as organisations from the political arena? This was the message we tried to put in the public debate. Here we were helped by the referendum in which we demonstrated against the government along with trade unions and other social groups (Interview with Hatuey Castro, FEDAP, 21/07/2008).[78]

The then President of FEDAP, Augusto César Castillo, made the following comment about the results of the referendum in 1998 in which the government lost:

> […] It reflects the unhappiness of the big national majority as a consequence of an economic pattern whose benefits are not yet perceived. Moreover, the sectors that have been more threatened with the model are blue collar workers, agricultural producers, native communities, professionals, public servants, teachers and industrial producers. They have not received any compensation from the government in order to repair the damage that the government has made with its decisions (in *El Panamá América* 04/09/1998).[79]

The messages in the press to cause a blockage to the FTA negotiation were rather harsh on negotiators and ministers in charge of conducting the FTA process. This rhetoric was answered in a rather passionate way by the ministers, especially the Minister of Finances Mr. Miguel Heras, who acted as a spokesperson on this negotiation. The government's counters sometimes had a hard tone, which benefited the cause of FEDAP to attract sympathetic support from civil society and affected the

77 Author's translation. Words in cursive added by the author of this work. There were similar words from Chilean diplomats according to an anonymous trade diplomat (26/07/2008). Chilean trade diplomat, Oscar Quina, after the negotiation stalled, described the position taken by medical doctors on the eventual removal of the nationality clause to work in Panama and on the hypothetical scenario that Panama will be invaded by doctors from Chile as "pathetic" (La Prensa 22/11/1998: 33A).

78 Author's translation.

79 Author's translation.

government negotiating agenda. FEDAP's mobilisation and rhetoric against the economic model as well as the answers from the government tended to escalate the politicisation level in a similar way to the spiral effects of hard bargaining.

The then Minister of Finances, Miguel Heras stated with regards to the non-participation of the association in the dialogue between negotiators and private sectors, that : "it is extremely irresponsible what this group is doing" (*El Panamá América* 01/07/1997: C1). He also said: "we have invited this association to talk, but apparently there is a group within FEDAP that only wants to complain through media. This association has an extremely intransigent and harmful position, which is sad because they could contribute a lot to the process" (*La Prensa* 23/05/1997: 21 A).[80] This type of rhetoric increased the gap between both sides. In fact, FEDAP and the government kept a tough dialogue through the press and media rather than through private channels.

To sum up, the politicisation level due to FEDAP's mobilisation to prevent and impede the liberalisation of its sector would in the negotiation with Chile played a decisive role in producing the failure of the negotiations. The politicisation level constrained the room to manoeuvre within the negotiation at the international level as the media were now intent on knowing the details of an international negotiation that is traditionally a closed process. Due to the lobbying of FEDAP, the Congress threatened to not ratify the FTA if the agreement with Chile was unbalanced and did not benefit all groups. FEDAP's articulation of clear messages as well as the intended provocations to make the government officials respond publicly over the course of the negotiations benefited the cause of this association of professionals. In addition, the internal dynamics of the negotiation over sensitive issue-areas, produced an extension and delay in the process, which was caught in an electoral year.

5.3.3.1 Elections

As previously discussed, in 1998 Panama witnesses a call for a referendum to amend the constitution to make the re-election of serving presidents possible. This call became a direct influence on the FTA negotiation between Chile and Panama. The political debate was highly focused on linking the referendum to the evaluation of the trade policy of the government (Gandásegui 1998, Sánchez 2007, *El Panamá América* 04/05/1997: B4).

The Congress, controlled by the president's party the PRD, approved a preliminary text for a constitutional reform and on 18 May 1998 the executive called for a referendum to be held in August of that year (*Gaceta Oficial Panamá*, 20/05/1998: no. 23546). However, the discussion of a possible constitutional reform had been debated since February 1997 (Rodriguez 1997: 4A). Though, as I argued above, the negotiating teams expected to have an agreement by May or June 1997, this became

80 Author's translation.

impossible to achieve due to the high divergence in the investment and services matters as well as in some agricultural products. The negotiators therefore moved the date to conclude the negotiation to September and then once again to November 1997 (*La Prensa* 24/10/1997: 31 A).[81]

By calling a referendum in 1998, Pérez Balladares automatically triggered an electoral race one year before it was supposed to be started, as the presidential elections were scheduled for 1999. The political parties sped up their proposal of presidential candidates as they knew the government would use the referendum as a political platform to legitimate its work and to initiate an electoral campaign for the re-election. Although some parties did not have a chance in the presidential race, they nominated their candidates and made them campaign in order to use the eventual voting support as a bargaining tool to negotiate with their possible allies in a coalition for the presidency (Gandásegui 1998).

Candidates opposing the government such as Mireya Moscoso, representing the Partido Panameñista -also known as Arnulfista Party-, and the outsider movement *Movimiento Nacional por la Soberanía del Pueblo* (with a diverse constituency of Labour Unions such as the "Central Nacional de Trabajadores de Panamá" (CNTP), the "Federación Nacional de Servidores Públicos" (FENASEP), and FEDAP) used a strong discourse against the economic model implemented under Pérez Balladares. Mireya Moscoso encouraged voters to vote for the 'no' option to impede the presidential re-election: "The poor people are getting poorer and the wealthy wealthier [...] The current government is governing for a small group of powerful men and not for the wide needy majority of this country" (in *La Prensa* 07/07/1998: 2 A).[82] Even the candidate Alberto Vallarino, who was coming from the financial world and representing a faction of the Arnulfista party, used a critical tone against the economic reforms of the government by calling for more emphasis on social policies and more state intervention (Harding 2006).

It seems that the articulation of a message against the economic policy, even for eventual pro-market politicians such as Alberto Vallarino was the only choice that would make their campaign gain electoral support.[83] The reason is that the voters that favoured market oriented reforms were likely to support the re-election of Pérez Balladares. In the case of Mireya Moscoso, the faction of the political party that she represented for both the referendum and the subsequent election in 1999 was traditionally linked to represent a popular base. The components of state intervention and strong social policies, at least in the message but not necessarily in practice, were

81 Yet four rounds and many informal talks were also conducted in 1998 to conclude the negotiations.

82 Author's translation.

83 "Vallarino is trying to make us believe is not a market oriented guy by using discourse on social policies" (González Henríquez 2001: 145). Author's translation.

beneficial to obtain the electoral support that in fact brought her to be the first female President in Panama in the period 1999-2004.[84]

In her victory speech before 25.000 supporters in Panama's national stadium, she pledged to eradicate social injustice and poverty. She also promised to review and possibly reverse some of the policies begun under Pérez Balladares, including the privatization of Panamanian state industries (Harding 2006: 130).

Therefore, every sensitive issue of foreign economic relations and internal economic affairs was subject to use for electoral purposes, constraining the power of initiative and execution in the policy-making of the government. In other words, the electoral process in Panama played a major role in bringing the negotiation to a standstill and in preventing the re-launching of it. Talking of and promoting the benefits of signing an FTA became unpopular for the government, and the costs of concluding the FTA negotiation with Chile became higher than expected. The government started to lose interest in pushing harder to conclude the negotiations. In addition, the government calculated that the extant electoral climate would have made the ratification another political problem for the government, with or without the issues of investment and services in the agreement (Gandásegui 1998: 16-20).

The results of the referendum became a final strike for the negotiation with Chile, since some Chilean and Panamanian negotiators and government representatives believed last attempts to conclude the FTA should be pursued. The then President Pérez Balladares lost the referendum which weakened its mandate and its capacity to continue with its economic reforms (Ferrer 2001: 179). Option 'yes' (acceptance of a presidential re-election for Pérez Balladares) received only 34.64 percent of the vote, and option 'no' received 64.31 percent (IFES Election Guide, Panama). Therefore, the possibility of launching a new round of negotiation with Chile disappeared because of the lack of popular support and the loss of control over the legislative agenda. Not only would the opposition have blocked the agreement, but it would also have blocked Perez Balladares' own coalition in Congress, whose representatives were also seeking re-election.

The then President Pérez Balladares (31/08/1998) referred to the electoral process and his defeat in the referendum in the following terms:

> For me it is always a motive of satisfaction to hear the voice of the people, and indeed we heard it. The nation of Panama has decided not to give itself the rights we have proposed [...] We accept this outcome with humility and with good will [...] I am also sorry that the referendum about constitutional reforms became an early presidential electoral competition, but today it is a day in which the nation won as its democracy is on a path towards strong consolidation.[85]

84 Once in office Mireya Moscoso continued implementing neoliberal policies, as with her predecessor, either for conviction or the external pressure exerted by the US, the IMF and the World Bank.

85 Author's translation.

The candidate appointed to run the electoral race for president in the PRD instead of Pérez Balladares was Martin Torrijos. In order to make the election of Torrijos possible and to keep a strong representation in Congress, Pérez Balladares tried to put a special emphasis on short-term social policies and also brought economic reforms to standstill, especially the planned privatization of water and social security (Adames Mayorga 2001: 26; see also Jované 2003). The presidency thus lost the momentum and power of initiative to conduct the economic policy of the country.

Within this scenario, the option of concluding the FTA with Chile did not have a chance as the government had to show a rapid shift in its in priorities if it wanted to position Martin Torrijos as a candidate with chances to win. Despite the fact that Torrijos lost the presidential race with 37 percent vis-à-vis 45 percent for the winning candidate Mireya Moscoso, by freezing liberal economic polices such as FTAs and further privatisations measures as well as by appealing to the personal attributes of each candidate, the PRD was able to maintain 33 out of 72 seats in Congress. The incoming governing Arnulfista Party won only 11 seats (Harding 2006: 129).

In this context of electoral processes, the FTA negotiation with Chile became a second priority during the campaign for the referendum. The existence of high divergent issues, which turned the negotiation into a zero-sum process, and the level of politicisation, acted as causes to slow down the negotiation. After the referendum there is no evidence of official attempts to revive the negotiation with Chile, nor did Chile push for reviving the negotiation with Panama as the Chilean negotiators did not want to include investment matters and financial services in the way proposed by Panama. In fact, Chile left the negotiation table on 14th August, two weeks before the referendum. Moreover, Chile's maintenance of a hard bargaining attitude was also taken by Panama as an indicator that Chile did not care that much about losing the agreement, and in fact Chile was the first country to leave the table.

The lack of interests in reviving the negotiation on Panama's side was partly because Chile used a rather tough bargaining to protect its position in the financial services and investment issues, and pushed extremely hard to liberalise professional services.[86] In addition, Chile was also coming to an electoral year. Chile was having elections in December 1999, and the Chilean government generally try to avoid negotiating commercial accords during election years in Chile or in the counterpart (interviews with Carlos Furche, DIRECON, 18/03/2008; Jorge Leiva, former Minister of Economy, 19/03/2008; Osvaldo Rosales, DIRECON, 19/03/2008; Marcela Klein, Ministry of Finances, 24/03/2008; Andrés Rebolledo, DIRECON, 25/03/2008). In light of this, I asked the same trade experts why the negotiation with Panama was continued in 1998 even though Panama was in an electoral year. The answers were rather similar, albeit with different emphasis: 'the negotiation was advanced enough to leave it even during an election'.

86 These issues will be analysed further in the next chapter which deals with the intergovernmental negotiation.

Although the electoral process in Chile was in 1999, the Chilean government was afraid that politicians running for Congress as well as the presidential candidate of the opposition could revive the issue of the outcome of MERCOSUR for agricultural producers as a source of politicisation, which may have had spill over effects on the ongoing and forthcoming FTA processes. Sensitive agricultural products were liberalised in the MERCOSUR agreement (Muchnik and Errazuriz: 1998: 406-409). The most sensitive items were mainly put on the list of those products to be liberalised in 15, 16 or 18 years. Yet MERCOSUR countries obtained certain quotas for beef and rice before the liberalisation period was over (ACE 35 Chile-MERCOSUR 1996: Annexes 2, 3, 5, 6, 7, 8 and 9).

Agricultural producers and their representatives in Congress -*Bancada Agricola*- which goes from the right to the left of the political spectrum, complained that the quotas given to MERCOSUR were endangering the local production, the reconversion plans and the programs to develop more competitiveness within these areas. Moreover, the side payments for agricultural producers i.e. compensation funds were not transferred or allocated as quickly as expected:

> The SNA is worried about the way the 500 million dollars, which were granted to this sector due to the signature of MERCOSUR accord, are being distributed. In general, the allocation of these resources is being distributed without a technical criterion, since the giving of money is for the rural and subsistence agriculture rather than for the commercial agriculture (*El Campesino* 1998: 46).[87]

Thus Chile did not overcharge its international trade agenda during 1999 because of the presidential race. This prevented the revival of negotiation with Panama and meant that another would only be launched if it was certain to be concluded rapidly.

5.3.4 Pro-FTA groups' Free-riding Option

The pace of the negotiation started to slow down in the second part of 1997, and during 1998. The aforementioned explanatory factors were key issues in slowing down the progress of the negotiation and in making pro-FTA groups lobby their governments to begin negotiations with countries whose trade exchange was more significant. Due to the time extension of the negotiation, and the perceived lack of political will, Panama's and Chile's pro-FTA groups started to focus on relevant markets such as Central America and the US in both cases, and also the EU in the case of Chile (SOFOFA Memories 1997-1998 and 1998-1999; interviews with John and Irving Bennett, APEDE, 25/07/2008). According to representatives of interest groups in Panama that favoured an open economy, Central America was more relevant, and the transport costs were lower than those to export to Chile,

87 Author's translation.

> We of course supported the negotiation with Chile but the enthusiasm was not that high partly because of the opposition and elections, and because many of our associates saw diffuse net gains in it. This was mainly due to the high transport costs that are involved if you want to send products to that market, while Mercosur countries with which some of our products should have competed were much lower. Mercosur already had a privileged access to Chile due to the accord they signed the year before our negotiations were launched. It was a matter of geographical distance (interview with Victor Cruz, SIP, 16/07/2008).[88]

In Panama, lobby groups pushing to open other negotiations, especially with the US and/or Central America after the new government of Mireya Moscoso came to power in 1999, were understood to want no more effort, time or economic resources to be put into this process with Chile. However, evidence of how pro-FTA groups started to lose interest in the negotiation with Chile can be traced back at least to May-June of 1997, as the formal talks extended beyond what was expected and the politicisation level and the electoral process increased. These months were when both countries expected to conclude the negotiation process. In other words, the time delay of the negotiations may have acted as a clear indicator that negotiations at the international level were becoming difficult to sustain as both countries started to use distributive bargaining over the sensitive issues. In addition, the pro-market domestic groups were participating in the next room, which means they could monitor what was going on in the intergovernmental negotiation (Interview with Bosco Quintero, and Carlos Berguido, APADEA, 18/07/2008).[89]

On a trip to Chile of different economic groups to explore business possibilities (*El Panamá América* 06/05/1997: C2), the difficult issues, which were hampering a final agreement, were discussed between the Chilean businessmen, representatives of the SOFOFA, and the Panamanian representatives and business groups. According to the representative of Panama's Chamber of Commerce, Manuel Ferreira (25/07/2008), the initial goal of launching joint-business opportunities during the meeting in Chile became about trying to make the Chilean position on services and investment more flexible: "During this trip we realised that instead of exploring business opportunities with the Chileans, we should focus on other markets such as the US and Central America".[90]

Because of the difficulties in the talks with Chile, Panama's pro-market groups started to lobby the government to launch FTA negotiations with Central America and insisted on trying to launch negotiations with the US (*El Panama América* 17/07/1998: E3; interview with Luis Garrido, MICI, 22/07/2008; Leda Arrué, MICI, 17/07/2008). According to Dario Selles (13/07/1998 in *El Panamá América*: E1), the former APEX president, "the APEX institution was even happy if the negotiation would end in no-agreement" as they perceived that Chile used unfair negotiating techniques to postpone services till the end, and made Panama accept certain

88 Author's translation.
89 Author's translation.
90 Author's translation.

unfavourable conditions in market access, thinking that financial services will be closed with a deal in the last rounds.

The then UNPAP representative, Carlos Pittí (07/07/1998: E1) was disappointed about the status of the negotiations and suggested that the government needs to launch new negotiations. He stated that "[...] the government has the obligation of achieving FTAs with a significant economic bloc that is attractive to Panamanian producers because of its size".[91] In other words, pro-FTA groups in Panama did not continue paying much attention to the developments of the FTA negotiation with Chile. In addition, they started to lobby the government for new FTA negotiations with more relevant economic markets that assure them the possibility of exporting large volumes of goods and services.

On the Chilean side, the groups who were directly benefiting from an agreement with Panama were the SME and the industrial groups joined under the umbrella of ASEXMA. In this regard, the priority of the government in Latin America was not only political but also a way to compensate those productive sectors with limited scope in the global markets but that are still competitive enough to sell in Latin America (Bull 2008). Yet these groups are less influential than big conglomerates such as banking, salmon, wine, wood and cellulose, and fruit exporters. The ASEXMA representative, which was one of the most interested groups in pursuing negotiations with countries from Central America as their markets are attractive for SME producing industrial goods, said that:

> They thought in advance that such negotiation was difficult to conclude when they heard from the Chilean negotiators the position of Panama on investment matters. We concluded that there was no way an agreement was possible if the loser of the agreement was the financial sector [...] Well it is self-explanatory to say why the financial sector will not be the loser of the agreement (interview with Roberto Fantuzzi, ASEXMA, 28/03/2008).[92]

This position is confirmed by Marco Veragua (24/03/2008), who represents a branch of the SME called CONAPYME. Although CONAPYME supported this negotiation, they could not sustain and articulate strong positions at the domestic negotiation table vis-à-vis the banking associations or the SNA. "What could we do? We are not the bankers. We owed them as most production sectors do, and the SNA is the SNA and the government heard them but not us".[93]

The strong economic sectors of Chile such as ASOEX, Salmón-Chile, SOFOFA, cellulose and wood producers (CORMA) and wine producers did not actively participate in the negotiation with Panama, although they supported the process all the same. The reason to give second priority to this negotiation was the size of Panama's domestic market. One way the government kept these groups interested in the process was to link the negotiation with the possibility of creating a storage centre in Panama in order to reduce the amount of time taken to distribute Chilean

91 Author's translation.

92 Author's translation.

93 Author's translation.

products in Europe, the Middle East and mainly in the US market (*Enlace* 1997: 3; interviews with Federico Mekis, Chilean Wine, 31/03/2008; Maria Teresa Arana, CORMA, 09/04/2008). Mario Agliati (quoted in *La Tercera* 03/03/1997: 23), former vice-president of the international relations division at the CNC, as a way to show support for the negotiation with Panama, stated that: "The idea will be to install some industries and a storage centre to store some of our products that go to the Middle East and other far away markets".[94]

Once the high divergences emerged and the politicisation process occupied the internal agenda in Panama, the pro-FTA groups including those big associations that supported the storage centre in Panama started to put pressure on Chile's government in order to focus more on the FTAA, the US, Europe, and Asia, countries that offer 'the big markets' for wine, salmon, fruits, and wood. In order to put pressure aside and show its commitment to its own domestic actors over the FTAA process, the Chilean government stated before the FTAA's first negotiating round that: "if the FTAA comes to exist then bilateral negotiations may be abolished between the Latin American countries" (Alejandro Jara in *El Diario* 12/06/1998: 27).[95]

As the FTAA could take a while to become effective, the industrial groups started to demand FTA negotiations with Central America. Here in an eventual negotiation with Central America played a major role ASEXMA, FEPACH the CONAPYME and SOFOFA. These groups were also able to attract other interest groups that were focusing on the US and Europe because a negotiation with Central America would be better than individual negotiations with each Central American country in terms of market size. However, ASEXMA and CONAPYME also had the second best option of negotiating bilaterally if the Central American states preferred. As Osvaldo Rosales (2008) argues, the accords with Central America have to be understood in a more developmentalist way as they boost the export of products that have more industrial value. Yet the condition for the big associations to actively support an FTA with the Central American countries was to negotiate with this region as a bloc and not individually.[96] Therefore, negotiating with Central America as a bloc was also perceived as a good opportunity for the exporters of commodities and the industrial sector,[97] although the priority was still the US[98] (Interview with Ronald Bown, ASOEX, 19/03/2008). In this regard, the big associations have not only the power to

94 Author's translation.

95 Author's translation.

96 The big-exporters would have also supported the negotiation with individual countries because of ideological commitments to the external trade policy, but this support would have been rather passive.

97 The negotiations with Central America were launched in 1999. This aspect will be analysed in the next chapter along with why Chile made an exception in negotiating an accord during an electoral year and how it was able to overcome a politicisation of this process due to its presidential elections.

98 On the priority of achieving an FTA with the US by joining NAFTA or going bilateral see van Klaveren (1998), Morande (2003), Porras (2003) and Silva (2001).

assure that their desired policy option will get through, but they also have the expertise in their business association to shape the trade agenda. This trade agenda is overall convergent with that of the government (Bull 2008), yet what is for discussion between these domestic associations and the government is which countries Chile should prioritise to negotiate first.[99]

Therefore, the pro-FTAs groups in both countries started to lobby their respective governments when the pace of the negotiation with Panama started to slow, due to the divergence on interests, the politicisation level, and the increased role of the elections. These factors encouraged the pro-FTA groups to free ride. Yet the free riding was not achieved through leaving the structure of negotiating FTAs. On the contrary, they lobbied their respective governments to focus on launching FTAs that were easier to achieve as well as those that can open markets with potential to export more attractive volumes of products and services than that of Chile and Panama. Whereas the representatives of the pro-FTA groups did not completely leave the table in Chile's and Panama's FTA negotiation, the lobbying to launch other negotiations empowered the protectionist lobby groups in this current FTA process. Protectionist lobby groups had more room to manoeuvre and use the access points to bloc an agreement that jeopardised their specific interest. Finally, establishing a storage centre in Panama to keep the big associations of exporters interested in this negotiation was not enough on its own, as these groups could also materialise this project without an FTA. A storage centre could also be pursued by using the legal frame provided by the BITs signed, but at that time not yet implemented, by Chile and Panama.

5.4 Concluding Remarks

This chapter assessed by what means the internal and external domestic conditions for the negotiation became constitutive elements for the failure of the FTA negotiation Chile-Panama. The main fact that slowed the pace of the negotiation was the divergent interests and high expectations domestic actors have in this process. The divergent interests also resulted in conflicting views between the negotiators and some domestic interest groups, especially the case of FEDAP. However, these divergent interests were to some extent produced by the fear of a certain trade policy or job insecurity that could be created by an FTA.

The problems faced when trying to achieve convergence on interests and the politicisation level driven and constructed by FEDAP extended the negotiation until it was caught in an electoral process. The politicisation level would have been there in any case, even if Panama had not had any elections, as FEDAP's mobilisations

99 Launching a negotiation is also about whether the eventual counterpart wants to negotiate an FTA with Chile. Despite the fact that the US was the main priority, this only became effective in 2003 due to the domestic dynamics in the US political arena.

started in 1997. Perhaps without elections the politicisation level would have been lower and FEDAP could not have linked its sectorial loss with the interests of a broader national coalition.

However, the domestic level of the negotiation is only one side of the story of an FTA negotiation. Whereas the domestic dimension analysed in this chapter has a lot of explanatory power that helps us to understand the failure of such FTA negotiation, it omits the state to state interaction. The final cause of a stalled FTA negotiation is that of the states. Understanding the international dimension of the negotiation is thus an essential component to map out the causes for such failure in the negotiations. The intergovernmental negotiation process as well as the international external conditions for negotiation may also reflect the high domestic divergences that were found in this chapter.

6. Intergovernmental Negotiation between Chile and Panama

6.1 Introduction

An FTA process at the international level also develops its own dynamic reflecting the strategies, leadership skills and the external influences of other simultaneous or future FTA negotiations. This chapter deals with the process and conditions at the intergovernmental level, which bring both states to stall an entire negotiation. It assesses the following specific conditions that brought the FTA negotiation to an enduring standstill such as the lack of clearly delineated non-negotiable issues at the outset of the process, the lack of displaying leadership skills, the overuse of value-claiming strategies, and the weight of other FTA negotiations. These conditions seek to complement those presented in the previous chapter. They have to be taken as an intertwined process in which the conditions originate, and are developed in a similar, yet not identical, timeframe.

6.2 Intergovernmental Factors

6.2.1 Non-negotiability

According to the former Chilean minister of Agriculture Carlos Madlinic (2000: 69), the most difficult part of an FTA negotiation is to negotiate what you are not willing to negotiate. Excluding issues from the accord is a sensitive process if the counterpart is expecting high benefits in that issue, but it can also be a conflict-absent process in the negotiation if both countries have concordant views on the exclusions. For example, if both countries considered 'corn' to be a sensitive issue, it may be the case that both countries agree on excluding this issue. If 'corn' is sensitive only for one side, but competitive in the other it will be a source of conflict as the sensitivity of this product is determined by the comparative advantages that govern the direct economic relationship between Chile and Panama. Nevertheless, in both cases the non-negotiability, paradoxically, has to be negotiated.

The non-negotiable issues can be negotiated in the pre-negotiating phase, which is the process in which both countries decide the mode and the extension of the negotiation (Gross Stein 1989). A concrete example of defining the non-negotiable goods and services at the pre-negotiating phase is the trilateral process of NAFTA, in which Mexico made clear, right from the beginning, the conditions and the exclusion of the issue of energy resources from the negotiating table. As Mexico knew that the US would hardly push for this issue, Mexico structured a strategy of five "NOs" to prevent the misunderstandings. In addition, it highlighted that any attempt to include the issue would mean the end of the talks. Nevertheless, Mexico was able to offer an attractive compensation package, mainly to the US, in exchange for excluding the energy sector from the agreement (see Ortiz Mena 2006).

There are other cases of FTA negotiations, like that of Chile and Panama, in which both sectors tacitly omit the signalling of the non-negotiable goods and services by not discussing them at the outset of the formal negotiation, or during the pre-negotiation phase. Though both parties can anticipate which issues will be sensitive, they think they can create an attractive deal that may overcome such eventual exclusions through the bargaining process, or they may think that the issue can be included in the final agreement with some 'cosmetic' changes that keep the pre-negotiation status quo. Here the sensitive products or services for one side may become a win for the counterpart if such issues are included, but they may also be a source of conflict during the negotiation. When these extremely sensitive issues become a source of conflict during the bargaining, the zone of agreement tends to narrow (Elms 2003; Singh 2008: 41; Raifa 1982; Holzinger 2001; Hopmann 1995).

As strategy, Chile does not signal its non-negotiable issues for tactical purposes whenever it negotiates an FTA. In fact Chile rhetorically pushes to have a trade agenda without exclusions. Chile's negotiators traditionally open their negotiations stating that 'Chile wants free trade in all items without any exclusion' (Interviews with Andrés Rebolledo, DIRECON, 25/03/2008; Osvaldo Rosales, DIRECON, 19/03/2008; Lorena Sepulveda, DIRECON, 25/03/2008). Yet this is tactical rather than real, since it is used to put the pressure of the negotiation on the counterpart as Chile is one of the countries with the lowest tariffs in the world.[100] As Mario Matus (DIRECON, 28/02/2008) stated:

> We learnt this in the FTA negotiation with Canada. In our first meeting with the Canadian negotiators we had a bunch of documents to show them that protection on key issues should be guaranteed, but we saw them and they only had a notebook and a pen! They told us, to state their position: 'we want zero tariffs on all items once the accord becomes into force'. We did not know what to say to that. We remained silent. As the negotiation developed we realised this was impossible to achieve for Canada, because they had a lot of sensible products, but they brought them up during the last rounds, so that they could protect their key issues in a better way. We learned all this with them and we have applied it in the following negotiations since then. Moreover we currently have a 6 percent tariff which is extremely low, so for us it is possible to deal with this claim quite well.[101]

This quote reflects the basic principle of Chile's strategy and how this claim has been mechanised in Chile's FTA negotiations, but it also shows that this position became a source of conflict for the negotiation with Panama. In other words, Chile neither assessed the viability of this statement in the negotiation with Panama nor

100 When it started the negotiation with Panama Chile had an 11 percent flat tariff, which is now at 6 percent.

101 Author's translation.

the possibility of adapting such initiatory statement according to the reality of each bilateral economic relationship. I argue that due to the already known liberal service sector in Panama (liberal relative to the conservative sector in Chile) the most logical option would have been to outline the issue of financial services as non-negotiable for Chile at the outset of the process.

Chile assumed from the beginning that the eventual demand of Panama to include the issue of, and liberalise, financial services, would be easy to neutralise by asking Panama to liberalise professional services. Moreover, Chile proposed a second option of validating the extant BITs (signed in 1996) as the governing body for the chapter about investment in the FTA, and a third option of adopting a WTO approach that ratifies each country's legislation, which would mean that financial institutions would have a double law to comply with (interviews with Catalina Bau, Ministry of Finances 11/04/2008; Lucy Gangas, Ministry of Economy, 07/04/2008).[102]

On Panama's side the government was preparing to conduct a banking reform to comply with the Basel regulations and also to show its Chilean counterpart that financial services would not jeopardise Chile's banking system and stability. This reform was planned in advance, but it became a necessity for the Panamanian government, when they realised that Chile did not want to include the issue in the accord. The reform of this sector became a tool to push Chile to accept the inclusion of this issue in the accord. This banking reform was conducted in 1997 in a parallel way to the FTA negotiations and negotiators used this law to exert pressure over Chile (Alexis Pineda, MICI, 18/07/2008; Leda Arrué, MICI, 17/07/2008; Anonimous 26/07/2008). Both positions show the bounded rationality of the negotiators, which made both countries misperceive what the other was willing to offer, negotiate and not negotiate in the FTA negotiation process. This bias was established before the formal negotiation was launched as both sectors thought that they could exclude in to a large extent their sensitive issue-areas by following a 'tit-for-tat' strategy (Interview with Camilo Navarro, DIRECON, 17/03/2008).[103]

Moreover, Chile could not account for or anticipate Panama's movement to change its legislation. In this regard, the reform of this sector in Panama was already planned. However, the refusal of Chile to include the issue in the agreement, after the negotiation was launched, sped up the reform (interview with official from the Ministry of Finances 31/07/2008).[104] Panama could not go beyond the bilateral ne-

102 These positions did not satisfy Panama as it wanted to assure its capacity to move their capital investment freely. The second best option (the third option) basically keeps the status quo as it ratifies what already exists and does not go further as it does not liberalise the investment regime.

103 Author's translation

104 The reform included the creation of supervisory institutions to prevent money laundering, regulate the financial transactions, and improve transparency and the good working of the financial system (Superintendency of Banks of Panama, www.superbancos.gob.pa). The Superintendency of Banks of Panama followed in its organisation and its roles the

gotiation and analyse Chile's reluctance to include this issue as a strategic move for subsequent negotiations such as the US. Therefore, the wait and see strategy, rather than that of stating the non-negotiable issues at the outset of the negotiation, proved to be the wrong mode of negotiating. This wrong path was costly in terms of time as it impeded the countries to devote more attention to finding issue-areas in which it was possible to create collaborative behaviour. This path was also costly in terms of strategy as both parties put an excessive focus on sensitive issues that made both countries develop value-claiming attitudes during the formal talks, which also had spill over effects on other issues related to market access and services that were conceived as low conflict. The non-signalling of the issues that were to be excluded from the negotiation narrowed the zone of the agreement as parties started to depict each other as pursuing a 'winner takes it all' strategy rather than an integrative one that allows the negotiation to frame specific issue-areas as a win-win game. The process leading to the lack of clearly outlined non-negotiability can be described in the following way:

The declarations of Panama's chief negotiator, Yuri Moreno, after the first round of negotiation in November 1996 reflect not only Panama's interests, but also Panama's misguided belief that financial services will be included in the agreement during the subsequent rounds. "When reporters asked Moreno, whether Panama proposed to Chile a wish to include the issue of financial services in the accord and he said, yes, we have in fact discussed this issue in our first meeting and this got a favourable reception" (*La Prensa* 22/11/1996: 25 A).[105] Moreover, Panama's negotiators assured its domestic constituencies that financial services were to be included in the negotiation and that Chile was willing to negotiate it (*El Panama América* 22/11/1996: C8). This tactic of Chile and the information given by Panama's negotiators to its domestic constituencies created high expectations of the inclusion of financial services in a favourable way for Panama in the accord. Chile and Panama progressed on market access, but they postponed the key decisions on services to the last rounds. It seems that Chile took advantage of Panama's inexperience on this type of negotiation, despite the fact that Chile was seen as a role model. Yet Panama's trade diplomats and representatives of economic associations with high stakes in the negotiation learnt that in the following negotiations both services and market access should be negotiated in a parallel way or at least use services to balance market access, because services were Panama's main asset. Using services to balance market access can give Panama more bargaining power with which they could protect sensitive agricultural and industrial products (*El Panamá América*

Superintendency created by Chile. The financial reform went along with reforms to modernise the code of commerce; create a national economic council (CENA); and to regulate insurance institutions and their financial operations (Gaceta Oficial-Panamá 09/07/1997; Gaceta Oficial-Panamá 01/08/1996)

105 Author's translation.

08/08/98, interviews with Victor Cruz, SIP, 16/07/2008, Diana Salazar, MICI, 30/07/2008, Melissa Davis, MICI, 17/07/2008, Samuel Moreno MICI, 22/03/2008).

The then vice-minister of foreign relations (1996-97) and then Minister of MICI (2004-08) Alejandro Ferrer (29/07/2008), said that

> we spent excessive time and resources over an issue that became the cause for the failure of the negotiation, but Chile was rather ambiguous on the issue. First they told us that the issue will be discussed later on, which made us optimistic about the prospects for including our main and most competitive sector of the national economy. Later Chile came up with a rather tough bargaining position opposing the liberalisation of financial services [...] the reluctance to include such issues made us look rather bad vis-à-vis our domestic sector which participated in the next room as we signalled to them that Chile got a favourable position on financial services after the first round of negotiation [...] After, when Chile started to say no over financial issues, we looked like fools as we were rather flexible on market access and we accepted most of Chile's sensitive issues for long phase outs or exclusions, waiting for what we expected to be a 'yes' from Chile on financial services.[106]

The then Chilean negotiator Carmen Paz Cortes (DIRECON, 25/03/2008), in charge of services, said:

> we did not know in detail how important financial services were for Panama. We thought we could balance or contain Panama's aspirations by exerting pressure on liberalizing professional services. We could not anticipate that Panama was willing to accept certain changes on professional services and we did not know much about the reforms on banking that this country was already implementing. They used these arguments to pressure us, but we knew we could not negotiate financial services for strategic reasons, and because what Panama was asking was impossible for us. Panama's positions on investment regime and cross-border financial services in principle could jeopardise the stability of our financial system [...]. [107]

Here this negotiator tacitly confirms the idea that Chile was thinking about other negotiations in which financial services could be used as a strategic bargaining chip as well as the lack of knowledge they have of Panama's economic reality. This lack of knowledge is not based on the poor preparation of the negotiator, but it may be linked to the conviction that this issue will be excluded from the agreement. The negotiator Oscar Quina (DIRECON, 08/04/2008) confirms that financial services were not up for negotiation in the way Panama wanted and it was not to be negotiated at all.

106 Author's translation.
107 Author's translation

> We did not say no straight away in the first round when Panama asked for financial services but we did not say yes either. We thought the issue will be protected by pushing professional services and other sensitive issues Panama had [...] A clear indicator that we were not thinking of including financial services in the accord was that we presented the text of the negotiation based on the FTA with Canada, which does not have a chapter on financial services.[108]

The minutes of the 4th and 5th round of the negotiation between Chile and Panama (3-4 March 1997; 24-26 March 1997) refer to the issue of services in general as "the parties were advancing fruitfully on issues as maritime services, cross border services, telecommunications, airfreight, competition policy, etc". When it comes to the issue of investment and financial services the parties stated that "they were exploring possibilities to include financial services, and that this issue was under study on the Chilean side". Moreover, the minutes refer in both cases to the fact that "the parties are trying to bring together their positions to work on a common ground". This diplomatic phrasing can be interpreted as stating that one another's positions were completely different and difficult to reconcile over the financial and professional services.

In the subsequent rounds, mainly from the 8th onwards, the main reason for the countries meeting was to unlock the negotiations on financial and professional services i.e. services in general, and close the remaining differences on beef, dairy products, sugar and sugar related issues, and some fruits such as melon and water melon, despite the fact that all the other issues were almost closed (Interviews with Oscar Quina, DIRECON, 08/04/2008; Rodrigo Contreras, DIRECON, 28/03/2008; Carmen Paz Cortes, DIRECON, 25/03/2008; Samuel Moreno, MICI, 22/03/2008; Alexis Pineda, MICI, 18/07/2008; Luis Garrido, MICI, 28/07/2008; Gabriela Díaz de Morales, Ministry of Agriculture, 30/07/2008; Diana Salazar, MICI, 30/07/2008). According to former Chilean negotiator on financial issues Catalina Bau (11/04/2008), Chile worked on excluding the issue of financial services, but it tried to create mechanisms to conclude the negotiation anyway i.e. by giving up professional services so that Panama would give up on financial issues, and by promising that entire service issues would be negotiated later on when the FTA was in force. Moreover, the idea was to protect investment by validating in the FTA the previous bilateral investment treaty which was already signed.

The issue of sugar was also kept opened during the negotiation, which shows the sensitivity of the issue. Panama was not willing to accept the exclusion of this issue, if Chile wanted to insist on increasing the market access for its food products based on sugar (FTA Chile-Panama's draft text, 24-26 March1997). Chilean negotiator Rodrigo Contreras (28/03/2008) suggested that Chile would have reduced its demand on more market access for sugar based food products, but Panama would have insisted on getting quotas for sugar anyway. However, sugar was put on a special scheme with Mercosur. It would start its progressive and linear liberalization after

108 Author's translation. When the formal negotiations were launched the parties started to draft a chapter on financial issues.

11 years and it will reach zero tariffs in 2012 (ACE 35 Chile-Mercosur: annex 8). This offer of starting a liberalisation of sugar after 11 years to reach zero tariff in 2012 was a second best option for Chile in the negotiation with Panama. This offer was presented at the end of the talks to close this issue. This second best option also meant that Chile should reduce its demands on food products by accepting Panama's proposal of a long-term phase out in food processed products, which use sugar as input (interviews with Rodrigo Contreras, DIRECON, 28/03/2008; Luis Garrido, MICI, 28/07/2008). This confirms the belief of FEPACH that when Chile negotiates with sugar producers food products are somehow sacrificed to protect the sugar industry, despite the competitiveness of the food industry. The sugar issue, although controversial, was not thought to be non-negotiable by Chilean negotiators. Therefore, the outlining of these issues as non-negotiable at the outset of the negotiation was out of the question. Keeping this issue open and asking for exclusion was strategic rather than real. The purpose was to get a good deal on sugar based food products so that Chile could then ask Panama for a liberalisation of sugar but according to what was negotiated with Mercosur and not beyond.

To sum up, Chile's overall strategy of claiming free trade on all issues at the outset of the negotiations in order to exclude the most sensitive issues during the following rounds proved to be the wrong path in the negotiation with Panama. Chile held the momentum of the negotiation as it was the experienced country on building these accords, and Panama conceived of Chile as its role model of economic transformation and integration to the global world. By not stating its non-negotiable issues, mainly financial services, and by adopting a wait-and-see position, Chile gave the illusion to Panama that financial services would be included. Perhaps this strategy would have been fruitful for Chile if Panama had not have been willing to make cosmetic changes in professional services and had not have been thinking of introducing a more restricted legal framework on financial operations.[109]

6.2.2 Lack of Leadership Skills

Chilean negotiators perceived the FTA process, before the formal talks were officially launched with Panama, as a negotiation in which a final agreement would be possible in the short-run. These trade diplomats sustained this perception due to the fact that Chile was seen as the expert and as the role model by Panama. These two labels were not empty vessels. On the contrary, they involved reputational skills attributed to Chile by Panama and recognised by Panama (interviews with Andrés Rebolledo, DIRECON, 25/03/2008; Rodrigo Contreras, DIRECON, 28/03/2008; Pablo Lazo, DIRECON, 25/03/2008; Carmen Paz Cortés, DIRECON, 25/03/2008; Camilo Navarro Ceardi, DIRECON, 17/03/2008). In negotiation theory, the terms

109 These legal changes in Panama became the main argument to sustain its position of including financial services during the rounds held in 1998.

expertise and role model can be translated into having more bargaining power; having a favourable setting to build an accord; and enjoying breadth to manoeuvre the negotiation in a win-win way. These qualities attributed to Chile are confirmed by Panama's trade diplomats. Then Panama's ambassador in Chile, Bruno Garisto (11/04/2008), talked about Chile as "the paradigm of economic transformation in Latin America and the country with most skills with regards to trade agreements". He also said in the interview with the author of this work, "For us Chile was the model of integration into the global economy we wanted to follow".[110]

According to Diana Salazar (MICI, 30/07/2008), Panama was willing to learn from Chile: "we saw Chileans negotiators as experienced and also as sincere and open to share their expertise".[111] This perception was also shared by then vice-minister of foreign relations (1996-97) and then minister of commerce and industries (2004-08) Alejandro Ferrer (29/07/2008), and by the then advisor to the minister of foreign affairs (1996-1997) Estif Aparicio (18/07/2008) as well as by Alexis Pineda (18/07/2008), Leda Arrue (17/07/2008), Melissa Davis (17/03/2008), and Brunilda de Castillo (17/03/2008), all of them trade diplomats from the Ministry of International Trade in Panama (MICI). Yet, what turned such a favourable negotiation setting into one in which the mutual perception changed to mutual distrust, and in which one side perceived the other as "creating" artificial issues to obtain more gains at the expense of the other? On top of the already analysed high divergent interests, the lack of clarifying the non-negotiable issues, the politicisation level, the role played by the elections, and the strategies to negotiate, the lack of displaying leadership skills at key junctures of the negotiation to keep such a favourable setting may in part explain the failure of this FTA.

The role of honest brokers in multilateral economic negotiations or in negotiations over geopolitical conflicts is usually conducted by third parties. However, in bilateral FTA negotiations this role is adopted by the same actors that negotiate and have concrete positions on the issues at stake but, at the same time, can adopt the role of facilitator and create bridges between the parties with the purpose of reaching an agreement. In other words, the negotiators or other government representatives may, in determined circumstances, play the role of party, and judge of the factual developments within the negotiation process. This role is difficult to fulfil, although it is not impossible, due to the fact that negotiators are focused on protecting their interests and pushing to get a better deal for their competitive sectors. However, negotiators face a dilemma of whether to push hard to maximise their gains until negotiation is at the edge of failure, or whether to redirect the process to make the spiral effect deescalate and in that way bring the process to an outcome of agreement.

110 Author's translation.
111 Author's translation.

The negotiators of this process could not detect the ripe moment to reduce the escalation level produced by an overuse of hard bargaining tactics that brought the negotiation into a vicious circle of contentious action and reaction (on spiral effects see Pruitt and Hee Kim 2004: 87-100).[112] Most negotiators confirmed that the definitive turning point of the negotiation came after the 5th round held in March 1997, as many issues were well advanced and the issue of services became the most important and the most sensitive to talk about. Yet not all the issues were closed as the minutes of the 5th round and the draft-text of the negotiation show. There were still low conflict aspects to be discussed within the areas of property rights, custom issues, safeguard clause, dumping and antidumping measures, as well as the low sensitivity issues in services and market access (FTA minute of the 5th round 24-26 March 1997).

> We negotiated easy issues in a rather hard way. We did not realise that we were pushing the counterpart hard to get more concessions. But we were hardly negotiating issues which are complementary in principle [...] I guess the problem was that we started to see each other as some sort of enemy that we have to defeat [...] What would produce such reaction I guess was the fact that Chile promised a lot of things at the beginning of the negotiation on services and our expectations were not fulfilled as promised (Luis Garrido, MICI, 28/07/2008).[113]

A notion in terms of a leadership vacuum in the negotiation was posed by Oscar Quina (DIRECON, 08/04/2008), who suggested that both parties could not use this positive initial setting to develop a good negotiation:

> There were episodes in which we needed solutions to continue and we did not have them. We were not creative enough to find solutions I guess. There was a certain fatigue with negotiating the same issues over and over again, and we could not move forward. None of us could come up with solutions on issues that may be seen as easy to solve.[114]

These words reflect the fact that there was no-one available to redirect the process whenever it got deadlocked. Whereas this evidence reaffirms the condition of high divergences over interests in key issues of these countries' economic relationship, it also shows the absence of facilitators within the negotiation to redirect and soften the hard bargaining whenever it started to escalate, as well as to facilitate the agreement over artificial controversies triggered in part by the development of a distrustful pattern between the parties. The initial perception of both parties was

112 Zartmann (1989, 2000) develops the ripeness theory which is presented a necessary condition to sit to negotiate after a conflict can no longer escalate due to a mutually hurting stalemate. Here both parties usually helped by a third party mediator may start to deescalate the conflict through a negotiation. I argue that such moment of ripeness is also present and may develop during the negotiation and when such process turns into a hard bargaining with escalating spiral effects.

113 Author's translation.

114 Author's translation.

that: "Panama has the potential on services as well as Chile; and moreover we are tropical fruits producers and Chile produces Mediterranean fruits. Therefore, there is not such a competition between both countries" (Bruno Garisto in *La Prensa* 25/02/1997: 17a).[115]

Elected leaders also tried to overcome the deadlocks of the negotiation. However, whether they displayed leadership skills is rather difficult to determine as presidents met privately to assess the bilateral relation in 1997 and then in 1998. However, the declarations and public discourses given by both presidents when they visited one another's country may give some clues as to whether a full commitment to back up the process was given, and on whether they use their leaderships skills to act as honest brokers to redirect the negotiation process.

The extant evidence on whether these leaders displayed leadership skills to overcome the deadlocks of the negotiation is rather ambivalent. On the one hand, the presidents of each country show ambiguous rhetoric on the difficulties of the negotiation during 1997. This is especially the case of then President Pérez Balladares, who visited Chile in October 1997 and talked directly about the FTA as a way to overcome the deadlocks. It is also the case of then President Frei who talked about the FTA negotiation in a rather indirect and vague way. At the same time both presidents signed a memorandum of understanding between both countries to cooperate in sanitary measures over agriculture and livestock production as well as to advance on the negotiations for an FTA.

It is also interesting to note that it was the then Minister of Foreign Affairs of Chile, Miguel Insulza, rather than the Chilean President who made declarations on the status of the negotiations during the presidential visit of the Panamanian President to Chile. "There are certain difficulties, such as the eventual revaluation of the Chilean peso because of the eventual arrival of dollars in a permanent base from Panama. Thus we had to be more cautious and slow than usual in this part of the negotiation" (Insulza 22/10/1997).[116] President Frei stated that "there is the intention of increasing the economic ties between both countries", but he did not directly refer to the FTA. Thus Frei's ambivalence could be taken as indifference on whether the FTA really made a difference for the economic relationship between Panama and Chile, as the increasing of economic exchange between both countries could exist with or without an FTA. In the words of Eduardo Frei (22/10/1997: 13):

> Panama is the main destiny of our exports and the main receiver of our FDI in the Central American Isthmus. These are concrete signals of our will to increase our economic exchange and to develop common projects between both countries' private sectors.[117]

115 Author's translation.
116 Author's translation.
117 Author's translation.

President Pérez Balladares (22/10/1997: E1) spoke directly on the issue of the FTA negotiation in the following way: "It seems that both pending issues will be solved within two to three months, and I hope that for the summit of Santiago in April I will have the chance to sign the accord".[118] The declarations of Pérez Balladares and Chile's presidential delegation to the Minister of Foreign Affairs about the responsibility to talk about the FTA negotiation suggest a certain asymmetry in terms of how important the FTA was for both parties. According to a former Panamanian negotiator (interview anonymous 26/07/2008), who was part of the delegation that visited Santiago of Chile: "we expected more from President Frei in terms of supporting the FTA".[119]

On the other hand, during the bilateral presidential meeting in September 1998 in Panama both presidents committed to overcome the problems of the negotiation and close it with a satisfactory outcome for both parties (*El Panamá América* 04/09/1998). Moreover, then president Frei also committed more directly to solving the issues that were hampering the FTA. "In the sphere of our economic relation, Panama is a great partner for Chile. It is for this reason that we will keep the good will to continue with the FTA negotiations" (Eduardo Frei 04/09/1998: 5).[120] Yet, President Frei also and in a implicit way lowered the expectations about the issues which were possible to include in the FTA, and/or on whether the FTA was likely to be concluded. Frei highlighted the importance of the upcoming FTAA, and made the link to the faltered bilateral negotiation:

> Beyond what can be achieved bilaterally we also highlight that the FTAA process has started. This FTAA has the purpose of creating a free trade accord for 2003, which will include all the countries of the Western Hemisphere (*El Mercurio* 04/09/1998: C3).[121]

Thus contradictory evidence that shows rather diffuse leadership skills in the presidential meeting in 1997 and then a commitment from the Chilean side in 1998, though with rather low expectations, bring into question why the exertion of leadership in 1998 did not result in agreement. First, it may be argued that the commitment was rather late in terms of timing as Chile already left the negotiation table in August that year. Second, the leadership exertion was diffuse and not direct as Frei lowered the expectations on the FTA and tacitly manifested that an outcome of non-agreement in the bilateral relationship may be overcome through the FTAA.[122] Finally, this invocation to resume the talks was merely a diplomatic gesture to Pérez Balladares as he lost the referendum a couple of days before Frei presidential visit.

118 Author's translation. During the Summit of the Americas in April 1998, there is neither evidence on a bilateral meeting between Panama's and Chile's Presidents nor a declaration on the FTA process. In this summit the Latin American countries plus Canada and the US signed a plan of action for the FTAA negotiation (www.summit-americas.org).

119 Author's translation.

120 Author's translation.

121 Author's translation.

122 The FTAA was expected to absorb the bilateral trade accords between the countries of the Americas (see Devlin and Giordano 2004).

Thus Pérez Balladares' ability to implement the internal and external trade policy was severely affected. A reduced group of authorities from the ministries involved in the negotiation met briefly (the morning of 4 September 1998) during the presidential visit, and this meeting did not involve the technical groups of negotiators. According to a Panamanian negotiator (anonymous 26/07/2008) "there was nothing to negotiate at that stage as the negotiations broke down in August and not in the best way as well as we knew Chile would say no again [...] It was mainly a protocol meeting".[123] There is no evidence that new meetings between the teams of negotiators were conducted after Frei's presidential visit. Thus the political context mattered for the outcome of the negotiation. However, it would be speculation to ask what would have happened if leadership skills would have been exerted in 1997 or in the first months of 1998 when the elections or referendums were far away, but divergences over interests were still high.

Nevertheless, it seems to be the case that the lack of leadership skills was more important in the day to day negotiation within the dynamics of the negotiating teams than at the presidential level. In this regard, neither the chief negotiators nor the head of each section of the negotiation acted as honest brokers or as facilitators, in order to bring the negotiation back to a path of a value creating strategy. The presidents' roles as such seem rather ambiguous and insufficiently resolute when trying to redirect the negotiation process.

6.2.3 Predominance of Value-claiming Strategies

Within the value-claiming strategy that Chile and Panama displayed in the FTA negotiation, there are different sets of tactics that qualify as value-claiming in both its defensive and offensive variants. On the offensive side one can find threats; holding and manipulating relevant information from the counterpart to control the negotiation; cheating behaviour; manipulating the BATNA i.e. either to worsens the counterpart BATNA or improve one's own; blaming the counterpart for the lack of progress and deadlock as well as avoiding taking responsibility for the problems; delaying an answer to proposals from the counterpart; breaking the principle of good faith on the counterpart by judging in advance that the other party is unable to deliver what it has promised to do even if they have the institutional tools to do it; asking for concessions with low or absent reciprocity; and stating that the counterpart's institutional transformations are not viable. On the defensive side, and to sum up, one can find reactive counteractions to such offensive variants (Odell 2000: 224-225).

123 Author's translation.

The above set of tactics corresponds to a value-claiming strategy in all type of negotiations. However, there are other elements that may become tactical either distributively or integratively depending on the negotiating context, i.e. whether the negotiation has developed mainly on a win-win track, or whether the negotiation has gone into a spiral effect of a value-claiming strategy. J. P. Singh (2008: 49) argues that some strategies fit both criteria and a third, which is a mixed strategy of integrative and distributive elements. What makes a tactic part of an integrative or distributive strategy in some cases is the context in which the negotiation is embedded. For example, a time factor may be used to obtain benefits either at the expense of the counterpart or after mutual concessions. Time is part of the negotiation process, and it may constrain or facilitate the negotiation as well as help or impede an agreement. Time may be manipulated to exert pressure on the counterpart to obtain concessions in a "take it or leave it" way, whereas time flexibility can mean that progress can be made later on, if the negotiation has been conducted in a win-win mode, and if the mutual trust within the process has increased rather than decreased.[124]

In this regard, the FTA negotiation between Chile and Panama presented tactics that were always hard bargaining, and others that became 'hawkish' due to the complex domestic and international negotiation dimensions, such as time constraints. As I have argued in previous subsections of this chapter, not only did Chile and Panama use hard bargaining over the most sensitive issues, but they also used it on others that were not sensitive as such, which increased the chances of failure as the zone of agreement narrowed. It has to be highlighted that Chile was the actor displaying most tactics associated with value-claiming strategy. This suggests that Chile had better external options, better bargaining power, and that this country perceived, rightly or wrongly, an asymmetric relation between both countries.

Chile's negotiators took an offensive position on the issue of professional services. Here Chile pushed hard on this issue with the purpose of defending itself when Panama put on the table the issue of financial services. Chile calculated that it did not have enough tools to protect its sensitive issues in agriculture and other services issues such as maritime transport, in which Chile perceived it was less competitive. Therefore, by using professional services it could neutralise Panama's offensive demands in financial services, but it could keep services as a whole as a pending issue for the last rounds (interview with Catalina Bau, Ministry of Finances, 11/04/1998). In fact, Chile always tied the advance in financial services to progress in professional ones. If there were open issues in services, this chapter of the FTA text was not possible to close at all. Therefore, all issues less sensitive than financial and professional services within this chapter remained open, which means they remained excluded from the FTA.

As Chile concentrated its strategy on protecting financial services but in pushing Panama to liberalise professional services, Chile's reluctance to include maritime

124 Giving concessions and building agreements based on mutual trust is called Rapport in negotiation theory.

transport was well covered in the rounds of negotiation with Panama. Chile did not develop major arguments to protect maritime services as the bargaining was, in a manipulative way, created to claim value on professional services to balance Panama's distributive tactics on financial services. The progress of maritime services was linked to the progress of financial and professional services. Maritime services were not up for negotiation in the way Panama wanted as the issue was linked to the investment regime. Panama wanted to liberalise maritime transport by being able to invest in this item in Chile under Panama's investment regime, whereas Chile wanted to protect the investment of its sector as they saw Panama as one of the most competitive countries in shipping and maritime cargo (interview with Rene Muga, CPC, 07/04/2008; Hugo Baierlein, SOFOFA, 26/03/2008). In other words, if progress would have been made on these two issues, it would have moved the other issues. Nevertheless, Chile could cover maritime services by claiming value on professional services, and tying it to progress on financial services.

These issues show a certain manipulation of information by Chile and Panama, but especially by the former country. Chile presented itself as fully committed to a free market, which was true due to its radical economic transformations in the mid 1970s, subsequent validation of the model under a democratic context, and early beginning in FTAs (Wehner 2009a). In defence of this economic pattern in the negotiation, Chile proposed a bilateral FTA with Panama without restrictions of any kind. This is also linked to the wait-and-see logic presented in the sub-section of non-negotiability. Chile defended its bargaining mode on professional services because of its position on free trade. Thus Chile tried to present the image that its proposals on professional services went beyond short term interests and that it did not have anything to do with tactical purposes (Interviews with Leda Arrué, MICI, 17/07/2008; Brunilda de Castillo, MICI, 17/07/2008; Samuel Moreno, MICI, 22/07/2008; Alejandro Ferrer, MICI, 29/07/2008; Alexis Pineda, MICI, 18/07/2008; Luis Garrido, MICI, 28/07/2008).

It is surprising that when Panama showed a more flexible position, after hard bargaining, to partially liberalise its professional services from the 7th round onwards, Chile did not do much to reciprocate Panama's move in order to close this issue, which remained open until the negotiation broke down. This suggests that Chile expected not to need to reciprocate liberalisation and instead to exclude one set of services (financial services) in exchange for the exclusion of another set (professional services). However, Panama decided not to give up on financial services even at the expense of accepting certain modifications on the issue of professionals (Interviews with Catalina Bau, Ministry of Finances, 11/03/2008; Carmen Paz Cortes, DIRECON, 25/03/2008; Estif Aparicio, MICI, 18/07/2008; Alejandro Ferrer, MICI, 29/07/2008, Melissa Davis, MICI, 17/07/2008; Diana Salazar, MICI, 30/07/2008).

Panama also manipulated information to its own advantage and as a way to make Chile's position on the sensitive issues more flexible. Panama implemented a banking reform to comply in part with Chilean demands and was also willing to change some parts of its law on professional services. These were reserved and not talked about in the first rounds of the negotiation. In fact, Chile received the news about the new legal frame for financial institutions from the newspapers and not through the channels of the FTA negotiation (interview with Carmen Paz Cortes, DIRECON, 25/03/2008). Once the reform on the financial sector was approved, Panama displayed a rather 'tough' bargaining position to negotiate on an equal basis the issue of investment and services with Chile as they though of the reform as a sufficient condition for including financial services under its own terms.[125]

Whereas the mutual trust *ante* the negotiation deteriorated by not outlining the non-negotiable issues at the outset, and by displaying tough bargaining, this mutual trust deteriorated even more when Chile started to question the quality of these reforms and their working in practice.

> Panamanians used the argument 'we have already implemented reforms that may satisfy the standards you are asking so there is no impediment to move forward on this issue' [...] We answered this request with 'well we need time to assess whether this new regulatory frame works in practice and this takes at least months and years and we are in hurry as both of us are going into electoral periods' (interview with Catalina Bau, Ministry of Finances, 11/04/2008).[126]

This statement reflects Chile's unwillingness to negotiate the financial services because it was seen as strategic issue for a future negotiation with structural powers. The statement also reflects Chile's judgment of the quality of Panama's institutions and their manipulation of the time setting in order to speed up the negotiation, though Chile did leave the issues of financial and general services out of the accord. After Panama reformed the banking legal frame, and showed willingness to concede on professional services, Chile's position weakened as there was no excuse not to negotiate. Chile's reluctance to include these issues in the accord also suggests that its desire to liberalise professional services in Panama was more of a tactic to prevent concessions on financial services than a core commitment to having an agenda without exclusions.

After Chile's tactical positions to defend its financial services were weakened by Panama's reform, Chile also started to manipulate Panama's BATNA in a more evident way. Chile, as a way of making Panama give up on the inclusion of financial services as part of the agreement, started to pressure Panama by stating that if they wanted more FTAs to come soon they needed to conclude this current negotiation. Moreover, Chileans argued that it will be extremely unlikely that other countries will accept these conditions on investment and services, and that financial services are usually not negotiable for most countries under such liberalising conditions, as experienced by Chile with Canada, Mercosur, and Mexico. Chile highlighted the fact that the reputational costs for Panama were higher than for Chile as the latter had already realised FTAs with other countries (interviews with Samuel Moreno, MICI, 22/07/2008; Melissa Davis, MICI, 17/07/2008). What can be deduced from

125 As presented in the previous chapter, the banking reforms were based on strengthening the regulatory system to prevent money laundering, assure transparency of the system, and to ensure that financial institution were solid enough in terms of patrimony.

126 Author's translation.

this is that Chile pushed Panama to accept the agreement without services with the promise that it will be reviewed in the future once the agreement becomes valid, arguing that the reputation damage will impact on whether any new country would negotiate an FTA with Panama. Therefore, Chile sought to burden the costs of an eventual non-agreement on Panama as a tactic to make the latter sign the accord.

The BATNA manipulation was also central to showing the external FTA options Chile and Panama had. In this regard, Panama did not consider as valid Chile's opinion that not signing the current agreement would prevent it from negotiating new FTAs. Panama stated that they had advanced conversations with the Central American regional grouping to start an FTA negotiation. Chile also showed that Central America was monitoring an FTA with Chile. In addition, Chile started to claim that the negotiation with the US was coming as the FTA with Mexico was being concluded almost in a parallel way to that of Panama.

In the previous chapter I described how the FTA negotiation was caught in a parallel game that affected the course of the negotiation, hampering the possibilities of reaching a final agreement. Because of the coming referendum, the high divergences over sensitive issues, and the deterioration of mutual trust increased by hard bargaining that escalated and spilled over to less sensitive issues, Chile started to use time as an ally to make Panama leave financial services and services in general out of the accord. During 1998, Chile started to use the fact that elections were coming in order to speed up a resolution and to make Panama cease demands for a chapter of services in the accord. As compensation Chile offered to confirm the extant Bilateral Investment Treaty signed in 1996 between both countries as a transitory measure.[127] Chile argued that if the negotiation wanted to be successful Panama and Chile needed to sign the agreement before August and confirm the FTA right away. This could be seen as an attempt to postpone meant sensitive issues for the future under a clause of revision in the text of the agreement. The clause of negotiating services in five years time does not necessarily mean that parties will reach an agreement over these issues in the future. Proposing to solve current negotiation problems in the future may reduce the interest of a country that is losing in the negotiation as there is no compulsory mechanism to assure an agreement. Therefore, revising or negotiating in the future due to this future negotiation clause in an FTA does not necessarily mean a new agreement over the exclusions and modifications to the text (Wehner 2007: 79).[128]

127 BITs protect investments but they do not liberalise it. The US has adopted a liberalising approach on services, which also seeks to protect investments in one another's country. If Panama's approach is comparable, it can be said that it was similar to that of the US. It is interesting to note that Chile started to follow the US approach on services and investment after it negotiated and achieved an FTA with the northern American country (see Reiter 2006).

128 It may be interesting to assess in future research how effective these revision clauses for the future are in these FTA agreements i.e. whether the parties feel obliged to open negotiations on these issues.

In June 1998, both parties agreed that Chile would revise and conduct a thorough study of how Panama's investment regime and financial services operate under the new legal frame. Panama provided the documents to Chile to show that the new legislation and the financial system will not jeopardise this South American country's financial system in any way. However, Chile delayed the answer for what Panamanian negotiators considered to be a rather excessive amount of time as Chile at that time already had conducted studies on Panama's investment regime and financial services. Then Minister of Finance, Miguel Heras (06/08/1998: 21 A) offered to the press the following statement about Chile's delayed answer on the issues of investment and financial services, unblocking the agreement and signing the accord: "To further postpone the conclusion of this accord will be detrimental to both countries". Minister of Trade and Commerce from May 1998 to July 99 Raúl Hernandez (30/07/1998: 31 A) stated that "the negotiations are done as we are only waiting for an answer from Chile". Chile had predicted that Panama really needed to close a deal soon to assure a de-politicised ratification in Congress, before the referendum affected the internal agenda (interview with an anonymous former analyst of the Central Bank 08/04/2008; former Chilean trade diplomat 11/04/2008). In this regard, it seems Chile miscalculated how important financial services were for Panama.

> At the end we were the ones calling Chile to ask whether they had an answer on our proposal and on the feasibility study they were conducting. The answer was always the same, 'we are waiting for the opinion and the final assessment of the minister of finances', as these issues are dealt by this institution and not DIRECON [...] The answer came in early August as we had a couple of weeks before the referendum to sign and approve the accord. The answer was 'no' but with the proposal of getting the accord done as it was and to validate the BIT and negotiate the issue of services as a whole later (Interview with Samuel Moreno, MICI, 22/07/2008). [129]

After using the time extension as a pressure-tactic in light of the forthcoming referendum, and the extant politicisation level in Panama, Chile pressed to close the agreement without services. The proposal was that all services would be reviewed through a revision clause in the future once the agreement came into force (interviews with Alejandro Ferrer, MICI, 29/07/2008; anonymous, Chile 04/04/2008; Diana Salazar, MICI, 30/07/2008).[130] Moreover, Chile based this offer on the fact that the negotiation was politicised and this would only increase because of the referendum and presidential election in Panama as well as the coming electoral process in Chile in 1999.

Even though Chile had a defensive position on market access, it controlled the momentum of the negotiation by using multiple tactics that belong to a value-claiming strategy. Whereas Chile opted for a offensive strategy, which helped them

129 Author's translation.

130 One of the interviewed was not sure whether it was five years or less in order to review the category of financial services and services. Nevertheless, the important part is Chile's offer to Panama, which was to use a clause in the accord to negotiate services in the future once the FTA becomes valid.

to administer the timing of the process, this strategy produced an escalatory effect since it affected the mutual trust within the negotiating parties. In many episodes, Panama answered in a rather defensive way in order to contain Chile's movements. In other episodes Panama also used an offensive value-claiming strategy towards Chile. The latter also answered in the same way, for example when Panama used the reforms it was conducting on banking legislation to push Chile in a hard way. Nevertheless it was Chile that created more mechanisms to manage the negotiation and regain bargaining power whenever it felt it was in a disadvantaged position vis-à-vis Panama. By increasing its bargaining power Chile pushed Panama to its resistance point. Whenever Chile felt that Panama was pushing too hard to reciprocate Chile's offensive moves, the latter threatened to leave the table, which is perhaps the most risky tactic when the win-set is rather small, the zone of agreement is not that broad, and the BATNA interesting for both sides. Finally, it was Chile that left the negotiating table in August, and that did not do much to solve the issues that blocked a final agreement.

6.2.4 The Weight of Other FTA Processes

The negotiation between Chile and Panama was not conducted in a vacuum. Other countries that negotiated, were negotiating, or were planning to negotiate FTAs with Chile and Panama, and/or those countries that Chile and Panama aspired to negotiate with, hampered the successful conclusion of the FTA talks between these two countries. In many ways the conditions in which external actors have an impact on the negotiation were created by Panama and Chile, in a rather inside-out way, with the purpose of enhancing their own or debilitating the other's BATNA. However, it is also possible to observe that the phenomenon of FTA was in vogue as there were ongoing negotiations in the Americas and in the world. Regional economic integration schemes and bilateral FTAs were triggered with a similar timing and sometimes as an answer to other FTAs and to cope with the global market forces. The proliferation of these accords was in part intended to prevent the trade deviation effect, producing a domino effect of FTAs as well as to create trade between the signatory countries of such agreements (see Viner 1950; Baldwin 2006: 1467-1468).

Although Panama and Chile knew which products were competitive and sensitive for each other, they did not know in detail how sensitive these were for their counterpart domestic groups and how embedded the governments were in these groups. Moreover, Panama did not know the detailed and specific dynamics in which Chile's previous FTAs or trade accords were conducted. What Panamanians did not know was which nested games Chile was involved in. In the FTA negotiation with Canada, the issue of investment was difficult to overcome, because Canada asked Chile to modify its 'encaje' system as well as to include financial services (Sáez 2006: 13). However, Chile refused to change this by using a mix of value-claiming and value-creating strategies. On the one hand, Chile stood strong to contain Canada's request, but on the other hand, it created compensation packages to broaden Canada's access on goods, especially in food and agricultural products as this North American country is one of the world's leading countries in the agri-food industry. This created a strong reaction from the SNA and jeopardised the Congress' approval of the accord (*El Diario* 04/12/1996: 26; *La Tercera* 01/07/1997: 21 and 23; Campbell 2006). In addition, Chile also granted juridical certainty to facilitate the investments on the mining sector, which was the main promoter of the agreement with Chile due to its high investments in the sector (64 percent of Canada's total investments in Chile in 1974-2002), and also granted certainty to their interest on developing new projects in this area (Caputo 2002: 11). Moreover, Chile also agreed to include a clause to start negotiations on financial services in the future if Chile's entrance to NAFTA did not come soon,

> If the negotiations for Chile's accession to NAFTA have not been engaged within 15 months of the entry into force of this Agreement, the Parties shall commence negotiations with a view to entering into an agreement, based on Chapter 14 on Financial Services of the NAFTA, by no later than April 30, 1999 (FTA Chile-Canada Annex G-01.3(b)).

In fact, the negotiations between both countries on financial services were only concluded in July 2007 (Foreign Affairs and International Trade-Canada 2009). The South American country could overcome Canada's pressure by committing to negotiate in the future. Canada accepted Chile's proposal by defining a time frame to conduct the negotiations if Chile did not join NAFTA soon. Moreover, Canada also believed that Chile would gain access to NAFTA, which could become true in the short run as the US, Canada and Mexico supported this (Zechner 2002: 24). Thus Canada knew that once Chile received NAFTA membership, Chile would adopt the NAFTA model on financial services as well as adopt further liberalisation such as the modification of its unremunerated reserve requirement for investments.[131]

If Chile did not include a chapter on financial services with Mercosur, Mexico and Canada, it would not grant this privilege to Panama that was seen as a small country with relatively small power to trigger such a change (interview with Catalina Bau, Ministry of Finances, 11/04/2008; Marcela Klein, Ministry of Finances, 24/03/2008; anonymous 04/04/2008). Chile thus misjudged not only its own bargaining power to protect this issue with Panama, but also misjudged Panama's decisive interest on including a financial services chapter in the agreement. Moreover, Chile was protecting the issue of financial services not from Panama, but from the US. Chile had the hope of starting a negotiation to enter NAFTA, or to negotiate a bilateral FTA with the US in the short-run. Chile knew that the US would put the issue of financial services on the negotiation table, since NAFTA includes a chapter on this issue (Sáez and Sáez 2006).

131 It is interesting to note that the time frame set by Canada was not respected as Chile waited until an agreement with the US was concluded to close a deal with Canada on financial issues. Yet, it is not clear whether Canada and Chile tried to negotiate financial services no later than April 1999.

Moreover, Chile took it for granted that the US would also ask to modify the *encaje* law for FDI as American investors complained about this mechanism. Canada's initial request to negotiate these issues was also taken as an indicator that the US would display all its structural and bargaining power to liberalise these issues. If this was the case, then Chile had to increase its bargaining power not necessarily to protect such issues, but to use it as a bargaining chip to get more concessions on other sectors, especially on market access for agricultural products, in which the US is highly protected (Saéz and Sáez 2006; interviews with Roberto Pizarro, DIRECON, 25/03/2008; Osvaldo Rosales, DIRECON, 19/03/2008; Mario Matus, DIRECON, 28/02/2008; Jorge Leiva, former Minister of Economy, 19/03/2008; Carlos Furche, DIRECON, 18/03/2008; Andrés Rebolledo, DIRECON, 25/03/2008; Raúl Opitz, Ministry of Agriculture, 10/04/2008). In other words, Chile's refusal to include financial services in the accord with Panama was a strategic move to enhance its bargaining power vis-à-vis the US.[132]

For Panama, the negotiation with Chile was also seen as a learning step with the purpose of negotiating an FTA with the US in the following years. In this regard, implementing domestic reforms to improve the transparency of the financial operations in Panama became imperative, once Panamanian negotiators realised that the issue may block not only the agreement with Chile, but also subsequent agreements. It may also have been a US requirement before starting the initial assessment for an FTA between both countries (*Enlace* 1998: 4-7). Only if Panama achieved international standards and established a regulatory framework on financial services, would an FTA negotiation with the US have been possible.[133] However, the implementation of these reforms changed the negotiation setting with Chile as the latter had decided to negotiate this issue only with the US or eventually the EU.

As the domestic and international conditions started to constrain the progress of the FTA talks between Chile and Panama, these countries also started to monitor possible new negotiations to satisfy the pro-FTA groups and to continue with the long-term economic foreign policy in order to keep the overall convergence between commercial interests of domestic groups and the economic national interest of the state. Both countries started to monitor the possibility of launching FTA negotiations with Central America (interviews with Estif Aparicio, MICI, 18/07/2008; Alexis Pineda, MICI, 18/07/2008; Alejandro Ferrer, MICI, 29/07/2008; Héctor Casanueva, ProChile, 07/04/2008; Francisco Prieto, ProChile, 15/04/2008). In addition, Chile started to devote more time to conclude its parallel negotiations of low scope trade agreement with Peru, which was concluded in 1998; and the FTA negotiation with Mexico also concluded in 1998.

132 This was confirmed when Chile continued refusing after Panama implemented banking regulatory reform in February 1998. See previous sub-sections of this chapter.

133 The FTA with the US is signed but it has not yet been approved by the American Congress, alongside the FTAs that the US signed with South Korea, and Colombia. The signed US-Panama FTA has a chapter on financial services (Office of United States Trade Representative 2009).

In the case of Chile, the negotiations with Central America were launched in 1999. However, Chile started the feasibility studies on launching these FTA negotiations in 1998. In fact, Chile and Central America announced the start of the negotiations in the summit of the Americas held in Santiago in April 1998 (see www.sice.oas.org). As discussed in the previous sections, president Frei did not refer to the FTA negotiation with Panama in this summit. Panamanians interpreted this announcement between Chile and Central America as Chile was ready to put less effort into concluding the FTA with Panama. They also interpreted the announcement as a way to put all of the pressure on their side in order to make Panama's position more flexible and close the deal (interviews with Diana Salazar, MICI, 30/07/2008; Alejandro Ferrer, MICI, 29/07/2008).

Therefore, Chile made an exception as the negotiation with Central America took place during an electoral year in Chile. The negotiation was launched in August 1998 and the normative text was concluded in September 1999, despite the fact that Chile and the Central American countries agreed to conclude the negotiation of a common normative frame by December 1998, and to start the negotiation of the bilateral protocols on market access and rules of origin in January (COMEX 1998: CP04). As the original times had passed Chile postponed the bilateral negotiations until after the presidential election, with the exception of that with Costa Rica. Chile and Costa Rica concluded with a bilateral market access and rule of origin protocol due to Costa Rica's pressure and under the promise of having a final agreement before the month of the elections in Chile (December 1999; interviews with Laura Rodriguez, COMEX, 08/07/2008; Roberto Echandi, COMEX, 26/06/2008). Even though Chile and Costa Rica concluded the negotiations in October and signed the bilateral protocol in November 1999, it only submitted the agreement for ratification to Congress after the election in order to prevent its electoral use. The agreement was only implemented in 2002 due to the slow pace of the ratification process in both Chile and Costa Rica (see Gobierno de Chile 14/02/2002: DTO-14).

Chile's conditions for negotiating with Central America were to exclude financial services and an investment chapter as such. Chile made clear the non-negotiability of these issue-areas and that it would only reaffirm the validity of the extant bilateral investment treaties (interviews with Oscar Quina, DIRECON, 08/04/2008; Camilo Navarro Ceardi, DIRECON, 17/03/2008). However, some cross-border services issues were included such as air-transport, telecommunications, and the temporary entry for business persons (FTA Chile-Central America, chapter 10-14). Chile's reason for establishing conditions and outlining the non-negotiable issues at the outset of the process was to prevent a similar negative experience to that of the FTA with Panama.

Panama also started to use its BATNA options to show Chile it also has possibilities of achieving other FTAs, even if the one with Chile failed in reaching an outcome of agreement. However, these possibilities were not secure. In this regard, the option of Central America was for Panama the most concrete option as they are natural trade partners. However, it was only in March 2000 that the Central American countries and Panama formally agreed to launch negotiations (see www.sice.oas.org, 2009). On the one hand, Panama did not have enough staff to conduct many parallel negotiations as the FTAA was also underway, and on the other hand the Central American countries put more emphasis on concluding the FTA talks with Chile (anonymous interview 26/07/2008). Nevertheless, Panama used the assessing phase with Central America, started in July 1998, to show Chile that it could get other trade partners. In addition, Panama started to focus its efforts on the FTAA as negotiations of this process were launched in April 1998 during the summit of Santiago.

To sum up, the possibilities of launching new negotiations and getting access to the US market through NAFTA or bilaterally for Chile, and bilaterally and in the FTAA process for Panama, played a decisive role in the use of hard bargaining within the negotiation. As a result of these factors they became real options for both sides. In fact, both actors were sure there were more potential trade partners 'out there' for both countries to continue growing or building a web of FTAs if the negotiation between Chile and Panama failed. In addition, Chile started to devote more attention to the parallel negotiations it was conducting as the progress on the FTA with Panama started to slow down. Yet Chile's previous FTA experiences also constrained what it could offer to Panama as any concession should also be granted to countries that had FTAs with Chile, or at the least these countries would have asked Chile to start negotiations on such issues. If Chile did not negotiate financial services and did not alter its encaje system with Canada or Mexico, it was not open for debate with Panama. One of the decisive aspects that increased the difficulty of converging on common positions in the FTA negotiation between Chile and Panama was Chile's decision to use the issue of financial services for strategic reasons in a future negotiation with the US.

6.3 Concluding Remarks

The elements presented in the state to state negotiation between Chile and Panama explain how the negotiation shifted from a setting in which mutual trust was high to one in which it started to deteriorate. The lack of a clearly outlined set of non-negotiable issues at the outset of the negotiation was based on the previous negotiating experience Chile had in the FTA process with Canada. Chile tried to structure a strategy based on balancing Panama's aspirations to include financial services by asking to liberalise professional services. Whereas Panama did not want to include this issue in the beginning, it made its posture more flexible in the following rounds, which altered, along with the reforms in the financial sector, the negotiating setting. This put the pressure of the negotiation on Chile, as they were reluctant to include a chapter on financial issues in this accord because of Panama's liberal legislation. Chile was also under pressure due to its desire to use financial issues as a bargaining chip in a negotiation with the US.

Moreover, as mutual trust started to deteriorate, the use of tactics which belong to a value-claiming strategy increased substantially and they were displayed in issue-areas and products that were in principle labelled as low conflict. In this regard, the lack of leadership skills within the process to redirect the negotiation was a missing element that may have induced de-escalation in the way Chile and Panama ended negotiation, which at the beginning was thought to be a win-win deal. Nevertheless, the evidence on leadership skills is rather ambiguous, especially concerning the role of political leaders, and it is certainly not conclusive enough.

This lack of leadership as a condition has to be understood as an intertwined process of convergence of forces, along with non-negotiability, the overuse of a value-claiming strategy, and the role of other external actors, who influenced and directed the course of this FTA negotiation. Therefore, these four conditions with different degrees of weight explain how and why the FTA negotiation between Chile and Panama failed to reach an outcome of agreement. Needless to say the conditions here described and those of the previous chapter played a decisive role in understanding the process, the dynamics, the timing and the divergent interests that made the negotiation between Chile and Panama fail.

7. The FTA Negotiation between Costa Rica and Panama: Domestic Dimension

7.1 Introduction

This chapter presents the domestic dimension of the trade negotiation between Costa Rica and Panama. It analyses the extant domestic conditions that are internal and external to the negotiation. In addition, I present an overview of the whole process including the negotiation of the FTA normative text between the Central American countries and Panama. In this negotiation of the normative text there were already sensitive issues, which are important for understanding the process that made the bilateral negotiation between these two countries fail. Finally, I assess the different internal and external domestic factors that brought this FTA negotiation conducted during 2002 to a long-term standstill.

7.2 An Overview of the Negotiation Process

Panama and Costa Rica are competitive trade partners.[134] In fact both countries signed a preferential trade agreement in 1973. However, the scope of this agreement is very limited. Therefore, Costa Rica and Panama as well as the other Central American countries sought to further deepen their respective trade relations by launching FTA negotiations.[135] The launch of an FTA negotiation was part of the new integration efforts in Central America and of the strategy of open regionalism that most Latin American countries adopted in the 1990s (Lizano 2001; Granados et.al. 2007: 21-25). In 1997, the Central American countries signed a general framework for the negotiation of an FTA (Ferrer 2001: 228). The formal launch of negotiation rounds was postponed for a number of reasons: the electoral climate in Panama; the loss of power of then President Pérez Balladares as a result of the referendum; the lack of staff to negotiate simultaneously for some Central American countries as they were also involved in the incoming negotiations with the Dominican Republic and Chile; and the reluctance of some domestic constituencies to en-

134 Costa Rica is Panama's fifth most important trade partner. In 2001Costa Rica imported from Panama USD 38,959.134 and exported to Panama USD 103,655.965 (MICI 2005: 1).

135 This FTA negotiation involved Costa Rica, El Salvador, Guatemala, Honduras and Nicaragua, and Panama. This FTA is only binding in bilateral terms i.e. the trade relation between each Central American Country vis-à-vis Panama.

gage in this process. It was only in April 2000 that the formal negotiations between Central America and Panama were launched (see www.comex.go.cr). The negotiation parties held eight formal rounds before concluding the normative framework, plus three extra sessions to solve the sensitive issue-areas such as services, investment, rules of origin and financial services, which were slowing the building of the normative framework (see table 4).

Table 4: Central America's-Panama's Negotiating Rounds

Rounds	Date
first	27-28 April 2000
second	6-8 June 2000
third	17-20 July 2000
fourth	22-24 August 2000
fifth	24-26 October 2000
sixt	30 January-2 february 2001
seventh	13-16 march 2001
eighth	15-16 May 2001
Special/extra rounds*	
services & investment	30 November-1 December 2000
	8-11 January 2001
rules of origin and Customs issues	4-6 December 2000
Bilateral Protocol-Panama-Costa Rica	
First	3-5 April 2002
Second	16-19 July 2002

* The special/extra rounds were conducted to solve sensitive issues

Sources: Comex available at:
http://www.comex.go.cr/acuerdos/Panama2/Paginas/Rondasnegociacion.aspx

The normative common frame was signed in May 2001 and in April 2002 the bilateral negotiation between Costa Rica and Panama started (www.comex.go.cr., www.mici.gob.pa). However, this negotiation stalled after two rounds during the same year (July 2002), due to the lack of agreement over a diverse array of issues-areas such as financial services, insurances, rules of origin, and different food, livestock and agricultural products (COMEX 14/03/2006: CP 597; COMEX

18/08/2006: CP 646).[136] However, informal meetings were conducted before and during the formal rounds to coordinate the negotiation and its different technicalities.

The antecedents of the previous negotiation on the normative framework suggest that the bargaining between Costa Rica and Panama would be difficult. The latter asked for some protective measures in the normative framework on agricultural issues, and the liberalisation of financial services. Costa Rica argued that the substantial part of financial services negotiation on whether to allow both bank branches and subsidiaries as Panama requested should be conducted in the bilateral process, and not in the normative negotiation (interviews with Gabriela Llobet, COMEX, 02/07/2008; Leda Arrué, MICI, 17/07/2008). Costa Rica allows the entry of international banks in the form of branches and it prohibits the operation of international banks in the form of subsidiaries (Barth, Caprio, and Levine 2006: 113).[137]

When the Central American countries and Panama launched their FTA negotiation, Costa Rica already had FTAs with Mexico (1994), the Dominican Republic (1998), Chile (1999), Canada (2001). Panama, on the contrary, signed its first FTA with the Central American countries in May 2001. This accord covered the normative frame of the FTA, and it kept the items of market access, and the details on services and rules of origin for bilateral negotiations between each Central American country and Panama (FTA Central America-Panama 2002). Panama's first FTA was signed with El Salvador in March 2002, in which both countries agreed to include liberal statements on financial services and excluding sensitive issues such as dairy products (see FTA Panama-El Salvador: bilateral protocol 2002). After assuring its first FTA with El Salvador, Panama started to more intensively monitor other possibilities of negotiations such as potential negotiation with the US, Taiwan and Singapore. They also began concluding the bilateral negotiations with Honduras, Nicaragua, Guatemala, and Costa Rica (Rivera 2005: 65-66). However, Costa Rica exerted pressure to be the second country to close a deal with Panama (interview with Melissa Davis, MICI, 17/07/2008; Laura Rodriguez, COMEX, 08/07/2008; Amparo Pacheco, COMEX, 02/07/2008).

The reasons to launch an FTA negotiation between Panama and Costa Rica followed an economic rather than political rationale. Therefore, both parties expected to have a tough bargaining process as they could detect one another's sensitive issues in the negotiation's normative frame. Moreover, the bilateral economic relationship between these two countries was affected by a sense of mutual distrust based on the historical fact that Costa Rica asked Panama for bilateral negotiations

136 For example, onions, tomato processed products, wheat flour, bakery products, poultry, beef, chicken, turkey, and pork meat, and milk products.

137 International banks can also enter Costa Rica's market through acquisitions. Yet there are two factors that hamper the entrance of international banks through these means: the size of the financial market and the restricted number of existing banks, and the legal restrictions to deliver some retail banking operations. These restrictions are presented in the following pages.

on market access in its accession to the WTO (Ferrer 2001).[138] This aspect played a role in the negotiation as both actors framed the negotiations as conflict-based rather than integrative-based. Moreover, in the following analysis we see that the bilateral economic relationship was built according to an inter-trade pattern rather than on possibilities of complementarity. Therefore, it is expected that this negotiation will present more conditions of politicisation within the process and high divergences over interests at the national level; moreover it is likely that we will find that the countries both searched for alternative options of other negotiations and used a large number of distributive strategies.

7.2.1 The Normative Frame between Central America and Panama

In a document to monitor the possibilities of launching FTA negotiations in 1998, Costa Rica divided the issues to be included in a possible negotiation with Panama into high intensity, low intensity and special issues categories. The high intensity issues were those that needed careful attention and those becoming the institutional pillars for a free trade zone with Panama. Amongst these issues were market access, rules of origin, Customs issues, safeguard measures, dispute settlement mechanisms and investment. The low intensity thematic issues, such as sanitary and phytosanitary measures, technical obstacles to trade, intellectual property, dumping and subsidies, had second priority because to some extent they were already covered by multilateral rules (COMEX 16/01/1998: 1-5). The special issues were government procurement and services. The main principle to negotiate these two issues was to assure national treatment. On the case of services, there was also the need to assure the protection of key strategic areas for Costa Rica such as telecommunications, financial services (banking and insurances), and the investment regime. Moreover, the services, which were not to be included in the FTA, were subject to future discussion under a clause of future negotiation or could be part of the so called non-conforming measures that were included in the annexes of the FTAs. These special issues were defined as such by Costa Rica, because there was not much experience between the parties in negotiating these areas. However, these issues were seen as important prerequisites for bringing the process to a final agreement as Panama was highly interested in these issues due to its competitiveness. This does not mean that a pro-liberalisation position in all issues was adopted. On the contrary, the convenience or inconvenience of adopting liberalisation positions was to be measured following a case by case logic. Moreover, the entire initiative to bring up these issues during the negotiation was given to Panama (Ibid.: 1-5).

Panama presented a liberal proposal on services in general and financial services in particular. In fact, Panama was the first country to present a first draft for a chapter on financial services (COMEX 06/04/2000: 070). Costa Rica's domestic groups

138 See Chapter 4, sub-section 4.2.1

from the banking sector overall agreed with Panama's proposal for a normative chapter on financial services as it showed a general commitment to facilitate the trade in financial services. Moreover, it lacked specification on which type of banks and which specific issues would be included as this was a matter to be negotiated in the bilateral rounds between each Central American country and Panama (COMEX 10/05/2000; SUGEVAL-COMEX 09/05/2000: 1-3; ABC-COMEX 08/05/2000; SUGEF-COMEX 08/05/2000: 1-3; Banco Central-COMEX 25/04/2000). Both Costa Rica and Panama were countries with higher stakes in the making of the normative framework of the FTA. This was especially the case for financial services, investment and telecommunications (interviews with Gabriela Llobet, COMEX, 02/07/2008; Diana Salazar, MICI, 30/07/2008). These issues were also analysed in a bilateral presidential meeting within the development of the FTAA negotiations held in Quebec in 2001. According to a memorandum sent by then Minister of International Trade Tomás Dueñas to the then President of Costa Rica Miguel Angel Rodríguez (09/03/2001), which included an analysis and the main talking points for the presidential meeting between the latter and Panamanian President Mireya Moscoso, Costa Rica wanted to speed up the completion of the normative framework to move on the negotiation to the bilateral protocols between both countries. This memorandum stated that Costa Rica's President should highlight the fact that concluding the normative frame,

> [...] is a significant step for Panama, because it is one of the few countries that have not signed an FTA yet, which affects its international image, taking into consideration that Panama will be the venue for the FTAA negotiation process for the next two years. This accord will be Panama's first one, which is very well advanced and it is inoffensive for its interests. Thus it makes sense to conclude such negotiation as soon as possible (COMEX 09/03/2001: 2).

In the same memorandum, Costa Rica expressed its concerns over the issue of telecommunications, in response to which Panama requested the option of entering this sector whenever Costa Rica privatised the area. Telecommunications in Costa Rica were a state monopoly sector controlled by the 'Instituto Costarricence de Electricidad' (ICE) at the time of these negotiations.[139] This issue was brought up by Panama as a way to protect its own defensive issues, but also as a way to increase its bargaining power in order to include the issues of insurances, and financial services in the accord (interview with Diana Salazar 30/07/2008). The document also argued that telecommunications as a public company should be protected: "This is an issue that has not been negotiated in previous FTAs due to the imposed restriction of the national law" (COMEX 09/03/2001:2).

Despite the fact that Panama proposed the inclusion of a clause to negotiate telecommunications in the future whenever Costa Rica's government privatised this sector (COMEX 05/03/2001), the final normative agreement indicates that this measure did not get a favourable reception. In fact, the FTA chapter about telecommunications is only valid for Panama and the rest of the Central American countries,

139 The ICE was liberalised in the negotiation of DR-CAFTA.

but not for the bilateral economic relationship between Costa Rica and Panama (FTA Central America-Panama 2002, chapter 13, article 13.01). Even though Panama did not achieve its goal, the trade-off offered to Panama was the inclusion of a broad definition of financial institutions that reflected the structure and nature of its financial sector. Costa Rica agreed on including Panama's position in the definition of *financial services* and *financial services of the counterpart*. This position was to include the words: "any company and financial intermediary which is authorised to **make business**" instead of: **to deliver financial services** as Central America proposed regarding financial services. And Central America under the lead of Costa Rica also accepted to include the wording "including **a branch**" regarding the meaning of a financial institution of the counterpart, as this word reflects the structure of Panama's banking system, which includes international banks (branches) located in this country (COMEX 03/07/2000: DGCE-331-00; COMEX 03/07/2000: DGCE 331-00: 172; FTA Central America-Panama 2002, chapter 12, article 12.01).

In addition, the trade-off also included the exclusion of Professional services from the trade discussions at the bilateral level. Costa Rica also acceded to negotiate financial services in an inclusive way, as well as to negotiate the issue of insurances and give a fair treatment to Panama's sensitive agricultural products in the subsequent bilateral negotiations. Yet in many ways these initial statements changed during the bilateral bargaining (Interviews with Joaquin Jácome, MICI, 17/07/2008; Melissa Davis, MICI, 17/07/2008; Alexis Pineda, MICI, 18/07/2008; Zereth Torres, MICI, 22/07/2008).

Most of the wording for these definitions and the coverage of the chapter of financial services were still broad and lack specification on the substance. The normative text of the FTA did not make clear which kind of financial institutions would be allowed to operate in Costa Rica (branches and/or subsidiaries; see FTA text Central America-Panama 2002). Moreover, it was not clear to what extent as well as how the issue of insurances would be covered, if at all, in the bilateral protocols of the FTA. These were the pending issues that were to be negotiated in the bilateral negotiation between each Central American country vis-à-vis Panama. The reason to negotiate this bilaterally was that both Panama and El Salvador had a liberal view on the issue, whereas Costa Rica, Honduras, Nicaragua and Guatemala had a rather defensive position on financial services. Costa Rica did not want to create divisions within its Central American partners. Therefore, they agreed to negotiate this issue bilaterally with Panama (interviews with Roberto Echandi, COMEX, 26/06/2008; Irene Arguedas, COMEX, 03/07/2008).

The negotiation of the normative part on market access was not conflictive for Costa Rica and Panama as such. The normative negotiation on market access included general commitments to liberalise under the principle of reciprocity the bilateral trade of goods and services. Moreover, the parties decided to grant each other national treatment; dismantle the extant NTB; and achieve non-discriminatory rules to facilitate trade on sanitary and phytosanitary measures, metrology, normalisation measures, and authorisation procedures respectively. In addition, the parties agreed to negotiate the specifics of rules of origin in the bilateral process (FTA text Central

America-Panama 2002: chapters 3, 4, 8, and 9). Moreover, the process of building the normative frame on market access did not establish the phase out periods and the quantities for the goods and services to be included in the agreement (DINECI 15/04/2000: 0059; Minute of the negotiation Central America-Panama 1-2/02/2001: 1-3).

Following the distinction in negotiation theory between a formula and a detailed phase, the normative framework on market access presents similarities to the formula phase of a negotiation as it was cooperative. And the detailed phase is the subsequent bilateral negotiation, in which tariff reductions, quotas, and transition periods are further discussed according to a distributive pattern (see Kremenyuk and Sjöstedt, eds. 2000: 25). Nevertheless, the making of the entire normative frame showed preliminary sensitive and divergent issues on financial services, and investment, which were conceived as strategic by each party, and which were likely to hamper the progress of the bilateral negotiation.

7.3 Domestic Factors

7.3.1 Divergent Interests

Costa Rica perceived itself as highly competitive in agriculture and industrial production vis-à-vis Panama. Industrial issues were not conflictive as there were two minor issues that were sensitive i.e. cardboard and plastic production (interviews with Luis Obando and Jack Liberman, CICR, 30/06/2008; Carlos Céspedes and Sergio Navas, CADEXCO,25/06/2008). The interesting issues for Costa Rica's producers, yet sensitive for Panama, were dairy products (except condensed and evaporated milk), pork meat, wheat flour, pasta, bakery, chicken meat, eggs, onions, and comestible oils. Panama was highly defensive regarding these products, and sought to exclude them from the agreement, while Costa Rica wanted immediate access. The proposals of Costa Rica's National Chamber of Agriculture, the Chamber of Food Producers (CACIA), dairy products representatives, industrial goods and agro-industry are shown in the table 5: 171.

It is interesting to note that the Chamber of Agriculture first proposed reciprocal free access on rice on September 12th 2000, and then resubmitted a new proposal with an amendment on the issue of rice, which was now excluded. The latter proposal was presented the 12th of November 2000 (Camara Nacional de Agricultura y Agroindustria 12/09/2000; and 28/11/2000). A CNAA representative (09/07/2008) mentioned that "the rice sub-sector did not measure the current deterioration of the national production at first due to the international prices. Once they realised there was a possible openness of this sector to Panama, due to Panama's lower costs of production, Costa Rica's rice producers would lose. Therefore, this group went for exclusion and we had to resubmit a new proposal". However, this issue did not become a source of conflict in the negotiation as Panama was also having problems with its rice production and therefore proposed that the sector should not be exposed to international competition (ANALMO, 04/2004: 4-12; interview with Denia de Sanjur, ANALMO, 23/07/2008).

Dairy products are another important aspect for understanding how these domestic interests became a source of conflict due to the extant divergence between the national sectors of Panama and Costa Rica. Costa Rica proposed immediate free trade for all its products (FTA Costa Rica-Panama's draft text 2002: Market access proposals, 0204-0202). Yet this initial proposal was not based on reciprocity as Costa Rica was very sensitive on condensed and evaporated milk vis-à-vis Panama. In order to contain Panama's eventual position for immediate free trade on these products, Costa Rica's milk producers went for free trade, but they clearly stated to the trade negotiators that the rules of origin would have to be restrictive (Interviews with Erik Montero, CNPL, 27/06/2008; Laura Rodriguez, COMEX, 08/07/2008; Tatiana Varela, COMEX, 26/06/2008; Alexis Pineda, MICI, 18/07/2008).

Table 5: Costa Rica domestic associations' positions

Association	Proposals on Goods and Services	Rules of Origin
CNAA	pork meat: immediate free access	
	sugar: exclusion	
	horticulture: free access	
	cattle industry: alive animals free access	
	cattle industry: beef meat: exclusion	
	apiculture: free access	
	coffee: free access	
	rice: free access initial/ then changed for exclusion	
	beans in all sorts: exclusion	restrictive
	diary: free access in all products	restrictive
UPANACIONAL	diary: free access in all products	restrictive
	chicken and turkey. Exclusion	
	beans in all sorts: exclusion	
CACIA	sauces, mayo and others: free access	flexible
	non-alcoholic beverages and juices: free access	
	Pastas, biscuits and bakery: free access	flexible

Sources: ANALMO, ANAPOR, ANAVIP; Chamber of Commerce, Industries and Agriculture; COMEX: FTA Costa Rica-Panama's draft text, proposals on market access (18/07/2002).

For Costa Rica, all the inputs for milk and milk related products should be produced within the national market or within the Central American region. In fact, in the draft of the FTA text on rules of origin, Costa Rica proposed that in order for the origin of milk products to be the same as the location of its production, the milk in its natural state or without processing must be from the same country in which the milk is processed. Conversely, Panama presented offers on most dairy products stating that the milk inputs for final dairy products should be produced in Panama or Costa Rica in a range from 20 to 50 percent of the total. This meant that the remaining 80 and 50 percent of the necessary inputs to elaborate final dairy products could be imported from a third country (FTA Costa Rica and Panama's draft text 2002: norms of origin: 0239-0238). Therefore, Costa Rica wanted to restrict Panama's importation of inputs to produce milk products from New Zealand, which is one of the world leading countries in dairy production (interview with Erik Montero, CNPL, 27/06/2008). Costa Rica's milk sector in the need to assure a restrictive rule of origin went so far as to ask the different associations of milk producers of Central American countries to sign a letter stating that the Central American and Caribbean Milk Producers Federation propose,

> [...] to keep the current Central American normative, which states that for a country to constitute the country of origin for a milk product this should be entirely processed with milk produced in that country, and/or in the Central American and Caribbean region, for any commercial negotiation and especially for the one between Central America and Panama. Only by assuring strict rules of origin, the national production and industrialisation of the dairy sector in the region will grow [...] (Federación Centroamericana y del Caribe del Sector Lácteo 22/03/2001).

From the positions presented in table 5, it could also be said that the food production sector perceived itself as highly competitive vis-à-vis Panama's food domestic sector. Despite the fact that tomato processed products were in jeopardy due to Panama competitiveness, the overall package for this economic sector was large. However, CACIA was not only afraid that Panama's defensive position on food products would hamper the achievement of its economic goals, but also that its own government could trade-off important food products in order to limit the scope of the talks on financial services and investment. CACIA did not want to be used as the bargaining chip for the protection of Costa Rica's financial and investment actors, which were considered strategic for Costa Rica. CACIA, on behalf of the wheat flour producers as well as pasta, bakery, bread, biscuits and cookies producers, manifested their concern about COMEX negotiation strategy,

[…] this sector requests that under any circumstance, the market access negotiated with Panama is below the one the rest of the Central American countries have negotiated or will negotiate with Panama. Therefore, we encourage COMEX to coordinate positions between Costa Rica and the rest of the Central American countries. Likewise, we prohibit, under any circumstance, the diminution of our potential to accede to Panama's market due to the sacrifice that the country -(Costa Rica)- should make whenever Panama requests free access to our services market (CACIA July 2000: 4).

This statement was intented to make noise and show the knowledge this group had on the dynamics of an FTA negotiation.[140] Whereas CACIA knew that COMEX's trade negotiators needed to offset certain pro-liberalisation interests in one area to protect its defensive positions in others, such as services in this case, this domestic group was not willing to be used as a bargaining chip as they saw high gains in this FTA (interview with Mario Montero, CACIA, 07/07/2008). The milk producers also aligned with CACIA's interests in the sense that they refused to be sacrificed in the deal if financial services were to join the bilateral economic negotiation (interview with Erik Montero, CNPL, 27/06/2008). These anticipatory measures taken by these domestic groups created inflexibility for the trade negotiators. The concrete impact was the narrowing of the room to bargain at the international level as well as the reduction of the initial win-set of the negotiation. This non-acceptance of lower conditions of market access had to do with the high expectations each domestic sector had of their potential access to Panama's market. These expectations increased the costs of what could be ratified at the domestic level by the legal mechanisms, if the negotiation would have concluded with agreement. A former trade negotiator from Costa Rica described the initial setting provided by domestic interests and how these created a strong influence and also conflict in the bilateral negotiation:

We negotiate for these groups, so these companies can have access to markets and make profits as well as increase the national production. Nevertheless, in the case of the FTA with Panama, we had big difficulties with containing the pressures of our own domestic groups; because they had excessive expectations as they saw the possibility of entering Panama which is an attractive market because of the level of wages (consumption); because we are border countries; and because it had high tariffs for food and dairy products, despite that fact we got some market access, but still insufficient. Therefore, our relative costs to send products to Panama vis-à-vis third countries were to be much lower if an FTA was signed. But these extremely high expectations created difficulties for us to manage the negotiation as none of our groups

140 Domestic interest groups' expertise in knowing the dynamics of the negotiation at the international level is to some extent given by the fact that some executives of these associations were formerly part of COMEX's trade negotiation team. Therefore, these people know that sometimes the exclusion of one economic sector or products is compensated for in other issue-areas and not necessarily within the same issue. This note is based on the observation I made when I conducted the interviews in Costa Rica, Chile and Panama, in which the most important economic associations attracted former trade negotiations as they knew the internal dynamics of the negotiations.

> wanted to lessen their demands. The different associations wanted "all or nothing" even when they wanted immediate free access as well as protection for tomato processed products and through a tight rule of origin for dairy products. I mean they did not want to give anything in exchange for protecting these issues. We tried to explain to these groups that we needed flexibility to accommodate all interests of the country, but they insisted on having the priority (Interview with Irene Arguedas, COMEX, 03/07/2008).[141]

As argued above, Panama presented an overall defensive position on food, livestock and agricultural products (see Table 6: 174). Yet Panama also sought to liberalise some specific agricultural and food products in which it had a better comparative advantage than Costa Rica such as bovine meat, evaporated milk, and condensed milk, beans, prepared or caned tomatoes, concentrated tomatoes, ketchup and tomato sauce. In most of these products Costa Rica proposed exclusion, while Panama proposed automatic free access (FTA Costa Rica-Panama's draft text: Bilateral Protocol 2002, Folder 380: 168-216).

With regards to services, Panama's position was offensive. In financial services and insurances, the position was to include these items in the negotiation. Panama wanted to include clauses that allowed banks to be established in the form of subsidiaries (Melissa Davis 20/09/2002) as this also was the way its banking system operates (Morales and Schipke 2005: 103). In addition, Panama wanted the subsidiaries to keep the name of the parent bank to help clients to identification and trust these subsidiaries (*La Prensa* 18/09/2002: 25 A). Conversely, Costa Rica did not allow the location of subsidiaries for financial operations. Panama thought that they could deliver competitive retail banking products in Costa Rica such as credits, mortgages, opening saving accounts, credit and debit cards, commercial accounts, accept deposits, and money transactions for people and companies (Interview with Panama's representative of the banking sector 23/07/2008).

141 Author's translation.

Table 6: Panama domestic association's positions

Association	Proposals on Goods	Rules of Origin
CCIA	diary products: exclusion with exceptions	flexible
	goat milk and cream: free access	flexible
	evaporated and condensed milk: free access	flexible
	butter and cheeses: free access	flexible
	potatoes: exclusion	
	fresh tomatoes: 10 years transition	
	onions: exclusion	
	beans all sorts: free access	
	bananas: free access	
	tropical fruits: free access except mango	
	strawberries, raspberries: exclusion	
	rice: exclusion	
	zugar cane: exclusion	
	coconut oil: exclusion	
	sunflower oil: exclusion	
	soya oil: exclusion	
	processed tomatos: free access	
	horticultere: free access few exceptions	
ANAPOR	alive animals: pigs: 10 years transition	
	pork meat: exclusion	
	hams: exclusion	
ANAGAN	alive animals: bovine sector: free access	
	beef meat: free access	
ANAVIP	alive chickens and turkeys: free access	
	chicken and turkey meat: exclusion	
	eggs: exclusion	

Sources: ANALMO, ANAPOR, ANAVIP; Chamber of Commerce, Industries and Agriculture; COMEX: FTA Costa Rica-Panama's draft text, proposals on market access (18/07/2002).

The introduction of international banks either through branches or subsidiaries has different legal and economic implications: "Bank subsidiaries are incorporated under the law of the host country" (Morales and Schipke 2005: 103). These institutions enter a market with the purpose of delivering and competing with local banks for retail clients. Thus they legally constitute a capitalised investment in the country where they locate (Cerutti, et.al. 2005: 1). On the contrary, branches of foreign banks have a head office located abroad and they mainly open centres in third countries to deliver wholesale and investment operations (Barth, Caprio, and Levine 2006; Morales and Schipke 2005). According to Cerutti, et.al. (2005: 1-5), international banks in the forms of branches and subsidiaries involve different levels of parent bank responsibility. Parent banks are responsible for the liabilities of their branches, and subsidiaries are separate entities from the parent bank, which means that the parent is not necessarily responsible for the way subsidiaries operate.

On the one hand, Costa Rica allowed branches as a way to keep control and make the parent bank abroad liable. On the other hand, Costa Rica's legal restrictions on the entrance of subsidiaries into its market is seen as a way to prevent external competition in a small financial market, and protect the local banking elite generated with the privatisation of some public banks in the 1980s and 1990s. Costa Rica has a mixed system of private and public banks. Moreover, the extant law tends to keep the present rent-seeking behaviour between the government and its 'clientele' within the public banks (see Castro 2003; Villasuso 2007: 263-277).

Costa Rica's government also limits the delivery of financial services to national private banks through increasing their operational costs in areas such as opening saving accounts. First, private national banks could only deliver saving services, if they were to keep a minimum credit balance for loans to the public banks of 17 percent once the compulsory reserve requirement is deduced. Alternatively, and second, the private bank should open four agencies within Costa Rica's regions of Chorotega, Central Pacific, Brunca, Huetar Atlántico, and Huetar North, as well as keep ten percent of its money raising for credits for the programs that the executive power will indicate in an obligatory way. These credits would be given to an interest rate that should not be above the basic passive rate calculated by the Central Bank to deliver saving operations (República de Costa Rica 1953, Ley Orgánica de Bancos, article 59 and Chapter V). The implementation of such measures is in no way related to keeping the financial stability of Costa Rica's banking system. Whereas some of these regulations have a developmental purpose, they also seek to prevent internal competition between national private and public banks. The fragmentation and exclusivity of financial operations have produced different and separated spheres of economic and political influence for private and public banks as well as for their controllers,

> The only achievement of the extant situation is the formation of groups of financial actors with privileges and comparative restrictions between each other. Each group defends its protections or privileges with strong force, stating that it is a matter of national interest to keep the status quo […] In our country, there are four or five groups with privileges, protected by the extant law and rules; they are associated with political groups who defend them as well as activate these pacts each time there is an attempt to pursue deep reforms on the financial sector (Barrenechea 2007: 246).

In addition, Panama also thought to include in the accord the issue of insurances, which is a state-owned sector in Costa Rica. Panama's argument was that Costa Rica had shown a systematic willingness to liberalise its services sector in the broad sense (interviews with Samuel Moreno, MICI, 22/07/2008; Melissa Davis, MICI, 17/07/2008), although it failed in some attempts as the case of 'El Instituto Costar ricense de Electricidad' (ICE) shows.[142] Nevertheless, Panama thought that the government of Costa Rica was willing to conduct internal reforms to gradually liberalise such economic sectors, including insurances. In other words, Panama perceived that an eventual liberalisation was a matter of time in Costa Rica; yet the latter needed to find the right moment to introduce such changes in order to minimise domestic opposition. Therefore, Panama's first option was to include insurance in the accord, and its second option was to include a clause stating that once Costa Rica liberalises or privatises this area, the issue will be automatically included in the FTA between both countries (interviews with Melissa Davis, MICI, 17/07/2008; Brunilda del Castillo, MICI, 17/07/2008; Diana Salazar, MICI, 30/07/2008; Leda Arrué, MICI, 17/07/2008; Alexis Pineda, MICI, 18/07/2008).

Costa Rica refused to include these issues –subsidiary banks and insurances- in the accord during the first and the second round and in the informal contact between the negotiators.[143] Costa Rica's trade diplomats argued that these requests were impossible to fulfil as they involved deep changes of its internal legislation.[144] According to the minutes of the negotiation during the first round (05/04/2002: 2),

> [...] the parties exchanged opinions about Costa Rica's argument that sustains that as a principle, Costa Rica does not seek to change its internal legislation through an international treaty. Panama suggested that it is necessary to make the following reflection 'that in the issue-area of goods the tariffs are part of the internal legislation of a country', and if this rule is applied then Costa Rica could not open this area in a bilateral accord. Costa Rica noted this observation.[145]

To sum up, the Costa Rica and Panama governments and domestic interest groups saw each other as threats in agricultural and food products, and financial services, which include the area of insurances. The high divergence on specific agricultural products produced by the offensive positions of Costa Rica's agricultural associations constrained the possibilities of the negotiators at the international level. This was due to excessive expectations of this economic sector to realise gains but not give compensations for protecting its sensitive issues. Needless to say Panama's associations were extremely defensive in order to protect its national production

142 The last attempt to privatise the ICE in 2000, by passing the so called Combo Law, was halted due to the strong popular opposition to such initiative. The ICE presents one of the most unique combinations in terms of delivery of services as it provides energy generation and its supply as well as telecommunications services. For a good analytical account of the process of failure of such reforms in Costa Rica, see Bert Hoffmann 2008. Finally, the ICE was included in the DR-CAFTA by allowing private competition into the system.

143 On one hand, Costa Rica was afraid of Panama's competitiveness and on the other hand, Costa Rica wanted to keep such issues for a future negotiation with the US. In other words, Costa Rica was in principle willing to liberalise these issues in a negotiation with the US after generous compensation in goods. This point is developed further in the next chapter.

144 Panama's trade negotiators stressed that the second option did not involve any concrete legal changes for Costa Rica, as it implies writing in a hypothetical scenario. As it is something for the future this involves a phrasing based on "if in case" (interviews with Diana Salazar, MICI, 30/07/2008, Leda Arrué, MICI, 17/07/2008).

145 Author's translation.

from what they considered predatory behaviour from Costa Rica's government and domestic groups.

Moreover, the high divergence of positions between the governments acted as a catalyst for domestic group demands within the area of services. This divergence also increased the mutual perception that there was a narrow zone of agreement to work with during the bilateral negotiation. During the negotiation of the normative frame such divergences were not as disruptive as during the bilateral process. In the normative negotiation, the divergence was transcended as the market access adopted a mode form and was not based on the details. Even though certain divergences in services were present in this previous process, Panama contained its aspirations in order not to jeopardise the negotiation with the other Central American countries. However, a narrow zone of agreement does not necessarily imply no-agreement in a negotiation as the win-set can be increased (or reduced) during the bargaining process (Singh 2008: 39). In other words, the high divergence of interests of domestic coalitions does not, on its own, explain the failure of this negotiation, although it provides a good explanation of why the process was so complicated to manage for the negotiators at the international level. Therefore, divergence of interests should complement a broader perspective with the other internal and external conditions to the negotiation that emerged in both the domestic (this chapter) and the international level (next chapter).

7.3.2. Job Insecurity

Panama's dairy producers, some sectors of the livestock industry, and food products were to be the most affected if Costa Rica's positions were put through in the agreement. On Costa Rica's side, the preferential free access to Panama would have generated certain negative consequences on the bovine meat industry and tomato sector. Costa Rica's most important sector to be affected by an FTA with Panama were the financial and insurance sectors. In addition, the recent conclusion of the FTA with Canada and the process of approving this accord in Congress were conducted in parallel to the FTA with Panama. This parallel approval created uncertainty and politicisation in the agricultural sector in general, and in the potato sector in particular, constraining the progress of the negotiation between Panama and Costa Rica. In other words, the inclusion of the most sensitive issues of each country in this negotiation, both affected powerful economic domestic groups within Panama and Costa Rica and hampered the negotiation at the international level. The reason was that these domestic groups started to politicise the process as they foresaw negative consequences such as the diminution of utilities and the loss of jobs.

In Panama, the possible impact on dairy producers was a concrete loss of jobs and the eventual closure of milk and milk related processing plants, if products from Costa Rica were to enter Panama's market immediately without tariffs (*La Prensa* 03/11/2002: 30a). Whereas some milk plants and industrial production would have been affected from the bottom to the upper part of the value chain due to the lack of competitiveness vis-à-vis Costa Rica, others would have been affected if an inflexible rule of origin would have been implemented under Costa Rica's terms. Most of the inputs to produce milk-related products, such as different sort of cheeses, butter, and condensed and evaporated milk, come from New Zealand (interview with Gabriela Díaz de Morales, MIDA, 30/07/2008).

Costa Rica asked for free access in all milk products not because it was more competitive than Panama in producing butter, cheeses and condensed and evaporated milk. On the contrary, Costa Rica was less competitive in these categories, but it still produced them, using national or imported inputs without restriction from the Central American free trade zone. With an inflexible rule of origin, Costa Rica could have delivered these items to Panama, but it would have impeded the latter to do the same in Costa Rica. As the representative of the milk sector in Panama stated (01/08/2008):

> An FTA with Costa Rica on those terms was too high a price to pay. Our industry is competitive in some products, but we need inputs from abroad. Imagine I tell my sector: 'okay from tomorrow Costa Rica has free access to our market and we cannot send any of our products there: It is the end for us' […] Nobody offered alternative options to make a good deal such as long term phase out periods, a package of aid to make the industry ready when such eventual phase out was over; to give some products quotas; to grant free access to certain products in exchange for free access for our competitive products; and to introduce flexible rules of origin. I mean, Costa Rica wanted immediate free access and all the inputs to be produced nationally or be bought to them, without giving us the right to import our inputs from wherever we think it was the best […] our proposal was exclusion for our products.

Panama's workers from the food sector also feared a deep liberalisation with Costa Rica would mean loss of competitiveness and a reduction of its market share in Panama. Moreover, they felt that the negotiation proposal of Costa Rica was not balanced as Costa Rica proposed to exclude the entire item of tomato processed products, which included tomato sauce, chopped tomatoes, ketchup, whole canned tomatoes, etc. At the same time, Costa Rica wanted free entrance on bakery products.

> In such a small market as Panama, the free entrance of products from a neighbouring country that subsidises its agriculture and grains production would have meant the saturation of the consumer market and the artificial predominance of Costa Rica due to the covered protection to food products (Interview with Gabriela Diaz de Morales, MIDA, 30/07/2008).

This sense of job loss was also present in the poultry industry as they saw Costa Rica pork producers as a regional champion.

> The pork meat and poultry sector as such was starting to prepare for globalisation; it was starting to adopt better organisation and more efficient production. In 2001 we started such a transformation so we could not risk to be openly exposed to one of the most competitive industries in all Central America […] If you ask me now whether we are - (2008) - ready to export to other markets, the answer is yes […] if we would not have opposed the FTA in 2001, we would not be the industry we are now (Interview with Aníbal Bocaranda, ANAPOR, 22/07/2008).

The aversion to liberalisation of these sectors show the asymmetry of Panama's economy as it is highly competitive in financial services in general, but reluctant to be exposed to FTAs in its agricultural and food related products (excepting a few such products). The economic general context in Panama was not that optimistic in those years as the national economy was still growing but was below the rates of the last years of the 1990s (see table 7).

Table 7: Panama's GDP (annual variation %)

1997	1998	1999	2000	2001	2002	2003
6,4	7,4	4,0	2,7	0,6	2,2	4,2

Sources: CEPAL (2005) Statistical Year for Latin America and the Caribbean, in www.cepal.org (Accessed 24/06/2009).

Moreover, the unemployment rate was still high and increasing. Therefore, the sense of job losses and economic uncertainty was reasonable for the economic sectors losing with the FTA (see Table 8). This is especially true for the agricultural, livestock, and forestry sectors that together provided around 20 percent of the job places in the national economy between 2001 and 2002. This is the largest economic sector in terms of people employed and related to such activities. It is only followed by the commercial activities –services- with 17 percent average and the government with 6.5 percent in the same 2001-2002 period (Contraloría General de la República de Panama 2007: 105).

Table 8: Panama's unemployment rate (%)

1999	2000	2001	2002
11,8	13,5	14,4	13,2*

* EIU estimate (No official rate available)

Sources: Economist Intelligence Unit, Country Report: Panama, September 2002, p. 11; Country Report Panama, December 2003, p.11.

The costs were also high for the government in terms of its office-seeking goals as the losing economic sectors represented around 20 percent of total working places in Panama. Nevertheless, the real impact of an eventual agreement is difficult to quantify as the FTA did not materialise. Yet, the sense of losing jobs is based on rhetoric to gain support from civil society groups and the promise of protection from the government. This rhetoric on losses was not based on total fabrication, in the sense that dairy producers knew that Costa Rica's producers could displace them from the market with the economic and social consequences that such liberalisation would bring to the national economy. This sense of job losses was also based on the past experience of economic transformations based on privatisation of key sectors of the national economy (Jované 2003; Leis 2003: 32). But there were also high expectations of gains for other economic groups within Panama such as the bovine sector, beans producers, and financial and insurance services. However, the potential win of these Panamanian domestic groups meant a high loss for Costa Rica's domestic groups in such areas.

Costa Rica's domestic groups losing with this FTA were also concerned about the possible implications for their sectors, if the accord would include their protected issue-areas or products. The case of tomato processed products, beans, and bovine meat producers, although small in numbers vis-à-vis the eventual winners of the FTA in the same area, was sensitive in the sense that they perceived they could be sacrificed for getting a deal and used as a way to lower Panama's demands in services. The uncertainty created by the possibility of being a bargaining chip produced the conditions for lobbying the negotiators and the government for exclusion. The bovine meat producers in terms of weight to lobby due to the importance in the economy had a larger impact on defending their position. The bovine sector, as a constitutive part of the cattle area, is considered a traditional one in Costa Rica, which represents the values of the countryside man. Therefore, the articulation of a message based on the erosion of this national tradition by these FTA talks got a favourable reception in the political arena, especially in the Congress which indicated that it would not ratify the agreement if this area was not protected (Interviews with CNAA representative 09/07/2008; CORFOGA representative 11/07/2008).

Despite the fact that the beans and processed tomato producers had a disadvantageous position vis-à-vis the bovine meat sector in terms of articulating a strong opposition against the FTA, they received attention from Congress by going along with the beef producers to lobby together against the accord. Moreover, these sectors used the politicisation level produced by the approval of the FTA with Canada which severely affected the interests of the potato producers. "We used the approval of the FTA with Canada to bring our issue up, and we got more support from Congress" (Interview with beans producer representative 10/07/2008). The information requested by congressmen on the FTA process with Canada shows the link between a specific FTA and the external trade policy of a country:

> The way COMEX authorities are conducting the FTA negotiations has created criticism from the agriculture of Cartago region - which is being affected by these negotiations –in reference to the FTA with Canada. Congressmen Nuñez González recalled the bankruptcy of many small companies, following external advice, that focused on "palmitos" (palm heart), and today they are out of the market. The boss of the orange faction also criticised an executive decree in which the norms to import beans were liberalised, which is extremely irresponsible and threatens the producers of these grains [...] Finally, Nuñez González stated that 'it will be another irresponsibility of the Legislative power to ratify the FTA with Canada without deeply studying the possible impact of the accord on the national production and knowing under what parameters and criteria the different compromises within this accord were reached' " (Boletin de Prensa Partido Fuerza Democrática fracción parlamentaria 25/05/2001: 1-2)

The most sensitive issue-area of the negotiation between Panama and Costa Rica was financial services, including insurances. The parties agreed on keeping talks on financial services. Private and public banks believe that an entrance of Panama's banking in form of subsidiaries might come with the FTA (interviews with Gustavo Guillen, COMEX, 27/06/2008; Ronulfo Jimenez and Daniel Castro, Banks Association-Costa Rica, 27/06/2008). Even though this was a speculative assumption, the economic sector lobbied through the different access points to make clear that they could not accept changes in the rules of the game.

> Our posture was to keep the status quo in the negotiation, but the banking and insurance sector were there anyway to let us know what the limits of acceptability for an FTA with Panama were. We also knew the limits on what to negotiate, and that was reflected in the negotiation, but we could not make public how the negotiation was developing (interview with Gabriela Llobet, COMEX, 02/07/2008).

Costa Rica's job insecurity factor was smaller than Panama's in terms of quantity. Nevertheless, these few economic sectors lobbied and articulated strong positions against the FTA due to their lack of competitiveness vis-à-vis Panama, which created a sense of uncertainty on the depth of the effect of eventual liberalisation. What was clear to these groups was the eventual impact of liberalisation on their utilities as much as on the eventual loss of jobs. The job insecurity factor was only limited to these sectors plus those jeopardised by the FTA with Canada as the unemployment index was 6.1 percent in 2001 and 6.4 percent in 2002. However, the GDP number created a sense of pessimism in the economy as it only grew at a rate of 1.8 percent in 2000, 1.1 percent in 2001, and 3 percent in 2002. These compared to the 8.4 percent of 1998 and 8.2 percent in 1999 were rather poor numbers (*Economist Intelligence Unit*, 2003: 5 and 21).

In this economic setting the non-liberalisation of these groups fitted the overall rhetoric of lack of economic growth in Costa Rica. Yet, to claim that this was a causal force on its own for the end of the talks with Panama would be excessive and does not deserve further explanation. Nonetheless, the sense of job insecurity for the already named domestic groups due to the FTA negotiation with Panama, along with the recent agreement with Canada that jeopardised agriculture; and the poor economic growth, served as a sine-qua-non for politicising the FTA talks conducted at the time.

7.3.3 Politicisation

Politicisation was increased by the highly divergent interests, which were due to the reluctance of domestic actors to be exposed to an open competition vis-à-vis economic sectors of their neighbouring countries. The interest groups losing with the FTA also sought to block the final agreement, or asked to exclude their respective issue-areas, through a variety of means, including: using the extant private channels provided by the negotiation (access points to lobby); getting support from civil society by declaring against the process in the media; and lobbying the Congress to send concrete signals the would not ratify the agreement if the sensitive issues presented were included in the final agreement (access points and veto players). Moreover, the negotiation between Panama and Costa Rica was caught in two intertwined parallel games which were the approval of Costa Rica's FTA with Canada and the presidential, congress and municipal elections held in 2002.

The impact of politicising an FTA negotiation creates a fault line for the government as on one side, it has to commit to the counterpart and to its long-term FTA policy, and on the other side it does not want to lose electoral support because of its aspirations to assure the re-election of its governing coalition. A similar reason is present for the role of Congress i.e. congressmen will tend to send signals of non-ratification if their domestic constituencies or electoral base for an upcoming election are being affected or are likely to be affected by the negotiation of an FTA (Mansfield, Milner, and Pevehouse 2007).

On the one side, the agricultural, food, and dairy sectors were losing in Panama and on the other side, the financial and the cattle sector were against the FTA in Costa Rica. These groups articulated messages to hamper the negotiation and also lobbied the government, negotiators and congress to achieve their goals of non-liberalisation. In the case of Panama, the dairy sector also used rhetoric, claiming that 'sacrificing their national production by granting free access to Costa Rica without reciprocal concessions such as exporting condensed and evaporated milk was a too unfair price to pay'. Moreover, not granting access to Costa Rica's financial services was also considered unfair as Costa Rica requested from Panama a deep and varied market liberalisation. Marco Ameglio, owner of the Panamanian dairy company BONLAC, stated that "the possibility of conducting an FTA negotiation in which we could maintain the competitiveness of the financial sector is something that we should seriously consider, as it is fair to analyse the negotiation that transcends individual productive sectors" (*La Prensa* 03/11/2002: 30a).[146] What Ameglio was suggesting was that if the financial sector did not win at all, it would be impossible to think about liberalising the dairy sector for Costa Rica. In addition, the same person also called the population not to forget how Costa Rica exposed Panama to unfair competition within Panama's negotiation to join the WTO.

> The national industry had to drain out because of the whim of Costa Rica's government to hamper our accession to the WTO [...] Panama was obliged to negotiate an agreement for dairy products, in which Costa Rica got access to our national market paying 15 percent tariffs. Meanwhile Panamanian dairy products have to pay more than a 150 percent tariff to enter Costa Rica's market (ibid.).[147]

The target of the critics on subsidies for dairy plants in Costa Rica was the company 'Dos Pinos', which is the largest dairy company in Costa Rica and received

146 Author's translation.
147 Author's translation.

support from the government (*El Panamá América* 21/05/2002: C5; *El Panamá América* 02/05/2002: C1).

The criticisms of Panama's dairy producers of the negotiation can be traced back to 1999, in which parties were monitoring the launch of FTA talks. Here the domestic concern regarding Costa Rica was rather diffuse as the dairy producers only called to be alert for the possible negotiation and the possible implications for the dairy sector (*El Martes Financiero* 09/02/2002: 4). According to Victor Cruz (SIP, 16/07/2008), the first goal of the negotiation on the normative frame was to be cautious, but once the bilateral process was ready to start, the different sectors losing with the negotiation started to bring their concerns to the media hoping to create an impact on the civil society and the negotiators. This move had the purpose of politicising the negotiation and increasing the costs for the government if excessive concessions, or concessions at all, were given to Costa Rica.

In the same vein of criticising the negotiation process with Costa Rica through media, the then president of the Panamanian Union of Industrials, Juan Kiener manifested his unhappiness with the current negotiation. He accused Costa Rica of having excessive expectations as they were asking for the liberalisation of the food sector, but they were unwilling to open the services sector (*El Panamá América* 18/07/2002: C2). "We have not seen any movement from Costa Rica to open the sectors of interest for Panama" (Kiener 25/07/2002: 33a).[148] Moreover, the SIP implied that Costa Rica had a double discourse on the negotiation as it also proposed to restrict the entrance of products from Panama to its national market (*El Panamá América* 06/06/2002, Finances section).

Food producers also manifested their concerns on the negotiation and how the national government under Costa Rica's request was putting them in jeopardy,

> We know that concessions have to be made in a negotiation, so if we publicly complain we make civil society, political parties and congress aware that something that we do not want at all is going to be included in the agreement. In the end, we were willing to give certain concessions if Costa Rica was willing to open the area of tomato processed products. Yet they were reluctant to concede anything, so we continue with this way of informing the public about how our interests were in jeopardy (Interview with Victor Cruz, SIP, 16/07/2008).[149]

The purpose of this behaviour was to politicise the negotiation and to increase the cost for the government, if the final package for food producers was imbalanced. In this regard, there is a dichotomy in the way negotiators and domestic groups conceive these types of negotiations, be these successful or failed cases. On the one hand, negotiators have an holistic approach to the negotiations and they will tend to link issue-areas in an horizontal way i.e. they will seek to liberalise one product to protect a different issue-area that may be unrelated to the one liberalised. On the other hand, domestic associations have a more narrow view of the process as their exclusive concern is to realise gains and prevent losses in their specific economic

148 Author's translation.
149 Author's translation.

sector. These two views clash and hamper the process. Yet the failure to reconcile these two views to conduct a successful negotiation depends on the internal and external context of the process.

A common goal of SIP and the Chamber of Commerce, Industries and Agriculture was to protect all the groups, as there were some sectors that were rather unsuccessful in politicising its eventual loss, such as the chicken sector. They also shared a common strategy: constantly referring to the losses of the FTA in a generic way i.e. 'Panama or Panamanians will be affected by this FTA' (interview Manuel Ferreira, Chamber of Commerce-Panama, 25/07/2008). In addition, these associations as well as sub-sectors like agriculture and livestock complained about the lack of information channels between the interest groups and the negotiators (*El Panamá América* 08/06/2002: C1). This criticism was more rhetorical than real inasmuch as these groups participated in the next room. Yet they wanted access to the texts of the negotiation to see whether or not their sectors were affected, and if they were affected to what extent (interviews with Luis Garrido, MICI, 28/07/2008; Leda Arrué, MICI, 17/07/2008). Another interpretation of the complaint about the lack of inclusion in the process was that it was intended to make Congress signal non-ratification as the process was conducted behind the interest groups. According to trade negotiators, these groups complained in this way by claiming they were excluded, but they were in the process and participated in the next room. The impossibility of granting access to the texts of the negotiation was based on the fact that this was a state diplomatic issue and as such it had to be kept secret (interviews with Diana Salazar, MICI, 30/07/2008; Melissa Davis, MICI, 17/07/2008; Samuel Moreno, MICI, 22/07/2008; Alexis Pineda, MICI, 18/07/2008; Zereth Torres, MICI, 22/07/2008).

> Imagine that we give access to the texts on market access to every group either that favour or oppose the negotiation; we will never end a negotiation. If the negotiation with Costa Rica was already politicised, imagine what could happen if we were giving every one a copy of the negotiation [...] In the next room, we give the relevant information, but not the specific details or product by product information (Interview with former Minister of International Trade, Joaquin Jácome 17/07/2008).

Costa Rica also politicised the FTA talks by exerting pressure on the negotiators as well as by calling Congress to possibly veto the accord. Moreover, the losing different groups articulated messages to protect their economic sectors. However, the level of politicisation was mainly structured by the bovine sector leadership and sometimes followed by the tomato processed products and beans producers. Yet the impact of the latter two was more limited as their representative sector CACIA and CNAA were favouring an overall and profound liberalisation of Panama's market. Nonetheless, both associations wanted to concede certain items to protect tomato processed products and beans respectively. However, the concessions were to be minimised and not in the most competitive products (interviews with CNAA representative 09/07/2008; Mario Montero, CACIA, 07/07/2008; Laura Rodriguez, COMEX, 08/07/2008).

The bovine sector alone could sustain the politicisation and lobbying against the FTA to protect its eventual loss on meat vis-à-vis Panama's producers. Moreover, this group linked the negotiation with Panama with the overall economic deterioration of their sector due to the growing imports of meat from different international markets, the diminution of meat exports, and the reduction of international prices. According to CORFOGA, Costa Rica imported around 1282 tons of meat in 2002. This group stated that "this meat is entering with all the required permissions but it is affecting us". Moreover, CORFOGA requested that the government controls the importation procedures, as by as early as mid-2002 Costa Rica had imported around 230 percent more meat than in 2001. This increase on imports deteriorated the meat commercialisation price. The price went down around 5 percent in 2001 (*La Prensa Libre* 31/05/2002, economic focus).

As Ricardo Castro, president of the CORFOGA, argued in a letter to then Minister of International Trade, Tomas Dueñas, to state the initial, and definitive, position of excluding its sector from the agreement, "we think that it does not represent any competitive advantage for Costa Rica to trade with Panama" (CORFOGA's Letter 31/07/2000). This position was also consistent with their claims on newspapers that expressed concern over the deterioration of the bovine sector (*El Financiero* 1-7/07/2002: 33):

> The majority of meat producers are small ones, whose ranches are not specialised. Most of these people produce meat as an alternative option for their economic subsistence so we cannot allow that the importation of meat jeopardise the investment of these people, and we cannot allow the prices to go down due to these imports (CORFOGA, in *El Heraldo* 31/05/2002: 6).

The lobby of CORFOGA, and in a minor degree of beans, and tomato processed producers hampered the ability of trade diplomats to structure a win-win process at the international level. In this regard, the negotiators had to work in an initial setting in which the win-set was already narrowed. Therefore, in order to include dairy and food products, and exclude financial and insurance, Costa Rica would have to offer high compensations to Panama such as the free entrance of, or quotas for, meat, and tomato processed products. These problems of how to compensate domestic groups without producing the eventual non-ratification of Congress were difficult to manage due to the increase in the politicisation level and in domestic group pressure on negotiators.

The financial and insurance sector politicisation process was difficult to trace as it seems to be the case that these groups used the formal channels of the negotiation to express their concerns, about the discussion of subsidiaries in the negotiation. The reason for this may be that bank owners are unlikely to go to the streets and demonstrate. Nevertheless these groups were exerting pressure on negotiators to protect its sector from Panamanian interests regarding bank branches and subsidiaries as well as the insurance sector (interviews with Ronulfo Jiménez, Bank Association, 27/06/2008; Eduardo Lizano, former President of the Central Bank-Costa Rica, 26/06/2008). Insurances was not politicised as it is a state owned sector. However, banking as a mixed system was and is a strong lobby force against any FTA, if the status quo is not likely to be preserved (interviews with Marvin Rodriguez,

COMEX, 07/07/2008; Laura Rodriguez, COMEX, 08/07/2008; Gustavo Guillen, COMEX, 27/06/2002; Amparo Pacheco, COMEX, 02/07/2008).

The FTA negotiation on Costa Rica's side was also caught in a parallel game that slowed down the pace of, and reduced COMEX's dedication to, the process with Panama. This parallel game was the approval of the FTA with Canada, which was signed 23rd April 2001. The difficulties with approving the accord in the Congress were based on the threat to potato producers posed by the world leading production of pre-fried chips by Canadian McCain Food Limited (Ramírez 11/06/2002: 17 A). First, the lobby went directly to COMEX before the negotiation between both countries was concluded. In a letter from UPANACIONAL, representing small agricultural producers, to the then Minister of International Trade Tomas Dueñas, this group manifested its strong opposition to the inclusion of potatoes in the accord with Canada. In addition, the same group criticise the pillars of FTA policy of the country.

> In conversations you have had with us in previous days with the purpose of convincing us to let Canada export industrial potatoes to Costa Rica with an asymmetrical phase out, we manifest our position for exclusion of this product. This is because we have had many years of fighting to get the necessary conditions for our agricultural sector, and we have not got a favourable reception from this or the previous governments. What we find is a deep deterioration of our sector which is truly provoking a crisis [...] it is important to remember that our association with 20000 members represent all the agricultural products. Therefore, our position is to defend all our sectors in an integral way from all these unequal policies in which you have put us. It is also good to remember that we are not afraid of liberalisation and free competition, but what we do not accept is the form and lack of conditions to achieve competitiveness. When these conditions start to be promoted by the government, then we can start to talk about FTAs (Fernandez, Rogelio, President of UPANACIONAL, 19/02/2001).[150]

Just days after this letter was sent five Congressmen -Carlos Villalobos, Ricardo Sancho, Oscar Campos, Daniel Gallardo, and Rodolfo Salas- sent a letter to President Miguel Àngel Rodriguez stating their concerns over the lack of information provided by COMEX on the FTA with Canada. Moreover, they suggested that not granting the information on the products excluded, and the initial position of domestic sectors, may affect the course of the FTA. These members of the legislative also stated that they were particularly interested in knowing the proposals of COMEX in the agricultural and livestock sector due to the growing vulnerability to which this area has been exposed in the different accords (Asamblea Legislativa Republica de Costa Rica, 20/02/2001: CVA-081-2001). Other letters were sent to COMEX, mostly from the representatives of the PLN party, requesting the negotiating texts and not the final ones under the argument that the outcome may have a strong social impact. In addition, the same political party also requested detailed analyses of why and how the negotiation parties reached agreement on the tariff, quotas and phase out periods for agricultural products (Asamblea Legislativa Republica de Costa Rica

150 Author's translation.

05/04/2001: CVA-098-2001; José Manuel Nuñez, Deputy 24/05/2001: JMN-372-2000/2001).

The lobby of agricultural groups and congressmen on behalf of potato producers was later replaced for public complaints and a direct politicisation. Meanwhile, domestic groups increased their level of complaints over the FTA with Canada through media channels and newspapers and the congressmen started to oppose the approval of the FTA (*La República* 26/04/2001). In fact, this accord could not be approved under the electoral campaign in 2001 and early 2002. The accord was only approved in Congress on 26 August 2002 (*El Financiero* 16/12/2001 to 5/01/2003: 8), once the implementation of radical and generous compensation packages were assured to the agricultural sector. The government promised to ensure resources to create a production and commercialisation project of different potatoes, to install an agroindustrial plant for vegetables, and to implement and transfers resources for programmes of technological transfers and better organisational management within this sector (*La Nación* 20/07/2002: 13). The compensation package had a cost for the government of 2000 millions 'Colones' (approx. 3.5 million dollars for the producers of one product; *La Nación* 19/07/2002: front page).

This process parallel to the FTA negotiation with Panama hampered the development of these FTA talks in the following way. First negotiators from COMEX could not compromise on offering access to Panama's most competitive products such as beans, tomato processed products, and bovine meat as it would have increased the politicisation level and it would have jeopardised the approval of the FTA with Canada even more. These three products belong to the same sector associations that were against the FTA with Canada such as UPANACIONAL, and CNAA in which CORFOGA is also embedded. Second, the producers of these sensitive products made their respective associations aware that these issues should not be included in the accord and they also made Congressmen aware that these issues should be protected in the FTA with Panama. Third, the negotiators' most reasonable option was to wait and see how the legislative process developed before agreeing with Panama on these issues, because Costa Rica did not want to have another negotiation in Congress, which includes financial compensations to approve a new FTA. Fourth, the lack of progress on these sensitive issues also prevented Panama from giving concessions on less sensitive dairy and food products until a clear commitment from Costa Rica to negotiate on these three areas was established. Finally, the lack of commitment on Costa Rica's side and progress on the negotiation was interpreted by Panama as lack of interest in the process, and in negotiating in a win-win mode (interviews with Laura Rodriguez, COMEX, 08/07/2008; Roberto Echandi, COMEX, 26/06/2008; Gabriela Llobet, COMEX, 02/07/2008; Irene Arguedas, COMEX, 03/07/2008; Francisco Chacon, COMEX, 14/07/2008). Once the governmental package of aid was approved by the UPANACIONAL and CNAA on 19th of July, the process of the negotiation with Panama stalled the same day. However, the executive in Costa Rica was not sure whether the package, which was still being negotiated on 19th July, was likely to be approved the same day by the agricultural sector. In addition, this package had to go through Congress for its legal ratification as well as the FTA text with Canada.

7.3.3.1 Elections

The FTA negotiation between Panama and Costa Rica was caught in an electoral process. First, Costa Rica had the presidential and legislative elections in February 2002, before the FTA bilateral process was launched. Yet some critics of the FTA policy of this country were used by the candidates for the presidency and the Congress, especially the candidate for president of the new political party Partido Acción Ciudadana (PAC), Otton Solís. This party was formed as a consequence of an internal division in the PLN. Otton Solís focused his message on eradicating corruption, motivating civil society participation beyond political parties, and implementing a fair treatment of the most vulnerable economic sectors that have suffered from globalisation, especially agriculture. This message of protection of agriculture obliged the two candidates with the higher chances to win –Abel Pacheco and Rolando Araya- to offer compensation packages and developmental programs to the agricultural sector (Sánchez 2002: 36). Within this election, the incumbent president Abel Pacheco (2002-2006) promised to implement compensation programs to protect the agricultural sector because of its deteriorating conditions and growing exposure to the forces of economic globalisation (*El Financiero* 22-28/04/2002; *La Nación* 20/11/2001; *La Nación* 24/01/2002: 6; *La Nación* 03/04/2002). Yet such programs or compensations were not detailed during the campaign. An indicator of the potential influence of the electoral process for an FTA was the non-approval of the FTA with Canada during the electoral campaigns in 2001 and the first two months of 2002. Here congressmen seeking to keep power for the candidates of their respective political parties as re-election is not allowed, exerted pressure by refusing to ratify the final FTA if the government did not implement and negotiate aid packages for the agricultural sector in general and for potato producers in particular (*La Nación* 06/04/2002: 8 A). Agriculture as an economic activity is present in most electoral districts in Costa Rica.

As required by Costa Rican electoral law, the presidential election went to a second round as none of the candidates got more than 40 percent of the votes cast. The run-off of the presidential election was held in the first days of April 2002 between the two most popular candidates, Abel Pacheco (Unidad Social Cristiana) and Rolando Araya (Liberación Nacional) (Wilson 2003: 510-514; Achard and González 2004: 47). Pacheco obtained 58 percent of the votes and Araya 42 percent in the 'ballotage' (*Panorama Centromaericano* 04/2002: 4). Araya criticised the neoliberal orientation of Pacheco's government as a way of presenting himself as the protector of those suffering from globalisation such as the agricultural sector (*La Nación* 01/04/2002: 6 A). This second round (7 April 2002) matches in length the first bilateral round of the negotiation held between the 3rd and 5th of April. Neither did the presidential elections in its first and second round nor the parliamentary elections provoke the outcome of non-agreement in the negotiation between Costa Rica and Panama. It seems to be the case that these electoral processes, especially the first one, only prevented the launch of the FTA negotiation rather than affecting its results. In this regard, the non-launch of the negotiations during the first round and parliamentary elections coincides with the overall view of trade negotiators about the inconvenience of conducting FTA talks during electoral process (interviews Indiana Trejos, COMEX, 24/06/2008; Tatiana Varela, COMEX, 26/06/2008; Alejandra Aguilar, COMEX, 04/07/2008). Nevertheless, the electoral campaigns for presidency and the legislative were focused around the economic problems that specific economic sectors were having due to globalisation. The negative consequences of economic globalisation were the centre of discourses in the electoral process, especially those of Otton Solís and Rolando Araya to criticise Pacheco's pro-market behaviour and his past support of the liberalisation of the ICE (Hamann and Wilson 2001; *La Nación* 01/04/2002: 6 A). In this regard, the criticisms of the FTA policy of Costa Rica and especially of the recent FTA with Canada targeted the candidates of PLN and PAC.

Costa Rica also had its city council elections for all its regional districts in December 2002 (Alfaro Redondo 2002). The fact that Costa Rica was in an electoral campaign through the entire year exposed the FTA policy of this country to criticisms. In this electoral process most of the criticism came from the different regions in which agricultural and rural areas were the electoral base for the winning president Pacheco and a large electoral base for the "Unidad Social Cristiana". During the electoral campaign the PAC and PLN continued highlighting the negative consequences of globalisation for rural regions and agriculture (interviews with representatives of the PAC 01/07/2008; PLN 04/07/2008).

Whereas the government gave aid packages to potato producers to pass the FTA with Canada, the compensations were also granted in order not to jeopardise the election of majors and aldermen from the governing party i.e. the USC. Moreover, the government also gave these packages of aid to prevent the deterioration of its international reputation. Not approving the FTA with Canada would have reduced the chances of launching an FTA negotiation with the US, which were likely to be started by the end of 2002 (*La Nación* 09/04/2002). Then Costa Rica's ambassador in United States Jaime Daremblum (in *La Nación* 07/07/2002: 2) subtly expressed the importance of the FTA between Canada and Costa Rica for the American administration: "The pattern of the FTA between Costa Rica and Canada is one of the most advanced and it is highly valued by the technicians on trade matters in the current American Administration".[151]

> The US would not have negotiated an FTA with us if we were not able to pass the one with Canada as this is also a NAFTA model agreement. Moreover, Canada and the US are close trade partners. The FTA with Canada was seen as stepping stone towards an FTA with the US

151 Author's translation.

> as it showed our strong commitment to market liberalisation and to the US FTA type of agreements (interview with Francisco Chacón 14/07/2008).[152]

The city council elections thus played a role in the failure of the FTA with Panama. The government was obliged to negotiate compensations to pass the FTA with Canada, but it did not want to repeat the experience with the cattle, beans and tomato sectors, especially if the FTA was with a small country like Panama. And the negotiators felt restricted to using these products as bargaining chips to create a balanced final agreement with Panama. In addition, negotiators could not offer small concessions to Panama on these agricultural products to protect the issue-area of insurance and banking, and to trigger concessions from Panama over Costa Rica's most competitive sectors such as food, agricultural and dairy products. Any concession on meat, beans, and tomato processed products should be made after the electoral process conducted in December 2002. The FTA negotiation with Panama stalled in July 2002.

In this regard, the time at which this bilateral negotiation was launched and conducted was not the most appropriate to assure an agreement. This shows the bounded rationality of Costa Rica's negotiators and decision makers when calculating the way the negotiation would differ if conducted during the city council electoral campaigns. Moreover, it seems to be the case that trade diplomats overlooked both the approval process in Congress of the FTA with Canada, and the influence of city council elections inasmuch as they perceived them as less important to the presidential or legislative ones. However, the governing political party and the presidential leader saw these elections as important processes for keeping their power and the possibility of realising its governing agenda. The negotiators were also biased in the sense that they perceived major gains for their domestic groups in the FTA negotiation with Panama, which made them overlook the importance of protecting important domestic groups that were also powerful political agents, such as the cattle sector.

7.3.4 Pro-FTA Groups' Free-riding Option

Even though Costa Rica's domestic groups such as dairy products, food producers and industry had a special interest in the negotiation, they also lobbied the government to establish trade relations with other countries and accelerate the launching of negotiations with the US if possible. This posture got a favourable reception from President Pacheco (*Panorama Centroamericano* 04/2002: 10; *La Nación* 20/07/2002: 22; interviews with Jack Liberman and Luis Obando, CIRC, 30/06/2008; William Cardoza, CANAVI, 01/07/2008; Mario Montero, CACIA,

152 Author's translation.

07/07/2008; Erik Montero, CNPL, 27/06/2008; Carlos Cespedes and Sergio Navas, CADEXCO, 25/06/2008). This move of these groups weakened their position in the negotiation table vis-à-vis meat producers, who remained strong until there was no chance to relaunch the negotiation in the short term. This was also the case of tomato processed and beans producers, who were highly defensive in the FTA negotiation with Panama. These interest groups persisted in asking for information and monitoring the FTA until the negotiation reached a definitive standstill as well as when the negotiations were already stalled (interviews with Gabriela Llobet, COMEX, 02/07/2008; Tatiana Varela, COMEX, 26/06/2008; Laura Rodriguez, COMEX, 08/07/2008).

The pro-FTA groups did not lobby to continue the negotiations with Panama after the second round, because they focused on the negotiations with the US, which were to be launched by the end of 2002 (interviews Carlos Cespedes and Sergio Navas, CADEXCO, 25/06/2008; Jack Liberman and Luis Obando, CIRC, 30/06/2008; Mario Montero, CACIA, 07/07/2008; Gabriela Llobet, COMEX, 02/07/2002; Francisco Chacon, COMEX, 14/07/2002; Amparo Pacheco, COMEX, 02/07/2002). As the US is Costa Rica's biggest and largest trade partner, the amount of lobbying and monitoring of the course of the pre-negotiation phase undertaken by different actors displaced the interests to insist on a negotiation with Panama. In addition, Panama and Costa Rica had a narrow initial zone of agreement to work with due to the differing interests. This zone of agreement narrowed even more during the bargaining because of the mutual aversion to concede to the counterpart over the most sensitive products. However, these sensitive products were attractive for the counterpart and thus some preferential treatment on these products and services became key issues to close a final deal.

As a parallel process to the FTA negotiation with Panama, COMEX's staff started to devote more attention to the coordination of common positions with Costa Rica's diverse economic actors for the coming negotiation with the US. This coordination was also carried out with the rest of the Central American countries as the negotiation was to be conducted as a regional grouping with the US (interviews with Francisco Chacon, COMEX, 14/07/2008; Roberto Echandi, COMEX, 26/06/2008; Alejandra Aguilar , COMEX, 04/07/2008). Basically the negotiation with the US involved the preparation of a negotiation of three levels i.e. domestic, regional (between Central American countries) and the US (international level; *Panorama Centroamericano* August-September 2002: 10-16). This enterprise with the US was attractive for most of the winners of the eventual FTA with Panama. Therefore, the difficulties with concluding the FTA talks with Panama and the amount of resources needed by an FTA negotiation with the US, led the eventual winners of the FTA with Panama to defect; they would thus not insist on launching a new round of negotiations until the process with the US was secured and underway.

Panama's most competitive sectors such as financial services and exporters of products such as melon, water melon, pineapples, cattle sector, beans producers, and others, did not have high expectations of the negotiation with Costa Rica. Once they realised that Costa Rica was not willing to give concessions on financial services, their expectations diminished as they saw that the advance of the negotiation related to the progress of the discussion of financial services i.e. granting accession to Panama's banks in the form of subsidiaries and granting preferential treatment for insurances, if and when this sector was to be liberalised. Here there was a convergence of interests between the financial sector and the government of Panama vis-à-vis not conceding agricultural issues to Costa Rica if there was no progress on financial services and insurances. The reason to grant concessions on sensitive agricultural issues only if financial services were liberalised was the strategy chosen by Panama's government and also promoted by domestic groups in order to make sure that Costa Rica included such issues in the negotiation (interviews with John and Irving Bennet, APEDE, 25/07/2008; Manuel Ferreira, Chamber of Commerce-Panama, 25/07/2008; Carlos Berguido, APADEA, 18/07/2008; Victor Cruz, SIP, 16/07/2008; Melissa Davis, MICI, 17/07/2008; Joaquin Jácome, MICI, 17/07/2008).

The reluctance of Costa Rica's trade negotiators to discuss market access and financial services in a hand by hand way indicated that this country was not willing to put this issue on the table, as Costa Rica expressed during the negotiation of the normative framework (interviews with Diana Salazar, MICI, 30/07/2008: Luis Garrido, MICI, 28/07/2008; Alexis Pineda, MICI, 18/07/2008; anonymous 19/07/2008). This fact, along with the lobbying of Panama's domestic economic groups that were likely to lose with the FTA with Costa Rica, brought the pro-liberalisation groups to concentrate their efforts on countries with which the probability of including financial services in the accord was high (interviews with Carlos Berguido, APADEA, 18/07/2008; Bosco Quintero, APADEA, 18/07/2008; Gabriela Diaz de Morales, MIDA, 30/07/2008). For example, Juan Francisco Kiener, President of the National Council of Private Companies, who was previously a supporter of further integration with Central America said: "it will be antipatriotic to continue giving market access to Costa Rica, if there is not reciprocity -referring to financial services and insurances- we as industrial and private sector cannot recommend the approval of an FTA like this" (quoted in *La Prensa* 18/07/2002: 3 A).

At the same time, domestic groups such as the Union of Industrial, ANAPOR, APEDE, the Chamber of Commerce, Industries and Agriculture, APADEA, and the banking association started to insist that they were not willing to accept an unbalanced agreement that did not include Panama's most competitive sectors (*La Prensa* 22/09/2002: 30 A; interviews with Aníbal Bocaranda, ANAPOR, 22/07/2008; Carlos González, APEDE, 21/07/2008; Manuel Ferreira, Chamber of Commerce-Panama, 25/07/2008; Carlos Berguido, APADEA, 18/07/2008; Victor Cruz, SIP, 16/07/2008; Banking Association representative 23/07/2008). Moreover, these domestic associations shifted the focus of their FTA preferences to the US. The attraction of negotiating an FTA with the US was not only based on the size of the market, but it was also the consequence of the negotiations that Central America and the US were likely to launch in the same year, 2002. In this regard, the economic relationship between Costa Rica and Panama was not only bilateral but also competitive i.e. gaining a preferential space on third markets (*La Prensa* 19/10/2002: 25 A; *La Prensa* 26/01/2002: 2 A). Panama's domestic groups lobbied to start FTA talks with the US as soon as possible and hopefully before their Central American counterparts. Both of these groups believed and had the experience of business to ensure that the one that arrives first to the market with preferential treatment via FTA has a higher chance of establishing exportation niches and keeping them, even if new actors get, preferential treatment after (interviews with Victor Cruz, SIP, 16/07/2008; Manuel Ferreira, Chamber of Commerce-Panama, 25/07/2008).[153]

Panama's domestic economic associations also lobbied the government to speed up its exploratory talks to analyse the possibilities of launching an FTA negotiation under Taiwan's initial interest (This FTA negotiation started in October 2002 and was successfully concluded after 5 rounds in August 2003; see www.sice.oas.org) Initially, Taiwan's proposal of negotiating an FTA did not receive much attention from domestic groups as Taiwan was considered a far away country. Moreover, the focus of the government was on creating the conditions to attract FDI rather than increase the exchange of goods. Yet, the willingness of Taiwan to negotiate conditions for FDI, to include a liberal chapter on financial services, and also increase the trade on goods and other services increased the attention of these domestic groups as the reluctance of Costa Rica to grant preferential treatment to Panama on financial services became more evident (interviews with Carlos Berguido and Bosco Quintero, APADEA, 18/07/2008; Joaquin Jácome, MICI, 17/07/2008). Moreover, the negotiation with Taiwan became an escape option for Panama, and also a possibility to conduct a depoliticised negotiation as the clashes of interest on goods were less perceptible for the agricultural sector in general. Moreover, this economic area had potential to open markets in Taiwan (Jimenez 12/08/2002; *La Prensa* 07/08/2002: 5 A; interviews with Luis Garrido, MICI, 28/07/2008; Gabriela Diaz de Morales, MIDA, 28/07/2008). Last but not least, Panama's domestic groups and also the government agreed that Taiwan had the potential to become a like-minded country due to their shared status as small powers that are hubs of their respective continents in maritime services and in their shared orientation to deliver world wide competitive financial services (interview with Diana Salazar, MICI, 30/07/2008; Carlos González, APEDE, 21/07/2002).

Having an FTA with one or both countries –the US and Taiwan- could outweigh Panama's government and domestic groups' costs of failing to reach a final agreement in the negotiation with Costa Rica. In other words, competitive sectors tended to free ride and realise their alternative options. Moreover, the domestic groups favouring an FTA with Costa Rica ended up adopting a passive attitude towards this

153 This idea that the one that enter first the market in a third country has a higher chance to keep the niche was also manifested in the interviews with business association representatives in Chile and Costa Rica (interviews in Chile: Ronald Bown, ASOEX, 19/03/2008; Rodrigo Infante, Salmon Chile,19/03/2008; Hugo Baierlein, SOFOFA, 26/03/2008; Roberto Fantuzzi, ASEXMA, 28/03/2008; Alvaro Marquez, Cámara de la Industria Cosmética, 02/04/2008; Marisol Figueroa, Chilealimentos, 17/04/2008; interviews in Costa Rica: Erik Montero, CNPL, 27/06/2008; Mario Montero, CACIA, 07/07/2008; Carlos Cespedes and Sergio Navas, CADEXCO, 25/06/2008).

negotiation vis-à-vis the eventual losers of the negotiation, when the costs of agreeing increased excessively. Therefore, focusing instead on promoting a negotiation with the US and Taiwan was a rational option for the pro-FTA domestic actors as they saw more economic gains and less difficulties in reaching an agreement with the US and Taiwan than in concluding the negotiation with Costa Rica.

7.4 Concluding Remarks

This chapter analysed the negotiation process at the domestic level. The divergence of interests and the job insecurity factor increased the level of politicisation and helped the articulation of domestic groups strategies to prevent making concessions on their sectors. An important factor that increased the politicisation level in Costa Rica was the games parallel to the FTA negotiation. The difficulties with approving the FTA with Canada increased the criticisms of political parties and domestic associations towards the way the government was conducting the FTA policy. Moreover, COMEX did not want to put its sensitive issues through the FTA with Panama until there was clarity on the costs of approving the FTA with Canada. Congress sent concrete signs that they would not ratify the FTA with Canada and others if sensitive agricultural products were not properly protected. In addition, COMEX had to devote its resources to ratify the agreement, displacing from the priorities the talks with Panama. This displacement of priorities was also due to the lack of progress in the negotiation with Panama. In addition, Costa Rica's domestic actors associations started to lose interest as they saw better conditions to achieve an accord with the US.

Panama had a restricted basket of goods to compete in Costa Rica. Therefore, it wanted the liberalisation of such products as well as the inclusion of subsidiary banks and insurance in the agreement. In addition, Panama did not want to grant concessions if these issues were not included in the agreement. Yet dairy, agricultural, and food producers perceived the demands of Costa Rica as excessive. Therefore, these sectors lobbied and politicised the negotiation to impede excessive concessions to the counterpart, and to prevent the government from using their products as bargaining chips to trigger favourable concessions in financial and insurance services. As the costs of agreeing with Costa Rica started to increase, pro-market domestic actors started to manifest their interests in pursuing negotiations with the US and Taiwan. They also started leave the negotiation with Costa Rica behind.

In addition, past experiences also mattered for the course of the negotiation. The previous negotiation between Costa Rica and Panama within the frame of the WTO made both sides depict each other as non-trustworthy, and as tough negotiators that pursued their interests in a predatory way rather than in a win-win mode. The conditions analysed in this chapter provide a partial explanation of why this FTA negotiation. To understand the whole process that converted this negotiation to a failed case, it is necessary to analyse the simultaneous process of the interstate negotiation.

8. Intergovernmental Negotiation between Costa Rica and Panama

8.1 Introduction

The state to state talks are to some extent based on the protection of interests of the domestic coalitions be these in favour or against an FTA. Yet, states also enjoy relative autonomy to pursue their own agenda in these FTA talks. The autonomy is relative because the state, to make decisions, takes into account the socio-political constraints i.e. the electoral costs of a decision; its ideological commitment to an economic model, in this case a neoliberal one; and the reputational impact of states decisions or non-decisions, and moves or non-moves in relation to other states. The interstate negotiation that made this FTA negotiation a failed case presents internal and external aspects of the bargaining process. The conditions -(non-negotiability, lack of leadership skills, overuse of value-claiming strategies and the weight of other FTA processes)- that constitute the setting for failure unfold within the same time-frame. The domestic conditions already presented and the ones to be presented here paved the way to failure in the FTA negotiation Costa Rica-Panama.

8.2 Intergovernmental Factors

8.2.1 Non-negotiability

In a negotiation, parties may outline the non-negotiable issues at the outset of the process or during the bargaining. In both cases, the exclusion of goods, services, and issue-areas that one or both parties are not willing to include in the agreement is potentially contentious, and may put the possibilities of reaching an agreement in jeopardy. A negotiation probably will not fail, if one party or both did not outline the non-negotiable issues at the outset of the agreement, if the zone of agreement and the win-sets are broad, or if the negotiation has been conducted using a joint problem-solving mode. In addition, if the BATNA are worse than the current negotiation, outlining the non-negotiables during the bargaining still helps the negotiation reach an agreement (on BATNA see Odell 2009).

If the initial setting is a favourable one, the parties have enough room to bargain and create solutions to expand the zone of the agreement, and use linkages and side-payment approaches to break resistance to the agreement their own domestic actors and their counterpart. Within this win-win context, the zone of agreement also expands during the negotiation rounds (Elms 2003). Thus, the wait–and-see negotiation strategy over the most sensitive issues of the process in such a setting will not hamper the ability of negotiators to find a mutually satisfactory agreement.

However, if the initial setting of the negotiation is a small zone of agreement and a narrow win-set, and the parties depict each other as non trustworthy from the beginning, the lack of outlining the non-negotiable issues will tend to further reduce the room to bargain. Thus the possibilities of having a balanced deal are reduced. Why did governments not outline the non-negotiable issues? A reason presented in the theoretical frame of this work and in the analysis of the case of Chile and Panama is that negotiators are rationally bounded (see Odell 2000).

In other words, trade diplomats from Costa Rica and Panama misjudged the ability of the counterpart and their own ability to create joint solutions in the negotiation. Trade diplomats from both countries believed before the negotiation that they could change the aversion of the counterpart to negotiate certain issues. They also thought they could offer minimum compensations to trigger the liberalisation of the counterpart's sensitive issues (interviews with Diana Salazar, MICI, 30/07/2008; Leda Arrué, MICI, 17/07/2008; Brunilda de Castillo, MICI, 17/07/2008; Melissa Davis, MICI, 17/07/2008; Alexis Pineda, MICI, 18/07/2008; Samuel Moreno, MICI, 22/07/2008; Amparo Pacheco, COMEX, 02/07/2008; Tatiana Varela, COMEX, 26/06/2008; Marvin Rodriguez, COMEX, 07/07/2008).

Another factor is that BATNA can be manipulated by the negotiating parties and a good BATNA can also emerge during the ongoing negotiation rounds due to the offer of third countries to negotiate an FTA with one or both members of the current negotiation (Odell 2009; Singh 2008).[154] The better the BATNA is, the more costly it becomes not to outline the non-negotiable at the outset of the negotiation process. Some hold talks on the non-negotiable issues at the outset of the process even before the formal rounds are launched and others use these issues as bargaining chip to trigger concessions from the counterpart (Mladinic 2000). This is the 'waiting and seeing strategy' on how the process develops to offer 'cosmetic' changes in certain issues with the purpose of making the counterpart open their sensitive areas. In principle the parties perceived, due to their bounded rationality bias, that small changes that do not affect the substance of the issues (that is, 'cosmetic changes') will in the end keep the status quo, as the concessions are minimum and imperceptible in terms of trade (interviews with Joaquín Jácome, MICI, 17/07/2008; Alejandro Ferrer, MICI, 29/07/2008; Amparo Pacheco, COMEX, 02/072008; Francisco Chacon, COMEX, 14/07/2008).

154 I develop this point further in the section concerning the weight of other FTA negotiations. In addition, BATNA as the status-quo before the negotiation is also an option. This is costly as most states in the 90s and 2000s were involved in this type of economic negotiations. Thus, the BATNA as the status quo is a costly option, that is, no FTAs for a country.

One successful experience in which one of the parties outlined its non-negotiable issues was the FTA negotiation of Chile and the Central American countries.[155] As a consequence of the failed experience between Chile and Panama, the former decided to outline the non-negotiability of services and financial services to the Central American countries in 1999. This shows that the negative experience with Panama became a learning experience for Chile's subsequent negotiations with countries with which the possibilities of high trade gains were reduced. Chile outlined the non-negotiability at the outset of the process as a way to conclude negotiations over the normative frame before Chile's electoral period in 1999 (interviews with Andrés Rebolledo, DIRECON, 25/03/2008; Camilo Navarro, DIRECON, 17/03/2008; Rodrigo Contreras, DIRECON, 28/03/2008). Finally, the Central American countries and Chile included in the FTA agreement the previous BIT signed between each Central American country and Chile, with a clause to review and negotiate a chapter on investment and services in the future (Wehner 2009b: 15). The team that dedicated full time to the preparation of the process with Central America was similar to the one, which conducted the negotiation with Panama. These agents asked themselves: why did the negotiation with Panama fail and how did it fail?

One answer was that they created excessive expectations on Panama's side on the issue of financial services and services in general by not stating clearly at the outset that these issues were not to be included in the agreement (interviews with Oscar Quina, DIRECON, 08/04/2008; Rodrigo Contreras, DIRECON, 28/03/2008; Andrés Rebolledo, DIRECON, 25/03/2008; Carmen Paz Cortés, DIRECON, 25/03/2008; Hugo Baierlein, SOFOFA, 26/03/2008). The creation of excessive expectations went along with the inability to create win-win situations and the extant narrowed zone of agreement they have to work with to create a final deal. Yet, how did this issue of not outlining non-negotiable issues become an element, amongst others, that made the negotiation between Costa Rica and Panama a failed case?

Panama and Costa Rica had a series of issues which both parties were unwilling to negotiate either because they were extremely sensitive, or because they were to be used as a bargaining chip in a future negotiation with the US. The negotiation between Panama and Costa Rica had non-negotiable issues that were solved without major problems as both countries presented the arguments that liberalisation over such issues would create strong problems for their domestic constituencies. These non-negotiables were sugar and rice (FTA Costa Rica-Panama's draft text 2002: 0191, and 0181). Whereas both countries outlined the non-negotiability of these issues, they were presented during the bargaining and not at the beginning of the process. Both parties followed a mirror approach on these exclusions, that is, sugar by sugar. Yet Panama perceived itself as highly competitive in banking and insurances as well as on beef, beans, and tomato processed products (industrial toma-

155 See also the successful Mexican experience to protect its energy resources by outlining its non-negotiability at the outset of the process from the US aspiration to liberalise such sector in the NAFTA negotiation; specifically see Chapter 6, sub-section 6.2.1 Non-Negotiability.

toes). And Costa Rica was likely to be the winner if Panama opened its market Costa Rican products such as dairy products, bakery products, and other food-products.

Following a mirror approach to exclude these sensitive issues was impossible because the bilateral economic relationship between two countries is governed by competitive advantages of one of the countries over the other in these items, and vice-versa. To some extent the issue of financial services and insurances were signalled wrongly by Costa Rica. In the negotiation of the normative frame Costa Rica claimed that the possibilities of allowing the location of subsidiaries and discussing the issue of services will be subject to discussion during the bilateral process (interviews with Gabriela Llobet, COMEX, 02/07/2008; Melissa Davis, MICI, 17/07/2008). According to trade diplomats from Panama, Costa Rica promised to negotiate such issues, whereas trade diplomats from Costa Rica agreed that they mentioned the possibility of talking about these issues, but they did not promise to negotiate them as such (Interviews with Diana Salazar, MICI, 30/07/2008; Melissa Davis, MICI, 17/07/2008; Leda Arrué, MICI, 17/07/2008; Amparo Pacheco, COMEX, 02/07/2008; Roberto Echandi, COMEX, 26/06/2008; Gabriella Llobet, COMEX, 02/07/2008; Irene Arguedas, COMEX, 03/07/2008).

The then Panamanian Vice-Minister of International Trade, Meliton Arrocha, confirms that parties did not outline the non-negotiables at the outset of the process and that this was taken to indicate that the sensitive issues were to be included in the final agreement. Arrocha (in *La Prensa* 19/10/2002: 25a) stated, with regards to the reluctance of Costa Rica to discuss financial services and insurances in the bilateral rounds, that:

> […] Costa Rica must remember that during the discussion of the normative frame, only Costa Rica's telecommunications sector was excluded from the FTA. Panama understood from that process that all the other issues were on the negotiation table. Yet, we also keep certain flexibility to assess cases in which exclusions are appropriate.[156]

The lack of outlining the non-negotiability of financial services and insurance from Costa Rica to Panama was based on the idea that trade diplomats from COMEX would be able to neutralise Panama's request. The diplomats would do so on the grounds that the financial services were negotiated in the normative part of the negotiation under the principle of keeping the status quo and assuring non-discrimination in the delivery of cross-border financial services. In fact, this was the argument COMEX negotiators used to convince its domestic actors from the financial sector of the convenience of accepting the normative chapter on financial issues. COMEX negotiators also argued that the chapter was inspired by NAFTA regulations (COMEX 10/05/2000; SUGEVAL-COMEX 09/05/2000).

In addition, COMEX negotiators expected to counterbalance Panama's aspirations of letting subsidiary banks operate, and facilitating the opening of bank branches and of offshoring societies in Costa Rica, by claiming that Panama was on the black list of tax havens in the OECD, and of non-cooperating countries in the

156 Author's translation.

Financial Action Task Force (see OECD 2000; Financial Action Task Force 2000).[157] This strategy was designed during the negotiation of the normative chapter on financial services in case Panama insisted on including offshoring and subsidiaries in this normative negotiation. As Panama and Costa Rica agreed to assess these issues in the bilateral negotiation, the strategy was to be displayed in this setting. COMEX negotiators faced a dilemma when they decided not to outline the non-negotiability of financial issues and insurances in the pre-phase of the bilateral negotiation as they thought Panama would not sit with them at all to conclude the bilateral protocols. Costa Rica also did not want Panama to negotiate with the rest of the Central American countries as being the last one to close a deal would have empowered Panama's positions on financial issues (anonymous interviews in Costa Rica 11/07/2008; 14/07/2008).[158]

Costa Rica's proposal for negotiating financial services in the bilateral protocol was to agree on the non-conforming measures by ratifying the extant valid law in each country (MICI 14/02/2002: 4). However, the initial strategy to counterbalance Panama's negotiating positions on financial services was impossible to implement as the IMF in August 2001 found that Panama's offshoring operations were compliant in 23 of 25 points of the Basel's Core Principles, including those of anti-money laundering. In June 2001, the Financial Action Task Force agreed to remove Panama from the list of non-cooperative countries to prevent money laundering (IMF 2001: 4 and 11). In addition, the OECD removed Panama from the list of countries with harmful tax practices in April 2002 (IMF 2002: 2).

By adopting a wait–and-see posture and not outlining these non-negotiables at the outset of the process, the setting to negotiate financial issues was changed by external factors to the process, as Panama displayed strong lobby efforts and implemented measures to comply with the Basel principles. Moreover, Panama's lobby efforts to be removed from these lists were with the purpose of improving their economic relations in general, and increasing their ability to attract foreign direct investment in particular. In fact, Panama signed a compromise with the OECD to improve transparency measures and the international organisation agreed to keep Panama off a new list of fiscal paradises (*El Panama América* 18/04/2002: Finance section: front page). Panama was not thinking of Costa Rica when it decided to lobby the international financial community to show that they complied with the Basel principles on banking issues. However, the removal of Panama from such lists affected Costa Rica's negotiation strategy in the FTA talks. There was no longer an excuse for not negotiating this issue-area on the basis of having harmful banking and

157 It has to be clarified that Panama was not on such lists when it negotiated with Chile as the first report from the OCDE to set standards of what qualify as harmful tax practices, which did not have countries names on it, came out in 1998.

158 These interviews were held with insiders of the process who want to remain anonymous as they thought these specific testimonies may create consequences for their job positions.

tax practices, or at least for not holding talks on whether it was possible to include such issues in the accord.

Once the normative negotiation started, there was no outlining of these non-negotiable issues between Central American countries and Panama, and this was also the case during the first negotiation round between Costa Rica and Panama (Minute of the First Round of Negotiation of the FTA Costa Rica-Panama 05/04/2002: 2). Yet, Costa Rica's refusal to negotiate financial services under Panama's position only emerged in the second round of the bilateral negotiation, in which both parties asked the counterpart to make their positions flexible on market access and financial services (Minute of the Second Round of Negotiation of the FTA Costa Rica-Panama 16-19/07/2002: 1).

Costa Rica's trade negotiator Gabriella Llobet publicly expressed the non-negotiability of financial services after the second round by claiming that this area is already open to external competition, as shown by foreign and Panamanian investment. Moreover, she claimed that Panama also have some sensitive issues in services such as professional services and transport systems (*La Nación* 20/07/2002: 25 A). Yet, the issue of transport was solved during the negotiation on the normative chapters in 2000-2001, and it was not subject to discussion in the bilateral process (FTA Central America-Panama 2002, annex 11.16). The two governments also solved an ongoing problem during the bilateral FTA talks about the entrance of people and cross-border transport from Panama that did not present insurances and load and were thus retained in Costa Rica. Moreover, Costa Rica tried to put pressure on its citizens to prevent them from buying in Panama's border city by asking for a tax on these products during the negotiation. An agreement was worked out between both governments (*Capital 10*-16/06/2002: 20). The issue of professional services, that is, eliminating nationality requirements, was neither discussed in the normative nor in the bilateral negotiation as Costa Rica also had some professions with nationality requirements. What was included in the normative agreement was the facilitation to allow the temporary entrance of business people (FTA Central America-Panama 2002, Chapter XIV, and annex 14.04).

The outlining of such issues after the second round of negotiations can be interpreted as a sign that Costa Rica wanted to address those issues during the upcoming rounds in order to neutralise Panama's aspirations, if the latter insisted on the banking issues (*El Financiero* 22-28/07/2002: 2; interview with Gabriela Llobet, COMEX, 02/07/2008). The issue of offshoring societies became part of the negotiation as Costa Rica was holding a public debate on the need to control offshoring operations. Offshoring societies are legally constituted outside of Costa Rica but in practice they operate in the country and they are not subject to any financial supervision. In this regard, the former president of Costa Rica's Central Bank, Eduardo Lizano, proposed a regulatory frame for such institutions. Panama had four groups of offshoring operations delivering services for Costa Rica's people (*El Financiero* 1-7/04/2002: 19). Yet, Panama wanted to state in the FTA that offshoring societies would not be discriminated (interview with Melissa Davis, MICI, 17/07/2008; Anonymous 19/07/2008). In principle this issue was not subject to negotiation as it emerged as a response of the ongoing internal debate in Costa Rica and the concern that eventual new regulations might affect Panama's offshoring societies.

Costa Rica believed that the issue of insurances was likely to be taken out of the negotiating agenda if they argued that this area was a state-owned company and its liberalisation would involve deep legal and constitutional changes that could not be pursued in an FTA negotiation (Minute of the Second Round of Negotiation of the FTA Costa Rica-Panama 16-19/07/2002). Such changes needed a deep national debate and a new legal frame in Costa Rica. Yet, Panama claimed as a second best option that this issue could be negotiated by using a phrasing that targeted the future, that is, if Costa Rica were to liberalise and privatise in the future, Panama would have a preferential treatment (interview with Joaquin Jácome, MICI, 17/07/2008). In this regard, by not stating the non-negotiability at the outset of the process, even during the normative negotiation, Costa Rica gave the illusion to Panama that such issues may be included in the agreement by using "if" and "in case" wordings. In other words, the lack of outlining these issues as non-negotiables was interpreted by the counterpart as a window of opportunity to negotiate them with the purpose of including such areas in the final package.

Panama had also its own non-negotiable issues, which were professional services, and some dairy and food products. Professional services were circumvented in the normative negotiation. Central American countries and Panama agreed on not negotiating this issue as most Central American countries have nationality requirements in certain professions. Yet, Costa Rica went out of negotiating possibilities to balance Panama's aspirations on financial services in the bilateral talks. Thus signalling the eventual discussion of professional services in the bilateral negotiation to some extent explains why Panama did not contribute much toward launching a third negotiation round. In fact, both countries agreed to more rounds after the second one (Minute of the Second Round of Negotiation of the FTA Costa Rica-Panama 16-19/07/2002), but the attempt to bring back an issue already agreed in the normative setting was considered as a cheating move on Panama's side, which eroded the fragile mutual trust the parties had. In addition, Panama also traded off this issue in the normative negotiation by not insisting on the liberalisation of telecommunications (interview with Diana Salazar, MICI, 30/07/2008; Joaquín Jácome, former Minister MICI, 17/07/2008; FTA Central America and Panama 2002, chapter 13, article 13.01).

Dairy and food products as well as beef were not outlined as non-negotiable by Panama and Costa Rica respectively at the outset of the bilateral process. However, the most sensitive goods became a problem for negotiators as these in principle could not be outlined as non-negotiables, inasmuch as one country had at least some competitive products within each category. Thus the producer of such products would want to export it to the counterpart under the preferential treatment that an FTA grants. This was the case with Panama for condensed and evaporated milk and butter within the dairy products category and tomato processed products within the food products category, and beef within the meat category. Yet in the vast majority of the areas in which these products are embedded, Panamanian producers were likely to lose. Beef was thought to be used by Costa Rica as a bargaining chip to make Panama's positions flexible on food and dairy products. However, the losses involved for the cattle sector (beef) and the link of this loss to external dynamics – potatoes in the FTA with Canada and politicisation- at the domestic level explain why beef was finally not used as a bargaining chip to trigger concessions in dairy products or to neutralise Panama's aspirations with financial issues. Thus the outlining of non-negotiables at the outset was more plausible for services rather than goods, which had to be negotiated as a constitutive element in the market access issue-area of a negotiation.

Finally, the lack of outlining the non-negotiables on services became an opportunity for the counterpart to press for including these issues in the agreement. However, as the negotiators could not manage all the dynamics that emerged domestically and internationally at the time of this negotiation, the option of not outlining the non-negotiables at the outset of the negotiation hampered their ability to take them out of the process. Thus, the space to negotiate a win-win deal narrowed. The factor of non-negotiables does not explain the whole failure of this negotiation process. Non-negotiability goes along with the domestic factors already explained, and the ones to be explained below. Together, they explain the failure of this negotiation.

8.2.2 Lack of Leadership Skills

Leadership is a skill that may be inherent in some people in all its forms or variants, that is, intellectual, entrepreneurial, and structural (Deese 2008; Young 1991), as well as political (Blondel 1987). However, it is also a skill that can be developed in a learning process. Politicians, negotiators, and diplomats use their leadership skills to direct the process in which they are participating though on other occasion the same people do not use such leadership skills to make parties reach an agreement.

Bilateral and multilateral economic negotiations, in this case an FTA negotiation, need the direct exertion of leadership skills to reach final agreement. In addition, leadership skills involve the ability to convince and attract the counterpart towards an agreement. Persuading the counterpart to change their initial choices in a soft way is about leadership skills. Leadership is not only based on resources and power. In other words, a leader is not a leader, because he is stronger than the other or because he has more economic weight than the counterpart (Deese 2008: 35). Leadership is also based on attracting the counterpart by making him want what you have and make the counterpart give you something in exchange, with the feeling that both sides are winners.

The exertion of leadership has been a key force to bring negotiations to an agreement in cases like the Doha round held in Qatar in 2001 within the WTO trade-based regime. And the lack of leadership also explains the failure of the involved parties to reach an agreement in the Doha rounds, such as that held in Seattle in 1998. Leadership in this setting took the form of mediation exerted by third parties or by officials of the same WTO (Odell 2009: 294-297; Deese 2008).[159] Third party mediation is a common practice in negotiations to settle conflicts of any type such as commercial, business, territorial, civil wars, etc (Raiffa 1982). Yet third party mediation as a form of leadership is rarely found in FTA negotiations between two governments. This role of honest brokers, and mediators has to be taken from one member from inside the FTA process if it is a bilateral talk. This can be unilateral or it could be a joint-leadership venture from members of each party. This role is usually reserved to presidents, ministers and chief negotiators.[160] The reason for this is that leadership skills are different to ordinary bargaining behaviour displayed by most negotiators (Malnes 1995: 100). Although a difficult task, a common negotiator can also use "the dress of a leader" and use their skills to redirect the process whenever it is at stake (Deese 2008; Malnes 1995).

In the case of the FTA negotiation between Panama and Costa Rica it is also possible to detect a lack of leadership skills to redirect the process whenever it was jeopardised by a divergence of interests, or by overusing distributive strategies that had an escalatory effect and also a spill over effect on other issues. The lack of leadership skills is also present in the inability of both parties to build up confidence and mutual trust. In this regard, both parties had a bias created by previous negotiations which affected the way the counterpart was depicted. There is no evidence of building mutual trust in this FTA negotiation. Mutual trust is not a symbolic label. It has material consequences in a bargaining process as one party may concede an issue with the "credible" promise from the counterpart that the conceding party will be compensated in the near future within or outside the frame established by the FTA as a regulatory institution. Trust may also trigger asymmetrical concessions from each party and may help both sides to take the other's argument as credible and not as cheating behaviour. Thus building trust as a rational enterprise to trigger concessions and reach a final agreement becomes essential (Malhotra 2004; Pillutla, Malhotra, and Murnighan 2003).[161]

The negotiation between Panama and Costa Rica lacked actors which were able to display leadership skills when the process was going towards impasse. Paradoxically leadership was exerted to launch the bilateral negotiation but not to conclude it. The then Panamanian President Mireya Moscoso and Miguel Angel Rodriguez met privately in the Summit of the Americas held in Quebec in April 2001 (COMEX 09/03/2001: 2). Here President Moscoso committed vaguely to start negotiations as she claimed that Panama was interested in the process but the agenda did not allow for the bilateral negotiations to begin straightaway. However, she committed to

159 Odell (2009: 276-279) also argues that a diminution of the quality of BATNA along with third party mediation explains the successful agreements in the Doha negotiation rounds such as Qatar 2001. However, when the quality of BATNA was high for the parties agreeing was extremely difficult, which produced impasses such as that in the Round held in Seattle 1998.

160 On how leadership exerted by heads of government can change a negotiation see Hermann (1995)

161 This process of concessions based on trust is known as Rapport (see List of Concepts).

starting the negotiations during her mandate and as soon as possible (interview with Joaquín Jácome, MICI, 17/07/2008; Gabriela Llobet, COMEX, 02/07/2008; Irene Arguedas, COMEX, 03/07/2008). In addition, President Rodriguez visited Panama in November 2001 in which the issue of launching FTA negotiations was once again discussed. As a consequence of this visit and the join commitment of Costa Rica's and Panama's presidents, negotiators started to coordinate a preparatory meeting for launching the formal rounds of negotiation.

> As I said to you on the phone and independently of the date we established for the coordination meeting, I would like to reiterate the importance of starting the first formal negotiation round as soon as possible. It is important to start these negotiations soon in order to fulfil the presidential mandate of President Moscoso and Rodriguez who agreed to start negotiations on 29 November in their presidential meeting and conclude them during the first term of this year (Fernando Ocampo 08/01/2002: DGCE-02-02).[162]

Panama answered in a positive way and proposed to start a first round in February over services and investment. This finally became a preliminary meeting to discuss the issues to be negotiated (interview with Joaquin Jácome, MICI; 1707/2008; Leda Arrué, MICI, 17/07/2008; Tatiana Varela, COMEX, 26/06/2008; Amparo Pacheco, COMEX, 02/07/2008). The letter states the following:

> I hereby would like to answer your note DGCE-02-02 with date 8 January 2002 directed to Vice-Minister of International Trade, S.E Melitón Arrocha, in which you propose a calendar to hold the bilateral negotiations between both countries as part of the Free Trade Agreement between Central America and Panama. In this sense, and given our various compromises of negotiations, we propose the 26 to the 28 of February for a first meeting for the table of Services and Investments to be held in Panama. We also propose the days 3 to 5 of April to have a meeting for the tables of market access, rules of origin, and services and investment which will also be held in Panama (Diana Salazar 14/02/2002, DINECI 137-02).[163]

Thus leadership skills to start the process were present for this but not to bring the negotiation to achieve agreement. What impeded the exertion of such leadership skills? Malnes (1995) argues that divergences on interests may be a reason for the hampered exertion of leadership skills. I would add that the initial setting matters when explaining the absence of leadership skills once the negotiation was underway. The lack of mutual trust along with the high divergence over economic interests may explain the difficulties with displaying such leadership skills but not the absence of them.

To make this clear, it is necessary to use some counterfactuals: the FTA negotiations between Panama and Costa Rica failed to reach an agreement in 2001, but the same negotiators were able to overcome similar sensitive issues to reach an agreement in August 2007 after relaunching the process in 2006. The problem was not the inherent inability of negotiators to make agreements as the majority of the team on both sides was almost the same, with few exceptions. In 2006, the issue of financial

162 Author's translation.
163 Author's translation.

services was also present, but not insurances as the US pushed Costa Rica to liberalise this item in the DR-CAFTA. Yet, beef, dairy products, and food products were once again sensitive and the parties were unwilling to grant concessions on these issues. In fact the absence of insurances made Panama pursue a rather tough bargaining strategy to push Costa Rica to grant more facilities for the location of bank branches as well as of opening subsidiaries. One common answer of negotiators was the political will of the heads of the state, but also the political will of ministers and vice-minister to break through resistant coalitions and to create balanced solutions on the sensitive issues (interviews with Laura Rodriguez, COMEX, 08/07/2008; Gustavo Guillen, COMEX, 27/06/2008; Tatiana Varela, COMEX, 26/06/2008; Leda Arrué, MICI, 17/07/2008; Samuel Moreno, MICI, 22/07/2008; Zereth Torres, MICI, 22/07/2008; Estif Aparicio, MICI, 18/07/2008; Diana Salazar, MICI, 30/07/2008). This so called 'political will' constitutes, to my understanding, leaderships skills, as negotiators claimed that they saw their bosses pushing to conclude a balanced agreement by using an integrative strategy.

Another example is the negotiation between El Salvador and Panama, which was not free of difficulties, despite the fact that the parties had more convergence on interests than in the case of Panama and Costa Rica. The negotiators from Panama were the same as those of the negotiation with Costa Rica. Both parties, especially the Vice-ministers or national directors of the sub-section of trade negotiations, exerted joint leadership on the different tables of negotiations to redirect the process whenever the value-claiming strategy started to predominate and whenever this mode of negotiating was going into a spiral effect. Bounded rationality and lack of mutual trust may have played a role not only in preventing Panama negotiators from using their leadership, but also on Costa Rica's side.

Going back to the negotiation setting between Costa Rica and Panama in 2002: the parties did not do much to make the spiral effect of value-claiming bargaining deescalate. This even affected the way parties negotiated lesser sensitive issues.

> The discussion over tobacco and cigarettes products was rather tough. Probably it was because we were the same negotiators holding the talks about dairy products, tomatoes, beef and these products. The way we saw each other and the way we felt Costa Rica was pushing on dairy products plus the restrictive rules of origin for our competitive milk-related products was too aggressive. We were also pushing hard to put our beef in Costa Rica's market. But we could not move each other from our initial positions. This affected other areas of the negotiation in market access [...] No, no one try to stop such a way of negotiating either from us, or from Costa Rica's or from both parties. We were so embedded in defending our interests that we did not have the time and will to do it. I mean Costa Rica and us were together responsible for not being able to solve issues that were not problematic, but we made these problems [...] Both sides stretched the elastic until it was cut (Leda Arrué, MICI, 17/07/2008).[164]

When the parties concluded the second round of negotiation the level of conflict was high. This is reflected in the words of Panama and Costa Rica. The latter criticised the inflexibility of Panama to open market access products in general and the

164 Author's translation.

former the inflexibility of Costa Rica to grant more facilities in financial services and insurances. Yet, Costa Rica's trade negotiators also stated that Panama should be willing to discuss professional services in the following negotiation rounds (*El Financiero* 22-28/07/2002). This fact prevented Panama agreeing to launching a new negotiation round to unblock the controversial issues and move the negotiation towards an axis of agreement.

> Perhaps it was not the best way of dealing with the conflict. We should not have announced in the newspapers, albeit tacitly, that we wanted to put professional services on the negotiation table, which obviously made Panama upset. We could have found other ways to exclude insurances and have a better talk on financial services. It was definitely not the best way to attract or invite Panama to the negotiation table (anonymous interview COMEX 30/06/2008).[165]

This quote reflects two constitutive aspects for failure. On the one side, it shows the lack of exerted leadership skills to redirect the process and convince Panama that solutions within the process of negotiation were still possible. It also shows that no one tried to make the tough bargaining and blaming deescalate. In fact the threat of putting professional services on the negotiation table through the press shows that escalatory effects were likely to continue. On the other side, this quote as well as the evidence presented in newspapers after the second round of negotiation confirms that offensive value-claiming was predominating in the bargaining, and was also likely to predominate if the parties decided to continue with the negotiation.[166] Thus, the non-display of leadership skills facilitated the escalatory effect; the absence of building mutual trust and the view of the other as non-trustworthy; and the predominance of offensive value-claiming strategies during the negotiation. The absence of leadership skills partly helps to understand how and why this negotiation process was brought to the edge of conflict and how it became a constitutive element that made this FTA experience a failed one.

8.2.3 Predominance of Value-claiming Strategies

There is an abundance of literature on negotiation that discusses the effects that an overuse of value-claiming strategies and the tactics that constitute such strategy may produce in different types of negotiations (Odell 2006; Odell 2009; Elms 2003; Raiffa 1982; Zartmann and Rubin 2000; Lebow 1996; Hopmann 1995). However, these scholars also agree that whether or not pure value-claiming will trigger failure to reach an outcome depends on the leverage capacity one or both parties have, given by their respective BATNAs (Singh 2008: 46). When the alternatives outside the agreement for one or both actors are worse than the current negotiation, the level of tolerance for distributive strategies may be higher (Odell 2009: 276). And when one party has a better BATNA than the counterpart, the former will tend to use more

165 Author's translation.

166 I analyse this aspect in depth in the following section.

value-claiming strategies to obtain more concessions at the expense of the counterpart, who will be more inclined to soften its demands (Singh 2008: 47).

An atypical case for the above mentioned literature is the negotiation between Costa Rica and Panama. The unusual element of this negotiation is that the leverage capacity was relatively similar for both countries, yet not equal, as both parties had or claimed to have similar external options. Both parties were less averse to display distributive strategies, but the danger of creating a spiral effect of using a value-claiming strategy over sensitive issues increased. Therefore, parties under these circumstances may be less averse to failure as both have external possibilities, and they will be more willing to press the counterpart hard.

The use of distribute strategies especially of the offensive variant played a decisive role in the course of the negotiation between Panama and Costa Rica. The display of tactics that constitute a value-claiming strategy was present from the beginning of the bilateral bargaining, and even in the contacts to launch the process. In the letter sent by Diana Salazar to the then General Director of International Trade in Costa Rica, Fernando Ocampo, with the confirmation of disposal to launch the negotiations, there was a tactical move from Panama. The letter stated that the first meeting was to be on Services and Investment matters which were the areas in which Panama was most competitive (Diana Salazar 14/02/2002: DINECI 137-02). This move of Panama was intended to make the parties focus on this issue, and to signal that the advance on market access will be tied to the progress on services and investment, in which financial services and insurances were embedded. Despite the fact that the meeting in February was a preparatory one, Panama's road map for the negotiation was unveiled.

Conversely, during the first negotiation round Costa Rica pressed to prioritise the discussion of market access, and argued that the negotiation of services and investment would be, in its substantial part, discussed later. The substantial part of the agreement to which Costa Rica was referring, was the discussion of subsidiaries, more facilities for branches, and insurances. In fact, the parties reviewed the non-conforming measures on investment and services of four of the six annexes during the first negotiating round (Minute of the First Round of Negotiation of the FTA Costa Rica-Panama 05/04/2002: 2). Costa Rica wanted to close dairy products, and protect beef and then move to the discussion of the areas of interest for Panama in the services.

Panama displayed a tactic of containment and forcing. On the one hand, Panama tried to contain the progress on market access by delaying the progress on this issue-area. On the other hand, slowing down the pace in market access was a mechanism to force Costa Rica to put financial services in the negotiation. Whenever Panama's negotiators noted that the progress of the services section was falling behind, they tried to even up and tie up the two issues by delaying the progress on market access. Perhaps this may have facilitated the spill over effect of using distributive strategies on issues that were conceived at the beginning of the negotiation as non-sensitive. By making up sensitivity on issues, and waiting to negotiate the real sensitive products, the zone of agreement was reduced and the escalatory effect of using threats and cheating tactics increased. In the end, negotiators spent a great deal of their time not only on including the counterpart sensitive issues in the accord, but also on discussing the mode of negotiating to prevent the inclusion of these issues, that is, first market access and then services (Costa Rica), and market access and services in a parallel way (Panama). In fact, one of the reasons for stopping the negotiation, and also a condition to seat again and conclude the FTA, was that services and market access should be discussed at the same time (*La Prensa* 25/07/2002: 33a; *El Panamá América* 24/07/2002: 24c; interviews with Joaquin Jácome, MICI, 17/07/2008).

Variants of cheating behaviour and threats were also present in the bilateral negotiation; at least this is the way one or both parties framed certain moves and statements from the counterpart. In the previous section it was mentioned that after the second round, Costa Rica threatened to put the issue of professional services on the negotiation table. Yet this was partly taken as a bluff by Panama to put the pressure on them and also put the costs of an eventual failure on their side (Interview with Melissa Davis, MICI, 17/07/2008; Samuel Moreno, MICI, 22/07/2008; Diana Salazar, MICI, 30/07/2008). As it was considered a bluff and the possibilities to retake the negotiations were low, Panama answered positively on the issue of professional services, saying that Panama was willing to put the issues of interests for Costa Rica on the negotiation table such as dairy products, professional services, transport, and publicity if Costa Rica was willing to include insurances and the known banking issues (*La Prensa* 19/10/2002: 25a). Panama thought that professional services could be counterbalanced by asking for liberalisation and the removal of the nationality requirements on some of Costa Rica's professions. Moreover, issues like transport and publicity services were not discussed top priorities, in case the counterpart asked for a non discriminatory treatment on these categories. Yet this was dependant on the concessions of Costa Rica on financial issues and its initiative to retake the talks. Panama's answer was also thought as a way of putting the cost of the impasse of the negotiation on Costa Rica (interview with Melissa Davis, MICI, 17/07/2008). Moreover, the two negotiating parties knew to some extent that the possibilities of sitting again were rather slim as the relation between both parties deteriorated due to the difficulties with reaching common positions and due to the rather public retaliatory statements in which each country blaming the other for the result of the second round.

After the second round, which became the last one, both parties also tried to place the responsibility for resuming the negotiation on the counterpart. On the one hand, Costa Rica and Panama blamed each other for the lack of flexibility needed to realise the FTA. On the other hand, both governments stated that resuming the talks had to be initiated by the counterpart. Phrases such as 'we are only waiting for the initial contact' or 'we are waiting for the phone call to resume the negotiation' were used after the second round (*La Prensa* 18/10/2002: 1 A; *La Prensa* 30/11/2002: 29 A; *La Prensa* 19/10/2002: 25 A). Whereas these phrases may seem part of an integrative strategy, they went, from Costa Rica's side, along with the message that banking, and insurances were no longer subject discussion. And if they were to be discussed, then talks on other services areas that were perceived as sensitive for Panama needed to be part of the negotiating agenda (interviews with Amparo Pacheco, COMEX, 16/07/2008; Luis Garrido, MICI, 22/07/2008).

The initial setting of the bilateral negotiation was also not the most favourable as the parties depicted each other as non-trustworthy and hard bargainers. The past experience that matters here was the negotiation between Costa Rica and Panama in market access as a requisite for completing the entrance of the latter into the WTO in 1997 (Ferrer 2001; interview with Roberto Echandi, COMEX, 26/06/2008). Here I do not claim that such depiction of the other is a path dependant process, and that this way of framing is always self-reinforcing and deterministic for failure, making probabilities of reversion of such behaviour or depiction of the other near impossible.[167] What I argue is that both negotiating parties did not spend time and human resources to change this mutual perception. Building mutual trust can also have material consequences, that is, it can facilitate the finding of a common ground to build a mutually satisfactory agreement, i.e. Rapport (see Elms 2006b). Costa Rica and Panama did not spend time on building mutual trust either in the normative or in the bilateral negotiation (interviews with Roberto Echandi, COMEX, 26/06/2007; Diana Salazar, MICI, 30/07/2008). Thus, the past experience of the negotiation within the frame of the WTO made both parties more inclined to use a distributive strategy, even in issues that were beforehand thought of as low conflict.

Remembering the external options to realise other FTAs and manipulating these options to increase the leverage in the present negotiation are common practices in these types of processes. BATNA manipulation is also conceived as a tactical move to lower the counterpart's demands and put through one's own issues at the expense of the counterpart (Odell 2000: 209-210, Fisher and Ury 2007; Raiffa 1982). However, it seems appropriate at this point to differentiate, for the sake of analytical clarity, between BATNA manipulation and the real BATNA, though they may overlap. Although BATNA is based on real fact, credibility, and/or real probability, the manipulation of BATNA in the case of launching other FTA negotiations over-exaggerates the external options and the diminution of the importance of the extant BATNA for the counterpart. It may be the case that both parties have external options with the same country and also with others.[168] BATNA manipulation as a tactic to lower the demands of the counterpart and insist on issues that are beneficial for oneself yet sensitive for the counterpart, is also based on the likely order and timing of the possible upcoming negotiations.

Concrete examples of BATNA manipulation in the FTA negotiation include the constant reference to a possible negotiation with the US. This country is the main

167 On path dependence and self-reinforcing patterns based on agent history see Pierson 2000; and Thelen 2000. On criticisms of path dependant theory and how this cannot account for endogenous change, that is, within the process, see Crouch and Farrell 2002; Deeg 2001; Peters .et.al, 2005.

168 BATNA can also be worse than the negotiation. The worse case scenario if you want to negotiate an FTA is that no one wants to negotiate with you.

trade partner of both countries and therefore using the possibility of having such an external option helped to exert pressure on the counterpart. As discussed above, both countries had this external option. Thus, the BATNA manipulation in this case facilitated the use of an offensive value-claiming strategy. As both countries have the US as their BATNA, these two countries started to signal to each other that they were likely to have a negotiation with the US before the other Central American country. For example, then Vice-Minister of International Trade of Panama Melitón Arrocha (19/10/2002: 25a) highlighted that "Panama still had the possibility of negotiating an FTA with the US, whereas this option for Costa Rica is an illusion".[169]

The then trade negotiator of COMEX Amparo Pacheco (02/07/2008) stated that:

> We mentioned to Panama during the normative process, to launch the bilateral and to hopefully conclude the FTA process, that our upcoming FTA negotiating agenda was rather full as a negotiation with the US was ready to be started [...] Of course this was to try to put some pressure to move the negotiation forward, but Panama also claimed the same, that is, they had also preliminary talks with the US to launch an FTA negotiation. We took this as valid as most countries were negotiating and ready to negotiate bilaterally, become part of NAFTA as well as enter the US market through the FTAA. I mean everyone knew that sooner or later for the countries following a market economy having an FTA with the US was a strong possibility. This started to matter the most was when we thought we had the first option vis-à-vis Panama.[170]

A related issue to that of BATNA manipulation is the use of time. As presented in the theoretical chapter, time can become a tactical instrument for both an integrative and distributive strategy. The setting makes time part of one of these two strategies. The negotiation had highly divergent issues; a counterpart's hopes for including these issues in the accord made time a tool that could be used to exert pressure on this counterpart. Time could be used to lower Costa Rica's aversion to include sensitive issues such as insurances and banking issues as well as to make Panama's position on food and dairy products more flexible. Panama used the time factor to delay its answers on the dates to launch the negotiation rounds, whereas Costa Rica used the lack of time to put pressure on Panama to have the negotiation rounds close to each other with the purpose of reaching an agreement as soon as possible.

It seems that Panama was not only trying to improve its own BATNA by claiming that the negotiations rounds with Costa Rica would have to wait, but also showing Costa Rica that their FTA talks had a second priority. Moreover, one could say that Panama had enough time to wait until its demands on insurances and banking issues were fulfilled as expected. Conversely, Costa Rica's rush to have the negotiations rounds without much time between each round reflected the fact that they saw more gains in the FTA with Panama. It also reflected the fact that the aversion to

169 Author's translation.

170 Author's translation. Other interviewees offered similar statements but with regards to Panama's option of having an FTA with the US and how this fact was used in putting pressure on Costa Rica (Melissa Davis, MICI, 17/07/2008; Diana Salazar, MICI, 30/07/2008; Joaquin Jácome, MICI, 17/07/2008; anonymous interview 26/07/2008).

stalemate was higher in Costa Rica than Panama, and that its future negotiating agenda was indeed demanding. Yet, this did not mean that Costa Rica was willing to make its position on services more flexible. Costa Rica's negotiators thought that they had a stronger bargaining position by highlighting the fact that they have multiples options not only restricted to the US, but with different countries. Once Costa Rica realised that Panama was not willing to negotiate again and as the negotiation with the US was forthcoming, Costa Rica highlighted the fact that if the negotiation with Panama should continue, it should be during 2003 (*La Prensa* 30/11/2002: 29 A).

Time manipulation was also present during the launching of the negotiation rounds and in the constant claims that the countries have busy negotiation agendas. It was mainly Panama that manipulated time to delay the progress of the talks and to improve its bargaining position. During the last day of negotiation in the first round:

Costa Rica indicated that its negotiators were available to meet again as soon as possible, for example, by the second quarter of May. Panama stated, due to its complex international trade agenda, that it could not give a date now. However, Panama said that during the week of the 15th of April, it would send a proposal to Costa Rica about the date to meet and the extension of the next meeting that would be held in San José, Costa Rica (Minute of the First Round of Negotiation of the FTA Costa Rica-Panama 05/04/2002: 2).[171]

During the second round, the parties tacitly recognised the difficulties the negotiation was experiencing in the minutes of the negotiation: "In the talks held in the three tables of negotiation there were only little progresses. The parties had the opportunity to explicitly express their interests and sensitivities" (Minute of the Second Round of Negotiation of the FTA Costa Rica and Panama 16-19/07/2002: 1).[172] This could reflect an incompatibility of interests; the phrase "explicitly express" may refer to the recognition of an ongoing open discussion over interests, and the predominance of a value-claiming mode for negotiating these sensitive issues. This is also confirmed in the second paragraph of the minutes of the second round negotiation, which shows how parties could not move forward in the negotiation: "Costa Rica made a call in order to have a greater degree of flexibility during the next round [...] Panama, reiterated its hope that Costa Rica makes its position more flexible with regards to financial services with the purpose of reaching a balance in the negotiation." However, time manipulation from Panama's side also became present in this round: "Costa Rica asked Panama to schedule the next round for 12 to 16 August 2002. Panama stated that due to its overcharged agenda it will analyse this proposal in its capital once its delegation is back in Panama and they will answer during the following days" (Ibid.).[173]

171 Author's translation.
172 Author's translation.
173 Author's translation.

It seems to be the case that it was Panama that left the negotiation table. Yet when parties ended the second round, they were still expecting to have a third round despite the high divergence of interests and the overuse of a value-claiming strategy that hampered the progress of the FTA talk. It is notable that one of the reasons for not coming back to the negotiation was the public threats that Costa Rica displayed through newspapers; that is, 'if Panama wants services, then negotiation over professional, transport and publicity services should also be included' (interview with Joaquín Jácome, MICI, 17/0/2002; anonymous 19/07/2002; Diana Salazar, MICI, 30/07/2002). However, Panama was also displaying a distributive strategy by delaying answers, and manipulating the BATNA. Neither Costa Rica did do much to try to bring the parties together. In fact, Costa Rica sought to place the costs of failure on Panama's side as well as give the responsibility for resuming the FTA exclusively to Panama. Such distributive bargaining behaviour from both countries was contained in the normative negotiation, but it showed its face in different tactics in the bilateral process, becoming a constitute element that brought this FTA negotiation to an outcome of non-agreement.

8.2.4 The Weight of Other FTA Processes

BATNA is not a static external option. Sometimes BATNA is there at the beginning of the process. At other times it rises during the process (Odell 2009, Singh 2008). In both cases, the negotiating parties manipulate the BATNA of the other and their own to increase the bargaining power during the negotiation. Yet, how realistic were the possibilities of Costa Rica and Panama launching more FTAs with other countries?

The US as an external actor is part of the so-called BATNA for both Panama and Costa Rica. However, the role of the US deserves further attention as it was and still is the main trade partner of these two countries. In addition, the US can be characterised as a hegemonic leader that exercises its structural power to shape and direct the system of global (economic) governance (Hurrell 2005; Ikenberry 2001; Keohane 1984; Cox 1994).[174] Therefore, the US is the main driver of the economic model of capitalism in a systemic sense and an active agent in promoting and realising the benefits of economic integration through multilateral institutions such as the WTO, regional institutions such as NAFTA and the FTAA, and bilateral FTAs. In fact the US has been the main promoter and driver of such economic integration process in

174 Keohane (1984) presents a liberal view on the relation of hegemony and institutions. Ikenberry (2001) develops an explanation of rational hegemonic power. Cox (1994) develops a Gramscian explanation of hegemony, socialisation, consent and enforcement in which he states that hegemony develops to accept the structure of domination, and Hurrell (2005) highlights the importance of norms and how these norms are used to legitimate the interests of the powerful. Without taking sides, these authors all highlight the importance of a hegemonic leader, although from different theoretical traditions.

Latin America since the conversion to market economies of the different countries in the early 1990s (Bulmer-Thomas and Page 1999)

Even before Panama and Costa Rica started to negotiate a bilateral FTA, these countries were thinking of the US as the main candidate. The importance of negotiating an FTA with the US for the Latin American countries in general was not only based on the size of the US market, but also on reputational aspects. Having an FTA with the US becomes a way of legitimising and locking-in internal reforms on the international level. Moreover, an FTA with the US was to be used as a 'quality stamp' by these countries in order to open new venues of economic negotiations with other potential trade partners (Wehner 2009a: 71-72).

The Ministry of Economy and Finances of Panama elaborated a plan for socio-economic development in 2000. This text highlights the relevance of deepening market reforms and investing in human capital in order to face the new challenges of the global economy in general, and that of the FTAA in particular (Ministerio de Economía y Finanzas-Panama 2000: 7). Panama's wish to achieve a trade accord with the US can be traced back to the very origins of the NAFTA and the Enterprise of the Americas proposed by George H. Bush. Panama's access to the WTO was also conceived as a stepping stone to reform its economy and to be able to join NAFTA or negotiate a bilateral with the US (Ferrer 2001: 78-79). The same former Minister of Internal Trade of Panama, Alejandro Ferrer (29/07/2008) maintained that the US was the main interest for Panama, and that the costs of liberalising the most sensitive areas of Panama's economy in an FTA with the US were lower than the potential economic gains. Conversely, in negotiations with small and middle sized economic powers the costs of liberalising sensitive issue-areas such as dairy products could not be out weighted by the potential economic gains of such accords (see also Ferrer 2001: 293). A similar argument was developed by Estif Aparicio (MICI,18/07/2007), who performed as chief negotiator in the FTA with the US.

Even though Panama was looking for an FTA negotiation with the US from 1994, the size of Panama's economy and the US preference to focus first on other trade partners delayed the start of an FTA negotiation. It was only in the beginning of 2002 that Panama started to display strong lobby efforts in Washington in order not to be left out of the web of agreements the US was building in the Western Hemisphere. A possible fact that precipitated this lobby effort from Panama was the announcement from the US president of the intention to launch FTA talks with the Central American countries on January 2002 (Bush 16/01/2002). On the one hand, Panama tried not to be forced to be part of such negotiations as part of the group of CAFTA, and on the other hand, it argued that due to its economic differences to the rest of Central America Panama deserves a bilateral negotiation (Ministerio de Economía y Finanzas 2002: 11; *La Prensa* 21/03/2002: 37 A).

Such negotiation with the US, despite the lobby efforts displayed from Panama, started to materialise in 2003, when the parties announced the launching of FTA negotiations. However, the US expected and made clear that the formal talks would have to wait until the first quarter of 2004 (Zoellick 18/11/2003). The reason for this was that the US was giving priority to CAFTA negotiations, Australia, Morocco, and the FTAA process (see www.sice.oas.org; www.ftaa-alca.org).[175] Despite the fact that Panama could not automatically start an FTA negotiation with the US after the breakdown of the talks with Costa Rica, it seems to be the case that the US also promised Panama that they would hold FTA talks soon. Whether this negotiation was to be launched in 2002, 2003 or 2004 was a pending issue, but the promise of the US was there (interview with Estif Aparicio, MICI, 18/07/2008). Nonetheless, the effect of having the certainty of launching negotiations with the US, although not knowing the date of start, made Panama's executive power more tolerant of another failed FTA process. It seems to be the case that Panama was not afraid of having a high rate of failed FTA experiences as its main trade partner –the US- was not intending to sanction such behaviour and loss of reputation. Therefore, the aversion to, or cost of, failure were kept low for Panama despite the failed experiences with Chile, and Costa Rica.[176]

In addition, the US did not produce an initial high divergence on domestic actor's interest as these groups saw a niche to explore in the American market (interview with Manuel Ferreira, Chamber of Commerce-Panama, 25/07/2008). However, difficulties with reaching an agreement with the US, and possibilities of a stalemate were also present but they were limited to agricultural issues. Financial services were not to be excluded from the agreement as the US was in favour of having a chapter on this topic as the NAFTA type of agreement shows. According to Alejandro Ferrer (29/07/2008) the US gave enough certainty to include the issue of financial services in the future FTA and ensured that the issue would not be an impediment for other FTAs. To wait to conclude the FTA with the US first and then resume with the stalled negotiations was the path that Panama chose.[177]

In a negotiation with the US the sensitive agricultural issues for Panama were to be liberalised a great deal as the gains in financial services as well as food and competitive agricultural products such as tropical fruits out weighted the costs for the government and the losers of the negotiation. In other words, the interests of pro-FTA domestic groups and those of the executive were convergent in pursuing an FTA with the US. Moreover the government also agreed that sacrifices in the non-competitive agricultural issues were necessary to reach an outcome of agreement with the US. Non-agreement with the US would have increased the costs of actualising Panama's external trade policy as the possibilities of negotiating with other countries thereafter would have been affected.

Panama was also dedicating its efforts to its the participation in the FTAA, which was also seen as a good possibility for realising economic gains in one go. The FTAA would have allowed Panama to have an FTA with the US. In addition, the

175 The FTAA process halted in 2005 due to the differences between the US and MERCOSUR countries lead by Brazil.

176 The FTA negotiation with Mexico also halted in 2002 (Novoa 25-30/04/2005).

177 The FTA between Panama and the US includes financial services (see FTA Panama-US 27/06/2007).

FTAA would have given Panama the chance of turning its previous failed negotiating experiences with Chile and Costa Rica into successful ones, since the FTAA would also have created a free trade zone between Panama and these countries. The FTAA was conceived as 'one agreement catches all the other previous ones' or was expected to absorb agreements of lesser scope and depth such as bilateral trade agreements between the Latin American countries (Devlin and Giordano: 2004: 174).[178] Moreover, the wave of FTAs was bringing different countries of the world to follow the policy of negotiating these accords. Thus, even before negotiating with the US, Panama had other FTA options that could include financial services. Panama and Taiwan signed a joint declaration to start FTA talks in August 2002 which formally started in 2003. This negotiation concluded with an outcome of agreement in August 2003. After this Panama dedicated full time exclusivity to prepare and coordinate the launching of FTA talks with the US. According to Estif Aparicio (MICI, 18/07/2008) there were no formal negotiations with the US as such in 2003, but there were many technical meetings with American representatives to prepare the process for 2004. This was a demanding process for a small country like Panama, which made the Ministry of International Trade dedicate all its trade diplomats, time and money to this national enterprise. This restricted the quantity of other FTA negotiations that Panama could take and also the possibilities of relaunching the dead negotiation processes with Costa Rica.

Costa Rica's real BATNA also involved an FTA with the US. In fact, it seems to be the case that Costa Rica's BATNA with regards to starting an FTA process with the US was slightly better than that of Panama as the US gave priority to the CAFTA process, which joined all the Central American countries in a negotiation with the US. The launching of this FTA process materialised only in 2002. In other words, Costa Rica also knew for sure that an FTA negotiation with the US would come when they started to negotiate the normative frame with Panama in 2000. Yet Costa Rica did not know how long it would take to start the formal process, and if this would be conducted in a bilateral way, or if Costa Rica would have to pursue its interests within the Central American regional grouping vis-à-vis the US. The official announcement of an FTA negotiation between Central America and the US came in 2002, before the negotiation between Panama and Costa Rica started (Bush 16/01/2002).[179] In fact, Costa Rica used the American announcement to exert pres-

178 The same authors also show scepticism on whether the FTAA will be able to absorb or subsume more complex structures of regional cooperation such as MERCOSUR. The FTAA may not be able to absorb such regional group, but it may act as a catalyst for MERCOSUR's reinvigoration. Thus, Devlin and Giordano claim that these two economic projects can coexist.

179 The US announcements of intending to start FTA talks with another country do not necessarily mean that formal rounds will be launched immediately. Starting the formal negotiation may take months or a year after the official announcement. In between there is also the official notification process to the American Congress of launching FTA negotiations. In the case of Central America (CAFTA) this happened 1st October 2002. The formal

sure on Panama in order not to delay their FTA negotiation further. The argument was that Costa Rica's trade agenda during the second part of 2002 would be overloaded.

Internally an FTA with the US was not subject to politicisation at least in the process of lobbying to launch this negotiation. Most domestic actors were likely to win in a negotiation with the US. The main reason was that the exportation of goods to the American market represented around 50 percent of Costa Rica's total exportations. In fact in 2003, in the year in which the CAFTA negotiation started, the Central American country exported 47 percent of its total goods to the US, and 42 percent of the total agricultural and agroindustrial goods were sent to the North American country (Jiménez 2005: 11).

Nevertheless, there were groups opposing the FTA negotiation with the US. These were the labour unions from the state-owned company of telecommunications ICE and the insurance sector. Yet Costa Rica's government surmounted these Labour Unions' and social movements' initial opposition by claiming that such issues would not be included in the FTA. In fact, the politicisation, mobilisation and the proposal of rejection to the DR-CAFTA started when the negotiation was almost concluded, and when Costa Rica publically confirmed that they were negotiating insurances and telecommunications with the US (Osterlof Obregón 2004: 31).[180] In addition, some of the sensitive issues in the negotiation with Panama were likely to win in the DR-CAFTA. Beef producers, which were for exclusion in the FTA with Panama, were now for free access to the American market (Interview with representative of CORFOGA 11/07/2008; Hathaway 2004: 228). Potato producers were not against the FTA with the US as such, yet they had status quo option, which means keeping importation quotas. In addition, they were well compensated in the FTA with Canada.[181] Other producers whose position was exclusion in the negotiation with Panama such as producers of sugar cane, and processed sugar were also pro-

negotiations for the DR-CAFTA were officially launched a year after George Bush announcement, that is, the 08/01/2003 (see www.sice.oas.org).

180 According to some anonymous people involved in the process, Costa Rica had a counterproposal ready for the US even before the latter put the ICE and insurances on the table. This means that Costa Rica's trade negotiators were willing to negotiate those issues, that the government was willing to assume the political costs of such decision in this FTA negotiation but not in previous ones, and that they knew in advance that US would make Costa Rica put such areas on the negotiation as a condition to close the deal. This fact of negotiating such issues triggered mobilisation and made the government put the ratification of the DR-CAFTA to the public scrutiny through a referendum. The DR-CAFTA was approved in Costa Rica with a slight majority of 51,6 percent vis-à-vis 48,4 percent of the population that rejected it. For the referendum process see Huhn and Löding 2007. For normative implications, and issues of democratic representation and accountability of double-track diplomacy processes in a general and normative level see Savage and Weale 2009.

181 Finally potatoes producers in Costa Rica were protected as the US got a quota of 300 metric tons which represent a 1.1 percent of Costa Rica's national production. Moreover, there is no reduction of the tariffs for such product (Jiménez 2005 28).

FTA (interview with CNAA representative 09/07/2008; see also Jiménez 2005: 19).[182] The beans sector was not against the FTA with the US, if protection was assured (interviews with CNAA representative 09/07/2008; beans sector representative 10/07/2008).[183]

Therefore, the number of groups favouring the FTA with the US was large and the government was willing to assume the political costs of including telecommunications and insurances in the final deal. Costa Rica refused to negotiate such issues with Panama. The reasons to assume such a decision of inclusion are varied. The most relevant ones are the size of the US market and Costa Rica's high dependence on this country for economic success. In addition, there is the fact that the US has more leverage to negotiate than Costa Rica due to its structural power capacity. For example, Costa Rica also wanted to close a deal and assume the costs of including the known sensitive services issues in order to create certainty for producers and products that were part of the Caribbean Basin Initiative (CBI). Costa Rica's textiles and tuna producers suffered from trade deviation with NAFTA. In order to remedy the situation the US passed a temporary law to include textiles and tuna within the CBI. Yet this was likely to come to an end in 2008. Costa Rica was also afraid that the costs of not including insurances and telecommunications in the DR-CAFTA, and not closing a deal would mean a restriction or temporary or definitive exclusion of the CBI as the US decides this in a unilateral way. The economic effects of an exclusion from the CBI would have affected all the productive sectors of Costa Rica without distinction (Jiménez 2005: 12-13).

An FTA with the US was the best possible scenario for Costa Rica. This BATNA was used in the negotiation with Panama, but it also created certain restrictions as Costa Rica was saving sensitive issues in the negotiation with Panama for the process with the US. Using telecommunications and insurances as bargaining chips in the process with the US meant a bigger openness of the American market to Costa Rica's agricultural products. Costa Rica, without privatising telecommunications and insurances, was able to liberalise such sectors. This meant that there would no longer be state monopolies but rather a competition between the state owned and private companies. The liberalisation and deregulation of state monopolies, or obfuscation without high economic dislocation, are seen as prepatory steps for possible privatisation, as they are intended to show the inefficiencies of public companies,

182 Sugar and beef producers got a tariff rate quota for entering the US market (COMEX 2004: 36). This was not the initial position of these sectors, but the US showed sensitivity on these two products. Therefore, the US got to protect its sugar and beef producers. However, some quotas to Costa Rica were granted (interview with Francisco Chacon, COMEX, 14/07/2008) A tariff rate quota means that a volume of imports in this case from the US is lower than the tariff charged for imports above the quota. Imports above the quota established face higher tariffs.

183 Beans entering Costa Rica's market from the US have a phase out of 15 years (COMEX 2004: 39). Uncooked, fresh and frozen beans entering the US market have free access (FTA DR-CAFTA 2004, Annex 3.3 US Schedule: 23-25).

which serves as a justification for privatising such companies later on (see Wilson 1999: 767). The need for keeping insurance, telecommunications and financial services out of any previous FTA agreement was strategic to gain bargaining power in the process with the US. In other words, Panama could not put such issues in the negotiation with Costa Rica due to its size, and its lack of structural power and because Costa Rica was hoping to use such issues in the upcoming negotiation with the US.

Costa Rica did not have other FTA concerns beyond the US when it was negotiating the bilateral protocols with Panama. Yet, Costa Rica constantly referred to its previous experience even with NAFTA countries such as Mexico and Canada as well as NAFTA possible candidates such as Chile. Costa Rica made these references in order to make Panama's position on banking, insurances and telecommunication – this last one during the normative process- more flexible and assume that Costa Rica was not up to negotiate such issues (interview with Gustavo Guillen, COMEX, 27/06/2008; Roberto Echandi, COMEX, 26/06/2008).

8.3 Concluding Remarks

This chapter presented the different internal and external factors to the interstate negotiation that made the governments of Costa Rica and Panama fail to reach an outcome of agreement in 2002. The four conditions outlined here –non-negotiability, lack of leadership skills, overuse of value-claiming strategies, and the weight of other FTA processes– played a decisive role in bringing this negotiation to an axis of failure. In addition, the lack of mutual trust contributed to an increasing narrow zone of agreement due to the past experience at the WTO, as it contributed to the overuse of distributive bargaining strategies during the negotiation. Nevertheless, the driving factor for such a narrow zone of agreement is the high divergence on interests that increased during the bilateral negotiation. This process of failure can be explained by both processes and extant conditions at both the domestic and international levels of this FTA negotiation. Costa Rica and Panama shared responsibilities for the outcome of non-agreement in the FTA process of 2002, inasmuch as they were not able to fulfil each other's economic expectations and built up a trustworthy relation. The conditions outlined in this chapter were together, and not on their own, constitutive elements for the outcome of non-agreement.

9. Comparing the Two Failed FTA Negotiations

9.1 *Introduction*

This chapter compares the two case studies of this research in their domestic and international dimensions. In the first sub-section of this chapter, I present the peculiarities of each negotiation process. In the second sub-section, I analyse the similarities of the two FTA negotiations, following the conditions that explain the process of failure. In a third sub-section, I discuss the different impact of the domestic and international conditions on the failed FTA negotiation processes of Chile and Panama, and Costa Rica and Panama. However, I also argue that the conditions that explain failed FTA negotiations have to be taken as part of a whole or as a multifactor process, despite the fact that there are some conditions that exerted a stronger influence on the outcome of non-agreement. In the second part of this chapter, I put the cases of Chile-Panama and Costa Rica-Panama in a broader comparative perspective. I introduce and give an overview of other cases of failed FTA negotiations.

9.2 *Differences of the Two FTA Negotiations*

The reasons to launch the FTA negotiations between Chile and Panama and Costa Rica and Panama were different. The former was launched because of political reasons and the latter because of economic reasons. This does not mean that there were no economic aspects involved in the launching of the FTA negotiation in the case of Chile and Panama, and that the political logic was absent in the FTA negotiation between Costa Rica and Panama. On the contrary such aspects were there, but they were secondary to the reasons already named.

The political logic for launching an FTA between Chile and Panama was based on Chile's need to redirect its foreign economic policy towards Latin America, and on Panama's view of Chile as its role model for its economic internationalisation. In the case of Chile, the priority of the US and Europe over Latin America was part of an internal debate. Yet, to some extent the dilemma of opting for the US or Europe over Latin America was artificial as shown by the open regionalism and the multitrack economic diplomacy adopted by Chile. This means that negotiating FTAs with the US, the EU, Asian countries, and Latin American countries did not exclude one another (Porras 2003: 37-56; Silva 2001; Van Klaveren 1998; Morande 2003).

Panama's reason to negotiate with Chile and also monitor FTA possibilities with other countries such as the US, was that Panama needed to continue to cement its domestic neoliberal reforms at the international level. Moreover, it also wanted to learn how to negotiate FTAs as a preparatory step for negotiating with the US, despite its previous economic negotiation experiences at the bilateral and multilateral level (interviews with Diana Salazar, MICI, 30/07/2008; Estif Aparicio, MICI, 18/07/2008; Alejandro Ferrer, MICI, 29/07/2008).

For Panama, Chile was the model to follow in terms of integration to the global economy and in terms of keeping the freedom of not becoming a full member of a regional grouping. Panama is a member of SICA, but it has not subscribed to the General Treaty on Central America Economic Integration (see www.sica.int). Panama identified itself with the Chilean way, as the South American country is only an associate member of MERCOSUR and has pursued its own way of proactive economic integration to the global markets through bilateral and multilateral FTAs (see Ferrer 2001). This resemblance and the option of pursuing Chile's way of economic integration was a key issue for Panama's decision to negotiate its first FTA with Chile (interviews with Samuel Moreno, MICI, 22/07/2008; Bruno Garisto, Ambassador of Panama in Chile, 11/04/2008).

Conversely, the economic rationale was more evident than a political logic in the launching of the FTA negotiation between Panama and Costa Rica. Costa Rica's decision to approach Panama for an FTA negotiation was due to the economic interests shown by its domestic actors (interviews with Laura Rodriguez, COMEX, 08/07/2008; Irene Arguedas, COMEX, 03/07/2008; Roberto Echandi, COMEX, 26/06/2008; Amparo Pacheco, COMEX, 02/07/2008). The domestic pressure to launch an FTA negotiation was not that evident in the case of Chile and Panama in 1996, since the decision of launching this negotiation responded to the national interests of the states. In the case of the FTA between Costa Rica and Panama, Costa Rica's domestic groups, especially, dairy, agricultural and food producers expected to assure a preferential treatment with Panama.

Panama was on the losing side of the story of market access with Costa Rica, with the exception of beef, beans and tomato processed products in the FTA negotiation; whereas it had an offensive position in the FTA negotiation with Chile in products such as sugar, coffee, melons, coconut oil, beef, and water melon. Even in food products Panama felt it could be competitive vis-à-vis Chile. The protection of sugar based food products was a strategic move from Panama rather than a consequence of Panama's lack of competitiveness in the negotiation with Chile. The purpose was to make this Southern Cone country grant quotas for processed and unprocessed sugar (interview with Leda Arrué, MICI, 17/07/2008).

Therefore, the sensitive and competitive products in both negotiations were determined by comparative advantages. Yet, the goods that provoked controversy in the market access section were different in each negotiation, with the exception of beef. However, beef did not play a major role in bringing the FTA negotiations with Chile to a standstill, although it did delay the negotiation process along with sugar and rice products (*El Diario* 18/01/1998: 29; interviews with Oscar Quina, DIRECON, 08/04/2008; Samuel Moreno, MICI, 22/07/2008). In the case of Costa Rica and Panama, the beef issue, along with dairy products, banking and insurances, was a constitutive element in the process towards failure in the FTA talks (FTA Costa Rica-Panama's draft text: market access and services, 2002).

Even though the main causes for the impasse of the two FTA negotiations lay within the financial services issue-area, the reasons for the respective divergences of interests are different. In the case of Chile and Panama, the latter requested that Chile facilitated the transfer of capital investment coming from Panama by granting an exception to the unremunerated reserve requirement –'encaje' - or by removing this mechanism. The former requested that Panama removed the nationality requirement in the area of professional services. Whereas Chile was sensitive on the 'encaje' with regards to Panama - it saw a possible impact on its monetary policy since the incoming of dollars from Panama could overvalue the Chilean currency - Chile was also thinking of reserving this issue-area for a negotiation with the US (Sáez and Sáez 2006; interview with Catalina Bau, Ministry of Finances, 11/04/2008). Thus, Professional services and 'encaje' to prevent speculative investment became the centre of the negotiation with Panama. Such issue-areas were not part of the sensitive issues of the negotiation over services in the case of Panama and Costa Rica.

The sensitive issues in services for Panama and Costa Rica were load and haulage, especially regarding the problem of Panama's trucks entering Costa Rica without insurances. However, this issue was solved in the negotiation. The most sensitive aspects for Costa Rica were Panama's request of facilitating the operation of bank branches, and the possibility of opening subsidiaries that would keep the name of the investing bank to help clients identify the brand. In addition, Costa Rica was not willing to include the issue of insurances in the agreement; not even in the form of future clauses or future phrasing, which Panama requested as a second best option (interview with Irene Arguedas, COMEX, 03/07/2008; Minute of the Second Round of Negotiation of the FTA negotiation Costa Rica-Panama 05/04/2002).

For Panama, the sensitive issues included professional services, as with the negotiation with Chile. The difference was that this issue, according to Panama's trade diplomats, was traded off with Costa Rica's exclusion of telecommunications in the normative FTA negotiation between Central America and Panama (interviews with Melissa Davis, MICI, 17/07/2008; Joaquin Jácome, MICI, 17/07/2008; anonymous 26/07/2008). However, the telecommunication chapter of the normative part explicitly states that this chapter does not apply to the economic relationship between these two countries. And the trade-off of telecommunications with professional services was only verbally assured and not written as part of the FTA text (interviews with Leda Arrué, MICI, 17/07/2008; Samuel Moreno, MICI, 22/07/2008).

Therefore, the possibility of agreeing was perceived as extremely limited due to the high divergence of interests. However, the specific topics discussed within services and financial services, which obstructed the progress of both FTA negotiations, were different, except in the case of professional services, though even in this case the nature and dynamic of negotiating the issue differed.

Another particularity of each process was with regards to the trust between the negotiation parties (on trust in FTAs see Elms 2006b). At the beginning of the process, the negotiators from Chile and Panama had a favourable perception of each other, whereas in the case of Costa Rica and Panama the parties depicted the other has non-trustworthy due to past experience at the WTO. Neither Costa Rica nor Panama enjoyed a trustful relation in the initial setting of the negotiation; nor could they build trust during the normative and the bilateral negotiation of the FTA.

Conversely, Chile and Panama trusted each other; however, the trust deteriorated during the process. The turning point during the negotiation that changed the initial trusting relation to one of increasing distrust, occured when the former started to pursue its interests in a tough way to protect its sugar and its financial sector, and when the latter pushed for the liberalisation of these issues.[184] Another turning point was when Chile pushed hard to liberalise Panama's professional services and get a better deal for its sugar based food products, and Panama adopted a containment position. Panama's position on professional services became more flexible in the second term of 1997 in order to use the issue to trigger concessions from Chile on financial issues. Yet, here Chile rejected such option showing its definitive unwillingness to include this issue-area in the final agreement. Chile's final offer was to sign the FTA without a chapter on services and financial services and negotiate these issues in five years time once the FTA became valid (interviews with Diana Salazar, MICI, 30/07/2008; Catalina Bau, DIRECON, 11/04/2008).

Chile and Panama perceived their relation as asymmetrical in terms of international experience, and economic and political power. Chile perceived that it had more power to move and manage the negotiation according to its own interests and Panama perceived Chile as more powerful. However, such power was not a threat for Panama as it believed that Chile's economic and international assets in Latin America would help Panama to enter into a growing web of FTAs. In addition, Panama acknowledged Chile's reputation in the international arena. The ascription of a powerful status to Chile by Panama did not mean that the latter lacked bargaining power in the negotiation, as it was the case that Panama strongly defended its professional services at the beginning of the process and pushed hard through the entire negotiation for a chapter on financial issues.

In the case of Costa Rica and Panama both actors perceived their economic and political bilateral relationship as symmetrical despite the fact that Panama could lose in agricultural issues in the negotiation. However, Panama thought they could be compensated for such losses with the inclusion of insurances and banking issues in the accord. Despite the fact that Costa Rica perceived itself as more experienced in FTAs than Panama, the former also depicted Panama as a hard negotiator. This means that both parties perceived each other as having or enjoying similar bargaining assets for the FTA process.

Each FTA negotiation had its own dynamic in its origin and development, and the reasons to launch the two negotiations were different. In addition, the sensitive issues that provoked a high divergence of interests and that to some extent explain the

184 On turning points in negotiation see Druckman 2001.

obstruction of these two FTA processes were different, although they lie within the item of services and market access. Despite the different dynamics in the initial setting of the process as well as the differences over the issues that provoked the aversion to liberalisation, both FTA negotiations ended with the same result in 1998 and 2002 respectively. The stalemates of the FTA negotiations between Chile and Panama, and Costa Rica and Panama are associated with underlying common aspects that are reflected in the conditions for failure I have presented.

9.3 Common Aspects of the Two Failed FTA Negotiations

9.3.1 Domestic Dimension

The initial conditions for an economic negotiation being conflictive are divergent interests. In both FTA negotiations it is possible to find a high divergence over interests. An important aspect of this divergence has to do with the bounded rationality of negotiators, which made them biased about the interests of the counterpart, and about the possibility of changing the initial position of the counterpart on specific issues. For example, Panama believed it could change Chile's position on financial issues, despite the fact that Chile's previous FTAs, even with the NAFTA countries –Canada and Mexico- did not include a chapter on financial services. In addition, Panama believed that Chile's aversion to liberalising financial issues was based on the impression they had of Panama as a potentially threatening tax haven. Whereas it is true that Chile thought this, Panama thought that the reforms to improve the control within its banking sector were enough to change Chile's initial position. Panama thought that by showing Chile the scope of the reforms conducted and how the banking system operates under the new legislation, it could convince Chile of the innocuousness of Panama's banking sector vis-à-vis Chile's financial system. In addition, Chile also believed it could change Panama's aspirations in the FTA by using distributive strategies and by signalling the eventual higher costs of failure to Panama. Costa Rica's negotiators were biased in a way that prevented them from detecting the profundity of Panama's sensitivity regarding agricultural issues, but at the same time, they thought they could change Panama's position without granting deep access on financial services and insurance. Trade diplomats from Panama also believed it could change Costa Rica's position on financial and insurances issues.

It is important to state that all countries showed bounded rationality as the negotiators lacked complete information and sometimes misinterpreted the extant incomplete information over the interests of the counterpart. The negotiation parties also ignored the eventual costs of the nested games for these two FTA negotiations. For example, negotiators from Costa Rica were unable to calculate the costs and ramifications of the politicised approval of the FTA negotiation with Canada for its ongoing negotiation with Panama. This ratification process and the domestic negotiation with the agricultural sector impeded the negotiators' ability to negotiate the beef item with Panama. In addition, Panama's negotiators could not understand the inability of Costa Rica to grant at least some quotas and progressive reductions of the tariff for beef. A similar experience was present in the case of Chile and Panama; Chile's negotiator took for granted Panama's inability to improve its supervisory regulations on banking issues and based their strategy on the fact that banking in Panama had a deficient structure and lack of international standards. Chile could not anticipate the effects of Panama's reforms on banking issues for the negotiation, which meant that Chile lacked tactics to protect the banking sector.

The lobbying from domestic groups that would lose with the FTAs was intense when directed towards the negotiators, but these interest groups also demand that the Congress send signals of possible non-ratification of the FTAs. However, in the case of Chile the Congress did not play a major role in the FTA talks with Panama as negotiators knew that the removal of the 'encaje' was impossible to pass in Congress given the size of Panama's market and the size of the economic gains. In the case of Costa Rica, Congress sent indirect signs of non-approval, which were related to the process of the FTA with Canada. Costa Rica's government limited negotiation of beef issues as it did not want to have a new domestic negotiation to compensate domestic groups to approve a new FTA in the future, as with potato producers in the negotiation with Canada. Panama's Congress sent concrete signals of non-ratification during both FTAs, warning that they would not agree to an FTA if the losses were high for agriculture and the gains for services rather limited.

In both FTA negotiations the economic relationships were governed by comparative advantages or an inter-trade logic. The possibilities for developing intra-trade were limited. Perhaps the reason for having limited possibilities for developing intra-trade was that the three cases concern developing countries and their production of industrial goods is small. However, the primacy of comparative advantages does not mean that intra-trade is not possible regarding agricultural products and/or commodities in developing and developed economies (Krugman 1992b). The recent FTA agreements of Chile with Australia and New Zealand prove this point as the three countries are agro-industrial countries and produce similar exportable products (Murray, and Challies 2004: 89-90, Challies and Murray 2008).

The lobby efforts to impede the inclusion of an issue-area, product or service in an FTA negotiation respond to the potential threat that such bilateral economic liberalisation may pose for an economic sector. Therefore, the job-insecurity factor was present in both FTA negotiations. The job insecurity factor was limited to FEDAP in the negotiation between Chile and Panama as the agricultural sector in Chile was more focused on the costs of the already approved MERCOSUR agreement. Yet, the potential economic loss for FEDAP acted as a sine-qua-non for politicising the negotiation with Chile on Panama's side.

In the case of Costa Rica, the job-insecurity factor played a role for the politicisation and mobilisation of agricultural producers; this was especially the case with beef as the cattle industry is a traditional sector in this country. The cattle industry was able to link its loss to the problems of potato producers who were fighting for either the non-approval of the FTA with Canada or generous side payments to compensate for the negative effects of the FTA. On Panama's side, the job-insecurity factor was latent in the dairy sector and food sector during the negotiation with Costa Rica. These two sectors saw Costa Rica as pushing for immediate access to its market, but at the same time they also maintained that Costa Rica's negotiators were obstructing the access of competitive dairy products by demanding tight rules of origin and by not granting a reduction of the tariffs on products such as cheeses, butter, and evaporated and condensed milk. In the Chile-Panama and Costa Rica-Panama FTA negotiations the job-insecurity factor became essential in constituting the opposition to the respective FTA negotiations. In both FTA negotiations, without the agricultural products already named and without the services known, an agreement did not make sense for the governments as the economic costs were higher than the possible economic gains for the parties.

The factors of divergence on interests and job-insecurity went along with the politicisation of the two negotiations. Here it also played a major role in the nested games in which each country was involved during these FTA negotiations. The politicisation was achieved by the eventual losers of the respective negotiations. Such politicisation also served as an indicator, noticeable to groups favouring these FTAs, that the talks held with Chile, Panama, and Costa Rica were likely to progress at a slow pace, if at all. Therefore, this politicisation and the inability to make domestic actors' positions more flexible made the domestic groups favouring the FTA free ride and lobby for other FTA negotiations.

The politicisation level would have been part of the negotiation at the domestic level even if the FTA talks would not have taken place during elections or referendums. In the case of Chile and Panama, the call for a referendum made the politicisation level stronger than it already was, and gave FEDAP the possibility of linking its sector loss to the economic transformation that was ongoing in this country. The results of the referendum became the last hit for an already dead FTA negotiation as then President Pérez Balladares lost his power of initiative. Neither did Chile do much to resume the negotiation as the gap between both countries' positions was difficult to close.

In the case of Costa Rica and Panama elections also increased the politicisation level of the FTA talks. Presidential and parliamentary elections in Costa Rica 2002 prevented the launch of the negotiation and increased the politicisation level of the approval of the FTA with Canada. These electoral processes prevented the launch of the talks but do not explain the failure. Costa Rica was also having City Council elections by the end of 2002, which impeded negotiators to use beef, beans and tomato processed products items as bargaining chip to obtain a better treatment from Panama in dairy and food products. The government of Costa Rica did not want to jeopardise the elections of the members of its political party –PUSC- in rural districts where most voters are agricultural producers and cattle growers.

The free-riding option did not mean that the domestic groups supporting the respective FTA negotiations left the process completely. On the contrary, the respective representatives of each sector favouring the FTAs remained in the process but the time spent in monitoring the talks decreased as finding a common ground between the governments became more difficult. Whereas the domestic groups in favour of FTAs started to lobby to initiate talks with other governments, giving little attention either to the Chile-Panama or the Costa Rica-Panama FTA talks, the eventual losers put all their efforts into lobbying the executive and legislative to exclude their sectors, or to send strong signals of non-ratification.

The three countries' interest groups that favoured the FTAs were seeking to actualise other FTA negotiations, especially with the US. In an eventual FTA negotiation with the US, the commercial interests of the groups in favour of this negotiation and the national economic interest of the state converged. The reason was that the potential gains for the states, consumers and producers were larger than the costs for some sensitive sectors. On the contrary, in the cases of the FTA negotiations analysed in this research, the zone of agreement was rather small and socio-political costs for the state were higher than the possible economic gains.

Hence, the implications of liberalising sensitive issues vis-à-vis the socio-political costs for the government, as well as the limited potential economic gains of the FTAs, served as incentives to change the governments' initial positions of agreement to one of non-agreement. However, these similar conditions at the domestic level do not explain the stalemate of the FTA negotiations between Chile and Panama, and Costa Rica and Panama if each condition is taken independently of each other. These conditions unfolded in the domestic level of the respective negotiations in a similar timing. Whereas the high divergence on interests, the job-insecurity, the politicisation level and the free riding of groups favouring the FTAs in the Chile-Panama and Costa Rica-Panama explain the obstruction of these negotiations, the decisions to leave the negotiations without agreement lay with the respective executive powers. Therefore, the international level is also a constitutive dimension for these failures.

9.3.2 International Dimension

Outlining the non-negotiability of issues at the outset of the negotiation process seems to work better in the service sector than in market access. Market access is still the core of trade negotiations and parties always have some agro-industrial products in which they are competitive. In these competitive goods, producers will lobby their government to assume a posture of opening its counterpart's domestic market to these competitive products. In the case of services which have diverse sub-sectors such as tourism, financial services, freight transport, maritime transport, publicity, professional services, etc., a government may be more inclined to exclude an entire item because of the impossibility of fragmenting these issues and negotiating them in small pieces, as is the case with the market access of goods.

In both FTA negotiations the non-negotiable services were not communicated at the outset of the process. The countries adopted a position to wait and see how the negotiation developed to express the issues they were not willing to negotiate. In addition, when countries did not outline the non-negotiability of services at the outset of the process, they precluded the dedication of time and human resources to find other areas in which collaboration was possible. The parties could not create innovative solutions to exclude the sensitive issues and compensate the counterpart with other items, products, and/or services either within the frame of the negotiation or in other areas unrelated to the negotiation such as political support for joining trade groups or regional forums, technical cooperation, academic exchange, and cooperation in defence issues.[185]

The analysed cases of Mexico in NAFTA, and Chile in the negotiation with Central America, show that it is more likely to have success when non negotiable issues are clearly outlined at the outset of the process. Yet, both Mexico and Chile in their respective experiences were also able to offer attractive compensation packages and worked with their negotiating counterparts to expand the zone of agreement. As such the lack of clearly outlined non-negotiable issues at the outset does not seem to be a sufficient condition for failure. Nevertheless, the lack of clearly outlined non-negotiable issues at the outset of the process created excessive expectations in the parties of these two FTA negotiations, insofar countries expected that such issues would be at least partially liberalised. In this regard, this condition of the intergovernmental negotiation has to be taken as a whole along with the other explanatory conditions to explain the result of non-agreement in both FTA negotiations.

Displaying leadership skills, or not, shapes the course of a negotiation at the multilateral level, such as those of the WTO (Odell 2009; Deese 2008; Malnes 1995). This is also the case in FTA negotiations; the presence of political leaders and their commitment was the first important step to launch the FTA negotiations of Chile-Panama and Costa Rica-Panama. However, the same role of leaders in a joint-venture was not perceived when the FTA negotiations started to show fault lines provoked by the divergent interests at stake. According to the testimonies of negotiators from the three countries, the exertion of leadership skills at key conjunctures of the negotiation was absent in both cases. The negotiators could not redirect the process whenever this was in jeopardy. The deterioration of the mutual trust in the case of Chile and Panama, and the initial distrust that increased in the negotiation between Costa Rica and Panama, may have prevented the exertion of such leadership. No negotiator adopted the role of mediator or honest broker to propose win-win deals either from one or both sides.

In both FTA negotiations, the countries negotiated using a distributive strategy, even to discuss areas, goods, and services which were not thought of as sensitive. The predominance of this type of negotiating strategy had an escalatory spiral effect. The tactics displayed by the negotiating parties were varied and included manipulation of information, the manipulation of their own and their counterpart's BATNA, and the use of threats. Due to the setting of the negotiation and the increasing prob-

185 On problem-solving negotiation see Wagner 2008.

lems with finding a common ground on which to work together, the time factor became an available tool for the hard bargaining of the three countries.

In these FTA negotiations, countries were more tempted to use a value-claiming strategy as their BATNAs were similar. These BATNAs were the US in the form of a bilateral negotiation, NAFTA, and the FTAA. In addition, the three countries also had the possibility of launching FTA negotiations with other countries as the phenomenon of FTAs was in vogue after the materialisation of NAFTA. As the external option was better for the countries, the aversion to overuse distributive strategies tended to disappear proportional to the reduction of the costs of failing to reach an outcome of agreement. Therefore, Chile and Panama as well as Costa Rica and Panama tended to go for all the possible gains, counteracted by only minimal or no concessions on their (most) sensitive issues, insofar as the possibilities outside these negotiations were better for these countries.

Since the 1990s with the beginning of the negotiation of NAFTA, the reinvigoration of the EU through the European Single Act in 1986 and through the Maastrich Treaty in 1992, the foundation of MERCOSUR in 1991, and the launching of SICA in 1991, most countries started to seek membership in regional economic groupings (Schirm 2002; Hurrell 1995).[186] Countries from the different continents also started to pursue their economic agenda bilaterally in order not to be left behind by this wave of trade arrangements. Therefore, Panama, Chile and Costa Rica had real external options to realise FTAs. Here it seems to be the case that previous failed experiences, or whether the countries needed certain 'quality stamps' to embark on this type of accord, were overlooked by other potential trade partners. Having failed experiences did not matter when finding trade partners. In fact, the best possible trade partner, the US, did not sanction Panama's lack of aversion to failure.[187] On the contrary, the US promised Panama it would negotiate an FTA by 2004. When the negotiation with the US was secured, Panama focused on this process not only because of the magnitude of this enterprise for a small country, but also, because of the belief that having an FTA with the US would make the previous failed cases easier to resume and conclude (Interviews with Diana Salazar, MICI, 30/07/2008; Melissa Davis, MICI, 17/07/2008).

The indirect presence of the US in these negotiations suggests that the FTAs were an US dominated phenomenon in the Western Hemisphere. These three countries were reluctant to liberalise certain items in their respective FTA negotiations as these areas were thought to be used in an FTA with the US.[188] In other words, bar-

186 On the process of regional integration of Central America in the 1990s see Sánchez Sánchez 2009: Chapters 7 and 8.

187 Ways of sanctioning the failed experiences of a country in these type of negotiations from third countries are: by not sitting to negotiate an FTA with those that have caused past failed FTA negotiations; or by postponing the launch of FTA talks until the record of the country with a high failure rate improves.

188 Eventually countries like Chile thought they could also liberalise such sensitive items with the EU. However, Chile's preference was for negotiation with the US (Interviews with Os-

gaining power vis-à-vis the US was likely to be gained if the most sensitive issues of a country were not liberalised in previous negotiations. Countries in these two FTA negotiations did not make clear to their counterparts that they were not thinking of negotiating the unremunerated reserve requirement (Chile), professional services (Panama), dairy products (Panama), insurances (Costa Rica), telecommunications (Costa Rica), and banking (Costa Rica) because of an upcoming negotiation with the US. Such a statement would have provoked an even stronger reaction from their counterparts as it would have showed they were willing to negotiate these items, but not with them. In fact, Chile and Costa Rica justified their unwillingness to negotiate these issues due to their sensitiveness by stating that in the previous FTA experiences financial services in the case of Chile, and insurances and banking issues in the case of Costa Rica, were excluded.

Moreover, the potential economic gains of an FTA with the US could outweigh the electoral costs for the governments, and the economic losses for some sectors of the respective national economies of Chile, Panama, and Costa Rica. It is important to mention that the convergence of the interests of the state and those of domestic groups in favour of an FTA with the US was maintained during the entire negotiation process, despite the strong lobby efforts of the domestic groups losing through this FTA (interviews with Fracisco Chacon, COMEX, 14/07/2008; Joaquin Jácome, MICI, 17/07/2008; Osvaldo Rosales, DIRECON, 19/03/2008). On the contrary, the national economic interests of the respective states converged with the commercial interests of domestic groups favouring an FTA negotiation between Chile and Panama, and Costa Rica and Panama. However, this initial convergence changed through the negotiation process, when the socio-political costs for the government started to increase vis-à-vis the potential economic gains of such FTAs, and when the lobby groups against these FTAs started to dominate the access points of the negotiation. Therefore, in the negotiations of Chile-Panama, and Costa Rica-Panama the influence of the groups favouring the FTAs decreased.

9.4 *The Different Force of the Conditions to Explain Failure*

The conditions that brought the FTA negotiations of Chile-Panama and Costa Rica-Panama to a long term standstill in 1998 and 2002 respectively are part of a whole process. These conditions together explain the failure of these FTA negotiations. It has to be highlighted that the negotiation between government and domestic actors, i.e. the domestic dimension, and the one conducted between states are developed simultaneously. This is true for most of the process, excepting the pre-negotiation phase in which the domestic and international negotiations are not synchronised.

valdo Rosales, DIRECON, 19/03/2008; Mario Matus, DIRECON, 28/02/2008). Moreover, the presence of the US in the Americas to launch trade accords was much stronger than that of the EU.

At the domestic level, the divergence of interests is a constitutive element for the lack of progress for the negotiation at the international level. The high divergence of interests means that the initial zone of agreement is narrow, and the convergence of interests implies that there is an initial broad zone of agreement for the negotiators to work with. Interests as such are the initial condition that predominates in FTA negotiations, and their high divergence creates the setting for a conflictive negotiation at the international level, as well as between the domestic groups and the government.

Another condition that seems to have had a stronger impact on the outcome of non-agreement was the high level of politicisation of the respective FTA negotiations. This politicisation level was augmented due to the electoral processes Panama and Costa Rica were facing in 1998, and 2002 respectively. The politicisation level acted as a clear indicator to the respective governments of the eventual electoral costs of agreeing with the negotiating counterpart and having an unbalanced agreement. The politicisation level served as a signal for the potentially high costs for the governments, if such agreements were signed and then sent for ratification to the respective national Congresses. The high politicisation level also became an element that convinced the governments (Panama in the negotiation with Chile, and Costa Rica in the negotiation with Panama) that they needed to protect the most sensitive issue-areas of the negotiation. The increasing politicisation level in Panama in the negotiation with Chile acted as a motivation for the change from agreement to non-agreement and for preventing further deterioration of the executive-legislative agenda. The politicisation level triggered in Panama was also as a motivation for change from agreement to non-agreement for the executive in Chile. This change from an initial governmental position of agreement to one of non-agreement due to the politicisation level originated in both countries in the case of the FTA negotiation of Costa Rica-Panama.

The free riding option of groups in favour of these FTAs is another strong factor to explain the process of failure of these FTAs. The decreasing interest of these groups in the respective FTA negotiations facilitated the labour of domestic groups opposing the negotiation as they could exert stronger influence to protect their issues at the lobbying access points. Groups favouring the FTAs weakened their representatives in the negotiation table as these groups started to lobby for other FTA negotiations in which the size of the economic gain would be large. The free-riding option of these groups in the negotiation of Chile and Panama, and Costa Rica and Panama was triggered by the external options of negotiating other FTAs, and the internal problems of the negotiation vis-à-vis the potentially realisable economic gains in a narrow zone of agreement.

At the international level, there are two conditions that have played a strong role: The overuse of a distributive strategy displayed by the negotiating parties, and the weight of other FTA processes. In both study cases, the parties displayed tactics that fulfil the criteria of a distributive strategy. Whereas distributive strategies are present in most trade negotiations, their overuse in these cases constrained the possibilities of broadening the zone of agreement, since overusing this strategy had a spill over effect on other issues of the negotiation. Every time the parties started to bargain in a zero-sum mode, the effect was to move the counterpart to its resistant point, increasing the chances of one country defecting or leaving the negotiation. It is important to note that a prior a distributive bargaining logic does not determine failure of a negotiation. In both FTA negotiations the overuse of a distributive bargaining affected other issues of the negotiation. The distributive bargaining increased the chances of failure, since the BATNA of the countries were similar and more attractive than the respective negotiations. Having a similar and attractive BATNA made parties less averse to failure.

The BATNA, or as it was labelled in this research, the weight of other FTA negotiations, had a strong explanatory power regarding the difficulties of these FTA negotiations. Leaving a negotiation incomplete did not matter for Panama as she knew she had external options that were unlikely to sanction her previous behaviour in these types of economic negotiations. Needless to say the cost of leaving these negotiations without agreement was also not costly for Chile and Costa Rica in terms of reputation or in terms of losing large economic gains, as they had already signed FTAs.

The impact of the negotiation strategy and BATNA confirms and validates most of the literature on negotiation theory that gives these two variables the explanatory power to explain both successful and failed cases (Odell 2000, 2006 and 2009; Singh 2008; Hopmann 1996; Elms 2006; Zartmann and Rubin eds. 2000; Kremenyuk and Sjöstedt eds. 2000; Landau 2000; Raiffa 1982). However, this literature also shows its limitations since BATNA and the overuse of a distributive strategy does not capture the whole process that brings two negotiating parties to leave a negotiation without an agreement.

This research introduced other conditions that perhaps do not have as much explanatory power as BATNA and negotiating strategies. However, they supplement these two conditions as they cover the areas where BATNA and distributive strategy cannot account for the difficulties of the FTA negotiation. What brought the negotiating parties to use distributive strategies was the initial condition of divergence on interests constituted at the domestic level. The governments' costs of agreeing increased insofar as the politicisation level increased and the support of domestic groups favouring an FTA policy for these negotiations decreased. The overuse of a distributive bargaining and its escalatory effects could have been reduced if trade diplomats had exerted leadership skills. These examples show the importance of the other explanatory conditions. Despite the fact that there are conditions that had a stronger impact on the outcome, they are unable to explain on their own the reasons for failure in these FTA negotiations. If only the strongest conditions for failure are put together as a multifactor process and the ones that have a lesser impact on the result of these FTA negotiations are kept aside, the process of what brought these negotiations to a standstill also seems incomplete. The interrelation of all the conditions analysed in this dissertation constitute a whole that explains in depth the process and the results of the FTA negotiations Chile-Panama and Costa Rica-Panama in 1998 and 2002 respectively.

9.5 *The Two Failed FTA Negotiations vis-à-vis Other Cases*

Failed cases of FTA negotiations are not as abundant as successful cases. Despite the small number of unsuccessful cases, it is possible to find other failed FTA negotiations between countries of the Americas, Asian countries, and cross-regional ones, i.e. between countries of the Western Hemisphere and Asia, or Europe and the Americas. Whereas some failed FTA negotiations have been retaken and concluded, such as Chile-New Zealand as part of the P4 agreement (Salazar 2005), Canada-EFTA (see www.dfait-maeci.gc.ca), and Chile-Guatemala (Ministerio de Economía. Política Comercial Externa, Guatemala 21/09/2007), others are still in a stalemate, such as Singapore-Mexico (see www.fta.gov.sg). Other processes are on the way to resumption and their prospects of conclusion are still unclear, such as the negotiations between New Zealand-Hong Kong, South-Korea-Japan, and Canada-Central America (except Costa Rica). Other cases had resumed but stalled once again, such as the negotiation between Canada and Singapore, which stalled in December 2003, resumed in 2007, and stalled within the same year (www.dfait-maeci.gc.ca). In the case of Mexico and South Korea, the parties agreed to resume the FTA negotiation in 2007 after the process halted in 2006. However there is no evidence that formal rounds have been carried out from 2007 to the present (see www.mofat.go.kr).

It is interesting to note the contribution of the most active negotiating countries to failed FTA negotiations. These cases of stalemate also involve the US, as it has a stalled FTA negotiation with Egypt. However, all these negotiations go unnoticed because the number of successful FTA experiences for the above named countries is much larger. In this regard, the case of Panama as central to this work is useful because at the time of negotiating with Chile and Costa Rica, Panama did not have a large number of FTA negotiations with an outcome of agreement. The impact of these failed experiences on Panama's FTA negotiation record has tended to reduce its importance as this country has already signed nine FTAs (see www.mici.gob.pa). In addition, the stalled FTA negotiations also go unnoticed because the countries always have the possibility of turning their previous negative experiences of FTAs into positive ones i.e. resuming and reaching a final agreement is still possible for the negotiating parties. Some stalled FTAs also do not receive much attention because of short amount of time between the stalemate and following resumption, as with the FTA between Chile and New Zealand within the frame of the P4. This negotiation was stalled in July 2003 and resumed in August 2004 (Salazar 2005: 6).

The analysis of other FTAs has to be taken as a preliminary assessment and with the purpose of putting the FTA negotiations between Chile and Panama, and Costa Rica and Panama in a broader comparative context. This section takes the route of describing the processes in a general way, presenting the divergent interests and plausible reasons for the stalemates of the FTA negotiations presented below.

9.5.1 New Zealand and Hong-Kong

New Zealand and Hong-Kong launched an FTA negotiation in April 2001 and after five rounds the talks were suspended in February 2002 due to technical issues (Trade and Industry Department, Government of Hong Kong 2009: 2). The technical differences that Hong-Kong refer to are related to the fact that the parties could not find a common ground on which they could solve their high divergence on interests pursued by their respective domestic actors and represented by the government. In addition, both governments could not overcome domestic opposition to the accord, possibly due to the possible economic consequences and socio-political costs involved.

The main area that brought the parties to a standstill in 2002 was the discussion of the rules of origin over goods such as textiles, footwear, and clothing (www.arena.org.nz; Rosenberg 2001a; New Zealand Council of Trade Unions-CTU 18/03/2002). Over rules of origin, New Zealand adopted a defensive position (Sutton 2001: 7). The conflict was due to the fact that Hong-Kong proposed a flexible rule of origin for these goods and New Zealand a restrictive one. Hong Kong's request was based on the fact that most of its textile goods are produced in China, but they retain Hong Kong origin due to a trade arrangement between these two countries. In other words, New Zealand was afraid of the triangulation of goods from China to its country via Hong Kong and of the low number of tools to trace the origin of the products, as they were labelled as originating in Hong Kong. Conversely, New Zealand's textile industry produces within the country. In addition, the transformative process of inputs from third countries is not high and is also made within the textile industry of this insular country (Edlin 2003).

Another sensitive issue, though less sensitive than that of rules of origin, was the discussion of services. Hong Kong has a lower commitment to GATT rules on services at the multilateral level than New Zealand. The latter has a competitive industry in issues such as education, tourism, environmental services, air transport, professional qualifications, and air services (Ministry of Foreign Affairs and Trade, New Zealand, 2001: 28-32). In these issues Hong Kong adopted a defensive position. However, the discussion of these issues was less sensitive than that of rules of origin.

Hong Kong adopted an offensive and an inflexible position about rules of origin. Fundamentally, Hong Kong wanted a mechanism that did not enforce rules of origin. Hong Kong's inflexible bargaining position on this issue to some extent was enhanced by its extant BATNA. New Zealand's defensive position on this issue was due to its domestic actors' fears of possible job losses (Rosemberg 2001b: 4). This negotiation also presented patterns of politicisation especially promoted by Labour Unions in New Zealand to protect the clothing, textile and foot wear industry (New Zealand Council of Trade Unions-CTU 18/03/2002).

Hong Kong's BATNA was a parallel FTA negotiation with China, which was signed in June 2003. China is one of the strongest emerging powers of the global economy and with good prospects of becoming a structural one (Hurrell 2006). As one representative of the employers and manufacturers association from New Zealand stated "[…] obviously the Hong Kong people were not anxious to forego an established trade practice with a country the size of New Zealand when they were hoping for much bigger fish". This quote was in direct reference to the ongoing negotiation with China (quoted in Edlin 2003: 1).

Without going in depth into the details of this negotiation, it is possible to appreciate some aspects that may in principle be similar to those of the FTA negotiations between Chile and Panama and Costa Rica and Panama, such as the divergence on interests, the fear of job losses on New Zealand's part, politicisation, distributive bargaining, and the weight of other FTA negotiations. Nevertheless, this is only an overview of the process and I make no generalisations as more research on this specific negotiation should be conducted.

9.5.2 South Korea and Japan

The rounds of the FTA negotiation between South Korea and Japan were officially launched in December 2003. This negotiation stalled after six rounds in November 2004. There have been at least three official attempts to resume this negotiation in 2006 (*China View* 14/12/2006) 2007, and in 2009 (*www.hani.co.kr* 12/05/2009). However, there is no evidence that other formal negotiations have been conducted beyond those of 2003-2004, despite the efforts to resume the FTA talks. The issue-areas that created the controversy and the aversion to conclude the negotiations were agricultural and fish products and cars as well as non-tariff barriers such as domestic laws. Japan was unwilling to grant a better deal to Korea on agricultural and fisheries, whereas the latter showed strong aversion to liberalise its car industry vis-à-vis Japan. During the FTA negotiation, the latter offered only 50 percent liberalisation to Korea on agricultural products and only quotas for fisheries industries (*Korea Times* 25/12/2007). In addition, it was estimated that if Korea lifted tariff restrictions on the importation of Japanese cars, as Japan requested, the decline of sales for Korean car makers would have been around 225000 units per year (*Digital Chosun Ilbo* 27/03/2006). Local electronics companies in Korea would also incur economic losses if free entrance was granted to Japan. This loss was estimated at 2.7 billion dollars in annual sales (*Asia Times* 28/03/2006)

These divergent interests and the aversion of domestic groups to be exposed to external bilateral competition became a key issue in the politicisation of the FTA process. The sense of job-insecurity for workers, especially from industrial and automotive sectors in Korea, made them articulate a movement against this FTA and these Unions mobilised and demonstrated in front of the place in which negotiations were held whenever Korea hosted the process.

Recently, the Seoul Japan Club -Organization of Japanese corporations in Korea-submitted to the Korean government a list of 13 regulations on labour they would like to see lifted. The list included decreasing the number of paid full-time trade union officials, severe punishment of illegal industrial action and facilitation in lay-offs. If these demands are included in the FTA under the name of 'non-tariff measures' (already deregulation of six labour-related measures are included in the KJFTA joint report, which forms the basis of the agreement), worker's lives will be devastated (KOPA 23/08/2004: 1-3).

The bargaining of the parties was also dependant on the external options both parties had or were likely to have in the future. The external options were also more attractive in the strict economic sense. Jeffrey Schott (2003), following economic model simulations conducted by others, argues that a Korea-Japan FTA is likely to reduce Korea's economic welfare as well as deteriorate its bilateral trade balance with Japan. It even makes more economic sense for Korea and also for Japan to promote a trilateral free trade zone with China. In fact, the positive part of this Japan-Korea FTA was, according to trade analysts mentioned by Jeffrey Schott (2003), that this bilateral accord could act as a catalyst for future negotiations with China on both sides, Korea and Japan.

It also seems to be the case that South Korea was thinking about reserving some of its most sensitive issues in the FTA negotiation with Japan, such as cars, to be used as bargaining chips in a negotiation with its main trade partner, the US. The US also had tariff and non-tariff barriers for the entry of Korean cars into the American market (Cooper and Manyin 2007: 4-5). However, in an eventual negotiation with the US Korea's agricultural products would potentially suffer losses, whereas in the case of the negotiation with Japan they were likely to win. Japan also had previous FTA experiences to show Korea the real sensitivity of agriculture, such as their FTA with Singapore signed in 2002. In this FTA the vast majority of agriculture was excluded from the final agreement (Cheong 2004: 4). Korea also launched a joint study group to initiate trade talks with Singapore in 2003. However, the formal negotiations started in 2005 (Ministry of Trade and Industry-Singapore 2009). Japan was also conducting a parallel negotiation with a competitive agricultural country such as Mexico. The early contacts for negotiating with Mexico started in 1999, but the negotiation rounds were launched in October 2002, and they were mainly conducted during 2003 and 2004. Hence, both countries had possibilities of still realising FTAs beyond their bilateral negotiation. These BATNAs reduced the costs of failure for both countries as the external possibilities to concrete FTAs were broad and not only restricted to Asia.

There are also principles common to this failed process and the cases discussed in this book, such as divergent issues, politicisation, job-insecurity, the weight of other FTA process, and the use of distributive strategies. It may be also the case that groups favouring an FTA in the case of Korea and Japan started to focus on future FTAs and the parallel FTAs that were progressing at a faster pace to that of Japan-Korea. Nevertheless, it is necessary to gather more empirical information to assess how similar (or different) these conditions are to those of the FTA negotiations of Chile-Panama and Costa Rica-Panama. More qualitative research with the protagonists of this negotiation is also necessary to find out whether conditions such as non-negotiable issues and the absence of leadership skills were factors that played a role in the stalemate of this FTA.

9.5.3 Other Cases of Failed FTA Negotiations

9.5.3.1 South Korea-Mexico

Both countries started to negotiate an FTA in February 2006. However, these two countries pursued joint meetings of experts to conduct feasibility studies from October 2004. In total six joint meetings were held prior to the official start of the FTA negotiation (Ministry of Foreign Affairs of South Korea 2004; and 2005). The first official round was held in February 2006 and the negotiation was halted during the third round in June 2006. South Korea showed high sensitivity in agricultural issues. This sensitivity was expressed in the mobilisation and politicisation of Korean farmers and the support of Congress representatives. In addition, Mexico car assemblers presented their opposition to the accord. This position was supported by trade unions. Other defensive positions in Mexico were taken by steel, textiles, chemicals, and automobile parts producers (*Reuters* 10/09/2005; Ministry of Foreign Affairs of South Korea 2006a).

In a press report the Ministry of Foreign Affairs of South Korea (2006b) stated over market access issues that the parties during the negotiation rounds "[...] were unable to make substantial progress in this area due to significant differences in perspectives regarding the degree of concessions and incorporation of items of mutual interest". Mexico also asked Korea to pledge investment to its car industry to close a deal in order to minimise the eventual negative impact of the entrance of Korean cars to the Mexican market and to create jobs in that sector. Korea, influenced by Hyundai's interests, refused to grant this concession as this company was more focused on activating its new plant in the US (*Korea Times* 25/08/2005). In this regard, Korean automakers were more likely to support an FTA with the US rather than investing in Mexico as an entrance door to the American market. This does not mean that Korean car makers did not have an interest in the FTA with Mexico. On the contrary, they have an interest in removing tariffs for their products, but they were not interested in opening assembling plants or car making plants in Mexico. Preliminarily, it is possible to observe certain notions of the divergence of interests, job-insecurity and politicisation level on both countries, and the role of external options such as the US for the case of Korea. These conditions may have prevented these two countries from reaching a final agreement in 2006.

9.5.3.2 Canada-Central America

Canada and four Central American countries –El Salvador, Honduras, Nicaragua, and Guatemala– launched FTA negotiations on November 2001. The reason for launching such talks was based on Canada's economic desire to maintain competitiveness with the US, which was likely to launch an FTA negotiation with Central America during 2003 (Department of Foreign Affairs and International Trade-Canada 21/11/2001). After ten rounds of negotiation the process stalled in 2004. One of the main reasons for the stall was Canada's unwillingness to lower its tariffs on textiles. This is one of the few sectors in which these four Central American countries are highly competitive (Goldfarb 2004: 6).

In addition, Central American countries did not want to leave the issue of sugar out of the negotiation, and Canada wanted to keep its system of restricted importation quotas for Central America (*Canadian Press* 04/07/2004). Honduras, Nicaragua, El Salvador, and Guatemala are all sugar producers. These four countries also presented some sensitive issues in food products in which Canada is world leading. Canada and Central America have attempted the negotiations throughout 2009. In fact, a first round after the stalemate of 2004 was held in February 2009 (Department of Foreign Affairs and International Trade-Canada 2009).

9.6 Concluding Remarks

This chapter compared the FTA negotiations of Chile-Panama, and Costa Rica-Panama by pinpointing their similarities and differences. Despite the different dynamics and initial settings of each negotiation, the outcome was the same in both cases. Even though the use of Panama as link for the two negotiations shows the peculiarity of its financial system, the problems of banking in the negotiation were different in the two FTA negotiations. In addition, the problems of the negotiations went beyond the issue of banking and involved other type of services as well as the traditional issue-areas of agricultural and agro-industrial products.

Despite the differences between each process, there are similarities between the FTA negotiations that reflect the relevance of the conditions that I have argued led to the failure of these FTA negotiations. These conditions also seem promising for understanding what brought other countries to disagreement in their FTA negotiations. Nevertheless, more empirical research is needed in order to analyse other failed experiences of FTAs that involve diverse countries from Asia, the Americas, and Europe. Qualitative research, i.e. interviews with the actors of the FTA negotiations, and the reviewing of the documents of the negotiation, may be an important step to analysing whether leadership skills were present or absent in the process that led to failure as well as to assess whether the lack of outlining non-negotiability at the outset of the process affected the result. Such qualitative empirical information would also be needed to establish the extent to which the conditions for the cases of

Panama-Chile and Costa Rica-Panama apply to other cases; the extent of similarities between the cases discussed in this book and other cases; and/or whether there are more differences and new elements that explain the results of other negotiations. Therefore, the general presentation of other cases in this chapter is only a contextual description to put the main cases of this research in a broader perspective. Nevertheless, this first approximation seems promising for applying the conditions for failure that explained the failed processes of FTA negotiations of Chile-Panama and Costa Rica-Panama to other cases.

10. Conclusion

10.1 The Key Questions Answered

This work examined two key questions. First, why do some FTA negotiations fail to reach an outcome of agreement? Second, under what conditions do these FTA negotiations fail? These two questions were applied to the Chile-Panama and Costa Rica-Panama FTA talks to find for the causes of non-agreement in these processes held in 1996-98 and 2002 respectively, as well as to show the need for the further research into other negotiation failures in the Americas, Asia, and cross-regional cases. This research becomes heuristic as it keeps the research questions open instead of asking the 'why and under what conditions' questions solely for the cases of Chile-Panama and Costa Rica-Panama.[189] This book is a call for further study of failed attempts to actualise FTAs and an invitation to add new cases to the framework and conditions presented here. This work does not make far reaching generalisations beyond the study cases of this research.

As has been argued throughout this book, it seems quite clear that the countries in the FTA negotiations of Chile-Panama and Costa Rica-Panama failed to reach an outcome of agreement because of the different conditions at the domestic and international levels. These conditions constituted and turned the initial setting and the hopes of these countries to failure. In addition, the conditions analysed are not only restricted to the internal process of a negotiation on its two levels, but include forces external to the bargaining. Factors external to the negotiation that unfolded at the domestic and international levels affected the outcome of non-agreement in these two FTA talks. Yet they mattered as much as the internal conditions of the negotiation. The external conditions are usually overlooked in negotiation theory, excepting BATNA. However, external conditions can complement the literature's focus on international economic negotiation strategies and tactics, as shown in this work. The political process matters for countries in a negotiation as much as the strategies and BATNA. The high domestic costs for the governments were critical motivations to leave these FTA negotiations without agreement in 1998 and 2002.

Yet an exclusive focus on conditions external to the negotiation also has its limitations. External factors such as job-insecurity, politicisation as well as BATNA

189 That is, the research questions of this work have been broader than simply asking: why did the FTA negotiations Chile-Panama and Costa Rica-Panama fail in reaching an outcome of agreement in 1998 and 2002 respectively? and: under what conditions did these FTA negotiations fail?

cannot account on their own for the outcome of non-agreement in these FTA talks. Therefore, this research sought to complement the internal and external conditions to explain the failure of these negotiations between these Latin American countries. My study has shown that only this complementary approach that takes specific internal and external conditions of the negotiation on its two levels can understand the result of non-agreement in these two negotiations.

10.2 Answering the questions through the process

The divergence of interests is a key factor that starts a negotiation with a narrow zone of agreement and restricts the number of possible win-sets. The governments in these two FTA negotiations defended and sought to represent the interests of domestic actors in the intergovernmental negotiation, be these in favour or against these specific FTAs. According to the liberal intergovernmental theory (Moravsick 1997; 2008) in most international processes, governments also enjoy some room to overcome or resist the demands of domestic actors through manipulation of the negotiation. However, it was the case that trade diplomats from Chile, Panama, and Costa Rica in these failed experiences did not have much of a margin in which to manoeuvre and pursue the governmental interests in the negotiation beyond those of the domestic actors losing in the agreement. The governments also started to pay more attention to the domestic actors who opposed these FTAs when the counterpart was not willing to fulfil the material economic expectations of their most competitive domestic actors. Thus, the initial position of agreement shifted to one of non-agreement when concessions on the most competitive sectors in the bilateral economic relationships were not granted.

The reasons for changing the initial position of agreement are based on the fact that some previous unseen costs started to appear during the negotiation that outweighed the potential economic gains from the FTAs. The increasing level of divergence on interests, and the increasing level of politicisation during the negotiation acted as a brake for the governments at the intergovernmental level, and prevented them from compromising with the counterpart. As the level of politicisation increased the Congress started to signal that they would not ratify the agreement if the final deal was unbalanced. The politicisation level also increased because of nested games; in these cases: electoral processes (Chile-Panama & Costa Rica-Panama) and ratification of already signed FTAs such as that between Costa Rica and Canada (Costa Rica-Panama). However, the high divergence on interests, and the increasing politicisation level acted as turning points of the negotiation, and indicated to groups favouring these negotiations that the costs of agreeing were much higher than expected when these talks were formally launched.

The fear of eventual job-losses was a strong factor for domestic actors advocating the exclusion and non-realisation of the FTAs. Groups such as FEDAP in the Chile-Panama negotiation, as Costa Rica's cattle farmers and beef producers and Panama's dairy producers in the Costa Rica-Panama negotiation, were successful in linking their sector loss to processes such as the referendum in Panama and the approval of the FTA of Costa Rica with Canada. The job insecurity factor also made the politicisation process possible. These two conditions pushed the groups in favour of these trade accords to seek alternative FTAs with third countries.

The intergovernmental process of the negotiation presented these diverging interests that originated at the domestic level. The countries could not find a common ground to bargain in a win-win mode; rather, they negotiated the most sensitive issues in a zero-sum way, giving little room for creative solutions, for offering side payments, and for issue-linkages with the purpose of breaking coalitions resistant to these FTAs or of offering an attractive deal to the counterpart. The defence of domestic interests losing with the agreement and the hard push to get concessions from the counterpart in the most competitive areas and products made the countries shift the initial position of agreeing to one of non-agreement. Despite the fact that the initial zone of agreement was narrow in both negotiations, this factor does not determine failure in a mechanistic way. On the contrary, negotiating parties can still reach agreement even if the zone of agreement is rather small. To do so, parties need to commit to the counterpart, and work together by using joint problem solving behaviour during the process to expand the size of the zone of agreement and augment the number of possible win-sets (Singh 2008).

Nevertheless, the Chile-Panama and Costa Rica-Panama FTA negotiations took a different path as these countries were incapable of gaining the acquiescence of the negotiating counterpart. Intergovernmentalism assumes that the states still have enough independence from domestic interests. For example, negotiators can still filter and select the information to be given to the domestic actors participating in the next room. However, Panama's governments, in a strategic move, with the purpose of committing the counterpart and preventing the exclusion of its most competitive issues as well as enhancing its own bargaining position, informed the domestic coalitions of the counterparts' willingness to negotiate the issues which were not for negotiation.

In this regard, the ambiguous announcement, or lack of announcement, from Chile and Costa Rica and also Panama over the issues which were not for negotiation at the outset of the process excessively raised the expectations of could be included in the final agreement. This meant that parties could not advance on other issues as the sensitive ones started to change the negotiation agenda. The focus on the most sensitive issues also made parties negotiate issues that were not conceived as sensitive in a distributive way rather than in a win-win mode. Therefore, the predominance of distributive strategies to negotiate these FTAs contributed to the failure of the processes. Moreover, the escalatory effect of using a distributive strategy was strong in these two FTAs. It was also the case that the absence of leadership skills made the escalatory effect possible, and difficult to de-escalate. Leaders were in the process: they displayed leadership skills when launching the negotiation, but not when they were needed to move the negotiation towards an axis of agreement.

The strong presence of actors external to the negotiation and/or other possibilities of realising FTAs also affected the outcome of the Chile-Panama and Costa Rica-Panama negotiations. The BATNA became a better option than getting an agreement without the issues of dairy products for Costa Rica, and financial services for Panama, and a better option than an agreement with the issues of financial services for Chile and Costa Rica. The real possibility of negotiating an FTA with the US in the short term played a strong role in the final outcome of the negotiation as these three countries declared their sensitive issues as non-negotiable in order to gain bargaining power when they had to negotiate with the US. In addition, the aversion to failure substantially decreased for the three countries, especially for Panama. The US and other possible trade partners did not impose performance requirements to negotiate an FTA, beyond a broad commitment to the free market and the global economy.

However, the BATNA for Chile, Panama and Costa Rica were not restricted exclusively to the US as most countries or regional groupings put all their efforts into achieving FTAs in any of their possible forms –through bilateral state to state or through a regional grouping. Therefore, the costs of leaving a negotiation without agreement became cheaper for these countries, especially, if a final deal without their most competitive sectors was not possible. In other words, Chile, Panama and Costa Rica tried to maximise all the possible gains not with the counterpart but at the expense of the counterpart as the extant BATNA became more attractive than the negotiations of Chile-Panama and Costa Rica-Panama.

After summarising and reviewing the explanatory power of the above conditions, it is necessary to asses the validity of the hypotheses of this work. These hypotheses related to two distinct elements of the negotiations, reflecting the two level game dynamics of the negotiations. This distinction between the two elements was solely for analytical clarity: the real process consisted of an inseparable combination of these elements. In particular, these elements unfolded simultaneously during the negotiation. It should be noted that, due to the complexity of the combination of these elements in the actual negotiations, the factors that led to negotiation failure should be thought of as more than simply the sum of these contributing factors.

Hypothesis I was: *If the defence of protected inter-trade areas of the national economy in the different spheres of the political process determines the course and the momentum of the negotiation by empowering protectionist interest groups which politicise the negotiation; by reducing the incentive for export-oriented groups to participate actively in the negotiation; and by increasing the socio-political costs for the government, then the initial governmental position of aspiring to an FTA is expected to change to a position of non-agreement.* This hypothesis focused on the domestic level of the negotiation; the explanatory conditions internal and external to the process at this level are encapsulated in such hypothesis. Thus, the explanatory power of these conditions (and of the hypothesis) is confirmed vis-à-vis the outcome of non-agreement in the Chile-Panama and Costa Rica-Panama FTA negotiations in 1998 and 2002 respectively.

Hypothesis II was: *If governments have limited room to manoeuvre in the inter-state negotiations as a result of their mutual distributive concerns over previous and current removal of TB and NTB; of not manifesting the non-negotiable issues of the negotiation at the outset of the process; of the lack of exerting entrepreneurial leadership skills; of prioritising other negotiations; and of predominantly using an offensive value-claiming strategy to get high concessions from the counterpart strategic inter-trade areas, then the negotiation is likely to stall.* This hypothesis is also validated by the empirical evidence analysed in the previous chapters. This hypothesis concentrated on the intergovernmental level; the explanatory conditions also have a strong contribution to explaining the failed FTA experiences of Chile-Panama and Costa Rica-Panama.

10.3 Theoretical Implications

As highlighted in this work, especially through the three first chapters, the extant theories on economics, IR/IPE, and negotiation could not capture the dynamics and process that brought Chile-Panama and Costa Rica-Panama to reach an outcome of non-agreement in 1998 and 2002.

As the different theories seemed insufficient to explain the process of failure in FTA negotiations, I used the benefits of analytical eclecticism (Katzenstein and Rudra 2004 & 2008; Moravsick 2008). However, my theoretical framework is not a link of theories and their explanatory factors, as a theory synthesis contribution to the field of IR. And certainly it is not an attempt to close a theoretical gap in the theory building in the international relations debate. Rather, I took existing different elements from theoretical lenses such as new trade theory in economic, liberalism, institutional and intergovernmental theory in international relations, and theory of negotiation, to build up a framework that allowed me to determine causes and conditions that explain why the Chile-Panama and Costa Rica-Panama negotiations failed to reach an outcome of agreement.

In this regard, the constitutions of domestic preferences based on inter-trade, intra-trade, the disposal of TB and NTB and the threat of removal of these protectionist measures determine whether domestic groups will advocate or oppose an FTA. Up until this point the theoretical framework has been useful to explain the domestic policy preferences regarding FTAs, be these successful or not. However, failure to achieve an outcome of agreement is based on the convergence of the interest of domestic actors against an FTA and the shift of the initial governmental position of agreement to one of non-agreement. In this process, the theoretical framework includes and validates the relevance of collective action theory. Domestic actors losing with the agreement dominate the access points to lobbying the negotiation, as lobbying for these groups is cheaper than for those in favour of an FTA. The same lobby groups losing with the FTA politicise the negotiations by making public their potential losses. They also take advantage of nested games and get full attention from the government if the costs of agreement start to increase. They also get the attention of Congress, which indicates that it will vetoe the accord if the electoral, economic, social, and political costs are higher than the economic gains that the FTA is likely to create. Socio-political costs are part of this frame as well as the defection of groups in favour of the FTAs. These groups favouring the accords devote less time to these FTAs and seek new options to reduce the costs of failure for the government. They also seek options to limit the cost of shifting from agreement to non-agreement, which becomes plausible if material economic expectations at the state to state negotiation are not being fulfilled.

The intergovernmental and domestic levels are connected through the logic of a two level game and through how the governments' decisions at the interstate negotiation are constrained by the eventual socio-political costs for both the government (electoral costs and popularity) and the domestic groups' interests. In this part I relied mainly on elements taken from negotiation theory (strategies, tactics, and bargaining positions), leadership theory, and liberalism and its form of republican and commercial liberalism. The conditions at the interstate negotiation focus on internal and external factors in which the aspects of negotiation theory such as strategies and BATNA have a stronger effect on the outcome of non-agreement. Nevertheless, the lack of leadership skills as well as the lack of outlining the non-negotiables at the outset of the process in these two FTA negotiations become supplementary forces for the failure of these trade negotiations.

The theoretical framework and the explanatory conditions embedded in this framework hold when attempting to explain the outcome of non-agreement in these two FTA negotiations. It would also be promising to analyse other cases of failed FTA negotiations, as chapter 9 shows. It seems to be the case that there are certain similarities between the negotiations analysed in this research and the failed experiences of Japan-Korea, Hong Kong-New Zealand, Mexico-Korea, and Canada-Central America. Yet, further research is needed on these cases and others to confirm the validity of the theoretical framework and its explanation of failure in the cases studied in this work. If this framework holds for other state to state cases it may be used as a starting point (and not beyond) to assess the reasons for failure in interregional trade negotiations such as those of the EU-MERCOSUR and the FTAA project. However, certain caveats and modifications may in principle apply such as adding a third level of negotiation as these interregional processes involve domestic, regional grouping coordination, and interregional levels.

Studying and establishing the reasons for other cases of failure in bilateral and interregional trade negotiations needs scholarly attention. And the framework and conditions set to explain the outcome in the Chile-Panama and Costa Rica-Panama FTAs in 1998 and 2002 may be a first step and starting point for such studies. Further studies about cases of failure could be useful to refine and challenge the theoretical framework of this research as well as its underlying assumptions.

10.4 For Future Research

Before closing this conclusion, it is pertinent to set a road map for future research, beyond those directions already mentioned in the last part of the previous section. As this work had the goal of explaining the reasons for failure of two FTA negotiations, it becomes necessary, after achieving the original goal of this research, to compare successful and failed experiences of FTAs using the same cases, Chile, Costa Rica, and Panama.

During this research there were also other aspects that emerged that were beyond the scope of this project. The strong presence of the US in the economic integration process in the Americas, as well as in Asia, opens a venue for assessing the extent to which this economic integration process is an US driven process and determining the goals for the US when it displays its structural power assets and pursues FTAs. Are the US goals related to the negotiation of the WTO trade based regime, or are its goals a reflection of domestic factors? Is this a unilateral race for the US or is it competing with someone in the realisation of this type of external trade policy? These aspects need further consideration and theory driven empirical research.

Another aspect that was present throughout this research was the re-launch of these negotiation processes, as the FTA negotiations of Chile-Panama and of Costa Rica-Panama were resumed in 2005 and 2006 respectively. These negotiations resumed and took the dynamics of new negotiations as the setting was different and the discussion over market access started from zero. These negotiations were also successfully concluded in 2006 and 2007 respectively. However, further attention needs to be paid to why and under what conditions these FTA negotiations resumed. Studying failed negotiations that were resumed and concluded neither diminishes the importance of analysing the previous setting as failed cases, nor the conclusions of this work. It only opens an important new venue for future research in the areas of international negotiations and trade diplomacy.

11. Epilogue: Re-launching Negotiations

11.1. An overview

11.1.1 Chile-Panama

In 2005, Chile and Panama started talks to re-launch the FTA negotiation stalled from 1998. These two countries signed the FTA in June 2006 (see www.sice.oas.org). However, the negotiation process started from zero as what was negotiated in the period 1996-98 regarding market access became anachronistic and did not represent the extant economic reality of the countries in 2005. Chile was now more competitive in the bilateral economic relation in agricultural issues such as beef and dairy products (DIRECON 12/03/2007). These goods were defensive interests for Chilean negotiators in 1996-98. The interests over services, especially financial services, remained similar. However, the parties showed more flexibility when discussing such items. The core of the negotiating teams were similar to those in the negotiation held in 1996-98 (interviews with Lorena Sepulveda, DIRECON, 25/03/2008; Rodrigo Contreras, DIRECON, 28/03/2008; Luis Garrido, MICI, 28/07/2008).

The context of the re-launch was different as Chile and Panama had other political leaders. In the case of Chile, the president of Chile was Ricardo Lagos (March 2000-March 2006), who was in the last year of his presidential mandate in 2005. The Chile-Panama FTA negotiation was successfully concluded in February 2006, a month before Lagos was to hand over power to the incoming President Michelle Bachelet (March 2006 to March 2010). However, President Lagos (socialist) and his predecessor, the Christian Democrat Eduardo Frei (March 1994-March 2000), belonged to the same governing coalition –La Concertación. The external trade policy did not and has not changed, despite the presidential changes. During the Presidency of Ricardo Lagos, Chile became the country with the most FTAs in the world and signed FTAs with its main trade partners such as the US, EU, and China. It also signed FTAs with Korea, and EFTA, and was negotiating trade agreements with New Zealand, Singapore, and Brunei within the frame of the P4 agreement; Japan, and Peru (see Wehner 2009b; Fuentes 2006).

At the time of retaking the FTA negotiation with Chile, Panama also had a new president, Martin Torrijos (2004-2009) from the PRD party. Torrijos was also part of the Government of Pérez Balladares serving as Vice-minister of Government and Justice. In fact, Torrijos ran as the PRD candidate for the Presidency in the elections in 1999, and was the candidate supported by the then government (Leis 2003: 33).

Even though then President Mireya Moscoso offered to change the course of neoliberal reforms once in power, she continued with the external trade policy of negotiating FTAs (see chapters 4, 5 & 6). In fact, under the presidency of Moscoso, Panama signed its first FTAs with Central America (normative agreement), El Salvador (bilateral protocols), Dominican Republic, and Taiwan. In addition, the FTA negotiations with Singapore and the US started under Moscoso's presidency (Jácome 2004: 1-8). Once Martin Torrijos took power, the FTA policy of Panama continued on the same track of seeking potential trade partners, and actualising new FTAs. In this context, Torrijos' Presidency started to pay attention to the stalled FTA processes from the previous presidencies, such as those with Chile and Costa Rica, with the purpose of re-launching and concluding the FTAs (interviews with Estif Aparicio, DINECI, 18/07/2008; Alejandro Ferrer, DINECI, 29/07/2008).

Chile achieved an FTA with the US, with whom Panama was also negotiating an FTA. Panama and the US were on their ninth round of negotiations when Chile and Panama re-launched their FTA negotiation, and there were few agricultural products to be excluded from the agreement with the US (Interviews with Gabriela Díaz de Morales, Ministry of Agriculture, 30/07/2008; Manuel Ferreira, Chamber of Commerce, 25/07/2008). The fact of having an FTA with the US in the case of Chile facilitated an eventual resumption of the negotiations as its position on services was perceived by Panama as more flexible (interviews with Bruno Garisto, Ambassador of Panama in Chile, 11/04/2008; Estif Aparicio, DINECI, 18/07/2008). In fact, once the FTA negotiation was resumed the countries agreed to use the FTA text of Chile and the US as the core text for the new negotiation (MICI 2005: 1-2). In other words, the different goods and the issue of services were no longer perceived as an impediment to reach an agreement, despite the divergent interests between the parties. The option of relaunching the negotiation on these grounds became attractive for these countries. The perception that the sensitive issues were liberalised in the FTA negotiation with the US made the parties more flexible and optimistic about concluding the pending FTAs.

The re-launch of the negotiation was also seen as a chance to advance other issues of foreign policy that were strategic for both countries. Chile needed the support of Panama to elect its candidate for General Secretary of the OAS, José Miguel Insulza. Chile asked for Panama's support and also offered to re-take the negotiations (Cooperativa 06/01/2005; Crítica en Línea 07/01/2005).[190] Panama also needed Chile's sponsorship to join APEC whenever new memberships were to be opened (see discourse of Samuel Lewis Navarro 27/06/2006: 146). These eventual issues may have facilitated the re-launch of the FTA negotiation and also its conclusion, as

190 Panama changed its voting in the OAS between the candidates from Honduras, Mexico, and Chile. In the last round of a total of five, Panama voted for the Chilean candidate (see El Clarin 12/04/2005; La Nación- Argentina 03/05/2005). According to trade diplomats from both countries, this last voting also acted as a way to sustain the negotiations once they were relaunched and to commit to finding an agreement.

this issue-linkage added to the number of issues under discussion i.e. "expanding the size of the gain".[191] Leaders played a major role in re-launching these negotiations as the Chilean Minister of Foreign Affairs went to Panama not only to ask for support for the Chilean candidate for the OAS, but also to relaunch the negotiations. President Torrijos and Lagos also supported the resumption of the negotiations (La Prensa 30/06/2005: 1 A; DIRECON 31/05/2005).

Internal lobbying was not so apparent on the Chilean side, as Panama is a small market, and the possibility of re-launching the FTA was to some extent linked to state matters. Nevertheless, business associations such as ASEXMA, PYMES, and SOFOFA supported the re-launching of the negotiations (interviews with Paulina Vasquez, ASEXMA, 31/03/2008; Hugo Beierlein, SOFOFA, 26/03/2008). The government sought to attract the domestic business associations to boost the support for this FTA. The government also started to present an FTA negotiation with Panama as essential for Chile's big exporters so that they could establish a storage centre in the Panama Canal to deliver its products in a shorter time to third markets (especially the US). The new building of a lock in the Panama Canal was also presented by the Chilean government as a business opportunity that would be increased by the juridical certainty that an FTA would give to the investors (DIRECON 12/12/2007).

11.1.2 Costa Rica-Panama

Costa Rica and Panama re-launched the FTA negotiation in 2006 and concluded it successfully in 2007. The parties held three rounds of negotiations in 2006 and four in 2007 (COMEX 2007a: 2). The teams of negotiators were similar to those in 2002 (interviews with Laura Rodriguez, COMEX, 08/07/2008; Diana Salazar, DINECI, 30/07/2008). The interest on market issues remained similar to the previous negotiation in 2002. Costa Rica had an offensive position in dairy, most agricultural products, and food products, whereas Panama was competitive in beef, beans, and tomato processed products. In addition, Panama was still interested in including a liberal chapter on financial services and it wanted to include insurances. Costa Rica's position on these issues did not substantially change from the previous to the new negotiation, except on the issue of insurances. Insurances were already included in the DR-CAFTA and as such were not difficult to agree upon. However, the inclusion of this item was dependant on the approval of the DR-CAFTA in the referendum of October 2007 (interviews with Melissa Davis, DINECI, 17/07/2008; Leda Arrué, DINECI, 17/07/2008; Tatiana Varela, COMEX, 26/06/2008; Amparo Pacheco, COMEX, 02/07/2008). In fact, the Costa Rica-Panama FTA established a future clause to review the issue of insurances a year after the FTA became valid

191 On expanding the size of the gain, creativity and joint gains, create value and/or expanding the pie in negotiation theory see Fisher and Ury 2007: 58-98.

(Bilateral Protocol Costa Rica-Panama of the FTA Central America-Panama 2007: Article 5).

Costa Rica and Panama also experienced a change of political leaders.[192] In the negotiation of 2002, the president was Miguel Angel Rodriguez from the PUSC. His term ended before the second bilateral negotiation round held in July 2002. This second round was held during the mandate of then President Abel Pacheco (2002-2006) also from the PUSC. The relaunch of the negotiation was under the Presidency of Pacheco, and the continuation of the process as well as the conclusion of the FTA occurred under the presidency of Oscar Arias from the National Liberation Party during the period 2006-2007 (COMEX 14/03/2006: CP-597; 14/08/2006: CP-644; 25/06/2007: CP-721). During these three presidencies in Costa Rica, there was a continuity regarding the external trade policy based on unilateral, bilateral, and multilateral liberalisation process (Lizano 2001). Costa Rica became one of the most proactive countries in pursuing FTA negotiations in the Central American region (Galván de Tuñon 2004: 15-18; see also www.sice.oas.org; www.comex.go.cr). Costa Rica has signed FTAs with Chile, Mexico, Canada, CARICOM, Dominican Republic, Panama and the US (DR-CAFTA). Under the Presidency of Oscar Arias (2006-2010), Costa Rica has been negotiating FTAs with China, the EU (Central America-EU), and Singapore.[193]

Despite the successful paths of economic integration pursued by Costa Rica, there was the pending case of concluding the FTA negotiation with Panama. In addition, Panama was also able to increase its performance in FTA negotiations inasmuch as it signed FTAs with countries from the Americas and Asia. Yet this performance of the two countries did not assure either a successful re-launching of the negotiations or the conclusion of such talks with an outcome of agreement. What factors help us to explain the re-launch of the Costa Rica-Panama FTA negotiations in 2006?

An important aspect was that Costa Rica liberalised its sensitive issues of insurances in the negotiation with the US and it also included a chapter on financial services in the DR-CAFTA agreement. In addition, Panama had already advanced agreement packages with the US over agricultural issues. In fact, when Panama and Costa Rica decided to approach each other to assess the possible re-launching of the FTA negotiations, agricultural issues did not have exclusions in the US-Panama negotiation. There were only eight products to be discussed including the issue of sugar (*La Prensa* 02/04/2006: 44a). In addition, the BATNA for Panama was worse than the resumption option as Panama's exporters expected to suffer from trade deviation in Costa Rica's market because of the already signed, yet not implemented, DR-CAFTA in Costa Rica. Panama's exporters had to deal with tariff barriers, whereas American exporters of agro-industrial products will enter Costa Rica's

192 I will not refer to the case of Panama here as I did so in the previous sub-section. Martin Torrijos was the president of Panama at the time of relaunching the FTA negotiation in 2006, and Mireya Moscoso was in power during 2002 when the negotiation stalled.

193 These negotiations were still ongoing at the time of writing this work.

market with a preferential tariff or without tariffs (*La Prensa* 22/01/2006: 43a). The same principle was also true for Costa Rica's exporters to Panama. As Panama had its FTA negotiation with the US well advanced and with positive prospects of concluding the FTA talks soon, the government and producers from Costa Rica wanted to retake the FTA negotiations with Panama in order to anticipate and avoid the possible trade deviation. Costa Rica wanted to assure an equal treatment in Panama's market to that of the US (interviews with Tatiana Varela, COMEX, 26/06/2008; Laura Rodriguez, COMEX, 08/07/2008). Not only was the BATNA worse than the option of retaking the negotiation, but also the domestic groups opposing the FTA in 2002 were perceived by negotiators as having more flexible positions, as their items were included in the respective negotiations with the US.

The re-launch option also became a key issue in Panama's foreign policy as Central America was expecting to launch an FTA negotiation as a group with the EU. The latter preferred that Panama become part of the interregional FTA negotiation (interview with Alejandro Ferrer, DINECI, 29/07/2008). Concluding the pending negotiations with Central America and joining the SIECA were perceived as conditions for being part of the negotiation between these two regional groupings (European Commission 2007: 14). Nevertheless, Panama only joined the negotiations between these two regional groupings as an observer (interviews with Roberto Echandi, COMEX, 26/06/2008; Diana Salazar, DINECI, 30/07/2008).[194]

11.2 Concluding Remarks

This epilogue had the purpose of describing the context in which the FTA negotiations between Chile and Panama as well as Costa Rica and Panama were re-launched. Studying the means by which these negotiations resumed and concluded under a new setting, after years of being stalled, constitutes the other side of the story about the bilateral economic relationships of Chile-Panama and Costa Rica-Panama. The importance of this topic is based on the consolidation of the market economy as a pattern of economic development for these countries, and the consequent deepening of the economic model through external economic integration. Whereas the benefits of freer trade is undisputed amongst promoters of economic globalisation, the means of achieving such economic integration as FTAs deserve further investigation. A starting point for such study of the means of economic integration is not only studying failure, as with this work, but also assessing how previously stalled FTA negotiations were re-launched

194 This interregional negotiation was ongoing at the time this work was written.

12. References

Abbot, A. (2004). Methods of Discovery: heuristics for the Social Sciences. New York: W.W. Norton & Company.

ABC-COMEX. (08/05/2000). *Reunión de Consulta con ABC*, (Minute of the meeting); in COMEX Centre of Documentation: Folders of the FTA between Central America and Panama.

Abrego, L. (2000). El Comercio Internacional de Panamá, su organización y el estado actual de la negociaciones a nivel regional e internacional. MA dissertation in Businnes Administration. Panama: Universidad de Panamá.

ACE 16 Chile-Argentina. (1991). *Acuerdo de Complementación Económica*, in: www.sice.oas.org (Accessed 02/11/2006).

ACE 22 Chile-Bolivia. (1993). *Summary*, in: www.direcon.cl (Accessed 20/10/2006).

ACE 23 Chile-Venezuela. (1993). *Summary*, in: www.direcon.cl (Accessed 22/10/2006).

ACE 24 Chile-Colombia. (1993). *Summary*, in: www.direcon.cl (Accessed 24/10/2006).

ACE 26Costa Rica-Venezuela. (1986). *AAP.A25TM N° 26*; in: www.sice.oas.org (Acessed 13/11/2006).

ACE 32 Chile-Ecuador. (1994). *Summary*, in: www.direcon.cl (accessed 24/10/2006).

ACE 35 Chile-MERCOSUR. (1996). *Acuerdo de Complementación Económica*; in: www.oas.sice.org (Accessed 02/02/2008).

ACE 41 Chile-Mexico. (1991). *Acuerdo de Complementación Ecónomica*, in: www.sice.oas.org (Accessed 10/10/2006).

Achard, D. and González, L. (2004). A Challenge for Democracy. Políticas Parties in Central America, Panama and Dominican Republic. Washington: Interamerican Development Bank.

Acuerdo de Alcance Parcial Costa Rica- Colombia. (1984). (AAP.A25TM N° 7), in: sice.oas.org (accessed 11/11/2006).

Adames Mayorga, E. (2001). Panamá. Decepciones y tareas pendientes. *Nueva Sociedad* 174, 25-32.

Adler, E. (2006). Constructivism and International Relations, in W. Carlsnaes, Th. Risse, and B. Simmons (Eds), *Handbook of International Relations* (pp. 95-118). London, Thousand Oaks, CA, and New Delhi: SAGE Publications Ltd.

Agliati, M. (03/03/1997). Oportunidades de inversion en Panamá, *La Tercera*, (Chile), p. 23.

Alfaro Redondo, R. (2002). Elecciones municipales y debilitamiento del respaldo electoral bipartidista en Costa Rica período 1986-2002, *Anuario de Estudios Centroamericanos* 28, no 1-2: 89-135.

Al-Ghamdi, S. (1999). "Success and Failure in Saudi-American Negotiations: American Views". *International Negotiation* 4: 23-36.

Ameglio, M. (03/11/2002). "La ANAGAN sostiene que sería un competencia desleal si se incluye este sector en las negociaciones con Costa Rica". *La Prensa*, (Panama), p. 30A.

ANALMO. (04/2004). Situación de la Actividad Arrocera en Panamá de caras a la negociación para un tratado de libre comercio con los Estados Unidos de América. ANALMO internal document.

ANBER. (2005). Presentación. In M. Bolivar Ruiz, et al. *El Libro Blanco del Azúcar: Una Historia de Proteccionismo...*, (pp. 9-16). Santiago: RIL Editores.

Anglade, C. and Fortin, C. (Eds.) (1990). *The State and Capital Accumulation in Latin America.* Vol. 2. London: Macmillan.

Arrieta, A. (2001). Aportes del Seminario Acuerdo de Libre Commercio Chile-EEUU: Las Preguntas desde el desarrollo sustentable. *Ambiente y Desarrollo* 17, no 4: 59-67.

Arrocha, M. (19/10/2002) Panamá no aceptará presiones de Costa Rica, *La Prensa*, Panama), p. 25 A.

Asamblea Legislativa, República de Costa Rica. (05/04/2001). *Carta a Lic. Tomás Dueñas, Ministro de Comercio Exterior Costa Rica*, CVA-098-2001. Folder 362(b), carpeta c201, pp. 0085-0084.

Asamblea Legislativa, República de Costa Rica. (20/02/2001). *Carta a Dr. Miguel àngel Rodríguez Echeverría, Presidente de la Reública*, CVA-081-2001, Folder 362(b), carpeta c201, pp. 0081-0080.

Asia Times. (28/03/2006). FTA to cut auto sales. In: www.atimes.com (Accessed on 11/08/2009).

Axelrod, R. (1984). *The Evolution of Cooperation.* New York: Basic Books, Inc., Publishers.

Balassa, B. *et al.* (1971). *The Structure of Protection in Developing Countries.* Baltimore: The John Hopkins University Press.

Baldwin, R. (1996) "The Political Economy of Trade Policy: Integrating the Perspectives of Economists and Political Scientists", in R. Feenstra, G. Grossman and D. Irwin, *The Political Economy of Trade Policy: Papers in Honor of Jagdish Bhagwati* (pp. 147-174). Cambridge, MA and London: The MIT Press.

Baldwin, R. (2006). Multilateralising Regionalism: Spaghetti Bowls as Building Blocs on the Path to Global Free Trade. *World Economy*, 29 (11): 1451–1518.

Banco Central de Costa Rica-COMEX. (25/04/2000). *Reunión con el Banco Central de Costa Rica, (Minute of the negotiation).* In COMEX Centre of Documentation: Folders of the FTA between Central America and Panama.

Barrenechea, M. (2007). Un Terreno Desigual: Bancos Comerciales del Estado en Competencia con Bancos Privados. In C. Ansorena (Ed.), *Restricciones Institucionales al desarrollo en Costa Rica* (pp. 241-261). San José: UNCR.

Bart, J., Caprio, G., and Levine, R. (2006). *Rethinking Bank Regulation.* Cambridge: Cambridge University Press.

Bhagwati, J. (1965). On the equivalence of tariffs and quotas, in R. Caves, H. G. Johnson, P.B. Kenen (Eds), *Trade, Growth and the Balance of Payments: Essays in Honor of Gottfried Harbeler* (pp. 53-67). Chicago: Rand-McNally.

Bhagwati, J. (2002). *Free Trade Today.* Princeton: Princeton University Press.

Bilateral Protocol Costa Rica-Panama of the FTA Central America-Panama. (2007). Article 5. in: www.sice.oas.org (Accessed 10/03/2008).

Blondel, J. (1987). Political Leadership: Towards a General Analysis. Beverly Hills, CA: Sage.

Boletín BCN legislativa. (11-24 March 2008). *Aprobado convenio de complementación económica con Cuba*, no. 78. Valparaíso-Chile: Congreso Nacional.

Boletín de Prensa Partido Fuerza Democrática Fracción Parlamentaria. (25/05/2001). no 404. San José-Costa Rica.

Bouzas, R. (Ed.) (2006). Domestic Determinants of National Trade Strategies : A Comparative Analysis of Mercosur Countries, Mexico and Chile. Paris: Chaire Mercosur, Sciences Po.

Boyer, M. (2000). Issue Definition and Two-Level Negotiations: An Application to the Foreign Policy Process. *Diplomacy and Statecraft* 11 (2): 185-212.

Brander, J. and Spencer, B. (1984). Trade Warfare: Tariffs and Cartels. *Journal of International Economics* 16: 227-242.

Bull, B. (2008) Policy Networks and Business Participation in Free Trade Negotiations in Chile. *Journal of Latin American Studies* 40, no. 2: 195-224.

Bulmer-Thomas, V. and Page, S. (1999). Trade Relations in the Americas: MERCOSUR, The Free Trade Area of the Americas and the European Union In V. Bulmer-Thomas, and J. Dunkerley (Eds.), *The United States and Latin America: The New Agenda* (pp. 75-97). London and Cambridge, Mass.: Institute of Latin American Studies, University of London, and David Rockefeller Center for Latin American Studies, Harvard University.

Bush, G. W. (16/01/2002). Fact Sheet—U.S.- Central America free Trade Agreement. For Immediate release. Washington: Office of the Press Secretary.

Business Latin America. (2007). Chile/Japan: Free Trade Accord takes Effect, 10 September 2007, pp. 1-2.

Cabezas, M. (2003). Tratado de Libre Comercio Entre Chile y Estados Unidos: Revisión de Estudios que Cuantifican su Impacto. Working Papers Central Bank of Chile 239. Santiago: Central Bank of Chile.

CACIA. (05/07/2000). Carta al señor Tomas Dueñas Ministro de Comercio Exterior de Costa Rica con propuestas para la negociación con Panamá del Sector Embutidor; in COMEX Folder 361 B. San José, Costa Rica

CACIA. (July 2000). Posición del Sector de Harina de Trigo Tratados de Libre Comercio: Costa Rica-Canadá y Centroamérica-Panamá. Posición avalada por CIA Nestle de Costa Rica, Productos Columbia, El Griego y CIA; Conos Victoria; Pastas Lucema; Roma Prince; Pasta Viena, Pastas Vigui; Musmanni, Pozuelo; y Cuétara; in COMEX Information Centre. San José, Costa Rica

Callario, D. (27/02/1997). En Junio se firma acuerdo comercial con Panamá. *El Diario*, (Chile), Economics Section.

Cámara Nacional de Agricultura y Agroindustria. (28/11/2000). Carta al señor Tomas Dueñas Ministro de Comercio Exterior de Costa Rica con propuestas para la negociación con Panamá; in COMEX Folder 361 B. San José, Costa Rica.

Cámara Nacional de Agricultura y Agroindustria. (12/09/2000). Carta al señor Tomas Dueñas Ministro de Comercio Exterior de Costa Rica con propuestas para la negociación con Panamá; in COMEX Folder 361 B. San José, Costa Rica.

Campbell, C. (2006). "Rough trade: the Canada-Chile Free Trade Agreement", *Canadian Business Magazine*, 11-24 September, in: http://www.bilaterals.org/article-print.php3?id_article=5981 (Accessed 07/06/2009).

Canadian Press. (04/07/2004). Free trade negotiations suspended between Canada and Central America, in: www.bilaterals.org (Accessed on 11/08/2009).

Capital. (10-16/06/2002) Despejan camino a intercambio comercial; Economía y Política, no 90, (Costa Rica), p. 20.

Caputo, O. (2002). Análisis crítico del tratado de libre comercio Chile-Canadá en la perspectiva del ALCA (Borrador para la discusión).

Carrizo, J. (1997). Frustante Participación. *El Panamá América*, 23 May 1997, p. C2.

Casanueva, H (2001). Chile: Apertura y Diversificación. In H. Casanueva, et al. *La Experiencia Chilena de Inserción Internacional e Integración Regional: Chile en el Mundo*. Santiago: Universidad del Pacifico and Chilean Government.

Castillo Araya, E. (2005). *El libre comercio entre Centroamérica y los Estados Unidos: estrategias y amenazas*. Serie Cuadernos de Historia de las Instituciones de Costa Rica 17, San José: Editorial de la Universidad de Costa Rica.

Castro, A. (2003). Ingerencia Política en el Sistema Bancario Nacional. Heredia: EUNA.

CEPAL. (2005). Statistical Year for Latin America and the Caribbean. In www.cepal.org (Accessed 24/06/2009).

Cerutti, E.; Dell' Ariccia, G.; and Martinez Peria, M. (2005). *How Banks Go Abroad: Branches or Subsidiaries?* World Bank Policy Research, WPS3753. In: http://econ.worldbank.org

Challies, E., and Murray, W. (2008). Towards post-neoliberalism? The comparative politico-economic of New Zealand and Chile. *Asia Pacific Viewpoint* 49, no. 2: 228-243.

Charpentier Brenes, S. (2004). La Negociación de la Deuda Externa de Costa Rica, 1986-1990. In G. López, G. and R. Herrera (Eds.), *Ensayos en Honor a Eduardo Lizano Fait* (pp. 161-204). San José: Academia de Centroamérica.

Checkel, J. (1997). International Norms and Domestic Politics: Bridging the Rationalist- Constructivist Divide. *European Journal of International Relations* 3 (4): 473-495.

Cheong, I. (2004). *East Asian economic integration: implications of a US-Korea free trade agreement*. (16 October 2004) Incheon: Inha University.

Chile-European Community Association Agreement. (2002). in: http://www.direcon.cl (accessed November 3, 2008).

Chile-Panama's Bilateral Investment Treaty. (1996). in: http://www.direcon.cl (accessed November 10, 2008).

China View. (14/12/2006). S Korea, Japan to discuss bilateral FTA next week. in: http://news.xinhuanet.com (Accessed on 11/08/2009).

Chumacero, R., Fuentes, R. and Schmidt-Hebbel, K. (2004). *Chile's Free Trade Agreements: How big is the deal?* Central Bank of Chile Working Papers. Santiago: Central Bank.

COMEX. (25/06/2007). *Costa Rica concluye histórico TLC con Panamá*. Comunicado de Prensa CP-721. San José, Costa Rica.

COMEX. (03/07/2000). Document on Costa Rica's positions on Panama's proposal for the chapters of services and investment. DGCE-331-00. To be shared with El Salvador, Guatemala, Honduras, Nicaragua. 03/07/2000. COMEX Information centre. San José, Costa Rica.

COMEX. (05/03/2001). *Tratado de Libre Comercio entre Centroamérica y Panamá: Temas pendientes y acciones por realizar*. Internal document, Folder 380 B, "sección varios", FTA Central America-Panama. San José, Costa Rica.

COMEX. (06/04/2000). *Carta de Gabriela Llobet Directora de Comercio Exterior a Claudia Umana, Sonia Lainfiesta, Reinaldo Osorio, Sonia Somarriba*. Document: DGE 171-00. (Folder 365 A, Box 204: p. 070). COMEX information centre. San José, Costa Rica.

COMEX. (09/03/2001). *Memorandum: Temas a tratar con la señora Mireya Moscoso, Presidenta de Panamá, el 15 de Marzo de 2001*. (Internal document, Folder 380-B, section: varios, FTA Central America-Panama, pp. 2). COMEX information centre. San José, Costa Rica.

COMEX. (10/05/2000). *Reunión Consulta con Cámara de Bancos Privados e Instituciones Financieras (Minute of the meeting)*, (Folders of the FTA between Central America and Panama). COMEX inforomation centre. San José, Costa Rica.

COMEX. (14/03/2006). Agilidad en negociaciones sera clave para TLC entre Centroamérica y Panamá. Comex apela a la voluntad política de los países. Comunicado de Prensa CP-597. San José, Costa Rica.

COMEX. (18/08/2006). Avanzan negociaciones del TLC entre Costa Rica y Panamá, CP-646. San José, Costa Rica.

COMEX. (14/08/2006). *Inicia Ronda de Negociación Costa Rica-Panamá*. Comunicado de Prensa CP-644. San José, Costa Rica.

COMEX. (16/01/1998). Documento Centroamericano de enfoque de las negociaciones para el TLC Centroamérica-Panamá. I and II coordination round of the FTA Central America and Panama. (Internal document, Folder 382 B, pp. 5). COMEX information centre. San José, Costa Rica.

COMEX. (2007a). Tratado de Libre Comercio Costa Rica-Panamá: Resumen Explicativo, Agosto. San José ,Costa Rica.

COMEX. (2006). Acuerdos Comerciales suscritos por Costa Rica: Principales resultados en el 2006. San José, Costa Rica.

COMEX. (2004). Tratado de Libre Comercio República Dominicana-Centro América-Estados Unidos. Documento Explicativo. San José, Costa Rica.

COMEX. (2003). Tratado de Libre Comercio entre la República de Costa Rica y la República de Chile: Documento explicativo. Costa Rica: Ministerio de Comercio Exterior.

COMEX. (2001a). El Comercio y la Inversión entre Costa Rica y Panamá: Evolución reciente. September. San José, Costa Rica.

COMEX. (2001b.) COMEX. Documento explicativo del Tratado de Libre Comercio entre el Gobierno de la República de Costa Rica y el Gobierno de la República de Canadá. San José, Costa Rica.

COMEX. (2000). *Comunicado de Prensa*, 4 September, CP-077. San José, Costa Rica.

COMEX. (2000a). Negociaciones comerciales con canadá y Panamá: resultados de la consulta y el diálogo con los costarricenses. Costa Rica: Ministerio de Comercio Exterior.

COMEX. (1998). *Comunicado de Prensa: Lanzamiento de las negociaciones del tratado de libre comercio entre Chile y los países Centroamericanos*. 17 de agosto de 1998, CP-004. San José, Costa Rica.

COMEX. (1998). Tratado de Libre Comercio Costa Rica-República Dominicana: Documento Explicativo. Costa Rica: Ministerio de Comercio Exterior.

COMEX. (1994). *FTA Costa Rica-Mexico: Documento Explicativo*. Costa Rica: Ministerio de Comercio Exterior.

Contraloría General de la República de Panamá. (2007). *Indicadores Sociales años 1999-2003*. Sección 012: indicadores sociales. Panamá: Serie Estadística Panameña de la Dirección de Estadística y Censo.

Cooper, W. and Manyin, M. (2007). *The proposed South Korea-U.S. Free Trade Agreement (KORUS FTA)*. 18 July. Washington: Congressional Research Service.

Cooperativa. (08/01/2005). Canciller Wlaker solicitó a Panamá apoyo para que Insulza asuma en la OEA. in: www.cooperativa.cl (Accessed 24/08/2009).

Cordero, A. and Jované, J. (1990). Estrategia y Nación. Reflexiones críticas sobre la Estrategia Nacional de Desarrollo y Modernización de la Economía. Panama: IDEN, Universidad de Panamá.

CORFOGA. (31/05/2002). Se tambalea producción nacional de Carne". *El Heraldo*, (Costa Rica), p.6.

CORFOGA's letter- Corporación Ganadera. (31/07/2000). *Carta de CORFOGA a Sr. Tomás Dueñas, Ministro de Comercio Exterior Costa Rica*. (Folder 361(a), section: meat and remains). COMEX information centre. San José, Costa Rica.

Corning, G. (2007). Japan's Bilateral FTAs: No Obstacles to Progress in the Doha Round. *East Asia* 24: 45-67.

Costa Rica-Panama preferential trade agreement. (1973). in: www.sice.oas.org (accessed on 12/01/2007).

Cox, R. (1994). Global Restructuring; Making Sense of the Changing International Political Economy. In R. Stubbs, and G. Underhill (Eds.), *Political Economy in Changing Global Order* (pp. 45-59). London: Macmillan.

Crítica en Linea. (07/01/2005). Canciller de Chile se reúne con su homólogo panameño. in: www.critica.com.pa (Accessed 24/08/2009).

Crouch, C. and Farrell, H. (2002). *Breaking the path of institutional development? Alternatives to the new determinism.* Discussion paper 02/05, Cologne: Max Planck Institute for the Study of Societies.

Crump, L. (2006). Competitively-Linked and Non-Competitively-Linked Negotiations: Bilateral Trade Policy in Australia, Singapore and the United States. *International Negotiation* 11: 431-466.

Davis, M. (20/09/2002). Los Bancos y aseguradoras frenana el TLC entre Panamá y Costa Rica. in: *americaeconomica.com* (Accessed on 14/02/2008).

Deardorff, A. and Stern, R. M. (Eds.) (1999). *Measurement of Nontariff Barriers.* Michigan: University of Michigan Press.

Deeg, R. (2001). *Institutional change and the uses and limits of path dependency: The case of German finance.* Discussion paper 01/6. Cologne: Max Planck Institute for the Study of Societies.

Deese, D. (2008). World Trade Politics: Power, Principles, and Leadership. Oxon: Routledge.

Department of Foreign Affairs and International Trade-Canada. (2009). *Canada-Central America Four (CA4). Free Trade Agreement Negotiations.* in: http://www.international.gc.ca/trade-agreements-accords-commerciaux/agr-acc/ca4.aspx?lang=en#contact(Accessed on 11/08/2009).

Department of Foreign Affairs and International Trade-Canada (21/11/2001). *News Release: Free Trade Negotiations Launched with Four Central American Countries.* in: www.dfait-maeci.gc.ca (Accessed on 10/05/2009).

Devlin, R. and Giordano, P. (2004). The Old and New Regionalism: Benefits, Costs, and Implication for the FTAA. In A. Estevadeordal, D. Rodrik, D., A. Taylor, and A. Velasco (Eds.), *Integrating the Americas. FTAA and Beyond* (pp. 143-186). Cambridge, Mass.: Harvard University Press.

Digital Chosun Ilbo. (27/03/2006). Possible Korea-Japan FTA could hurt conglomerates. English edition. In: http://english.chosun.com (Accessed 11/08/2009).

DINECI. (15/04/2000). Dirección Nacional de Negociaciones Comerciales Internacionales: Carta a Gabriela Llobet Directora General de Comercio Exterior de Comercio Exterior Costa Rica de Diana Salazar Directora Nacional de DINECI. DINECI no. 358-00. (COMEX, Box 204, Folder 365 (a): 0059). COMEX information centre. San José, Costa Rica.

Dirección de Estadística y Censo-Panamá. (2001). *Panamá en Cifras.* November, Panama: República de Panamá.

DIRECON. (2008). Informe: Comercio Exterior de Chile. Cuarto Trimestre 2007. Santiago: Gobierno de Chile.

DIRECON. (12/12/2007). *Minuta Panamá.* (Documento Interno del DIRECON). Santiago: Departamento de Comunicaciones DIRECON.

DIRECON. (12/03/2007). *Minuta Tratado de Libre Comercio (TLC Chile-Panamá)*. Santiago: Departamento de Comunicaciones DIRECON.

DIRECON. (July 2006). *Antecedentes de la negociación del TLC Chile-Panamá*, in www.sice.oas.org (accessed 01/04/2008).

DIRECON. (31/05/2005). Comunicado de Prensa. Chile y Panamá Iniciaron diálogo para negociar un TLC. Santiago: Departamento de Prensa DIRECON.

DIRECON. (2006). *Intercambio comercial Chile-Panamá*. Santiago de Chile: Departamento de Estudios DIRECON. in:

http://www.direcon.cl/documentos/panama/intercambio_comercial_panama_julio_2006.pdf (accessed 04/07/2007).

Druckman, D. (2001). Turning points in International Negotiation: A Comparative Analysis. *Journal of Conflict Resolution* 45, no 4: 519-544.

Dür, A. (2007). Regionalism in the world economy: building block or stumbling stone for globalization? In S. Schirm (Ed.) *Globalization: State of the art and perspectives,* Oxon and New York: Routledge.

Economist Intelligence Unit. (2006). Panama: Country Report, December 2006.

Economist Intelligence Unit. (2005). Panama Country Report, December 2005

Economist Intelligence Unit (2003). Panama Country Report, December 2003.

Economist Intelligence Unit. (2003). Costa Rica Country Report, September 2003.

Economist Intelligence Unit. (2002). Panama Country Report, September 2002

Economist Intelligence Unit.(1998a). Panama: Country Report, First Quarter 1998.

Economist Intelligence Unit. (1998b). Panama: Country Report, December 1998.

Economist Intelligence Unit. (1996). Panama: Country Report, December 1996.

Edlin, B. (2003). *Made in Hong Kong or made in China?* in: www.arena.org.nz (Accessed on 11/05/2009).

Ehrlich, S. (2009). Constituency Size and Support for Trade Liberalization: An analysis of Foreign Economic Policy Preferences in Congress. *Foreign Policy Analysis* 5(3): 215-232.

Ehrlich, S. (2008). The Tariff and the Lobbyist: Political Institutions, Interest Groups Politics, and U.S. Trade Policy. *International Studies Quarterly* 52(2): 427-455.

Ehrlich, S. (2007). Access to Protection: Domestic Institutions and Trade Policy in Democracies. *International Organization* 61: 571-605.

El Campesino. (1998). Disminución del PIB agricola en 1997. (Chile), March-April 1997, vol. CXXIX, no 3.

El Clarin. (12/04/2005). Tras 5 votaciones con empate la OEA aplaza la elección de su jefe. (Argentina). in: www.clarin.com (Accessed 24/08/2009).

El Diario. (18/01/1998). El Tratado con Panamá se firmará este año. (Chile), p. 29.

El Diario. (15/01/1998). El Tratado con Panamá se firmará este año. (Chile), Economía, p. 29.

El Diario. (04/12/1996). El Acuerdo nos protegerá de los vientos proteccionistas. (Chile), p. 26.

El Financiero. (16/12/2002 to 5/01/2003). Hábil negociador. (Costa Rica), p. 8.

El Financiero. (22-28/07/2002). Entrabado TLC. (Costa Rica), p. 2.

El Financiero. (1-7/07/2002). Carne de Nicaragua y Panamá gana terreno. (Costa Rica), no 368, p. 33.

El Financiero. (22-28/04/2002). Agro y comercio, dilema del próximo gabinete. (Costa Rica).

El Financiero.(1-7/04/2002). Offshore pagaron 480 millones al fisco. (Costa Rica), p. 19.

El Financiero.(18-31/03/2002). Ex-Pdte CONASSIF Arnoldo Camacho. (Costa Rica), p. 18.

El Martes Financiero. (09/02/2002). Costa Rica, un socio comercial de cuidado. (Panama), p. 4.

El Mercurio. (04/09/1998). Chile Pretende Afianzar Su Presencia en Centroamérica. (Chile), p. C3.

El Panamá América. (24/07/2002). Costa Rica bloquea acceso al sector de servicios. p. 24 C.

El Panamá América. (18/07/2002). Pretensiones desmedidas de Costa Rica en el TLC: Kiener. p. C2.

El Panamá América. (08/06/2002). TLCs son "inconsultos" según el sector agropecuario. p. C1.

El Panamá América. (06/06/2002). Pretensiones de Costa Rica son desmedidas dice Kiener. Front Page, Finances section.

El Panamá América. (21/05/2002). Industriales están alertas por tratados comerciales. p. C5.

El Panamá América. (02/05/2002). Los lecheros temen introducción de productos subsidiados. p. C1.

El Panamá América. (18/04/2002). Panamá firma carta compromiso con la OCDE. Finance section: first page.

El Panamá América. (05/09/1998). Frei acepta que Panamá es líder en servicios financieros. E 1.

El Panamá América. (04/09/1998). Profesionales cuestionan a Pérez B. No page.

El Panamá América. (17/07/1998). Panamá puede formar parte del TLC norteamericano. p. E3.

El Panamá América.(22/11/1997). Panamá tendrá que renegociar techos arancelarios con Chile. p. E-3.

El Panamá América. (13/09/1997). Panamá y Chile, unidos por un comercio y futuro marítimo. p. 5 C.

El Panamá América.(01/07/1997). Heras confirma que TLC con Chile se firmará en octubre. p. C1.

El Panamá América. (23/05/1997). Panamá en la recta final para firmar TLC con Chile. p. C 1.

El Panamá América. (06/05/1997). Misión empresarial viaja a Chile. p. C2.

El Panamá América. (05/05/1997) Temor infundado por tratado con Chile. p. C5.

El Panamá América. (04/05/1997) Traer al debate público la reelección es sofocar el país innecesariamente. p. B4

El Panamá America. (23/04/1997). Profesionales temen negociación con Chile. Finances, p. C1.

El Panamá America. (09/04/1997). FEDAP questiona al gobierno. Finances, p. C4.

El Panamá America. (22/11/1996). Concluye primera negociación con Chile. p. C8.

Elms, D. (2006a). How Bargaining Alters Outcomes: Bilateral Trade Negotiations and Bargaining Strategies. *International Negotiation* 11: 399-429.

Elms, D. (2006b). Trust in Trade: Negotiating U.S. Free Trade Agreements. Paper Prepared for the International Studies Association Meeting, San Diego, California, March 2006.

Elms, D. (2003). *When the Status Quo is not Acceptable: Resolving U.S. Bilateral Trade Disputes*. PhD dissertation in Political Science University of Washington.

Engel, E. and Navia, P. (2006). Que Gane "El Más Mejor". Mérito y Competencia en el Chile de Hoy. Santiago: Arena Abierta.

Enlace. (1998). Presidente Carles renovó compromiso de fortalecer la empresa privada Panameña. May, no 101, (pp. 1-11). Panama: Panamanian Chamber of Commerce, Industries and Agriculture.

Enlace. (1997). Prochile evalúa proyecto de centro de acopio en Panamá. no 93, (p. 3). Panama: Cámara de Comercio, Industrias y Agricultura de Panamá.

Esser, H. (2004). Die 'Logik' der Verständigung. Zur Debatte um 'Arguing' und 'Bargaining' in internationalen Verhandlungen. In F. Pappi, E. Riedel, P. Thurner and R. Vaubel (Eds.), *Die Institutionalisierung internationaler* Verhandlungen, Frankfurt: Campus.

European Commission. (2007). *Panama. Country Strategy Paper 2007-2013.* 29 March 2007 (E/2007/482).

Evans, P. (1995). *Embedded Autonomy: States and Industrial Transformation.* New Jersey: Princeton University Press.

Evans, P., Jacobson, H. and Putnam, R. (Eds.) (1993). *Double-Edged Diplomacy: International Bargaining and Domestic Politics.* Berkeley, Los Angeles and London: University of California Press.

Faure, G.O. (2005). Deadlocks in negotiation dynamics. In W. Zartman and G.O. Faure (Eds.), *Escalation and negotiation in international conflicts.* Cambridge: Cambridge University Press.

Faust, J. (2004). Blueprint for an Interregional Future? The European Union and the Southern Cone. In V. Aggarwal and E. Fogarty (eds), *EU Trade Strategies between Regionalism and Globalism* (pp. 41-63). New York: Palgrave McMillan.

Fazio, H. (2004). *TLC. El amarre del modelo.* Santiago: LOM ediciones.

FEDAP. (25/08/1997). Comunicado al País. *El Panamá América*, p. C2.

Federación Centroamericana y del Caribe del Sector Lácteo. (22/03/2001). *Carta al señor Lic. Tomas Dueñas Ministro de Comercio Exterior de Costa Rica.* (Folder 361 B). COMEX information centre. San José, Costa Rica.

Fermandois, J. (2005). *Mundo y fin de mundo : Chile en la política mundial 1900-2004.* Santiago: Eds. Universidad Católica de Chile.

Fernández, M. (2005). Condiciones generales de competencia en Panamá. *Serie Estudios y Perspectivas* 37. Mexico, D.F.: CEPAL.

Fernández, R. (19/02/2001). Carta de Rogelio Fernández, Presidente de UPANACIONAL al Licenciado Tomás Dueñas, Ministro de Comercio Exterior de Costa Rica, S:G: 045-2001. (Folder 362(b), pp. 071-070). COMEX information centre. San José, Costa Rica.

Ferrer, A. (2001). Accession of Panama to the WTO: Implications for Deeveloping Countries Joining the World Trade System. Panama: Círculo Editorial y de Lectura.

Ffrench-Davis, R. (2005). Entre el Neoliberalismo y el Crecimiento con Equidad: Tres décadas de política económica en Chile. Third edition. Santiago: J.C. Sáez editor.

Financial Action Task Force. (2000). Review to Identify Non-cooperative countries or territories: increasing the world wide effectiveness of anti-money laundering measures FATF Secretariat, OECD, Paris, June 22.

Fisher, R. and Ury, W. (2007). *Getting to Yes: negotiating an Agreement without Giving In.* Reprinted. Reading, Berkshire: Random House Business Books.

Foreign Affairs and International Trade-Canada (2009) Free Trade Agreements. In: www.international.gc.ca

Foxley, A. (2003). Intervenciones en la Sesión del 6 de agosto de 2003 en que sé aprobó el proyecto de Ley 19897 sobre nueva banda de precio para el azúcar. In M. Bolivar Ruiz, et al. (2005) *El Libro Blanco del Azúcar: Una Historia de Proteccionismo...*(pp. 217-219). Santiago: RIL Editores.

Frei, E. (1998). *Palabras de S.E. el presidente de la república, D. Eduardo Frei Ruiz-Tagle. Press Conference in Panama.* 3 September 1998. Republic of Chile, Press Secretary. Pd-54/02, available at Frei's Foundation-Santiago of Chile.

Frei, Euardo (04/09/1998) "Discurso de S.E. el president de la república , Don Eduardo Frei Ruiz-Tagle", en la Cámara de Comercio, Industrias y Agricultura Panamá. Press Secretary, Pd-54/02, available at Frei's Foundation-Santiago of Chile.

Frei, E. (22/10/1997). Chile y Panama suscribieron acuerdos de complementación. *La Tercera.* (Chile). p 13.

Frieden, J. A. and Rogowski, R. (1996). The Impact of the International Economy on National Policies: An Analytical Overview. In R. Keohane, and H. Milner (eds), *Internationalization and Domestic Politics* (pp. 25-47). Cambridge: Cambridge University Press.

Friman, H. R. (1993). Side-Payments versus Security Cards: Domestic Bargaining Tactics in International Economic Negotiations. *International Organization* 47 (3), 387-410.

FTA Central America-Panama. (2002). in: www.sice.oas.org (accessed December 17, 2008).

FTA Chile-Canada. (1996). in: http://www.direcon.cl (accessed March 13, 2008).

FTA Chile-Central America. (1999). in: http://www.direcon.cl (accessed May 15, 2007).

FTA Chile-Japan. (2007). in: http://www.direcon.cl (accessed September 12, 2008).

FTA Chile-Mexico. (1998). in: http://www.direcon.cl (accessed May 27, 2008).

FTA Chile-Panama. (2006). in: http://www.direcon.cl (accessed April 2, 2008).

FTA Chile-Panama's draft text. (24-26 March 1997). Requested in DINECI's information centre. Panama.

FTA Chile-South Korea. (2003). in: http://www.direcon.cl (accessed July 30, 2008).

FTA Chile-US. (2003). in: http://www.direcon.cl (accessed August 7, 2008).

FTA Costa Rica-Panama's draft text: Bilateral Protocol. (2002). *Market Access Proposals.* (Folder 380, pp. 168-216). COMEX information centre. San José, Costa Rica.

FTA Costa Rica-Panama's draft text: Bilateral Protocol. (2002). *Norms of Origins Proposals.* (Folder 380). COMEX information centre. San José, Costa Rica.

FTA DR-CAFTA. (2004). in: www.sice.oas.org (Accessed on 08/09/2009).

FTA Panama-El Salvador. (2002). *Bilateral Protocols.* In: www.sice.oas.org (Accessed 15/12/2006).

FTA Panama-US. (27/06/2007). in: www.mici.gob.pa (accessed 20/02/2009).

Fuentes, C. (2006). La apuesta por el "poder blando": política exterior de la Concertación. In R. Funk (Ed.), *El Gobierno de Ricardo Lagos* (pp. 105-122). Santiago: Diego Portales University Press.

Gaceta Oficial, Républica de Panamá. (20/05/1998). *Legislación de la Républica de Panamá no 23546.* in: http://www.asamblea.gob.pa (Accessed 04/12/2007).

Gaceta Oficial-Panama. (09/07/1997). Decreto Ley no 5 (2 de Julio de 1997) "por la cual se modifican y se adicionan algunos artículos del código de comercio con el objeto de modernizar algunas instituciones, se modifica la ley 1 de 1984 sobre fideicomisos, y se dictan otras dispocisiones" y decreto ley no 7 (2 julio de 1997) "por la cual se crea el consejo economico (CENA) y se modifican algunas disposiciones de la ley no 56 de 27 de diciembre de 1995. Año XCIII, no 23.327. Published 09 July 1997. Panama: Republic of Panama.

Gaceta Oficial-Panama. (01/08/1996). Asamblea Legislativa Ley no 59 (de 29 de julio de 1996) "Por la cual se reglamentan las entidades aseguradoras, administratdoras de empresas y corredores o ajustadores de seguros; y la profesión de corredor o productor de seguros; y Ley no 60 (de 29 de julio de 1996) "por la cual se regulan las operaciones de las aseguradoras cautivas". Año XCII, no 23.092. Published 01 August 1996. Panama: republic of Panama

Galván de Tuñon, J. (2004). Acuerdos de Libre Comercio de los Países Centroamericanos. Temas de Administración. October. San José, Costa Rica: IICA.

Gandásegui, M. (2003). El ALCA y sus difíciles combinaciones: Comercio, salud y ambiente. *Nueva Sociedad* 183: 106-118.

Gandásegui, M. (1998). Panamá, la derrota neoliberal. *Nueva Sociedad* 158, November-December: 12-20.

Gandolfo, G. (1998). *International Trade Theory,* Heidelberg: Springer-Verlag Berlin.

Garisto, B. (25/02/1997). Panamá considera "primera prioridad" el tratado con Chile. *La Prensa*, (Panama), 25 February, p. 17a.

Genna, G. (2007). *Trade Triangulation: The Stalemate of the FTAA and EU-MERCOSUR FTA Negotiations*, Paper presented at the 48th Annual Convention of the International Studies Association, March 3, Chicago, IL.

George, A., and Bennett, A. (2005). *Case Studies and Theory Development in the Social Sciences*. Cambridge, MA and London, England: MIT Press.

Gerber, J. (2000). Cruzando fronteras: políticas nacionales y los límites de la integración internacional. J. Gerber, et al., *Inserción Económica Internacional de América Latina* (pp. 31-62). Santiago: Flacso-Chile.

Gilpin, R. (1987). *The Political Economy of International Relations*, Princeton: Princeton University Press.

Gobierno de Chile. (14/02/2002) .Promulga el Tratado de Libre Comercio entre Chile y Centroamérica y el Protocolo Bilateral a dicho Tratado Suscrito con Costa Rica. DTO-14. In: www.bcn.cl (Accessed 21/03/2007).

Gobierno de Chile. (1995). Crea Comité Interministerial de Negociaciones Económicas Internacionales; DTO-419; 7 April 1995.

Goldfarb, D. (2005). *U.S. Bilateral Free Trade Accords: Why Canada Should Be Cautious About Going the Same Route*. C.D. Howe Institute Commentary, no. 214, August.

Gomes, L. (2003). *The Economic and Ideology of Free Trade: A Historical Review*. Cheltenham, UK and Northampton, MA, USA: Edward Elgar.

Gonzalez, C. (2006). Deconstructing the Mythology of Free Trade: Critical Reflections on Comparative Advantage. *Berkeley La Raza Law Journal* 17 (1): 65-93.

González Henríquez, S. (2001). *Los dilemas de la transición: constituyente y democracia.* Panama: Instituto de Estudios Políticos e Internacionales.

Grabowski, R. (1999). *Pathways to Economic Development.* Cheltenham, UK: Edward Elgar.

Granados, J., et.al. (2007). Costa Rica: ante un nuevo escenario en el comercio internacional. INTAL-Documento de Trabajo 32.

Grieco, J. (1993). Understanding the Problem of International Cooperation: The Limits of Neoliberal Institutionalism and the Future of Realist Theory. In D. Baldwin, (Ed.), *Neorealism and Neoliberalism: The Contemporary Debate.* New York: Columbia University Press.

Grieco, J. (1990). *Cooperation Among Nations: Europe, America, and Non-tariff Barriers to Trade*, Ithaca: Cornell University Press.

Grieco, J. (1988). Anarchy and the limits of Cooperation: A realist critique of the newest liberal institution. *International Organisation* 42: 485-507.

Gross Stein, Janice (Ed.) (1989). *Getting to the table: the processes of international prenegotiation.* Baltimore: John Hopkins University Press.

Grossman, G. and Helpman, E. (1999). The Politics of Free-Trade Agreements. In J. Bhagwati (Ed.), *Trading Blocs: Alternative Approaches to Analyzing Preferential Trade Agreements.* Cambridge, MA and London: The MIT press.

Habermas, J. (1984). The Theory of Communicative Action, Vol. 1: Reason and the Rationalization of Society, Boston, MA: Beacon Press.

Hague, R., Harrop, M., and Breslin, S. (1992). *Political Science: A Comparative* Introduction. New York: St. Martin's Press.

Hall, P. and Soskice, D. (2001). An introduction to varieties of capitalism. In P. Hall, and D. Soskice (Eds.), *Varieties of Capitalism. The Institutional Foundations of Comparative Advantage* (pp. 1-68). Oxford: Oxford University Press

Hamann, K., and Wilson, B. (2001). Surviving the Political Consequences of Neoliberal Economic Policies. *Journal of Contemporary Politics*, 7(2):129-147.

Harding, R. (2006.) *The History of Panama.* Westport, CT: Greenwood Press.

Harding, R. (2001). *The Military Foundations of Panamenian Politics*. New Brunswick: Transaction Publishers.

Hart, J. and Prakash, A. (2000). Globalization, Governance and Strategic Trade and Investment Policies. In J. Hart, and A. Prakash (Eds.), *Globalization and Governance* (pp. 243-266). Reprinted edition. London and New York: Routledge.

Hathaway, D. (2004). The U.S.-Central American Free Trade Agreement: Main Effects on Agricultural Products. In M. Jank (ed.), *Agricultural Trade Liberalization: Policies and Implications for Latin America.* Washington: Inter-American Development Bank.

Helpman, E. (1999). Politics and Trade Policy. In R. Baldwin (Ed.), *Market Integration, Regionalism and the Global Economy.* Cambridge: Cambridge University Press.

Helpman, E. and Krugman, P. (1999). *Trade Policy and Market Structure.* Cambridge, MA and London: The MIT Press.

Heras, M. (06/08/1998). Tratado de Libre Comercio Chile y Panamá podrían firmar en Septiembre. *La Prensa*, (Panama), p. 21 A.

Hermann, M. (1995). Leaders, Leadership, and Flexibility: Influences on Heads of Government as Negotiators and Mediators. *Annals of the American Academy of Political and Social Science,* Vol. 542, November: 148-167.

Hernandez, R. (30/07/1998). Panamá, a un paso de firmar TLC con Chile. *La Prensa*, (Panama), p. 31 A.

Hiscox, M. (2002). International Trade and Political Conflict: Commerce, Coalitions, and Mobility. Princeton: Princeton University Press.

Hoffmann, B. (2008). Why reform fails: The 'politics of policies' in Costa Rican Telecommunications Liberalization. *European Review of Latin American and Caribbean Studies* 84: 3-19.

Holzinger, K. (2001). Negotiations in Public-Policy Making: Exogenous Barriers to Successful Dispute Resolution. *Journal of Public Policy* 21 (1): 71-96.

Hopmann, T. (1996). The Negotiation Process and the Resolution of International Conflicts. Columbia: University of South Carolina Press.

Hopmann, T. (1995). Two Paradigms of Negotiation: Bargaining and Problem Solving. *Annals of the American Academy of Political and Social Science* 542: 24-47.

Hornbeck, J.F. (2004). The US-Chile Free Trade Agreement: Economic and Trade Policy Issues. In A. Miller (Ed.), *Free Trade: Current Issues and Prospects* (pp. 31-64). New York: Novinka Books.

Huhn, S. and Löding, T. (2007). Zentralamerika: Sozialer Konflikt um CAFTA um Seine Folgen. *GIGA Focus*, no 10.

Huneeus, C. (2000). *El Régimen de Pinochet*. Santiago: Editorial Sudamericana.

Hurrell, A. (2006). Hegemony, liberalism and global order: what space for would-be great powers? *International Affairs* 82, 1: 1-19.

Hurrell, A (2005). Power, Institutions and the Production of Inequality. In M. Barnett, and R. Duvall (Eds.), *Power in Global Governance* (pp. 33-58). Cambridge: Cambridge University Press.

Hurrell, A. (1995). Regionalism in the Americas. In L. Fawcett, and A. Hurrell (Eds.) *Regionalism in World Politics* (pp. 250-282). Oxford: Oxford University Press.

IFES Election Guide, Panama. in: http://www.electionguide.org/results.php?ID=887 (Accessed 12/03/2008).

Ikemberry, G. J. (2001). After Victory: Institutions, Strategic Restraint, and the Rebuilding of Order After Major Wars. Princeton: Princeton University Press.

IMF. (2001). *Panama. Module 2-Banking Sector Assessment.* August 2001. Washington: Monetary and Exchange Affairs Department.

IMF (2002) *IMF Concludes 2002 Article IV Consultation with Panama.* Public Information Notice (PIN), no. 02/74, July 18. Washington: IMF.

Insulza, J. (22/10/1997). Chile y Panama suscribieron acuerdos de complementación. *La Tercera*, (Chile), p 13.

Izam, M. (2003). Rules of Origin and Trade Facilitation in Preferential Trade Agreements in Latin America. *Serie Comercio Internacional* 31, CEPAL, Santiago.

Jácome, J. (2004). Memoria de gestión 1999-2004. Ministro de Comercio e Industrias. Panama: MICI.

Jana, Á. (2005). La protección del Azúcar en Chile", in Bolívar Ruiz, M. et.al., *El Libro Blanco del Azúcar: Una Historia de Proteccionismo*...(pp. 135-185). Santiago: RIL Editores.

Jara, A. (12/06/1998). El 17 de junio parte en Buenos Aires primera ronda negociadora de ALCA. *El Diario*, (Chile), p. 27.

Jiménez, R. (2005). El TLC de Centroamérica, República Dominicana y Estados Unidos: ¿Qué Dice?, y ¿Cuáles son las opciones? Documentos 15, Septiembre, Academia de Centroamérica.

Jimenez, T. (12/08/2002). Taiwan y Panamá firman delcaración de reinicio de negociaciones de TLC. in: *www.roc-taiwan.org.pa* (Accessed 16/07/2009).

Jované, J. (2003). *Neoliberalismo, desarrollo y Seguridad Social.* Serie. Panamá Hoy 9, Panamá: CEASPA.

Kaplisnki, R., and Morris, M. L. (2001). *A Handbook for Value Chain Research*, Institute of Development Studies, University of Sussex and School of Development Studies: University of Natal. Available in: www.ids.ac.uk/global

Kapstein, E., and Landa, D. (2000). Pluses and minuses of globalization. In M. Plattner, and A. Smolar (eds), *Globalization, Power and Democracy* (pp. 133-148), Baltimore and London: The John Hopkins University Press.

Kateznstein, P. and Sil, R. (2008) Eclectic Theorizing in the Study and Practice of International Relations. In C. Reus-Smit, and D. Snidal (eds.), *The Oxford Handbook of International Relations* (pp. 109-130).Oxford: Oxford University Press.

Katzenstein, P., and Sil, R. (2004). Rethinking Asian Security. A Case for Analytical Eclecticism. In J. Suh, P. Katzenstein, and A. Carlson (Eds.), *Rethinking Security in East Asia. Identity, Power, and Efficiency* (pp. 1-33). Stanford: Stanford University Press.

Keohane, R. and Milner, H. (eds) (1996). *Internationalization and Domestic Politics*, New York: Cambridge University Press.

Keohane, R. (1984). After Hegemony: Cooperation and Discord in the World Political Economy. Princeton: Princeton University Press.

Kesner, I. F. and Shapiro, D. L. (1991). Did a 'Failed' Negotiation Really Fail? Negotiation Journal 7 (4): 369-376.

Kibritçioglu, A. (2002). On the Smithian origins of "new" trade and growth theories. *Economics Bulletin* 2 (1): 1-15.

Kidder, L. (1987). Breaking a Stalemate with a Creative Alternative. *Negotiation Journal* 3, no. 2: 141-146.

Kiener, J. (25/07/2002). Panamá acusa a C.R. de rigidez en negociación. *La Prensa*. (Panama), p. 33A.

Kiener, J. (18/07/2002). Rechazan un TLC con Costa Rica. *La Prensa* (Panama), p. 3A.

Kjeldsen-Kragh, S. (2001). *International Trade Policy.* Copenhagen: Copenhagen Business School Press.

KOPA. (23/08/2004). *We denounce the Korea-Japan FTA!* in: http://antiwto.jinbo.net (Accessed on 11/08/2009).

Korea Times. (25/12/2007). FTA talks with Japan to resume. in: www.koreantimes.co.kr (Accessed 11/08/2009).

Korea Times. (25/08/2005). Mexico FTA talks stall. in: www.bilaterals.org (Accessed on 14/08/2009).

Kotzian, P. (2007). Arguing and Bargaining in International Negotiations: On the Application of the Frame-Selection Model and its implications. *International Political Science Review* 28 (1): 79-99.

Kratochwill, F. (1989). Rules, norms, and decisions: On the conditions of practical and legal reasoning in international relations and domestic affairs. Cambridge: Cambridge University Press.

Kremenyuk, V and Sjöstedt, G. (eds) (2000). *International Economic Negotiation: Model versus Reality*, Cheltenham, UK and Northampton, MA, USA: Edward Elgar.

Krueger, A. (1997). Trade Policy and Economic Development: How We Learn. *American Economic Review* 87: 1-22.

Krugman, P. and Obstfeld, M. (2006). *International Economics: Theory and Policy*, Seventh Edition. Boston: Pearson International Edition.

Krugman, P. (1992a). Does New Trade Theory Require a New Trade Policy. *The World Economy* 15 (4): 423-441.

Krugman, P. (1992b). Import Protection as Export Promotion: International Competition in the Presence of Oligopoly and Economies of Scale. In G. Grossman (Ed.), *Imperfect Competition and International Trade*, Cambridge, MA and London: The MIT Press.

Krugman, P. (1991). Is Bilateralism Bad? In E. Helpman and A. Razin (Eds.), *International Trade and Trade Policy*, Cambridge, MA and London: The MIT press.

Krugman, P. (1989). New Trade Theory and the Less Developed Countries. In G. Calvo, R. Findlay, P. Kouri, and J Braga De Macedo (eds), *Debt, Stabilization and Development: Essays in Memory of Carlos Díaz-Alejandro* (pp. 347-365). Oxford and Cambridge, MA: World Institute for Development Economic Research of the United Nations University, Helsinki,

La Epoca. (12/09/1996). Derecha: gobierno debe cumplir su palabra. (Chile), p. 3B.

La Nación. (03/05/2005). Tras disputa, se impuso Insulza en la OEA. (Argentina). In: www.lanación.com (Accessed 24/08/2009).

La Nación. (12/08/2002). Agro vigilará los TLC. (Costa Rica), section país, p. 4.

La Nación. (23/07/2002). Aprobado el TLC con Canadá. Costa Rica. (Costa Rica), section país, p. 1.

La Nación. (20/07/2002). Cinco Columnas. (Costa Rica), p. 22.

La Nación. (20/07/2002). Paperos firmaron acuerdo por TLC. (Costa Rica), p. 13

La Nación. (20/07/2002). Sigue Choque con Panamá. (Costa Rica), p. 25 A.

La Nación. (19/07/2002). Vía Libre a TLC con Canadá tras acuerdo. (Costa Rica), front page.

La Nación. (07/07/2002). País procura reforzar lazos con EE. UU. (Costa Rica), p. 2.

La Nación. (09/06/2002). Buscan opciones a paperos. (Costa Rica), section: el país, p. 6 A.

La Nación. (09/04/2002). Pacheco fija prioridades. (Costa Rica), p. 4 A.

La Nación. (06/04/2002). TLC con Canadá paralizado en el Congreso por tiempo electoral. (Costa Rica), p. 8 A.

La Nación.(03/04/2002). Pacheco reafirma sus compromises. (Costa Rica), p. 4.

La Nación. (01/04/2002).Choque por nombres. (Costa Rica), p. 6 A.

La Nación. (24/01/2002). Pacheco por agro y turismo. (Costa Rica), p. 6.

La Nación. (20/11/2001). Transcripción completa del debate de los candidatos Rolando Araya y Abel Pacheco. (Costa Rica), in: www.lanacion.com (accessed 10/03/2007).

La Prensa. (02/04/2006). El panorama comercial entre Panamá y sus vecinos centroamericanos ya no es el mismo de hace cuatro años. (Panama), p. 44 A.

La Prensa. (06/03/2006). Panamá relanzará el próximo juves negociaciones para un Tratado de Libre Comercio (TLC) con los países de Centroamérica. (Panama), p. 45 A.

La Prensa. (22/01/2006). Panamá deberá poner al día su agenda comercial con Centroamérica. (Panama), p. 43 A.

La Prensa, (30/06/2005), Ayer el Palacio las Garzas recibió importantes figuras: el presidente chileno, Ricardo Lagos, el magnate méxicano Carlos Slim y el ex-presidente del Gobierno E-spañol Felipe González. (Panama), p. 1 A.

La Prensa. (30/11/2002). Costa Rica prolonga TLC con Panamá. (Panama), p. 29 A.

La Prensa. (03/11/2002). La ANAGAN sostiene que sería un competencia desleal si se incluye este sector en las negociaciones con Costa Rica. (Panama), p. 30A.

La Prensa. (19/10/2002). Panamá no aceptará presiones de Costa Rica. (Panama), p. 25 A.

La Prensa.(18/10/2002). Peligra el TLC con Costa Rica. (Panama), p. 1 A.

La Prensa. (22/09/2002). ABP dispuesta a sacrificarse en TLC con Costa Rica. (Panama), p. 30 A.

La Prensa. (22/09/2002). Panamá no aceptará presiones de Costa Rica. (Panama), p. 25 A.

La Prensa. (18/09/2002). Costa Rica pone obstáculos a los bancos y seguros panameños. (Panama), p. 25 A.

La Prensa. (07/08/2002). Taiwan busca afianzar sus lazos con Panamá. (Panama), p. 5 A.

La Prensa. (25/07/2002). Panamá acusa a C.R. de rigidez en negociación. (Panama), p 33a.

La Prensa. (21/03/2002). Panamá debe negociar un TLC bilateral con EU. (Panama), p. 37 A.

La Prensa. (26/01/2002). Panamá y Costa Rica buscan TLC con EU. (Panama), p. 2 A.

La Prensa.(25/08/2000). Avances moderados en TLC. (Panama), Business Section.

La Prensa.(22/11/1998). Los secretos del gigante del comercio suramericano y los restos y ventajas de asociarse con él. (Panama), p. 33 A.

La Prensa. (07/07/1998). Los pobres están cada vez peor en Panamá: Mireya Moscoso. (Panama), p. 2A.

La Prensa. (15/11/1997). Imposible renegociar tratado de neutralidad. (Panama), p. 5 A.

La Prensa. (24/10/1997). Panamá y Chile: Ministros esperan concluir negociaciones en Noviembre. (Panama), p. 31A.

La Prensa. (09/06/1997). Solo restan dos rondas para firmar TLC. (Panama), p. 35 A.

La Prensa. (23/05/1997) Panamá y Chile podrían firmar acuerdo comercial en agosto. (Panama), p. 21 A.

La Prensa. (05/05/1997). Tratado con Chile no provocará 'inundación' de profesionales. (Panama), p. 2 A.

La Prensa. (22/11/1996). Panamá y Chile inician conversaciones para un TLC. (Panama) , p. 25 A.

La Prensa. (21/11/1996). Panamá espera firmar en abril acuerdo con Chile. (Panama), p. 33 A.

La Prensa Libre. (22/06/2002). Definen prioridades. (Costa Rica). Section: nacionales, front page.

La Prensa Libre. (08/06/2002). TLC en controversia: Optimismo en horticultores. (Costa Rica), section: economic focus.

La Prensa Libre. (31/05/2002). Disconformidad con importaciones de carne. (Costa Rica). Economic Focus.

La República. (31/05/2002). Gobierno mercadea TLC con Canadá. (Costa Rica), national section, p. 17.

La República. (26/04/2001). TLC con Canadá. ¿Quiénes ganan?. (Costa Rica); written by Lizbeth Ulett, no page.

La Tercera. (28/08/1997). Acuerdo Chile-Panamá avanza a pesar de protestas. (Chile), p. 24.

La Tercera. (01/07/1997). Razones para nueva postergación del TLC con Canadá. (Chile), pp. 21 & 23.

La Tercera. (03/03/1997). Oportunidades de inversión en Panamá. (Chile), p. 23.

Ladewig, J. (2006). Domestic Influences on International Trade Policy: Factor Mobility in the United States, 1963 to 1992. *International Organization* 60: 69-103.

Lamy, S. (2001). Comtemporary mainstream approaches: neo-realism and neo-liberalism. in S. Smith, and J. Baylis (Eds.), *The Globalisation of World Politics. An introduction to International Relations*. 2nd edition, Oxford: Oxford University Press.

Landau, A. (2000). Analyzing International Economic Negotiations: Towards a Synthesis of Approaches. *International Negotiation* 5: 1-19.

Landman, T. (2000). Issues and Methods in Comparative Politics: An Introduction, London: Routledge.

Le Fort, G. and Lehmann, S. (2003). El encaje y la entrada neta de capitals: Chile en el decenio de 1990. *Revista de la Cepal* 81: 33-64.

Lebow, R. N. (1996). *The Art of Bargaining*. Baltimore and London: The Johns Hopkins University Press.

Legislación sobre Seguros. (1999). *Colección Textos Jurídicos*. Second edition. Vol. 2. Panama: Sistemas Jurídicos, S.A.

Leis, R. (2003). Panamá: la encrucijada del centenario. *Nueva Sociedad* 186: 28-35.

Lewis Navarro, S. (26/06/2006). *Discursos Política Exterior Abril 2006 a Septiembre 2006* (pp. 145-146). República de Panama, Ministerio de Relaciones Exteriores.

Lewis, J., and Ritchie, J. (2003). Generalising from Qualitative Research. In J. Ritchie and J. Lewis (Eds.), *Qualitative Research Practice: A Guide for Social Science Students and Researchers* (pp. 263-286). London: SAGE Publications.

Ley Bancaria Panameña. (1998). Decreto-Ley No 9 De 26 de Febrero de 1998, por la cual se reforma el régimen bancario y se crea la superintendencia de bancos. Panama: Cultural Portobello.

Ley de Lavado de Dinero. (2001). Legislación Bancaria Panameña sobre el Control de Lavado de Dinero y el Blanqueo de Capitales. Panama: Editorial Portobello.

Linklater, A. (1995). Neo-realism in Theory and Practice. in K. Booth, and S. Smith (Eds.), *International Relations Theory Today*. Cambridge: Polity Press.

Lizano, E. (2003). *Visión desde el Banco Central 1998-2002*. San José: Academia de Centroamérica.

Lizano, E. (2001). La Política de Comercio Exterior de Costa Rica. Academia de Centroamérica. Documentos 4, Agosto, San José-Costa Rica.

Looney, R. (2005). US Middle East Economic Policy: The Use of Free Trade Areas in the War on Terrorism. *Mediterranean Quarterly* 16 (3): 102-117.

López Giral, D. (2006). La apertura comercial de Chile y México: un análisis comparado. *Comercio Exterior* 56, no. 8: 703-718.

López, G. and Herrera, R. (eds.) (2005). Volatilidad y Vulnerabilidad: El Caso de Costa Rica, veinte años (1984-2004) sin crisis. San José: Academia de Centroamérica.

López, G. and Herrera, R. (eds.) (2004) *Ensayos en honor a Eduardo Lizano Fait*. San José: Academia de Centroamérica

Malhotra, D. (2004). Risky Business: Trust in Negotiation. *Negotiation* 7, no. 2 (February 2004).

Malnes, R. (1995). 'Leader' and 'Entrepreneur' in International Negotiations: A Conceptual Analysis. *European Journal of International Relations* 1 (1): 87-112.

Mansfield, E., Milner, H., Pevehouse, J. (2007). Vetoing Co-operation: The Impact of Veto Players on Preferential Trading Arrangements. *British Journal of Political Science* 37: 403-432.

March, J., and Olsen, J. (1998). The Institutional Dynamics of International Political Orders. *International Organization* 52: 943-969.

Marrewijk, C. V. (2002). *International trade and the world economy*. Oxford: Oxford University Press.

Martes Financiero. (25/11/1997). ¿Tratados, para qué? (Panama), p. 10-11.

Martes Financiero. (08/07/1997). Las Negociaciones. (Panama), p. 2.

Maxwell, J. (2004). Using Qualitative Methods for Causal Explanation. *Field Methods* 16, no 3: 243-264.

Mayer, F. (1992). Managing Domestic Differences in International Negotiations: The Strategic Use of Internal Side-payments. *International Organization* 46 (4): 793-818

Mesa, W. and Pinto-Agüero, C. (2004). Evaluación de los Tratados de Libre Comercio de Chile. *Estudios Sociales* 114: 153-198.

Mesquita Moreira, M. and Blyde, J. (2006). Chile's strategy: Is There Room for Improvement? Working Paper 21. Buenos Aires: IDB-INTAL.

Messalles, L. and Céspedes, O. (eds.) (2007). Reformas para el Crecimiento Económico de Costa Rica. San José: Academia de Centroamérica.

MICI. (2007). Documento Explicativo del Tratado de Promoción Comercial (TPC) entre Panama y Estados Unidos de América. Panama: Ministerio de Comercio e Industrias.

MICI. (2005). Beneficios de Contar con Un Tratado de Libre Comercio entre Panamá y Chile. In: www.mici.gob.pa (Accessed 25/08/2009).

MICI. (2005). *Relación Comercial entre Costa Rica y Panamá*. April. Panama: Ministerio de Comercio e Industrias.

MICI. (14/02/2002). *Reacción de Panama a la propuesta de Costa Rica*. Panama: Ministerio de Comercio e Industrias.

MIDEPLAN. (2007). La situación de la pobreza en Chile. Serie análisis de resultados de la encuesta de caracterización socioeconómica (CASEN 2006). Santiago: Gobierno de Chile.

Milner, H. (2006). International Trade. In W. Carlsnaes, T. Risse, and B. Simmons (Eds.), *Handbook of International Relations* (pp. 448-461). London: Sage.

Milner, H. and Rosendorff, P. (1996). Trade Negotiations, Information and Domestic Politics. *Economics and Politics* 2 (8): 145-189.

Milner, H. (1988). *Resisting Protectionism*. Princeton: Princeton University Press.

Ministerio de Economía y Finanzas-Panamá. (2002). *Informe económico anual 2002: La economía Panameña*. Panama: Gobierno de Panamá.

Ministerio de Economía y Finanzas-Panamá. (2000). Plan de Desarrollo Económico Social y Financiero con Inversión en Capital Humano. Panama: Gobierno de Panamá.

Ministerio de Economía. Política Comercial Externa, Guatemala. (21/09/2007). *Evaluación Negociación con Chile*. in: http://www.mineco.gob.gt/ComercioExterior.aspx (Accessed on 19/08/2009).

Ministry of Foreign Affairs and Trade New Zealand. (2001). Hong Kong and New Zealand: Initial analysis of the bilateral trade and economic relationship as background to a possible "closer economic partnership" agreement. in: www.mfat.govt.nz (Accessed on 10/05/2009).

Ministry of Foreign Affairs of South Korea. (2006a). *Outcomes of the 1st Round of Korea-Mexico SECA Negotiations*. in: www.mofat.go.kr (Accessed on 11/05/2009).

Ministry of Foreign Affairs of South Korea. (2006b). *Outcomes of the 3rd Round of Negotiations on the Korea-Mexico SECA*. in: www.mofat.go.kr (Accessed on 11/05/2009).

Ministry of Foreign Affairs of South Korea. (2005). *Results of the 4th Meeting of Korea-Mexico Joint Experts Group*. in: www.mofat.go.kr (Accessed on 11/05/2009).

Ministry of Foreign Affairs of South Korea. (2004). *Results of the 1st Meeting of the Korea-Mexico Joint Experts Group*. in: www.mofat.go.kr (Accessed on 11/05/2009).

Ministry of Trade and Industry, Singapore. (2009). *FTA with Korea*. in: http://www.fta.gov.sg/fta_ongoingneg.asp (Accessed on 12/07/2009).

Minute of the 5th round of negotiation Panama-Chile. (24-26 March 1997). Requested at DINECI's information centre. Panama.

Minute of the 4th round of negotiation Panama-Chile. (3-4 March 1997). Requested at DINECI's information centre. Panama.

Minute of the second round of negotiation of the FTA Costa Rica-Panama. (16-19/07/2002:1). COMEX information centre. San José, Costa Rica.

Minute of the first round of negotiation of the FTA Costa Rica-Panama. (05/04/2002). Requested at COMEX's information centre. San José, Costa Rica

Minute of the Negotiation Central America-Panama (1-2/02/2001) *Reunión de Vice-ministros in Managua-Nicaragua*. (Box: 206; Folders 366 B; pp. 3). COMEX information centre. San José, Costa Rica.

Mladinic, C. (2000). *Apertura al Exterior y Negociaciones Comerciales: lecciones y Experiencias del Caso Chileno.* Santiago: Instituto Interamericano de Cooperación para la Agricultura (II-CA), Agencia de Cooperación en Chile.

Mon, J. (1995). Domestic Institutions and International Bargaining: The role of agent veto in two-level games. *The American Political Science Review* 89 (4): 914-924.

Monge, R. and González Vega, C. (1995). *Economía Política, Proteccionismo y Apertura en Costa Rica.* San José: Academia de Centroamérica y Centro Internacional para el Desarrollo Económico.

Morales, A., and Schipke, A. (2005). Regional Integration and Financial System Issues. In M. Rodlauer, and A. Schipke (Eds.), *Central America: Global Integration and Regional Cooperation.* Occasional Paper 243, July. Washington DC: International Monetary Fund.

Morandé, J. (2003). Chile: The invisible hand and contemporary foreign policy. In F. Mora, and J. Hey (Eds.), *Latin American and Caribbean Foreign Policy* (pp. 243-264). Oxford: Rowman & Littlefield Publishers, Inc.

Moravsick, A. (2008). The New Liberalism. In C. Reus-Smit, and D. Snidal (Eds.), *The Oxford Handbook of International Relations* (pp. 234-254).Oxford: Oxford University Press.

Moravcsik, A. (1997). Taking Preferences Seriously: A Liberal Theory of International Politics. *International Organization* 51(4): 513-553.

Moravcsik, A. (1993a). Preferences and Power in the European Community: A Liberal Intergovernmentalist Approach. *Journal of Common Market Studies* 31 (4): 473-524.

Moravcsik, A. (1993b). Introduction: Integrating International and Domestic Theories of International Bargaining. In P. Evans, H. Jacobson, and R. Putnam (Eds.), *Double-Edged Diplomacy: International Bargaining and Domestic Politics* (pp. 1-42). Los Angeles: University of California Press.

Muchnik, E. and Errrazuriz, L. F. (1998). Desafíos a la agricultura y al comercio exterior agropecuario en Chile en los años noventa. In L. Reca, and R. Echeverría, (Eds.), *Agricultura, medio ambiente y pobreza rural en América Latina.* Washington DC: Intermaerican Development Bank.

Mughan, A., and Lacy, D. (2002). Economic Performance, Job Insecurity and Electoral Choice. *British Journal of Political Science* 32: 513-533.

Muñoz Gomá, O. (2007). El modelo económico de la Concertación: 1990-2005 ¿Reformas o cambio? Santiago: Flacso Chile y Catalonia.

Murray, W., and Challies, E. (2004). New Zealand and Chile: partnership for the Pacific century? *Australian Journal of International Affairs* 58, no 1.: 89-103.

Nash, J. (1950). The Cooperative Problem. *Econometrica* 18: 155-162.

Navia, P. (2006). Chile: Erfolgsmodell des linken Liberalismus. *Nueva Sociedad,* Sonderheft: 44-53

New Zealand Council of Trade Unions-CTU. (18/03/2002). *CTU concerns over Hong Kong trade deal confirmed.* Media Release. in: www.arena.org.nz (Accessed on 10/05/2009).

Novoa, M. (25-30/04/2005). Tras Acuerdos Comerciales. *Martesfinanciero.com* (Accessed 31/07/2009).

Nowak-Lehmann, F, Herzer, D., and Vollmer, S. (2007). The Free Trade Agreement between Chile and the EU: Its Potential Impact on Chile's Export Industry. *Applied Econometrics and International Development,* Vol. 7, No. 1.

Nuñez, J. (24/05/2001). *Carta, Asamblea Legislativa, Fracción Fuerza Democrática a Ministro de Comercio Exterior Sr. Tomás Dueñas*. JMN-372-2000/2001. (Folder 362(b), carpeta c201, p. 0091). COMEX information centre. San José Costa Rica.

Ocampo, F. (08/01/2002). *Carta al Viceministro de Comercio Exterior de Panamá, S.E Melitón Arrocha, DGC-02-02*. Ministerio de Comercio Exterior de Costa Rica, available at COMEX information centre. San José, Costa Rica.

Odell, J. (2009). Breaking Deadlocks in International Institutional Negotiations: The WTO, Seattle, and Doha. *International Studies Quarterly* 53, no 2: 273-299.

Odell, J. (2006). Introduction. In J. Odell (Ed.), *Negotiating Trade: Developing Countries in the WTO and NAFTA*. Cambridge: Cambridge University Press.

Odell, J. (2000). *Negotiating the World Economy*. Ithaca, NY: Cornell University Press.

OECD. (2000). *Toward Global Tax Cooperation in identifying and eliminating harmful Tax practices*. Report to the 2000 Ministerial Council Meeting and Recommendations by the Committee on Fiscal Affairs. OECD Paris, June.

Office of the United Status Trade Representative. (2009). *Free Trade Agreements*. in: http://www.ustr.gov/trade-agreements/free-trade-agreements

Okamoto, J. (ed) (2003). *Whither Free Trade Agreements? Proliferation, Evaluation and Multilateralism*. Chiba, Japan: Institute of Developing Economies (IDE), JETRO.

Olekalns, M., Smith, P., and Walsh, T. (1996). The Process of Negotiating. Strategy and Timing as Predictors of Outcomes. *Organizational Behavior and Human Decision Processes* 68 (1): 68-77.

Olson, M. (1982). The Rise and Decline of Nations: Economic Growth, Stagflation, and Social Rigidities. New Haven: Yale University Press.

Olson, M. (1965). The Logic of Collective Action: Public Goods and the Theory of Groups. Cambridge, MA: Harvard University Press.

Onuf, N. (1989). World of Our Making: Rules and Rule in Social Theory and International Relations. Columbia: University of South Carolina Press.

Ortiz Mena, A. (2006). Getting to "No:" Defending against demands in NAFTA energy negotiations. In J. Odell (Ed.), *Negotiating Trade: Developing Countries in the WTO and NAFTA* (pp. 177-216). Cambridge: Cambridge University Press.

Osterlof Obregón, D. (2004). Costa Rica. In N. López Carrión (ed.), *DR-CAFTA. Impacto sobre sectores sociales menos favorecidos en América Central* (pp. 23-70). Managua: Frierich Ebert Stiftung;.

Palmer, D. (2006). US Relations with Latin America during the Clinton Years: Opportunities Lost or Opportunities Squandered? Gainesville: University Press of Florida.

Panorama Centroamericano. (August-September 2002). Autoridad de Promoción Comercial (TPA) y el futuro TLC de Centro América con Estados Unidos. no. 185-186, Reporte Político, pp. 3-16.

Panorama Centromaericano. (04/2002). La Unidad Social Cristiana repite en el poder por primera vez; abstencionismo alacanza su nivel más alto en lo que va de la nueva República. no 181, Reporte político, pp. 1-10.

Paredes, G. and Morales, J. (2007). Compentencia y regulación en la banca: el caso de Panamá. *Serie estudios y perspectives* 86, September. Mexico: CEPAL.

Patomäki, H. (2009). Reassessing Long-Term Political Economy Developments: possible future crisis and the politics of Global Governance. *Arena*, forthcoming.

Payne, R. (2001). Persuasion, Frames and Norm Construction. *European Journal of International Relations* 7(1): 37-61.

Pérez Balladares, E. (22/10/1997). Tratado con Chile se firmará en abril. *El Panamá América*, p. E 1.

Pérez Balladares, E. (31/08/1998). Ganó el No. *El Panamá América*, front page.

Peters, B.G., Pierre, J. and King, G. (2005). The politics of path dependency: political conflict in historical institutionalism. *Journal of Politics* 67(4): 1275-1300.

Pettman, R. (2000). Common Sense Constructivism: or the making of world affairs, New York: M.E. Sharpe.

Phillips, N. (2004). *The Southern Cone Model*. Oxford & New York: Routledge.

Pierson, P. (2000). Increasing returns, path dependence and the study of politics. *American Political Science Review* 92(4): 251-267.

Pillutla, M., Malhotra, D., and Murnighan, J. (2003). Attributions of Trust and the Calculus of Reciprocity. *Journal of Experimental Social Psychology* 39, no. 5: 448-455.

Pitti, C. (07/07/1998). Panamá en desventaja arancelaria. *Panamá América*, p. E1.

Plantey, A. (2007). International Negotiation in the Twenty-First Century. Oxon: Routledge-Cavendish.

Pollack, M. (2006). *Rational Choice and EU Politics*. Arena Working Papers Series 11/2006.

Pólya, G. (1957). *How to Solve It*. Garden City, N.Y.: Doubleday.

Porras, J. (2003). La Estrategia chilena de acuerdos comerciales: un análisis político. *Serie comercio internacional* 36, CEPAL, Santiago.

Preferential Trade Agreement Panama-Colombia. (1993). in: www.sice.oas.org (accessed 13/12/2006).

Preferential Trade Agreement Panama-Dominican Republic. (1985). in: www.sice.oas.org (accessed 13/12/2006).

Preferential Trade Agreement Panama-El Salvador. (1970). in: www.sice.oas.org (Accessed 12/12/2006).

Preferential Trade Agreement Panama-Guatemala. (1975). in: www.sice.oas.org (accessed 11/12/2006).

Preferential Trade Agreement Panama-Honduras. (1974). In: www.sice.oas.org (accessed 11/12/2006).

Preferential Trade Agreement Panama-Mexico. (1985). in: www.sice.oas.org (accessed 11/12/2006).

Preferential Trade Agreement Panama-Nicaragua. (1974). in: www.sice.oas.org (accessed 11/12/2006).

Pruitt, D. and Hee Kim, S. (2004). *Social Conflict: Escalation, Stalemate, and Settlement*. New York: McGraw Hill.

Pruitt, D. (1995). Flexibility in Conflict Episodes. *Annals of the American Academy of Political and Social Science*, Vol. 542, November: 100-115.

Pruitt, D.G. (1983). Strategic choice in negotiation. *American Behavioral Scientist* 27: 167-194.

Putnam, R. (1988). Diplomacy and Domestic Politics: The Logic of Two-Level Games. *International Organizations* 42: 427-460.

Quinteros de Aguilera, L. (2000). El Comercio en Centroamérica. In E. Robles (Ed.), *Centroamérica y la Integración Económica hacia el Siglo XXI* (pp. 457-462). San José: IICE.

Quinteros, C.; Ochoa, M.; and Salcedo, D. (2005). Impacto del Tratado de Libre Comercio entre Estados Unidos y Centroamérica en los actors sociales centroamericanos. *Revista Centroamericana de Ciencias Sociales* 2, no 1: 9-44.

Raiffa, H., Richarson, J., and Metcalfe, D. (2002a). *Negotiation Analysis: The Science and Art of Collaborative Decision Making*, Cambridge, MA & London: The Belknap Press of Harvard University Press.

Raiffa, H. (2002b). Contributions of Applied Systems Analysis to International Negotiation. In V. Kremenyuk (Ed.), *International Negotiation: Analysis, Approaches, Issues* (pp. 5-21). Second edition. San Francisco: Jossey Bass.

Raiffa, H. (1982). *The Art and Science of Negotiation*. Cambridge, MA and London: Harvard University Press.

Ramírez, L. (11/06/2002). Papas, paisaje y democracia. *La Nación*. (Costa Rica), 17 A.

Rappaport, A. (1960). *Fights, games and debates*. Ann Arbor: University of Michigan Press.

Rebolledo, A. (2003). Negociaciones Comerciales Internacionales. Boletín Mensual 1, November 2003, FACEA UCEN.

Rebolledo, A. (1996). *Historia y desafíos de la política comercial chilena, 1974-1994*. Documento de trabajo de la facultad de Ciencias Económicas y Empresariales Universidad Complutense de Madrid. No. 5.

Reiter, J. (2006). International investments rules. In S. Woolcock (Ed.), *Trade and Investment Rule-Making: The Role of Regional and Bilateral Agreements* (pp. 208–240). Tokio-Nueva York-Paris: United Nations University Press.

República de Costa Rica. (1953). *Ley orgánica del sistema bancario nacional: Ley no 1644* (with its reforms). Updated in January 2002.

Républica de Panamá. (2008). *Código de Trabajo*. Edición 2008. Panama : Librería y Editora Interamericana S.A.

Républica de Panamá. (1994). *Constitución Política de la Républica de Panamá*. in: http://www.panama1.com/constitucion.php (Accessed 02/03/2008).

Reuters. (10/09/2005). South Korea, Mexico to push for limited trade talks. in: www.bilaterals.org (Accessed on 11/05/2009).

Risse, T. (2000). 'Let's Argue': Communicative Action in World Politics. *International Organization* 54:1-39.

Rivera, H. (2005). Los Tratados de Libre Comercio de Panamá, sus consecuencias, impactos y las futures negociaciones con otros países. In Cuadernos Nacionales, Tercera època (2005) *Globalización, TLC y Privatización*; no. 5. Panama: Universidad de Panamá; pp. 63-81.

Rodriguez, R. (1997). Critican Intenciones del PRD de Discutir Reelección Presidencial. *La Prensa* 19/02/1997. (Panama), p. 4A.

Rodriguez-Clare, A., Sáenz, M., and Trejos, A. (2004). Análisis de crecimiento económico en Costa Rica, 1950-2000. In M. Agosin, R. Machado, and P. Nazal, (Eds.), *Pequeñas economías, grandes desafíos. Políticas económicas para el desarrollo en Centroamérica* (pp. 111-117). Washington DC: Banco Interamericano de Desarrollo.

Rodrik, D. (1997). *Has Globalization Gone Too Far?* Washington, DC: Institute for International Economics.

Rogowski, R. (1989). Commerce and Coalitions: How Trade Affects Domestic Political Alignments. New Jersey: Princeton University Press.

Rojas Bolaños, M. (1997). Los años ochenta y el futuro incierto. *Nuestra Historia 20*. San José: UNA/UNED.

Rosales, O. (2008). Integración regional: Propuestas de renovación. In J. Altmann, and F. Rojas (Eds.), *Las paradojas de la integración en América Latina y el Caribe* (pp. 33-66). Madrid : Fundación Carolina y Siglo XXI.

Rosemberg, B. (2001a). *Hong Kong Free Trade and Investment Agreement: Deal not done yet.* in: www.arena.org.nz (Accessed on 10/05/2009).

Rosemberg, B. (2001b). Globalisation by Stealth: The proposed New Zealand-Hong Kong Free Trade Agreement & Investment. ARENA: Action, Research & Education Network of Aotearoa; March.

Sáez, R. (2006). *Trade in Financial Services: The Case of Chile.*, LCR Study, Background Paper, December. Free Trade Agreements and Financial Services in Latin America and the Caribbean Finance, Private Sector and Infrastructure Department Latin America and the Caribbean Region, Washington: The World Bank.

Sáez, S and Sáez, R. (2006). Las negociaciones de servicios financieros de Chile. *Serie Comercio Internacional* 75, Santiago: CEPAL.

Sáez, S. (2002). *La formulación de la política comercial en Chile: Una evaluación.* In Banco Intermaricano de Desarrollo, Inter-American Dialogue y Munk Centre for International Studies, Ibidem.

Sáez, S. and Valdés, J. G. (1999). *Chile and its "Lateral" Trade Policy. Cepal Review* 67: 85-131.

Saied, D. and Estribí, H. (2004). Panamá. Competitividad Sistémica en Panamá: Nuevo enfoque de análisis y búsqueda de soluciones a los problemas socioeconómicos del país. In N. Obed López (Ed.), *Competitividad sistémica en América Central : nuevo enfoque para el análisis y busqueda de soluciones a los problemas socioeconómicos de los países de la region* (pp. 318-391). Managua: Fundación Friedrich Ebert;

Salazar, D. (14/02/2002). Carta al Licenciado Fernando Ocampo. Director General de Comercio Exterior, Ministerio de Comercio Exterior de Costa Rica. DINECI 137-02. In COMEX information centre. San José, Costa Rica.

Salazar, J. (2005). *A Chile-New Zealand CEP?: The Concept of Coopetition and the Politics of Trade Liberalization. A Lecture: "Diplomatic Conclusions."* Political Science and International Relations Programme, Victoria University of Wellington; 15 March.

Salvatore, D. (2005). *Introduction to International Economics.* Hoboken, NJ: Wiley, John Wiley & Sons, Inc.

Samuelson, P., and Nordhaus, W. (2005). *Economics.* Eighteen Edition. Boston: McGraw Hill International Edition.

Sánchez Sánchez, R. (2009). *The Politics of Central American Integration.* New York: Routledge.

Sánchez, F. (2002). Desalineamiento electoral en Costa Rica. *Revista de Ciencias Sociales* IV, no 98: 29-56.

Sánchez, P. (2007). *Panama Lost? U.S. Hegemony, Democracy, and the Canal.* Gainesville: University Press of Florida.

Sauvé, P. (2006). Trade and investment rules: Latin American perspectives. *Serie Comercio Internacional* 66. Santiago: ECLAC.

Savage, D. and Weale, A. (2009). Political representation and the normative logic of two-level games. *European Political Science Review* 1: 1, 63-81.

Scapini, J. (2006). *Los gremios empresariales en Chile.* Santiago: Tajamar Editores.

Schirm, S. (2004). *Internationale Politische Ökonomie.* Baden-Baden: Nomos.

Schirm, S. (2002). Globalization and the New Regionalism: Global Markets, Domestic Politics and Regional Cooperation. Cambridge: Polity Press.

Schott, J (2003). *Korea's FTA Conundrum*. Peterson Institute for International Economics. in: www.iie.com (accessed 11/08/2009).

Selles, D. (13/08/1998). Exportadores aplauden fracaso de TLC con Chile. *El Panamá América*, p. E1.

Sen, S. (2005). International Trade Theory and Policy: What is Left of the Free Trade Paradigm? *Development and Change* 36 (6): 1011-1029.

Silva, V. (2004). Chile: A multi-track market access strategy", in M. Lengyel and V. Ventura-Dias (Eds.), *Trade Policy Reforms in Latin America* (pp. 27-43).New York: Palgrave MacMillan.

Silva, V. (2001). Estrategia y agenda commercial chilena en los años noventa. *Serie Comercio Internacional* 11. Santiago: CEPAL.

Simon, H. (1957). Models of Man, Social and Rational: Mathematical Essays on Rational Human Behavior in a Social Setting. New York: Wiley.

Singh, J.P. (2008). *Negotiation and the Global Information Economy*. Cambridge: Cambridge University Press.

Smith, P. (2001). Strategic Options for Latin America. In J. Tulchin and R. Espach (Eds.), *Latin America in the International System* (pp. 35-72). Boulder: Lynne Rienner Publishers.

Snidal, D. (2006). Rational Choice and International Relations. In W. Carlsnaes, T. Risse, and B. Simmons (Eds.), *Handbook of International Relations* (pp. 73-94). London: Sage.

SOFOFA. (1997-1998). *Memoirs* (Memorias Anuales). Santiago of Chile.

SOFOFA. (1998-1999). *Memoirs* (Memorias Anuales). Santiago of Chile.

Solís, M., and Katada, S. (2008). Understanding East Asian cross-regionalism: an analytical framework. *Pacific Affairs* 80, no 2: 229--57.

Spector, B. (2006). Resiliency in Negotiations: Bouncing Back from Impasse. *International Negotiation* 11: 273-286.

Spector, B. (1995). Creativity Heuristics for Impasse Resolution: Reframing Intractable Negotiations. *Annals of the American Academy of Political and Social Science*, Vol. 542, November: 81-99.

SUGEF-COMEX. (08/05/2000). *Reunión de Consulta con SUGEF,* (minute of the meeting). (Folders of the FTA between Central America and Panama; pp. 3). COMEX information centre. San José, Costa Rica.

SUGEVAL-COMEX. (09/05/2000). *Reunión de Consulta con SUGEVAL*, (Minute of the meeting). (Folders of the FTA between Central America and Panama, pp. 3). COMEX information centre. San José, Costa Rica.

Superintendency of Banks of Panama (2009) Reseña Histórica. in www.superbancos.gob.pa (Accessed 27/05/2009).

Sutton, H. J. (2001). *New Zeland-Hong Kong Closer Economic Partnership Negotiations: Submission on Discussion Paper.* Office of the Minister for Trade Negotiations. Cabinet External Relations and Defence Committee; 06055584.01; Approved 23/07/2001. in: www.mfat.govt.nz (Accessed on 10/05/2009).

Tansey, O. (2007). Process Tracing and Elite Interviewing: A case for Non-probability Sampling. *PS: Political Science and Politics* 40, no 4: 765-772.

Teichman, J. (2001). *The Politics of Freeing Markets in Latin America: Chile, Argentina, and Mexico.* Chapel Hill and London: The University of North Carolina Press.

Terra/EFE. (31/01/2006). Panamá y Chile retoman negociaciones para un TLC. In: http://php.terra.com/templates/imprime_articulo.php?id=ACT330668 (Accessed 28/01/2008).

Thelen, K. (2000). Timing and Temporality in the Analysis of Institutional Evolution and Change. *Studies in American Political Development* 14: 101-108.

Tonra, B. (2001). The Europeanisation of national foreign policy Dutch, Danish and Irish foreign policy in the European Union. Aldershot: Ashgate.

Tornell, A. (1991). On the Ineffectiveness of Made-to-Measure Protectionist Programs", in E. Helpman, and A. Razin (Eds.), *International Trade and Trade Policy*. Cambridge, MA and London: The MIT press.

Torres Abrego, J. (2000). Los pies de barro de la estrategia financiera del gobierno (¡¿Nuestro compromiso para el cambio?!). Panama: Universidad de Panamá.

Trade and Industry Department, Government of Hong Kong. (2009). *Hong Kong and New Zealand. A Possible Closer Economic Partnership Agreement: Consultation Document*. In: www.tid.gov.hk (Accessed on 10/04/2009).

Trans-Pacific SEP Agreement among Chile, New Zealand, Singapore and Brunei Darussalam. (2002). in: http://www.direcon.cl (accessed November 13, 2008).

Tsebelis, G. (2002). *Veto Players: How Political Institutions Work*. New Jersey: Princeton University Press.

Tsebelis, G. (1991). *Nested Games: Rational Choice in Comparative Politics*. Berkeley and Los Angeles: University of California Press.

Ulett, L. (2001). TLC con Canadá ¿Quienes Ganan? *La República* 26 April 2001. (Costa Rica).

Ulloa Urrutia, A. (2003). Chile's Trade Policy and the Chile-United States Free Trade Agreement. In Cuba in Transition: Papers and Proceedings of the Thirteenth Annual Meeting of the Association for the Study of the Cuban Economy (ASCE), vol. 13. Coral Gables, Florida, 7-9 August.

Underdal, A. (1983). Causes of Negotiation 'Failure'. *European Journal of Political Research* 11 (2): 183-195.

Urbina, C. (2001). *La Aseguradora Cautiva Offshore*. Panama: Universal Books.

Urriola, R. (2000). Apertura económica y control del flujo de capitales externos en Chile. *Nueva Sociedad*, no 168 (July-August): 129-137.

Ury, W. (2007). Getting Past No: Negotiating in Difficult Situations. New York: Bantam Books.

Van Klaveren, A. (1998). Inserción Internacional de Chile. In C. Toloza, and E. Lahera (Eds.), *Chile en los noventa* (pp. 117-160). Santiago: Dolmen ediciones.

Vargas Solís, L. (2007). *La estrategia de liberalización económica (Período 1980-2000)*. Serie Cuadernos de Historia de las Instituciones de Costa Rica 9. San José: Universidad de Costa Rica.

Vargas Solís, L. (2002). Costa Rica, 1985-1997: Liberalización y Ajuste Estructural o la Autodestrucción del Neoliberalismo. San José: EUNED.

Venables, A. (2003). Winners and Losers from Regional Integration Agreements. *Economic Journal* 113: 747-761.

Venables, A., and Smith, A. (1986). Trade and Industrial Policy under Imperfect Competition. *Economic Policy* 1: 622-672.

Vergara Hernández, S. (2008). Interpretación finalista de las reglas de origen en los TLC : investigación tributaria. Santiago de Chile : Nova Lex.

Villalobos de Tapia, L. (1997). La Eventual Firma de los Tratados de Libre Comercio de Panama con Mexico y Chile, y sus posibles efectos socioeconomicos para Panamá y el Canal. MA dissertation in Business Administration. Panama: Universidad de Panamá.

Villasuso, J. M. (2007). Dimensiones Institucionales del Sector Financiero Costarricense y sus efectos sociales: Un Cambio de Modelo de Desarrollo. In C. Ansorena (Ed.), *Restricciones Institucionales al desarrollo en Costa Rica* (pp. 263-279). San José: UNCR.

Viner, J. (1950). *The Customs Union Issue*. New York: Carnie Endowment for International Peace.

Wagner, L. (2008). *Problem-Solving and Bargaining in International Negotiations*. International Negotiation Series. Leiden: Martinus Nijhoff Publishers.

Walton, R., and McKersie, R. (1965). A Behavioral Theory of Labor Negotiations: An Analysis of a Social Interaction System. New York: McGraw Hill.

Waltz, K. (1979). *Theory of International* Relations. New York: McGraw-Hill; Reading: Addison-Wesley.

Watkins, M. and Passow, S. (1996). Analyzing Linked Systems of Negotiations. *Negotiation Journal* 12(4): 325-339.

Wehner, L. (2009a). Más Allá de la Lógica Económica: Poder e Instituciones en los TLCs de Chile y México. *Asian Journal of Latin American Studies* 22(2): 47-82.

Wehner, L. (2009b). *Power, Governance and Ideas in Chile's Free Trade Agreement Policy*. GIGA Working Paper Series 102, May, Hamburg-Germany.

Wehner, L. (2007). The Free Trade Agreement Negotiations between Japan and Chile: Causes for Reaching a Rapid Agreement. *Journal of Current Japanese Affairs*, 6/2007, pp.72-86.

Wendt, A. (1999). *Social Theory of International* Relations, Cambridge: Cambridge University Press.

Wesley, M. (2008). The strategic effects of preferential trade agreements. *Australian Journal of International Affairs* 62, no 2: 214--28.

Williamson, J. (2009). Exchange Rate Economics. *Open Econ Review* 20: 123-146.

Wilson, B. (2003). The Elections in Costa Rica, February and April 2002. *Electoral Studies*, 22(3): 509-516.

Wilson, B. (1999). Leftist Parties, Neoliberal Policies, and Re-election Strategies: The Case of the PLN in Costa Rica. *Comparative Political Studies* 32(6): 753-780.

Witker, J (2004). Las reglas de origen en los tratados de libre comercio. Santiago: LexisNexis.

Woolcock, S. (2006). Introduction: The interaction between the levels of rule-making in international trade and investment. In S. Woolcock (ed), *Trade and Investment Rule-making: The Role of Regional and Bilateral Agreements* (pp. 1-26). Tokyo, New York and Paris: United Nations University Press.

www.hani.co.kr (12/05/2009). S. Korea, Japan prepare to resume FTA talks this summer (Accessed on 11/08/2009).

Young, O. (1991). Political Leadership and Regime Formation: On the Development of Institutions in International Society. *International Organitzation* 45: 281-308.

Zartman, W., and Rubin, J. (ed) (2000). *Power and Negotiation*. Ann Arbor: The University of Michigan Press.

Zartmann, W. (2000). 'Ripeness: The hurting stalemate and beyond'. In P. C. Stern, and D. Druckman (Eds.), *Conflict resolution after the Cold War*. Washington D.C.: National Academy Press.

Zartmann, W. (1989). *The ripe for resolution: Conflict resolution in Africa*. (2nd edition). New York: Oxford University Press.

Zartman, W., and Berman, M. (1982). *The practical negotiator*. New Haven, Connecticut: Yale University Press.

Zechner, C. (2002). Expanding NAFTA: Economic Effects on Chile of Free Trade with the United State. Berlin-Hamburg-Münster: LIT Verlag.

Zoellick, R. (18/1172003). *USTR Notifies Congress of Intent to Initiate Free Trade Talks with Panama.* Office of United States Trade Representative 2009. In: www.ustr.gov (accessed 23/05/2009).

12.1 Internet Pages

www.aladi.org	(Asociación Latinoaméricana de Integración).
www.sofofa.cl	(Sociedad Fomento Fabril- Chile)
www.cpc.cl	(Confederación de Producción y Comercio)
www.sica.int	(Sistema Integración de Centro América)
www.mici.gob.pa	(Ministerio de Comercio e Industrias-Panamá)
www.summit-americas.org	(Free Trade Area of the Americas)
www.comex.go.cr	(Ministerio de Comercio Exterior-Costa Rica)
www.direcon.cl	(Dirección de Relaciones Económicas Internacionales-Chile)
www.sice.oas.org	(Organisation of the American States, Trade division)

12.2 Interviews

Chile

a) Negotiators

1. Alegría, Constanza. Current Institution: DIRECON. Role in the Negotiations: Negotiator. Date of Interview: 07.04.2008. Place: Santiago of Chile.
2. Banda, Leonardo. Current Institution: ProChile. Role in the Negotiations: Chief for The Latin American Region. Date of Interview 25.03.2008. Place: Santiago of Chile.
3. Bau, Catalina. Current Institution: CONAF. Role in the Negotiations: Negotiator of Financial Services, Ministry of Finances. Date of Interview: 11.04.2008. Place: Santiago of Chile.
4. Belmar, Carolina. Current Institution: DIRECON. Role in the Negotiations: Negotiator on intellectual property rights. Date of Interview: 14.04.2008. Place: Santiago of Chile.
5. Casanueva, Hector. Current Institution: Cervantes University. Role in the Negotiations: Head of ProChile. Date of Interview: 07.04.2008. Place: Santiago of Chile.
6. Contreras, Rodrigo. Current Institution: DIRECON. Role in the Negotiations: Negotiator on Market Access. Date of Interview: 28.03.2008. Place: Santiago of Chile.
7. Cortes, Carmen Paz. Current Institution: DIRECON. Role in the Negotiations: Negotiator: Market access and rules of origin. Date of Interview: 25.03.2008. Place: Santiago of Chile.
8. Culagousky, Jorge. Current Institution: DIRECON. Role in the Negotiatons: Negotiator on Trade Remedies. Date of Interview: 28.03.2008. Place: Santiago of Chile.

9. De la Fuente, Julio. Current Institution: DIRECON. Role in the Negotiations. Negotiator, Latin American Region. Date of Interview: 17.03.2008. Place: Santiago of Chile.
10. Furche, Carlos. Current Institution: DIRECON. Role in the Negotiations: General Director DIRECON and former Negotiator on Agricultural issues ODEPA, Ministry of Agriculture. Date of Interview: 18.03.2008. Place: Santiago of Chile.
11. Gangas, Lucy. Current Institution: Ministry of Economics. Role in the Negotiations: Advisor on International Trade Issues. Date of Interview: 07.04.2008. Place: Santiago of Chile.
12. Guardia, Alexis. Current Institution: DIRECON. Role in the Negotiations: Director of Studies. Date of Interview: 08.04.2008. Place: Santiago of Chile.
13. Klein, Marcela. Current Institution: Ministry of Finances. Role in the Negotiations: Advisor on International Trade Issues (Financial Issues). Date of Interview: 24.03.2008. Place: Santiago of Chile.
14. Lazo, Pablo. Current Institution: DIRECON. Role in the Negotiatons: Negotiator. Date of Interview: 25.03.2008. Place: Santiago of Chile.
15. Leiva, Jorge. Current Institution: Chile 21. Role in the Negoations: Advisor on International Economic Relations at the Ministry of Economic 1997-98; and Minister of Economics 1998-2000. Date of Interview: 19.03.2008. Place: Santiago of Chile.
16. Matus, Mario. Current Institution: Embassador of Chile at the WTO. Role in the Negotiations: Negotiator/ Chief Negotiator. Date of Interview: 28/02/2008. Place: Geneva-Switzerland.
17. Navarro, Camilo. Current Institution: ALADI. Role in the Negotiatio: Negotiator/ Chief Negotiator for Latin America. Date of Interview: 17.03.2008. Place: Santiago of Chile.
18. Ocampo, Catalina. Current Institution: ProChile-Embassy of Chile in Panama. Role in the Negotiations: Input Giver on the economic and political situation in Panama. Date of Interview: 31/07/2008. Place: Panama City.
19. Opitz, Raul. Current Institution: Ministry of Agriculture. Role in the Negotiations: Advisor on International Trade Issues and Negotiatons. Date of Interview:10.04.2008. Place: Santiago of Chile.
20. Pizarro, Roberto. Current Institution: DIRECON. Role in the Negotiations: Advisor/Negotiator for Latin America. Date of Interview: 25.03.2008. Place: Santiago of Chile.
21. Prieto, Francisco. Current Institution: ProChile. Role in the Negotiations: Advisor/ Negotiator on Services, DIRECON. Date of Interview: 15.04.2008. Place: Santiago of Chile.
22. Quina, Oscar. Current Institution: DIRECON. Role in the Negotiations: Negotiator for Latin America. Date of Interview: 08.04.2008. Place: Santiago of Chile.
23. Rebolledo, Andres. Current Institution: DIRECON. Role in the Negotiations: Chief Negotiator and Negotiator. Date of Interview: 25.03.2008. Place: Santiago of Chile.
24. Rosales, Osvaldo. Current Institution: ECLAC. Role in the Negotiations: Negotiator/ Chief Negotiator in the FTA with US, South Korea and the EU. Date of Interview: 19.03.2008. Place: Santiago of Chile.
25. Sepulveda, Lorena. Current Institution: ProChile. Role in the Negotiations:Negotiator of DIRECON. Date of Interview: 25.03.2008. Place: Santiago.

b) Interest Groups

26. Arana, Maria Teresa. Current Institution: CORMA. Role in the Negotiations: Interest Group/ Wood and Cellulose Producers/ Manager on Economic Studies. Date of Interview: 09.04.2008. Place: Santiago of Chile.
27. Baierlein, Hugo. Current Institution: SOFOFA. Role in the Negotiations: Interest Group/ General Manager in International Trade/Former Negotiator DIRECON. Date of Interview: 26.03.2008. Place: Santiago of Chile.
28. Bown, Ronald. Current Institution: ASOEX. Role in the Negotiations: Interest Group-Fruits Exporters- ASOEX. Date of Interview: 19.03.2008. Place: Santiago of Chile.
29. Budinich, Ema. Current Institution: SNA. Role in the Negotiations: Interest Group/ Agricultural Association/Manager of the Department of Studies. Date of Interview: 09.04.2008. Place: Santiago of Chile.
30. Farah, Christina. Current Institution: ABIF. Role in the Negotiations: Interest Group/Banking Association/Advisor in International Trade Issues. Date of Interview: 26.03.2008. Place: Santiago of Chile.
31. Fantuzzi, Roberto. Current Institution: Private. Role in the Negotiations: Interest Group - Exporters of Industrial Goods ASEXMA. Date of Interview: 28.03.2008. Place: Santiago of Chile.
32. Figueroa, Marisol. Current Institution: Chilealimento. Role in the Negotiations: Interest Group-Director of the Department of Studies. Date of Interview: 17.04.2008. Place: Santiago of Chile.
33. Garcia, Marcela. Current Institution: CNC. Role in the Negotiations: Advisor on internal and international trade issues. Date of Interview: 18.03.2008. Place: Santiago of Chile.
34. Garcia, Mario. Current Institution: INTECH-textil. Role in the Negotiations:Interest Group/ Textile Association/ President INTECH. Date of Interview: 03.04.2008. Place: Santiago of Chile.
35. Gatica, Guillermo. Current Institution: ASIMET. Role in the Negotiations: Interest Group/ Advisor in International Trade Issues. Date of Interview: 27.03.2008. Place: Santiago of Chile.
36. Gática, Jaime. Current Institution: ANBER. Role in the Negotiations: Interest Group/ Refreshments products/General Manager. Date of Interview: 01.04.2008. Place: Santiago of Chile.
37. González, Cristian. Current Institution: EXPORLAC. Role in the Negotiations: Interest Group/ Dairy Products/Executive Manager. Date of Interview: 31.03.2008. Place: Santiago of Chile.
38. Infante, Rodrigo. Current Institution: Private. Role in the Negotiations: Interest Group-Salmon/ General Manager of Salmon Chile. Date of Interview: 19.03.2008. Place: Santiago of Chile.
39. Lothholz, Werner. Current Institution: ASIQUIM. Role in the Negotiations: Interest Group/ Quimics Products (President). Date of Interview: 10.04.2008. Place: Santiago of Chile.
40. Marquez, Alvaro. Current Institution: Chamber of Comestics. Role in the Negotiations: Interest Group/Beauty Products/General Director. Date of Interview: 02.04.2008. Place: Santiago of Chile.
41. Mekis, Federico. Current Institution: Wines of Chile. Role in the Negotiations: Interest Group/ Wine/Executive Manager. Date of Interview: 31.03.2008. Place: Santiago of Chile.
42. Muga, Rene. Current Institution: CPC. Role in the Negotiations: Interest Group/Manager on International Trade/Former negotiator DIRECON. Date of Interview: 07.04.2008. Place: Santiago of Chile.

43. Munoz, Osvaldo. Current Institution: ANIC. Role in the Negotiations: Interest Group/ Poultry and Pork Sausages/Executive Manager. Date of Interview:04.04.2008. Place: Santiago of Chile.
44. Pitto, Hernan. Current Institution: Chamber of Glass Producers. Role in the Negotiations: Interest Group/former governmental advisor on negotiatons. Date of Interview: 02.04.2008. Place: Santiago of Chile.
45. Pucchi, Victor Hugo. Current Institution: Salmon Chile-Aqua. Role in the Negotiations: Former President of Salmon Chile/ Owner of AquaChile. Date of Interview: 20.03.2008. Place: Santiago of Chile.
46. Sánchez, María Angélica. Current Institution: ASILFA. Role in the Negotiations:Interest Group/Farmaceutical Products/Executive Director. Date of Interview: 03.04.2008. Place: Santiago of Chile.
47. Schmidt, Luis. Current Institution: SNA. Role in the Negotiations: Interest Group-Agricultural Association (President). Date of Interview:01.04.2008. Place: Santiago of Chile.
48. Vásquez, Paulina. Current Institution: ASEXMA. Role in the Negotiations: Interest Group/ Industrial Goods/Manager of International Trade. Date of Interview: 31.03.2008. Place: Santiago of Chile.
49. Veragua, Marco. Current Institution: CONAPYME. Role in the Negotiations: Interest Group SME/ Executive Director. Date of Interview: 25.03.2008. Place: Santiago of Chile.
50. Vergara, Jorge. Current Institution: ASIPLA. Role in the Negotiations: Interest Group/ Plastic Goods/General Manager. Date of Interview: 14.04.2008. Place: Santiago of Chile.

c) Anonymous

51. Anonymous. Current Institution: Governmental. Expert and Adivsor on Financial Services. Date of Interview: 04.04.2008. Place: Santiago of Chile.

Costa Rica

a) Negotiators

1. Agüero, Esteban. Current Institution: COMEX. Role in the Negotiations: Negotiator. Date of Interview: 02.07.2008. Place: San José, Costa Rica.
2. Aguilar, Alejandra. Current Institution: COMEX . Role in the Negotiations: Negotiator. Date of Interview: 04.07.2008. Place: San José, Costa Rica.
3. Arguedas, Irene. Current Institution: Private. Role in the Negotiations: Negotiator/ General Director of International Trade Negotiations. Date of Interview: 03.07.2008. Place: San José, Costa Rica.
4. Chacón, Francisco. Current Institution: Private. Role in the Negotiations: Former Vice-Minister COMEX 1994-97/ Negotiator/Private Advisor on Trade Issues/Head of the Movement for the Yes option for the Referendum to approve the DR-CAFTA. Date of Interview: 14.07.2008. Place: San José, Costa Rica.

5. Echandi, Roberto. Current Institution: Chief negotiator COMEX, FTA Central America-EU. Role in the Negotiations: Negotiator. Date of Interview: 26.06.2008. Place: San José, Costa Rica.
6. Guillén, Gustavo. Current Institution: COMEX. Role in the Negotiations: Negotiator COMEX. Date of Interview: 27.06.2008. Place: San José, Costa Rica.
7. Llobet, Gabriela. Current Institution: Private. Role in the Negotiations: Former Director COMEX/Vice-Minister COMEX/ Negotiator. Date of Interview: 02.07.2008. Place: San José, Costa Rica.
8. Miranda, Silvia. Current Institution: COMEX. Role in the Negotiations: Negotiator. Date of Interview: 27.06.2008. Place: San José, Costa Rica.
9. Pacheco, Amparo. Current Institution: Vice-Minster COMEX. Role in the Negotiations: Vice-minister COMEX/negotiator. Date of Interview: 02.07.2008. Place: San José, Costa Rica.
10. Rodriguez, Laura. Current Institution: Implemnetation of FTAs-COMEX. Role in the Negotiations: Former Chief Negotiator COMEX/ negotiator. Date of Interview: 08.07.2008. Place: San José, Costa Rica.
11. Rodriguez, Marvin. Current Institution: COMEX. Role in the Negotiations: Former Advisor of CIRC / Negotiator. Date of Interview: 07.07.2008. Place: San José, Costa Rica.
12. Trejos, Indiana. Current Institution: COMEX. Role in the Negotiation: Negotiator. Date of Interview: 24.06.2008. Place: San José, Costa Rica.
13. Varela, Tatiana. Current Institution: COMEX. Role in the Negotiations: Negotiator Market Acesses and Rule of Origins. Date of Interview: 26.06.2008. Place: San José, Costa Rica.

b) Interest Groups

14. Cardoza, William. Current Institution: CANAVI. Role in the Negotiations: Interest group/ Executive Manager CANAVI. Date of Interview: 01.07.2008. Place: San José, Costa Rica.
15. Castro, Daniel. Current Institution: Bank Association. Role in the Negotiations: Interest group/ Legal Advisor Bank Association. Date of Interview: 27.06.2008. Place: San José, Costa Rica.
16. Céspedes, Carlos. Current Institution: CADEXCO. Role in the Negotiations: Interest group/ tecnical manager in International Trade-CADEXCO. Date of Interview: 25.06.2008. San José, Costa Rica.
17. Jiménez, Ronulfo. Current Institution: Bank Association. Role in the Negotiations: Director of the central Bank (1998-2003)/ Representative of the Bank Association/ Former Advisor on Economic Issues of President Abel Pacheco. Date of Interview: 27.06.2008. Place: San José, Costa Rica.
18. Liberamn, Jack. Current Institution: CICR. Role in the Negotiations: President of CICR. Date of Interview: 30.06.2008. Place: San José, Costa Rica.
19. Lizano, Eduardo. Current Institution: La Academia de Centroamérica. Role in the Negotiations: Former President of Costa Rica's Central Bank between 1984-1990, and 1998-2002. Date of Interview: 26.06.2008. Place: San José, Costa Rica.
20. Montero, Erik. Current Institution: CNLP. Role in the Negotiations: Interest group/ Executive Director-CNLP. Date of Interview: 27.06.2008. Place: San José, Costa Rica.
21. Montero, Mario. Current Institution: CACIA. Role in the Negotiations: Interest group/ Executive Vicepresident-CACIA. Date of Interview: 07.07.2008. Place: San José, Costa Rica.
22. Navas, Sergio. Current Institution: CADEXCO. Role in the Negotiations: Interest group/ General Manager CADEXCO. Date of Interview: 25.06.2008. Place: San José, Costa Rica.

23. Obando, Luis. Current Institution: CIRC. Role in the Negotiations: Advisor in International Trade Issues-CIRC. Date of Interview: 30.06.2008. Place: San José, Costa Rica.

c) Anonymous

24. Anonymous. Role in the Negotiations: Former COMEX. Date of Interview: 30.06.2008. Place: San José, Costa Rica.
25. Anonymous. Role in the Negotiations: Representative PAC. Date of Interview: 01.07.2008. Place: San José, Costa Rica.
26. Anonymous. Role in the Negotiations: Representative PLN. Date of Interview: 04.07.2008. Place: San José, Costa Rica.
27. Anonymous. Role in the Negotiations: CNAA Representative. Date of Interview: 09.07.2008. Place: San José, Costa Rica.
28. Anonymous. Role in the Negotiations: Beans sector Representative. Date of Interview: 10.07.2008. Place: San José, Costa Rica.
29. Anonymous. Role in the Negotiations: CORFOGA Representative. Date of Interview: 11.07.2008. Place: San José, Costa Rica.
30. Anonymous. Date of Interview: 11.07.2008. Place: San José, Costa Rica.
31. Anonymous. Date of Interview: 14.07.2008. Place: San José, Costa Rica.

Panama

a) Negotiators

1. Aparicio, Estif. Current Institution: Private. Role in the Negotiations: Negotiator MICI/Adivisor Ministry of Foreign Affairs / Legal Director of MICI, department of International Economic Negotiations 1998-2000/Chief Negotiator MICI 2004-2006. Date of Interview: 18.07.2008. Place: Panama.
2. Arrué, Leda. Current Institution: MICI. Role in the Negotiations: Negotiator MICI, Market Access. Date of Interview: 17.07.2008. Place: Panama.
3. Davis, Melissa. Current Institution: MICI. Role in the Negotiations: Negotiator/Chief Negotiator. Date of Interview: 17.07.2008. Place: Panama.
4. de Castillo, Brunilda B. Current Institution: MICI. Role in the Negotiations: Negotiator. Date of Interview: 17.07.2008. Place: Panama.
5. Díaz de Morales, Gabriela. Current Institution: MIDA. Role in the Negotiations: Director of External Trade Policy Issues-MIDA. Date of Interview: 30.07.2008. Place: Panama.
6. Ferrer, Alejandro. Current Institution: Private. Role in the Negotiations: Deputy Minister Ministry of Foreign Affairs 1996-1997/ Ambassador-Member of the Foreign Relations Committee 1997-1999. Minister MICI 2004-2008. Date of Interview: 29.07.2008. Place: Panama.
7. Garisto M., Bruno. Current Institutution: Ambassador.Role in the Negotiations: Ambassor in Chile. Date of Interview: 11/04/2208. Place: Santiago of Chile.
8. Garrido, Luis. Current Institution: MICI. Role in the Negotiations: Negotiator. Date of Interview: 28.07.2008. Place: Panama.

9. Jácome, Joaquín. Current Institution: Private. Role in the Negotiations: Minister of MICI (1999-2004). Date of Interview: 17.07.2008. Place: Panama.
10. Moreno, Samuel. Current Institution: MICI. Role in the Negotiations: Negotiator MICI, rule of origin and market access. Date of Interview: 22.07.2008. Place: Panama.
11. Pineda, Alexis. Current Institution: MICI. Role in the Negotiations: Negotiator MICI, rules of origin and market access. Date of Interview: 18.07.2008. Place: Panama.
12. Salazar, Diana. Current Institution: MICI. Role in the Negotiations: Negotiator/Chief Negotiator MICI. Date of Interview: 30.07.2008. Place: Panama.
13. Santoya, Alexander. Current Instituion: MICI. Role in the Negotiations: Negotiator MICI. Date of Interview: 28.07.2008. Place: Panama.
14. Torres, Zereth. Current Institution: MICI. Role in the Negotiations: Negotiator MICI. Date of Interview: 22.07.2008. Place: Panama.

b) Interest Groups

15. Benett, Irving. Current Institution: Private. Role in the Negotiations: External advisor to negotiations/Former President APEDE. Date of Interview: 25.07.2008. Place: Panama.
16. Benett, John. Current Institution: Private. Role in the Negotiations: Former President APEDE. Date of Interview: 25.07.2008. Place: Panama.
17. Berguido, Carlos. Current Institution: APADEA. Role in the Negotiations: Director APADEA. Date of Interview: 18.07.2008. Place: Panama.
18. Bocaranda, Aníbal. Current Institution: ANAPOR. Role in the Negotiations: Interest group/ President ANAPOR. Date of Interview: 22.07.2008. Place: Panama.
19. Castro, Hatuey. Current Institution: FEDAP. Role in the Negotiations: Interest Group/Former President of FEDAP. Date of Interview: 21.07.2008. Place: Panama.
20. Cheng, Luis. Current Institution: FEDAP. Role in the Negotiations: Interest Group/ President and Director of FEDAP. Date of Interview: 21.07.2008. Place: Panama.
21. Cruz, Victor. Current Institution: SIP. Role in the Negotiations: Interest group/ Economic Advisor SIP. Date of Interview: 16.07.2008. Place: Panama.
22. Ferreira, Manuel. Current Institution: Chamber of Commerce, Industries, and Agriculture. Role in the Negotiations: Interest Group/ General Manager for International Trade Issues. Date of Interview: 25.07.2008. Place: Panama.
23. Garisto P., Bruno. Current Institution: University of International Trade. Role in the Negotiations: Chamber of Commerce Chile-Panama. Date of Interview: 16.07.2008. Place: Panama.
24. González, Carlos Ernesto. Current Institution: Private. Role in the Negotiations: Former Negotiator of the access to the WTO/ Representative of APEDE. Date of Interview: 21.07.2008. Place: Panama.
25. Quintero, Bosco. Current Institution: APADEA. Role in the Negotiations: Interest group/ Executive Director APADEA. Date of Interview: 18.07.2008. Place: Panama.
26. Sandoval de Sanjur, Denia. Current Institution: ANALMO. Role in the Negotiations: Interest group/Director ANALMO. Date of Interview: 23.07.2008. Place: Panama.

c) Anonymous

27. Anonymous. Date of Interview: 19.07.2008. Place: Panama.
28. Anonymous. Role in the Negotiations: Representative of the Banking Association. Date of Interview: 23.07.2008. Place: Panama.
29. Anonymous. Role in the Negotiations: Former Negotiator. Date of Interview: 25.07.2008. Place: Panama.
30. Anonymous. Role in the Negotiations: Former Negotiator. Date of Interview: 26.07.2008. Place: Panama.
31. Anonymous. Role in the Negotiations: Representative AZUCALPA. Date of Interview: 28.07.2008. Place: Panama.
32. Anonymous. Role in the Negotiations: Ministry of Finances. Date of Interview: 31.07.2008. Place: Panama.
33. Anonymous. Role in the Negotiations: Dairy Sector. Date of Interview: 01.08.2008. Place: Panama.
34. Anonymous. Role in the Negotiations: Representative of CMP. Date of Interview: 04.08.2008. Place: Panama.

FSC
www.fsc.org
MIX
Papier | Fördert gute Waldnutzung
FSC® C083411

Kolibri 360 GmbH
Ferdinand-Jühlke-Straße 7
99095 Erfurt, Deutschland
produktsicherheit@kolibri360.de